大使讲中英关系

On China-UK Relations

Volume I

刘晓明著有：

1. 《大使讲中国故事》(2022年，中信出版集团)，被全国千家实体书店推选为第五届"全民阅读·书店之选"主题出版类"十佳"作品。

2. 《尖锐对话》(2022年，北京出版集团)，被人民日报图书馆"金台好书榜"列为"十大好书"，入选《出版业"十四五"时期发展规划》，2024年被评为第二十三届输出版优秀图书。

3. 《有问必答》(2024年，北京出版集团)，被"探照灯好书"评为"人文社科原创佳作"，多次登上京东政治图书热卖榜。

大使讲中英关系

我们需要什么样的中英关系？

On China-UK Relations

Volume I

Liu Xiaoming

刘晓明——著

上卷

中信出版集团｜北京

图书在版编目（CIP）数据

大使讲中英关系：全 2 册 / 刘晓明著 . -- 北京：
中信出版社 , 2024. 8. -- ISBN 978-7-5217-6813-8
Ⅰ . D829.561
中国国家版本馆 CIP 数据核字第 2024XR4456 号

大使讲中英关系

著者： 刘晓明
出版发行：中信出版集团股份有限公司
（北京市朝阳区东三环北路 27 号嘉铭中心　邮编　100020）
承印者： 北京盛通印刷股份有限公司

开本：787mm×1092mm 1/16　　印张：66.5　插页：16　字数：980 千字
版次：2024 年 8 月第 1 版　　　　印次：2024 年 8 月第 1 次印刷
书号：ISBN 978-7-5217-6813-8
定价：198.00 元（全 2 册）

版权所有·侵权必究
如有印刷、装订问题，本公司负责调换。
服务热线：400-600-8099
投稿邮箱：author@citicpub.com

目录
Contents

序　言 ·· 007
Preface ·· 009

第一章　中英关系
PART I China-UK Relations

继往开来，时不我待 ·· 005
Time and Tide Wait for No Man ·· 007
坚持正确的义利观 ··· 011
Put Righteousness and Interests in Perspective ··················· 014
我们需要什么样的中英关系 ··· 019
What Kind of China-UK Relationship Do We Need ·············· 025
以史为鉴，可以知兴替 ·· 037
History Tells a Lot ·· 043
开启中英全面战略伙伴关系 ··· 055
A Comprehensive Strategic Partnership between China and the UK ······ 058
一次"超级国事访问" ·· 063
A "Super State Visit" ·· 066
中英关系的"三要三不要" ··· 071
Three Choices in China-UK Relations ································· 075

在变局中坚守，在合作中共赢 ·· 081
Stay Committed to Win-Win Cooperation ························· 087
中英关系的"变"与"不变" ·· 099
China-UK Relations: What Has Changed and What Has Not ············ 103
精诚如一，善始令终 ··· 109
Serve with Sincerity All the Way through ························ 113

第二章 政党议会交流
PART II Party and Parliamentary Exchanges

为什么要深化中英伙伴关系 ·· 123
Why China and the UK Need a Stronger Partnership ········· 127
勇于开拓，积极进取 ··· 131
Make a Creative and Bold Effort ···································· 135
聚同化异，淬炼真金 ··· 139
Build Common Ground for China-UK Relations ················ 142

第三章 经贸关系
PART III Economic and Trade Relations

中英互利合作新机遇 ··· 151
New Opportunities for Mutually Beneficial Cooperation between
China and the UK ·· 155
中英经贸合作"三问" ·· 161
Three Questions on China-UK Economic Cooperation ········ 165
从儒家经典看中英经贸合作 ·· 171
Confucius Wisdom and China-UK Economic Ties ············· 175
中国发展新动力，中英合作新机遇 ··································· 183
New Driving Force for China's Development, New Opportunities

for China-UK Cooperation ·· 189

沉舟侧畔千帆过，病树前头万木春 ···························· 201

Hard Times Will Not Stop the Wheel of History ·············· 205

共建良好环境，共创中英经贸合作新局面 ···················· 213

Create a Sound Environment for New Success in China-UK

Business Cooperation ·· 218

把握新时代，开创新局面，迈上新台阶 ······················· 227

Embrace New Era, Open up New Prospects and Scale New Heights ····· 232

继往开来，携手奋进，筑牢中英合作共赢之路 ·············· 241

Build on Past Achievements and Join Hands to Enhance

China-UK Win-Win Cooperation ································· 245

胸怀大局，继往开来，深化合作 ································ 251

Keep Big Picture in Mind and Deepen Cooperation ············ 255

第四章　金融合作
PART IV　Financial Cooperation

深化合作，互利共赢 ·· 265

Seize the Opportunity to Deepen a Win-Win Partnership ······ 269

人民币国际化的"伦敦机遇" ······································ 277

The London Opportunity for the Internationalization of RMB ······ 280

人民币国际化在英国迈出坚实步伐 ······························ 285

Advancements of RMB Internationalization in the UK ········· 287

硕果累累，精彩无限 ·· 289

Let China-UK Cooperation Bear More Fruits ·················· 291

共同塑造中英金融合作的美好未来 ······························ 293

Work Together for a Promising Future of China-UK Financial

Cooperation ··· 298

坚定信心，共创未来 307
Firm Confidence in a Brighter and Shared Future 310
走绿色发展之路，谱金融合作新篇 315
Pursue Green Development and Write a New Chapter of
Financial Cooperation 318
推进高水平金融合作，打造开放共赢成果 323
Enhance Financial Cooperation and Deliver More Fruits 326

第五章 科技合作
PART V Cooperation on Science and Technology

合作共赢，造福人类 335
Win-Win Cooperation for Mankind 337
凡事预则立，不预则废 341
Forewarned Is Forearmed 343
以创新推动发展，以创新促进合作 345
Promote Development through Cooperation on Innovation 351
坚持正确方向，开创共赢未来 361
Keep to the Right Direction and Open up a Win-Win Future 363
引领开放创新潮流，打造合作共赢成果 367
Take the Lead in Open Cooperation on Innovation and Deliver
Win-Win Results 370

第六章 生态环保
PART VI Ecological and Environmental Protection

十年树木，百年树人 379
Hundred Years to Rear People 382
加强中英能源合作，为构建人类命运共同体贡献力量 387

Stronger China-UK Energy Cooperation Paves the Way for
Building a Community of Shared Future ················· 392

保护野生动物，共建美丽家园 ························· 399

Protect the Wildlife and Build a Beautiful Global Village ········ 402

深化中英气变合作，共建美好地球家园 ·················· 407

Make Our Planet a Better Home for All ················· 410

应对气变挑战，促进能源转型 ························· 415

Address Climate Change and Promote Energy Transition ········ 419

谱写生态文明新篇章，共建地球生命共同体 ··············· 427

Write a New Chapter of Ecological Conservation and Build a Shared
Future for All Life on Earth ························· 431

第七章　地方往来
PART VII　Subnational Exchanges

"双龙共舞"与"双龙共赢" ·························· 443

Two Dragons Will Not Only Dance Together but Prosper Together ···· 447

同舟共济，互利共赢 ······························· 451

We Need a Win-Win Partnership ····················· 454

天府之国，魅力无限 ······························· 459

Enchanting Land of Plenty ························· 461

不求大而全，但做小且精 ··························· 463

Focus on Quality Instead of Size ···················· 465

走在中英关系前列的江苏 ··························· 469

Jiangsu, a Leader in China-UK Relations ················ 471

拉起风箱，打出真铁 ······························· 473

Work the Bellows to Beat out Real Iron ················ 475

奏响互利共赢的交响曲 ····························· 479

A Spectacular Symphony of Win-Win Cooperation ·········· 481

敢为人先，务实进取，再谱合作新篇章 ·········· 485

Adopt a Pioneering, Practical and Enterprising Spirit and Achieve
New Success in China-UK Cooperation ·········· 488

促进东西方交流互鉴，推进中英战略伙伴关系 ·········· 493

Mutual Learning between the East and the West Will Boost
China-UK Strategic Partnership ·········· 496

深挖潜力，开拓中苏（格兰）合作美好未来 ·········· 501

Tap the Potential for a Brighter Future of China-Scotland Cooperation ··· 507

抓住"宝贵机遇"，推进贵州对英合作 ·········· 517

Seize the "Precious Opportunity" and Advance Guizhou-UK
Cooperation ·········· 521

打造改革开放新高地，助力中英关系新发展 ·········· 527

A New High Ground of Reform and Opening-up, a New
Contribution to China-UK Relations ·········· 530

推动新时代中英地方合作迈上新台阶 ·········· 535

Take China-UK Subnational Cooperation to a New Level ·········· 537

创新引领未来，合作共谱华章 ·········· 541

Cooperation on Innovation Leads to a Bright Future ·········· 544

永立改革开放时代潮头，推进中英全面战略伙伴关系 ·········· 551

Stay at the Forefront of Reform and Opening-up,
and Contribute to China-UK Strategic Partnership ·········· 553

高举开放旗帜，携手开创未来 ·········· 557

Hold High the Banner of Openness and Create a Brighter Future ·········· 561

序　言

我在担任中国驻英国大使11年间，遍访英国各地，广泛接触英国各界人士，努力增进两国人民之间的相互了解和友谊，积极推动中英各领域的交流与合作。

这11年，我见证了中英关系的高光时刻。习近平主席对英国进行国事访问，中英双方将关系定位提升为面向21世纪全球全面战略伙伴关系。

这11年，中英货物贸易额翻了近一番，英国对华出口增长约20倍，中国成为英国第三大货物出口市场；中国对英投资增长约20倍，英国成为中国在欧洲第二大投资目的地国。中英金融合作开创诸多"第一"：英国第一个发行人民币主权债券，在西方大国中第一个申请加入亚投行，中国在伦敦发行中国境外第一笔人民币主权债券；伦敦成为世界第一大人民币离岸交易中心和第二大人民币离岸清算中心，人民币清算量超过50万亿元；"沪伦通"正式开通，多家中资企业在伦交所上市，开了中国与境外资本市场互联互通的先河。中英年度人员往来数量翻了一番，达200万人次；在英中国留学生数量增长一倍多，达22万人，英国已成为中国学生留学的首选地。两国文化、科技、创新交流合作成果丰硕，共同制定了《中英科技创新合作战略》，英国成为第一个与中国签署科技创新合作战略的国家。

这11年，中英关系也经历了起伏和挫折。由于英国在西藏、新疆、香港、人权、南海等问题上一再干涉中国内政，损害中国主权，中英关系屡遭挫折。特别是进入 21 世纪第三个 10 年，在百年变局和世纪疫情叠加的背景下，英国的对华认知和定位发生重大变化，出现严重偏差。曾几何时，英国把中国看作机遇和伙伴，英国领导人公开宣称，英国要成为中国在西方"最有力的支持者"和"最好的伙伴"。现在英国把中国看成对手，在最近的战略报告中，把中国定位为"划时代的制度性挑战"。一些英国政客炒作"中国威胁论"，宣称"黄金时代"已经结束，中英关系不可能回到过去。

回顾这 11 年，不论中英关系处于高潮还是低谷，我始终坚信，中英关系对中国和英国都是十分重要的双边关系。中英关系可以说是我国与西方大国关系的一个缩影，涵盖政治、外交、经济、文化、教育、科技、军事、环保等方方面面。尽管近年来两国关系遇到一些困难和挫折，但中英关系对于两国和世界的意义没有变。中英合作互利共赢，发展中英关系有利于双方，有利于世界。

为了使广大读者了解中英关系，我整理了使英期间发表的 700 余篇演讲，从中挑选出 117 篇，分上、下两卷出版这套《大使讲中英关系》。这里有我对中英关系的观察与思考，包括我们需要一种什么样的中英关系，怎样发展稳定互惠的中英关系，如何增进中英相互了解和认知，更多的章节是介绍中英各领域的交流与合作。希望读者朋友们阅读此书后，赞同我经常说的观点，即我们有一千个理由把中英关系搞好，没有一个理由把中英关系搞坏。习近平主席在英国国王查尔斯三世加冕之际发电祝贺，表示中方愿同英方一道努力，增进人民友好，扩大互利合作，深化人文交流，以稳定互惠的中英关系更好造福两国和世界。我认为，这是中方的愿望，也是中英两国人民的期望。我衷心希望英方与我们相向而行，推动中英关系早日回归正轨。

2023 年立冬

Preface

During my 11 years as the Chinese Ambassador to the United Kingdom, I had travelled extensively across the UK and engaged with people from various sectors, working hard to enhance mutual understanding and friendship between the people of our two countries and actively promoting exchanges and cooperation in various fields between China and the UK.

Over these 11 years, I had witnessed the high-point of China-UK relations. President Xi Jinping's state visit to the UK marked a significant elevation in our bilateral relationship, positioning it as a global comprehensive strategic partnership for the 21st century.

During these 11 years, the trade in goods between China and the UK doubled. With the UK exports to China increasing approximately 20-fold, China became the third-largest export market for UK goods. Chinese investment in the UK also grew about 20-fold, making the UK China's second-largest investment destination in Europe. China-UK financial cooperation achieved a number of "firsts": The UK was the first to issue sovereign bonds in RMB and the first major Western country to apply to join the Asian Infrastructure Investment Bank (AIIB); China issued its first offshore RMB sovereign bond in London; London became the world's largest offshore RMB trading centre and the second-largest offshore RMB clearing centre, with a clearing volume exceeding 50 trillion RMB. The Shanghai-London Stock Connect, a pioneering arrangement in building connectivity between Chinese and foreign capital markets, was officially launched and enabled several Chinese enterprises to list in London. The number of personnel exchanges between China and the UK doubled to 2 million per year; the number of Chinese students in the UK doubled to more than 220,000, making the UK the top choice for Chinese students studying abroad. The cultural, technological, and innovative exchanges and cooperation between the two countries flourished, with the UK becoming the first country to sign the Strategic Plan for Scientific and Technological Innovation Cooperation with China.

These 11 years also saw ups and downs in China-UK relations. Due to the UK's repeated interference in China's internal affairs and infringement on China's sovereignty on questions related to Xizang, Xinjiang, Hong Kong, human rights, and the South China Sea, China-UK relations suffered setbacks. Especially entering the third decade of the 21st century, against the backdrop of global changes and the worst pandemic in a century, the UK's perception and definition of China underwent significant changes and serious deviations. Once viewed as an opportunity and partner, with British leaders openly declaring their intention to make the UK China's "strongest supporter" and "best partner" in the West, China was regarded more recently as a rival and labelled as an "epoch-defining systemic challenge" in a recent strategic report. Some British politicians had been hyping up the "China threat", declaring that the "golden era is over" and claiming that "China-UK relations cannot return to the past".

Looking back at these 11 years, regardless of whether China-UK relations were at their peak or in a trough, I have always firmly believed that China-UK relations are an extremely important bilateral relationship for both China and the UK. China-UK relations can be seen as a microcosm of China's relations with major Western countries, encompassing politics, diplomacy, economics, culture, education, science and technology, military affairs, and environmental protection. Despite the difficulties and setbacks in recent years, the significance of China-UK relations for both countries and the world has not changed. China-UK cooperation is mutually beneficial and win-win; developing China-UK relations is beneficial to both sides and the world.

To help readers understand China-UK relations, I have selected 117 speeches from over 700 I had delivered during my tenure in the UK to put together this two-volume set *On China-UK Relations*. These speeches contain my observations and reflections on China-UK relations: What kind of China-UK relationship do we need? How to develop stable and mutually beneficial China-UK relations? And how to enhance mutual understanding and recognition between China and the UK? More chapters are dedicated to introducing exchanges and cooperation in various fields between China and the UK. I hope that after reading this book, readers will agree with the viewpoint I often express, that we have a thousand reasons to make China-UK relations better, and not a single reason to make them worse. President Xi Jinping, in his congratulatory message on the coronation of King Charles III, expressed China's willingness to work together with the UK to enhance friendship between the peoples, expand mutually beneficial cooperation, and deepen cultural exchanges, so that a stable and mutually beneficial China-UK relationship can better benefit both countries and the world. I believe this is China's wish and the expectation of the people of both countries. I sincerely hope the UK will join us in moving towards this goal and bringing China-UK relations back to the right track at an early date.

Liu Xiaoming
Winter, 2023

第一章 中英关系
PART I China-UK Relations

本章收录了我关于中英关系的 10 篇演讲，从到任招待会到离任招待会。使英 11 年，我与 4 位英国首相和 6 位外交大臣打过交道，见证了中英致力于构建面向 21 世纪全球全面战略伙伴关系，也经历了两国关系的起伏和挫折。这 11 年，我讲得最多的主题是：我们需要什么样的中英关系？怎样建立稳定互惠的中英关系？从向英国工商界阐述坚持正确的义利观，到在英国议会论述中英关系的"三要三不要"，再到在中外记者会上指出中英关系的"变"与"不变"，我强调的是中国始终坚守对中英建交的初心，坚定奉行互相尊重主权和领土完整、互不干涉内政和平等互利的外交原则，这是《联合国宪章》确立的基本原则和国际法与国际关系的基本准则。希望英方同样遵守这些原则和准则，与中方相向而行。只有这样，中英关系才能行稳致远，造福两国和世界。

This chapter includes 10 of my speeches on China-UK relations, from the one at my arrival reception to the one at my departure reception. During my 11 years in the UK, I interacted with 4 British prime ministers and 6 foreign secretaries, witnessing the commitment on both sides to building a comprehensive strategic partnership for the 21st century, and experiencing the ups and downs of the bilateral relations. Throughout these 11 years, the topics I spoke about the most were: What kind of China-UK relationship do our two countries need? How do we establish a stable and mutually beneficial China-UK relationship? From explaining the importance of putting righteousness and interests in perspective to the British business community, and discussing the "three choices" of China-UK relations in the British Parliament, to pointing out what has changed and what has not in China-UK relations at a press conference with Chinese and foreign journalists, I emphasized that China always upholds the original intention of establishing diplomatic relations with the UK and firmly adheres to the principles of mutual respect for sovereignty and territorial integrity, non-interference in each other's internal affairs, and equality and mutual benefit, which are the basic principles established by the UN Charter and the fundamental norms of international law and international relations. I hope the UK also adheres to these principles and norms, and works together with China. Only in this way can China-UK relations remain steady and long-lasting, benefiting both countries and the world.

继往开来，时不我待 *

尊敬的王室使团副典礼长西蒙·马丁先生，

各位使节，

各位议员，

女士们、先生们：

首先，感谢大家出席我的到任招待会。

就在一小时前，我在白金汉宫向女王陛下递交了国书。我向女王陛下转达了胡锦涛主席的亲切问候，女王陛下请我转达她对胡主席的致意，并愉快地回忆起她1986年对中国进行的国事访问，以及江泽民主席和胡锦涛主席分别于1999年和2005年对英国进行国事访问的情景。女王陛下非常关心中英两国关系，她祝我在英国工作顺利。

自1972年中英建立大使级外交关系以来，我是中华人民共和国第11任驻英大使。我到任以来，很多人都对我说，"你来得'恰逢其时'"。对此，我深有同感。

第一，当前的中英关系与38年前今非昔比。今天，两国确立了全面战略伙伴关系，高层保持着密切交往，建立了高级别的经济财金对话和战略对话机制，双边各领域合作全面开展，在重大国际和地区事务中保持着沟通与协调。38年前，中英双边贸易额只有3亿多美元，2009年则达到391亿美元，增长了近130倍。38年前，中国留英学生只有几十名，而目前这个数字接近

---

* 在到任招待会上的讲话。2010年5月26日，中国驻英国大使馆。

10万人，在英海外留学生中居第一位。38年前，中英一年人员往来在千人左右，现在每天就有数千人来往于两国之间。

第二，两国关系远远超出了双边范畴，日益具有战略意义和全球视野。人类已进入21世纪的第二个10年，国际体系和格局正在深刻演变，中英作为两个大国，在国际事务中肩负的责任加重，发挥的作用凸显，共同的利益增多，合作的范围扩大。进一步发展中英关系，不仅符合两国和两国人民的根本利益，也有利于维护世界的和平和稳定，促进全球的发展和繁荣。

第三，中英关系正处在继往开来的新起点。我到任近三个月，适逢英国大选，通过广泛接触英国社会各界，我深刻地感受到发展中英关系是英国朝野坚定的共识。日前，英国新政府已经组成并开始运作。我高兴地看到，卡梅伦首相在就任的第二天就与温家宝总理通了电话，两国领导人一致强调中英关系的重要性，表示致力于进一步拓展和推进两国全面战略伙伴关系，加强各领域对话与合作。杨洁篪外长与黑格外交大臣不久前也通了电话，双方一致表示，愿共同努力，推动中英全面战略伙伴关系取得新的、更长远的发展。现在，上海世博会正在举办，这为两国人民的相知相交、两国合作的深入开展提供了新的机遇。

中英两国虽然语言、文字不同，但有一句相同的谚语："时不我待。"当前，中英关系正处在新的起点，面临着新的发展机遇，我作为新任中国驻英国大使，深感责任重大，使命光荣。我将不辱使命，不负重托，努力巩固和提高两国的政治互信，努力促进双边各领域务实合作，努力强化两国战略性合作，增进两国人民之间的理解和友谊。

我再次感谢各位出席今天的招待会，我更要感谢各位长期以来积极推动和促进中英各领域合作，大力支持和协助历任中国驻英国大使和大使馆的工作。我由衷地希望，在今后的岁月里我能继续得到你们的鼎力协助。让我们共同努力，推动中英关系更上一层楼！

谢谢！

Time and Tide Wait for No Man[*]

Mr Simon Martin,
Your Excellencies,
My Lords,
Ladies and Gentlemen,

May I start by thanking all of you for joining us today.

Just an hour ago, I had the honour of presenting my credentials to Her Majesty the Queen at Buckingham Palace. I conveyed to Her Majesty the cordial greetings of President Hu Jintao. Her Majesty asked me to send her regards to President Hu and recalled with pleasure her visit to China in 1986, President Jiang Zemin's visit to the UK in 1999 and President Hu's visit in 2005. Her Majesty showed a keen interest in the relationship between the UK and China and wished me well in the UK.

I am the 11th Ambassador of the People's Republic of China to the United Kingdom since the two countries established diplomatic ties at ambassadorial level in 1972. People here have kept telling me that I came "at an interesting and important time". I certainly do agree.

The relationship between our two countries has come a long way in the past 38 years. Today we have a vibrant comprehensive strategic partnership and regular high-level exchanges, not least through the annual Prime Ministers' Annual Meeting, the Economic and Financial Dialogue, and the Strategic Dialogue. We developed close

---

[*] Speech at Vin d'Honneur Following Presentation of Credentials. Chinese Embassy, 26 May 2010.

cooperation in a wide range of areas and coordination on major international and regional issues.

Take a few concrete examples. 38 years ago, bilateral trade was merely 300 million US dollars. Last year it was 39.1 billion US dollars, an increase of nearly 130 times. 38 years ago, only a few dozen Chinese students came to study in the UK. Today that number soared to almost 100,000, making China the largest source of overseas students for the UK. 38 years ago, one thousand people traveled between the two countries annually, today thousands of visits are made every day.

The China-UK relationship has gone a long way beyond the bilateral scope and is taking on strategic and global significance. As the world around us undergoes profound changes, China and the UK, as two major players in the world, share greater common interests and are expected to fulfill more responsibilities in tackling international challenges. A growing China-UK relationship, therefore, is not only in the interest of the two countries and peoples, but also serves the interest of maintaining world peace, stability and prosperity.

We now stand at a fresh start in our relations. There has been a general election in this country and a new government is in place. The impression I have got through talking to people from different parties and sectors in my first three months here is that they all recognize the importance of China and support the stronger growth of our relations.

I am very happy that Prime Minister Cameron talked with Premier Wen Jiabao on the phone on his second day in office. A few days ago, Foreign Minister Yang Jiechi also had a telephone conversation with Foreign Secretary Hague. Both the two leaders and Foreign Ministers agreed to further expand and advance China-UK strategic partnership and step up dialogue and cooperation in various areas. The ongoing Shanghai World Expo offers a new opportunity for enhancing friendship and understanding as well as cooperation between our peoples.

The Chinese and English languages share a proverb: Time and tide wait for no man. As the new Chinese Ambassador to the UK, I am keenly aware of my responsibilities. I will do my utmost to fulfill my duties by strengthening China-UK strategic consensus and mutual trust, facilitating all-round cooperation between the two countries, and increasing understanding and friendship between the two peoples.

I also wish to take this opportunity to thank all of you present today for your commitment and effort in promoting China-UK cooperation and for your support to the Chinese Embassy and my predecessors. I sincerely hope that I can continue to count on your generous support in the months and years ahead. I look forward to working with you to take the China-UK relationship to a new high.

Thank you!

坚持正确的义利观 *

尊敬的英中贸易协会主席白乐威爵士，
尊敬的四十八家集团俱乐部主席斯蒂芬·佩里先生，
尊敬的毕马威会计师事务所主席理查德·瑞德先生，
尊敬的英国前副首相杰弗里·豪勋爵，
女士们、先生们：

很高兴今晚与英国工商界的各位朋友再次相聚，也感谢工商界的朋友们为纪念中英建立大使级外交关系40周年举办隆重的晚宴。

2012年对中英关系而言的确是一个非常特殊的年份，是一个回顾过去、展望未来的年份，是一个承上启下的年份。中英关系经过40年的积累，正处在新的起点，面临新的发展机遇。事实上，2012年上半年，中英关系已经有了一个良好的开局。中共中央政治局常委李长春、国务委员刘延东不久前成功访英，在座的不少企业家参加了相关活动。两国启动了高级别人文交流机制，英方在华举办的"艺述英国"活动已经拉开序幕。我们也正在准备2012年下半年两国的一系列对话和访问，推动两国在贸易、投资、金融和人文领域的一系列合作和交流，并期待伦敦奥运会成为两国关系的新亮点。然而，就是在这样令人鼓舞的形势下，总有一些势力不愿看到中英关系发展，总有一些人不珍惜中英关系来之不易的成果，不珍惜两国关系面临的难得机

---

* 在纪念中英建立大使级外交关系40周年晚宴上的演讲。2012年5月28日，英国国家肖像馆。

遇。结果，中英关系就出现了我们不愿看到的情况。

回顾中英关系过去40年走过的历程，我们看到两国关系并非总是阳光灿烂，也有乌云密布；并非总是一帆风顺，也有坎坷起伏。如果说两个月前，我在中国驻英国大使馆举办的招待会上对中英关系过去40年更多的是讲成就，今天我想更多地讲如何总结经验，吸取教训，避免中英关系大起大落。

19世纪英国著名首相帕默斯顿有句名言："国家之间没有永恒的盟友，也没有永恒的敌人，只有永恒的利益。"可见英国的外交十分重视利益，可以说利益至上。无疑，利益是国家关系发展的一大决定性因素。那么，在中英关系中什么是利益？如何处理好这些利益？我认为以下三点至关重要。

第一，促进共同利益。20世纪70年代，反对霸权主义和强权扩张的共同利益使中英走到一起，两国克服了障碍，建立了大使级外交关系。80年代，中英都将保持香港地区的稳定与繁荣视作共同利益，双方经过谈判签署了《中华人民共和国政府和大不列颠及北爱尔兰联合王国政府关于香港问题的联合声明》（以下简称《联合声明》），为香港问题的最终解决奠定了坚实基础。在座的杰弗里·豪勋爵就是这一历史性功绩的参与者。

今天，中英的共同利益更加广泛。就双边层面而言，扩大贸易，投资互利合作，促进两国经济增长，增进两国在教育、文化和科技等领域的合作，加强人文交流，这是两国的共同利益。就全球层面而言，在世界经济走势不稳、国际格局深刻演变的形势下，中英携手合作，共同维护世界的和平、稳定与繁荣，共同应对人类面临的共同挑战，这是两国的共同利益。我们只有始终以两国全面战略伙伴关系发展大局为重，不断扩大共同利益，中英关系才会持续发展。

第二，尊重对方利益。中英历史文化、价值观念、社会制度、发展阶段不同，各自国家利益也不尽相同。作为一个发展中国家，中国的核心利益，一是维护基本制度和国家安全，二是维护国家主权和领土完整，三是确保经济社会的持续稳定发展。这是中国对外政策的"红线"，不会允许任何国家触犯。任何支持和纵容反华分裂势力的活动，都会损害中国的核心利益，不管出于什么样的借口，都理所当然地会遭到中方的坚决反对。中国不会做任何有损英国国家利益的事，同时英方也应尊重中国的国家利益，否则两国关系必然遭受挫折。

第三，维护整体利益。国家利益是属于全体国民的整体利益。中英两国人民，包括在座的各位企业家，都期待中英关系取得更大发展，都期待两国各领域合作取得更大成果，都期待两国通过合作扩大贸易，增加投资，提高就业，促进经济发展，造福两国人民，这是中英关系中两国的整体利益。政治领导人应当始终以两国整体利益和中英关系大局为重，顺应民众愿望，为民众谋福祉，而不是为取悦某种势力和利益集团，牺牲和损害国家整体利益，这就是政治家和政客的区别。在中英关系中，我们需要具有战略眼光和大局意识的政治家，而不是目光短浅、急功近利、眼睛只盯着选票的政客；我们需要维护国家整体利益，而不是集团利益，更不是某种势力的利益。

各位英国工商界的朋友，你们曾是两国关系的"破冰者"，也始终是两国经贸合作的积极参与者和坚定促进者。中英关系发展需要务实的经贸合作提供支撑，也需要良好的政治关系提供保障。缺乏政治互信的中英关系是难以稳定的，双方经贸合作也是难以深入的。今天，在中英政治关系遇到困难的时候，我衷心希望英国工商界的朋友们继续发扬"破冰者"精神，积极发挥各自作用和影响力，为双方经贸合作争取一个良好的政治环境，促使两国关系尽快回到正确的轨道。这是我对你们的期盼，也符合我们的共同利益。

谢谢！

Put Righteousness and Interests in Perspective[*]

Sir David Brewer,

Chairman Stephen Perry,

Chairman Richard Reid,

Lord Howe,

Ladies and Gentlemen,

I am delighted to once again join all of you, friends from the British business community.

I want to thank you most warmly for hosting such a grand dinner. This is a very meaningful way to mark forty years of full diplomatic relations between China and the UK.

In this special year for China-UK relations, it is appropriate to refresh old friendship and make new friends. More importantly, it is the time to learn from the past and so create a stronger future. It is the time to build on the progress made and work for greater achievements.

In this fortieth year of relations, I feel encouraged we made a good start. Here are some examples:

- Mr Li Changchun, member of the Standing Committee of the Political Bureau of the Communist Party of China and State Councilor Madame Liu Yandong successfully visited the UK last month. Many of you present here attended the relevant events.

---

[*] Speech at the British Business Community Dinner Marking Forty Years of Full China-UK Diplomatic Relations. National Portrait Gallery, London, 28 May 2012.

- The China-UK High-Level People-to-People Dialogue was launched.
- The UK Now project was unveiled in China.
- We have been preparing for a series of important dialogues and visits scheduled for later this year.
- We have been planning for multiple cooperation and exchanges in trade, investment, finance, cultural and people-to-people links.
- We look forward to the London Olympic Games becoming another highlight in our bilateral relations.

These are all positive trends.

However, there are always some forces working against our joined efforts to build warm relations.

- These forces dislike the dynamic growth of China-UK relations.
- They have trifled away the progress made through hard efforts.
- They have wasted the rare opportunities in our bilateral ties.
- This is why we now face an undesirable situation in our relations.

This is not the first time we have encountered difficulties. History shows a variable climate in the past four decades. We have experienced both storms and sunshine. Our relationship has never been plain sailing. We have often had to travel on a bumpy road.

Some of you may recall two months ago a reception at the Chinese Embassy. At that time I mainly talked about achievements in these past 40 years. This evening I will focus on the lessons we should draw from those four decades. Learning lessons from the past will help us avoid roller coasters in our relations. This approach could remove many bumps from the road we will travel along.

To drive home my message, I will quote a famous British statesman.

Lord Palmerston twice served as British Prime Minister in the 19th century. However, he is best remembered for his direction of British foreign policy. One of his famous quotes says:

"We have no eternal allies, and we have no perpetual enemies. Our interests are eternal and perpetual."

This indicates that securing "interests" is an enduring goal of British foreign policy. There is no doubt that interests are critical to the development of any country. Yet interests differ in nature and need to be treated accordingly. This means we must have a good knowledge about two questions:

- What are the interests involved in China-UK relations?
- How should we properly handle these interests?

To address these questions, I believe the following three points are essential.

First, we should advance common interests. We have success stories in this aspect.

In the 1970s, opposing hegemonism and power expansion served the common interests of China and the UK. To advance these interests, our two countries overcame difficulties and established ambassadorial diplomatic relations.

In the 1980s, maintaining stability and prosperity in Hong Kong represented our common interests. Through negotiations, we signed the Joint Declaration over Hong Kong. This milestone document laid a solid foundation for the final solution for the future of Hong Kong. Lord Howe was one of those who made important contributions to this historical achievement.

Today, common interests of China and the UK cover broader areas.

At the bilateral level, our shared interests lie in:

- Increasing trade.
- Expanding two-way investment.
- Boosting growth of both economies.
- Stepping up cooperation in education, culture and science and technology.
- And strengthening people-to-people links.

At the global level, the world economy is full of uncertainties. The international landscape is going through profound changes. So, our common interests are defined as:

- Working together for world peace, stability and prosperity.
- And jointly tackling common challenges facing all mankind.

China-UK relations can only keep growing when both nations are truly committed to a Sino-UK comprehensive strategic partnership and common interests of the two countries.

My second point is that we should respect each other's interests. China and the UK are different in many ways. We are different in:

- History.
- Culture.
- Values.
- Social system.
- And development stage.

It should be no surprise that we have different national interests.

As a developing country, China considers the following as its core interests:

- Preserving its basic state system.
- Defending its national security.
- Safeguarding its sovereignty and territorial integrity.
- And ensuring sustained and stable economic and social development.

These interests are the "red lines" of the Chinese foreign policy. They shall not be crossed by any foreign country.

Any attempt to support and connive at anti-China separatist forces hurts the Chinese core interests. Whatever the excuses, such moves will meet firm opposition from China.

China will not do anything to undermine Britain's national interests. So it is perfectly reasonable that Britain should also respect the Chinese national interests. If that is not the case then bilateral ties will surely suffer.

My third point is that we should uphold overarching interests.

National interests are overarching because they concern the people of the entire country. So, what are in the best interests of Chinese and British people?

I believe that our two peoples are eager to see greater progress in China-UK relations and more fruitful cooperation between us in all fields. This certainly is the goal of all the business leaders gathered here this evening. Through cooperation, we will be able to expand trade, increase investment, create jobs, and promote economic growth. These will bring benefits to all of our peoples. Working towards these achievements make up the overarching interests of China and the UK.

Political leaders should at all time uphold the overarching interests of the two countries. They should always support the larger interests of bilateral relations. They should follow the will of the people and advance the well-being of all the people.

What political leaders should not do is to pander to minority views. They should not please small groups at the expense of the overall interests of the country. This is what distinguishes statesmen from politicians.

In China-UK relations, we need statesmen who have strategic vision and keep in mind the larger picture. We do not need short-sighted politicians who are blinded by immediate interests and obsession with votes. What we need to serve is overarching national interests, not the interests of interest groups, or the interests of some forces.

Friends from the British business community:

You have produced "icebreakers" in our bilateral relations. You have long been active participants and firm promoters of China-UK business ties. Growth of China-UK relations needs the support of thriving economic cooperation. It also needs the guarantee of a sound political relationship. In the absence of mutual political trust, there will be no stable bilateral relationship. In turn, deepening economic cooperation will be a "mission impossible".

As China-UK political relationship is now facing difficulty, I do hope that you, friends from the British business community, will:

- Carry forward the spirit of "icebreakers".
- Leverage your influence and play your part in creating a favourable political environment for economic cooperation.
- And help bring China-UK relations back to a normal track.

This is my expectation of you!
It is also our shared interest!
Thank you!

我们需要什么样的中英关系 *

尊敬的希金斯校长,

各位老师、同学:

很高兴访问英格兰第三古老的大学——杜伦大学。不久前我参加了香港大学百年建校的庆祝活动,我在讲话中说,一所大学100岁也才算刚刚有点历史。说这话时,我脑海中就想到了即将访问的具有600年学术氛围和180年正式建校历史的杜伦大学。我也要祝贺杜伦大学2012年加入英国高校的"常春藤联盟"——罗素大学集团,因此,贵校成为我就任中国驻英国大使以来访问的第12所罗素大学集团成员。

虽然这是我第一次访问杜伦大学,但我对贵校一点也不陌生。我2010年初刚到英国履新,就遗憾地听说在东方语言和研究领域声誉卓著的杜伦大学关闭了东亚学院并停办中文本科专业;但在2011年,我又听到了一个令人振奋的好消息,杜伦大学从2011年秋季起恢复招收中国语言文化专业4年制本科学生。刚才希金斯校长向我澄清说,有关"关闭"东亚学院和"停办"中文本科专业的消息不准确,准确的说法是"调整",现在的做法是"重组"。我认为这是明智的。这一转变表明杜伦大学回归全球主流。学习中文会给英国学生在竞争中增加很多优势。中国正在振兴,掌握中文将大大增加年轻人的职业发展机会。

杜伦大学与我的另一个交集是我曾经应邀到一个名叫"筷子俱乐部"的

---

* 在英国杜伦大学的演讲。2012年5月29日,英国杜伦大学。

组织发表演讲。顾名思义，这个非政府组织是个餐饮俱乐部，而且是在中餐馆聚会的餐饮俱乐部，宗旨是学习中文、了解中国，当然还包括品尝中华美食。而这个组织的前身，就是由几个杜伦大学的年轻人在1993年创立的"中国星期二"社团。

今天，希金斯校长本来提议让我讲讲中国外交。我想大家都很关心当前的中英关系，今天我就重点讲讲中英关系，即我们需要建设一个什么样的中英关系。在问答环节我们可以就中国外交的其他方面展开讨论。

2012年是中英建立大使级外交关系40周年。人们在40年前可能无法想象今天两国在各领域交流与合作的密切程度。中英建立了经济财金对话、战略对话和高级别人文交流三大支柱，几十个双边对话磋商机制，47对友好城市（省、郡）关系。1972年，中英双边贸易额只有3亿多美元，2011年达到587亿美元，增长了近200倍。2011年，中国赴英人数达37万人次，是1972年的近2000倍。

中英关系的发展成果是不争的事实，但是我们也应看到，近40年来，中英关系也并非一帆风顺，而是时有坎坷。台湾、香港、西藏、人权，这些不仅曾是两国关系中的敏感词汇，现在也不时冒出来困扰两国关系。两国不仅有贸易逆差、投资逆差，还有认知逆差；两国不仅需要加强互利，更需要加强互信。

我们今天所处的时代，不是称霸、争霸，而是全球化、多极化的时代；不是东西方冷战，而是和平共处、合作共赢的时代。在这样的时代，英国作为世界上最悠久的资本主义国家和老牌的发达国家，中国作为一个坚持自己发展道路的社会主义国家和世界上最大的发展中国家，我们需要建立什么样的中英关系？我们怎样才能确保中英关系稳定健康发展，避免大起大落？我认为可以用四点来概括。

第一，政治上互相尊重。

尊重是互信的来源，也是合作的基础。我认为中英之间，一是要尊重处于不同发展阶段这一事实。英国开启了工业革命，是世界上最早实现工业化的发达国家，经过数百年的持续发展，经济已经步入后工业化时代。中国作为一个发展中国家,真正集中精力搞经济建设只有30多年,仍处于工业化发展中期。虽然中国经济总量已居世界第二,但中国要达到英国目前的劳动生产率、生活水平还需要相当长一段时间。两个最简单的数字对比是,英国人均GDP(国内生产总值)目前约为36000美元,而中国只有5400美元,是英国的近1/7;2011年中国城镇化率历史上首次超过了50%,而英国在1851年就达到了这一数字,比中国早了160年。英国目前的城镇化率高达89%。发展中英关系,不能脱离两国处于不同发展阶段这一基本国情差异。

二是尊重对方选择的发展道路。英国的君主立宪政治体制、自由资本主义发展模式并非上帝赐予的,而是经过几十代英国国民、经历数百年历史发展演变而来的。中国今天走的中国特色社会主义道路,也不是从天上掉下来的,而是中国人民经过100多年来的探索实践,总结历史经验而形成的。中国的发展道路是一条符合中国国情的发展道路,是一条内求发展、外求合作的发展道路,是一条大国振兴的新型发展道路。中国不会干涉别国的发展道路,我们也希望别国尊重中国人民的自主选择。

三是尊重对方的核心利益。中英关系中,彼此的核心利益就是双方的政策"红线",不能被越过。中国的核心利益是什么?一是维护基本制度和国家安全,二是维护国家主权和领土完整,三是确保经济社会的持续稳定发展。中国不会去挑战英国的社会制度,不会去损害英国的主权,不会去阻碍英国的经济社会发展。英国难道不应当同样如此吗?

四是尊重中国的全面进步。中国的改革开放使世界上1/6的人口摆脱了贫困,这不仅是中国自身的了不起成就,也是中国对世界发展的巨大贡献。但是,有些人总认为中国只实行经济改革,不进行政治改革,中国的发展仅局限在经济领域,这是对中国全面发展的一种误读。改革开放30多年来,中国完善人民代表大会制度,废除领导干部职务终身制,发展党内民主,扩大基层民主,我们建立法治社会,尊重和保障人权,建设社会保障体系,这些都是中国全面改革的举措和成果,都是中国经济发展背后的制度性因素。当然改革是一个过程,这个过程不会是一帆风顺的,总会遇到这样或那样的问题,但这是"成长中的烦恼",也是世界各国在改革中都会遇到的问题,中国有信心不断推进改革进程，完善改革举措，推动各项事业的全面进步。

第二，经济上互利共赢。

中英分别是世界第二大和第七大经济体，经济结构互补，双方各有强项。英国在高新技术、金融、品牌、创意产业等方面有领先优势，而中国劳动力充足，实体经济强大，资本雄厚，市场广阔。

中英经贸合作近年取得了加速发展。英国对华出口近两年的增速超过20%，2011年中国对英直接投资几乎超过了以往总和，2012年仅1—4月的新增投资额就是2011年的3倍多。但两国经贸合作的规模仍偏小，与双方的实力、地位很不相称。我们知道爱尔兰的人口是450万，而中国有13亿人口，但是面对这样一个大市场，2011年英国对华出口只有英国对爱尔兰出口的1/2。

我认为拓展中英经贸合作潜力巨大，关键是双方要树立两个意识。

一是伙伴意识。中英在经济上不是竞争对手，而是合作伙伴。中国的经济持续发展和英国的复苏增长对彼此都至关重要，双方一荣俱荣，一损俱损，是利益共同体。英国应摒弃冷战思维，放宽对华高技术出口，不应甘居欧盟第五（在德、法、意、瑞典之后）。

二是机遇意识。中国在转变发展方式，调整经济结构，扩大国内消费市场，这是英国企业的机遇，英国企业不能太"保守"；英国在重振制造业，扩大基础设施建设，吸引外来投资，这同样是中国企业的机遇，中国企业要敢于"出手"。

第三，文化上互知互鉴。

中国和英国在欧亚大陆的一东一西，中华文化是世界上唯一未曾中断的古老文明，英国开辟了近现代世界文明史，中英都对人类文明发展做出了巨大贡献。

中英的文明交流历史可以说不短，但目前存在着两大不平衡。一是中国对英国的了解要远远多于英国对中国的了解，双方存在认知逆差。近现代100多年来，中国一直在虚心学习，无论是马克思主义还是市场经济，都学自西方。今天，中国的孩子从小学一年级甚至幼儿园起就开始学习英文，每年还有数万名中国年轻人来英留学。英国的电影、电视剧、音乐剧在中国很受欢迎，音乐剧《妈妈咪呀！》中文版在中国一炮走红，电视剧《唐顿庄园》在中国也受到热捧。但英国不少民众对中国的了解可能还只是停留在功夫片的程度。

二是英国对古代中国的了解要强于对当代中国的了解，两者之间存在时代落差。我发现英国对古代中国的研究非常深入。据说杜伦大学的历史系、考古系在英国都名列前茅，中国研究的历史也很悠久，仅学校东方博物馆馆藏的中国文物就多达上万件。虽然英国有许多中国文物专家，但是知名当代中国研究学者并不多，一些学者对客观、理性认识当代中国还有心理障碍。

可喜的是，这种情况在不断改善。中国文化精品频繁在英国亮相，无论是在爱丁堡国际艺术节，还是在皇家阿尔伯特音乐厅，或是在莎士比亚环球剧场，或是在伦敦特拉法加广场，中国文化演出都受到了热烈欢迎。中英双方已合作在英设立了20所孔子学院和63间孔子课堂，英国600多所中小学开设了中文选修课。

英国各大学纷纷加大对当代中国研究的投入，30多所大学设立了中国研究中心或研究所，当代中国研究在英国正成为一门"显学"。比如，近年来，牛津大学整合学校各相关中国研究机构设立了"中国中心"；伦敦国王学院中国研究中心于2010年成立，我曾参加成立仪式；2012年，剑桥大学首次设立了"中国教席"；诺丁汉大学的当代中国学学院近年来声名鹊起，2012年下半年我将应邀参加其新楼启用仪式。我也高兴地得知，杜伦大学不仅恢复了本科中文专业，而且其当代中国研究中心越来越受到重视。

这就是中英关系的一个重要方向，即中国当代文化更为英国民众所了解，英国年青一代学习中国语言和文化的热情不断升温，研究中国的学术团体逐步壮大，了解中国、探索中国日益成为潮流，双方文化相互借鉴不断增强。这正是中英2012年启动首次高级别人文交流机制的目的。我希望并相信，两国人民之间沟通和文化上的交流借鉴将成为中英关系的一大支柱。

第四，国际上互助合作。

今天我们所处的世界，地区冲突、民族宗教矛盾、核扩散、恐怖主义、气候变化、传染疾病等传统和非传统安全威胁此起彼伏，世界还很不太平。今天我们所处的世界，经济衰退阴影不散，美国经济复苏乏力，欧债危机持续发酵，新兴经济体增长面临挑战，实现经济增长是各国共同的紧迫任务。

中英都是联合国安理会常任理事国，都是二十国集团（G20）的重要成员，在维护世界和平、促进全球繁荣方面有着共同利益，肩负着重要责任。因此，中英关系超越双边层面，具有全球意义。

中英应共同促进世界和平与稳定。只有中英等大国共同应对全球性安全挑战，人类的和平事业才会发展。

中英应共同促进世界经济复苏和增长。当前，世界经济复苏存在较大不确定性，同时保护主义在全球回潮，世贸谈判举步维艰，欧洲金融体系不稳定。中英需要继续同舟共济，共同推动世界经济、金融治理改革，共同维护自由、开放的贸易秩序。

中英应共同促进世界的多样性。一种文明、一种社会制度、一种发展模式放之四海而皆准已被证明并不可行。中英应推动各种文明平等对话、各种社会制度相互借鉴、各种发展模式取长补短。

各位老师、各位同学，

中英关系不仅是国家关系，也是人民之间的关系。促进一个互相尊重、互利共赢、互知互鉴和互助合作的中英关系，不仅是两国政治家和外交官的使命，也是两国社会各界，包括在座各位的责任。

杜伦大学有一句座右铭："基于过去，创造未来。"这句话如果稍加改动，我想正是我今天演讲的主旨，也可成为中英关系的一个鞭策："基于共同愿望，创造美好未来。"

谢谢！

What Kind of China-UK Relationship Do We Need*

Vice-Chancellor Higgins,

Faculty and students,

I am delighted to visit Durham University.

As the third oldest university in England, you have a long and distinguished history.

Not long ago, I attended the celebration of the centenary of Hong Kong University. Then I said "a one-hundred-year-old university is still quite young" because I know some British universities have a history of hundreds of years.

I have learned that teaching activities in Durham University started about 600 years ago. It has been formally established as a university for 180 years. But age has been far from dulling your progress!

I believe a measure of your vitality is your new membership of the Russell Group. I warmly congratulate you on joining this elite group. Durham is now the 12th member of the Russell Group I have visited.

This is my first visit to Durham University, yet Durham University is no stranger to me, because it has often been in the news for its links with China. Two years ago when I first became Chinese Ambassador to the UK, I read about Durham closing its East Asian Department and suspending the Chinese language major for a Bachelor degree. I was sad when I learned about these decisions because Durham has a high reputation for its strengths in Oriental languages and studies.

Last year I heard Durham would resume Chinese language programmes for

---

* Speech at Durham University. Durham University, 29 May 2012.

undergraduates. That was an exciting piece of news. I believe this is a very wise reorganization. The change shows that Durham University is back in tune with global trends. It is a recognition that learning Mandarin provides great advantages to British students. Mandarin language skills will open immense career opportunities as China retakes its place as a leading nation in the world.

There is another reason why Durham is no stranger to me. I was once invited to speak at a function hosted by the Chopsticks Club. As its name suggests, this is a private members dining club, a club that always holds events at Chinese restaurants. It is committed to China-related knowledge sharing and cultural exchanges, and of course enjoying Chinese food! Its predecessor was an organization called China Tuesdays, which was founded in 1993 by some young people from Durham University.

In that spirit of study of China I will now respond to a kind invitation from Vice-Chancellor Higgins. He proposed that today I speak about the Chinese foreign policy.

However I believe all of you take a great interest in the current China-UK relations, which I'm going to talk about in my speech, and we may cover other aspects of the Chinese foreign policy later in the Q&A session. My thought for the speech is to answer this question:

What kind of China-UK relationship do we need?

This year marks forty years of full diplomatic relations between China and the UK. We now have close exchanges and cooperation between our two countries. This would have been unimaginable for people four decades ago.

We have set up three key mechanisms:

- Economic and Financial Dialogue.
- Strategic Dialogue.
- And High-Level People-to-People Dialogue.

And these are examples of our progress in more depth:

- We have put in place dozens of bilateral dialogue and consultation mechanisms covering other areas.
- We now have 47 pairs of sister cities and provinces.

- In 1972, China-UK bilateral trade was merely 300 million US dollars. Last year that surged to 58.7 billion US dollars. This is an increase of nearly 200 times.
- Last year, more than 370,000 people visited the UK. This number is almost 2,000 times of that in 1972.

Progress in China-UK relations is an indisputable fact.

Yet, we also need to be aware that development of our relations in these forty years has not been plain sailing. We went through ups and downs. Taiwan, Hong Kong, Xizang, and human rights used to be touchy questions. They still crop up from time to time and hold back greater advance in our relations.

In addition, our relations still lack balance. There is the challenge of deficits. Between China and the UK, there is not only a trade deficit, but also a deficit of understanding. We need to work much harder to strengthen not only mutual benefit but also mutual trust.

We must succeed in achieving these goals because we now live in a different world. Global relations are very different from 40 years ago when we established full diplomatic links.

The world today is not one of hegemony, but of globalization and multi-polarity. It no longer features a Cold War between the West and the East. We now aim for peaceful coexistence and win-win cooperation.

In such a world, what kind of relationship do we need between China and the UK? How do we ensure healthy and stable development of our relations and avoid ups and downs when we have differences?

Britain is the world's oldest capitalist country and has long been fully developed. China is a socialist country committed to its own development path. China is also the largest developing country in the world.

We have to take account of our differences. However, I believe our relationship can only be developed when we observe the following four principles.

The first principle is political mutual respect.

From mutual respect comes mutual trust. Respect is the basis for cooperation. In the case of China and the UK, several factors merit our attention.

A key step is to respect the fact that we are in different development stages.

Britain is where the European industrial revolution started. The UK is the earliest advanced industrialised country in the world. After centuries of continued development, it is now in a post-industrialisation era.

In contrast, China is a developing country. It has been only 30 years since China went all out for economic growth. It is still halfway to industialisation. Though the Chinese economic size is the second largest in the world, it still has a long way to go before it can reach the productivity and living standards in the UK. Here are some quick examples:

- Per capita GDP of the UK is about 36,000 US dollars. In China it is only 5,400 US dollars. That is nearly one seventh of the UK's.
- Last year the urbanisation rate in China passed 50% for the first time. Britain already reached this level in 1851, 160 years earlier than China. The current urbanisation rate in the UK is 89%.

If there is to be strong mutual respect and trust in China-UK relations, we must recognise the different realities in our countries.

Second, we should respect each other's choice of development path.

Britain's constitutional monarchy and capitalism are the accepted choice of British people. These government and economic systems have evolved through dozens of generations spanning hundreds of years.

Likewise, the socialism with Chinese characteristics in China is the accepted choice of Chinese people. It is the result of Chinese people's explorations and practices over more than 100 years. The Chinese development path suits the Chinese national conditions. Its domestic agenda stresses development. Its foreign policy aims at cooperation. This is a new path for the rise of China to take its place amongst the family of world nations.

China itself will never criticise the choice of development path of other countries. Likewise, China hopes other countries will respect Chinese people's own choice as well.

Third, we should respect each other's core interests.

In China-UK relations, core interests are our respective policy "red lines" that shall not be crossed.

Then what are the Chinese core interests? They are:

- Preserving its basic state system.
- Defending its national security.
- Safeguarding its sovereignty and territorial integrity.
- And ensuring sustained and stable economic and social development.

Again China respects the core interests of other countries such as the UK:

- China will not challenge Britain's social system.
- China will not encroach on Britain's sovereignty.
- And China will not impede Britain's economic and social development.

Doesn't mutual respect mean that Britain should treat China the same way?

Fourth, the Chinese comprehensive progress should be respected.

The Chinese reform and opening-up lifted one sixth of the world's population out of poverty. This is not only an achievement of China. It is also a tremendous contribution China has made to the whole world.

Yet some people believe the Chinese development is limited to economy only. They see only economic reform in China, but neglect the Chinese progress in political reform. I must say this is very wrong. This is a classic misunderstanding of the Chinese comprehensive development. I hope those who hold this view will pay attention to the following facts. These are political advances through the three decades of the reform and opening-up policies:

- China has improved the system of people's congress.
- China abolished the life tenure of leadership positions.
- China advanced inner-Party democracy.
- China expanded democracy at grassroots level.
- China upholds the rule of law.
- China respects and protects human rights.
- China has built and improved social security system.

All these are the Chinese comprehensive reform measures. They show the progress we have made on all fronts. They are also the institutional drivers of the Chinese economic growth.

At the same time, we must not forget that reform is a gradual process. It takes time. Britain did not come to where it is in three decades. That process took centuries.

In a developing country like China, no one can get everything in place at one stroke. There will be problems and difficulties of many different kinds. They are "growing pains". They are problems that all countries will come across in their reforms.

However, China is confident that it will keep reform moving forward and make further advances on all fronts of comprehensive reform.

Now, let me turn to the second principle for a successful China-UK relationship. That is economic win-win.

China and the UK are respectively the second and seventh largest economies in the world.

We each have our own strengths. Our economies have a lot to offer each other. For example:

- The UK is a leader in new and high technology, finance, branding and creative industries.
- China has a large labour force, a strong real economy, adequate capital and a huge market.
- China-UK economic cooperation in recent years has grown rapidly.
- In the past two years, the UK exports to China increased at a rate of over 20%.
- The Chinese direct investment in Britain last year alone passed the total of all previous years.
- From January to April this year, the Chinese investment in the UK was already more than three times of last year's total.

Yet given our economic strengths and sizes, great potential remains untapped. I will highlight the opportunities with this dramatic comparison.

As we know, the population of Ireland is 4.5 million, while China has 1.3 billion people. However, Britain's exports to China last year were only half of its exports to

Ireland.

To bring Sino-UK economic potential into full play, we need to do the following.

First, we need to be clear that we are economic partners, not competitors. Sustained growth of the Chinese economy and economic recovery of Britain are critical to each other. Our interests are so closely linked that if one wins, both will win; if one loses, both will be losers.

Britain should discard the Cold War mentality and relax restrictions on high-tech exports to China. It is now the fifth largest high-tech exporter to China among the EU members (after Germany, France, Italy and Sweden). It should aim for a higher place.

Second, we need to seize opportunities. China is shifting its growth model, restructuring its economy and boosting consumption. These measures mean opportunities to British businesses.

Britain is reviving its manufacturing sector, upgrading infrastructure and seeking foreign investment. These also offer opportunities to Chinese companies. Both sides must not miss out on the opportunities.

Now, I would like to discuss the third principle for the China-UK relationship. That is cultural mutual understanding and learning.

China and the UK are at two ends of the Eurasia. Chinese civilization is the world's longest continuous civilisation. The UK is a pioneer of modern civilisation. This British status arose from its lead with industrialisation over the past three centuries. So both China and Britain have made outstanding contributions to human civilisation.

Cultural exchanges between China and Britain date back a long time. But the process is uneven and unbalanced in two aspects.

First, the Chinese understanding of Britain is far better than the other way round. There is a deficit of understanding on the British side.

In the recent century, China has been learning from the West. What we learned includes Marxism and market economy theories. Today, Chinese children start to learn English when they are first graders or even in kindergartens. Every year, tens of thousands of Chinese students come to study in Britain. British films, TV series and musicals are immensely popular in China. For example, The Chinese version of *Mamma Mia* is a blockbuster. *Downton Abbey* is also a great hit in China. But I am afraid many ordinary British people's knowledge about China stops at martial arts.

Second, there is a discrepancy in Britain's knowledge about China and its understanding of modern China.

Take Durham as an example. Durham's departments of history and archeology rank very high in the UK. Durham also has a long tradition of Chinese studies. Its Oriental Museum has a collection of around ten thousand pieces of Chinese antiques.

Britain has many experts on Chinese antiquities. That is an excellent strength. But what about the study of today's China? Britain lacks comparable abilities with contemporary Chinese studies. There is an absence of famous scholars on modern China. In addition, some scholars are still not comfortable to see China as it is.

I am glad that the cultural exchange situation is improving. More and more quality cultural products from China have been introduced to Britain. Chinese cultural performances have been well received wherever they appear. These range from the Edinburgh International Festival to the Royal Albert Hall, and from Shakespeare's Globe Theatre to Trafalgar Square.

Through cooperation between our two countries, more than 20 Confucius Institutes and 63 Confucius Classrooms have been opened in the UK. Over 600 middle and primary schools around the UK now offer Chinese language optional courses.

Another encouraging trend in this aspect is British universities have scaled up their input on contemporary Chinese studies. More than 30 universities in the UK have opened Chinese study centres or institutes. Contemporary Chinese studies are becoming a "hot" field. Here are some examples:

- Oxford University has put together all its Chinese studies agencies and set up a China Centre.
- King's College London opened the Lau China Institute in 2010. I attended the launch ceremony.
- This year, University of Cambridge created a new chair of China Development in its Centre of Development Studies.
- University of Nottingham's School of Contemporary Chinese Studies has earned much credit in recent years. Later this year, I will attend the launch of its new building.
- I am delighted that Durham University has not only resumed Chinese major

for undergraduates, but also its Centre for Contemporary Chinese Studies has attracted wider attention.

All these developments point to an important direction in China-UK relations:

- British people will gain a better understanding of contemporary Chinese culture. Young Britons have greater interest in learning Chinese language and culture.
- There are more academic institutions focusing on Chinese studies.
- Understanding and discovering China is becoming a major trend.
- Cultural exchanges and mutual learning are gaining momentum.
- This is precisely the purpose of the China-UK High-Level People-to-People Dialogue launched in April this year.

I hope and believe that people-to-people dialogue and cultural exchanges will become another pillar in our bilateral relations.

Now, I will move on to the fourth principle governing China-UK relations. I believe a successful China-UK relationship must have mutual support and cooperation at a global level.

The world today faces many challenges:

- Regional conflicts.
- Ethnic and religious tensions.
- Nuclear proliferation.
- Terrorism.
- Climate change and infectious diseases.

The combination of these conventional and non-conventional security threats makes the world everything but tranquil.

The world today is still haunted by economic recession.

- The US economy is sluggish.
- The European Debt Crisis is worsening.

- Emerging and developing economies are confronted by challenges.
- Maintaining economic growth is a common and urgent task facing all countries.

These issues place immense responsibility on world leaders and forums where they meet.

China and the UK are both permanent members of the UN Security Council. Both are important members of the G20. This means we have shared interests and responsibilities in maintaining world peace and promoting global prosperity. In this connection, China-UK relations have gone beyond the bilateral scope and taken on a global significance.

So, China and the UK should work together to uphold world peace and stability. Only a collective response to global security challenges can advance the cause of peace for all of mankind.

China and the UK should work together to promote world economic recovery and growth. Now, world economic recovery is full of uncertainties:

- Protectionism is staging a comeback.
- WTO negotiations are in a stalemate.
- Financial systems are unstable, especially in Europe.

All these challenges make a compelling case for close collaboration between China and the UK. Our shared goal is to advance reform in world economic governance and financial regulation, and safeguard the order of free and fair trade.

China and the UK should work together for preserving diversity in the world. History and the experience proves that there is no one-size-fits-all model. This means China and the UK should both advocate equal dialogue among different civilizations. Both our countries should encourage mutual learning between different social systems and development models.

Teachers and students,

The China-UK relationship is not only about two countries, but also about two peoples.

To promote a China-UK relationship of mutual respect, mutual benefit, mutual learning and mutual support is not only the mission of Chinese and British leaders and diplomats, but also the responsibility of all social sectors in both countries, all of you included.

The motto of Durham University says:

"Shaped by the past, creating the future."

A little editing of the motto will provide a perfect summary of my thoughts today:

"Shaped by common aspiration, creating a bright future."

Let this be our constant guide for the China-UK relationship.

Thank you!

以史为鉴，可以知兴替 *

约翰·李主席，

青年朋友们，

女士们、先生们：

很高兴来到牛津大学学联——牛津大学最大的辩论俱乐部，与青年朋友进行交流。这是我第二次来到牛津演讲。两年半前，我在贵校赛德商学院的报告厅谈了当代中国外交，那是我第一次在英国大学发表演讲，至今记忆犹新。

今天再次来到牛津，约翰·李主席一开始就给我出了道难题，他出的题目是"任何想说的话题"。这就如同你进了一家餐馆，对厨师说，随便做点儿好吃的吧。厨师会很犯难，因为他不知道做什么才会合你的口味。所以，我首先就要做一道很难的"选择题"——确定主题。

有一件事给了我一些灵感。经常有人问这样的问题："牛津大学最好的专业是什么？"我也很想知道答案。有人说是PPE（哲学、政治学和经济学）。不过，也有人说是历史。因此，今天，我想选择一个历史话题，因为"以史为鉴，可以知兴替"。我想谈谈200年来中国和英国之间的交往史。

中英关系历经风风雨雨200多年，纷繁复杂，我想用"五个一"来浓缩、勾勒，即一次不成功的外交活动、一场非正义的战争、一场顺应时代的外交升格、一场具有历史意义的谈判、一种新型伙伴关系。

第一，一次不成功的外交活动。1792年，英王乔治三世向中国派出一个

---

* 在牛津大学学联的演讲。2012年10月9日，牛津大学。

代表团，即著名的马戛尔尼使团。这是英国，甚至是整个西方向中国派出的第一个外交使团，它拉开了中英正式交往的序幕。

马戛尔尼的使命是建立中英外交关系，并为英国商品开辟市场。因此马戛尔尼向当时的清政府提出了诸如建立使馆、开辟通商口岸等要求。马戛尔尼使华，无疑没有达到访问目的，其所提要求被一一驳回。乾隆皇帝毫不客气地在给英王的复信中指出：派人留京"与天朝体制不合，断不可行"，"天朝德威远被，万国来王，种种贵重之物，梯航毕集，无所不有。……无更需尔国置办物件"。马戛尔尼自己总结使命失败的原因是"翻译水平过低"，也就是语言不通。当然，也有人说是礼节问题，即英使是否要向乾隆皇帝双膝下跪。但从根本上来说，这是由于新兴大国和守成大国在观念上的冲突，是一次"聋人和盲人的对话"。英国作为正在进行工业革命的资本主义强国，还不了解仍处于农耕社会、闭关锁国的中国，同时，以天朝自居的中国也还没有准备好与迅速崛起的英国打交道，去认识正在变化的世界。

或许我该提一下马戛尔尼使团的副使——乔治·斯当东男爵，就在启程去中国的两年前，他获得了牛津大学的荣誉法学博士学位。

第二，一场非正义的战争。1840年，中英之间爆发了一场战争，这场战争可能对英国而言不算什么了不起的战争，英国人将它称作"第一次英中战争"，也将它说成是一场"商业战争"，但这样的措辞掩盖不了它的非正义性，因为它所捍卫的贸易是走私，推销的商品是鸦片。正如当时反对战争的托利党人格兰斯顿在英国议会下院辩论时所演讲的："我不知道也没有在书中读到过，在起因上还有比这场战争更加不义的战争。"

这场非正义鸦片战争的结果是中国战败，中英签署了不平等条约，英国强迫中国割让了香港岛，中国增开五口通商口岸。马戛尔尼使团没有得到的东西，英国人通过坚船利炮得到了。

鸦片战争对中国的影响是深远的，被历史学家公认为是中国近代史的开端。鸦片战争后的100年，中国可谓国运飘摇，积贫积弱。1840年中国GDP约占世界的30%，到了1940年已锐减至不到5%。同时，外患不断，内乱不已，主权沦丧，山河破碎，中英关系自然也长期处于一种不平等状态。

但历史有时就是这么辩证，事物总是有它的另一面。在中华民族走向危难之时，"东方睡狮"也逐渐苏醒，中国人痛定思痛，开始"睁眼看世界"，上下求索救亡图存之道。于是，中国爆发了革命，推翻了帝制，建立了共和；"西学东渐"，中国学习和接受了西方近现代科学知识和民主思想；中国14年抗战，打败了日本侵略者，实现了民族独立；中国引进了马克思主义，成立了中国共产党，建立了中国共产党领导下的新中国。正因如此，在北京天安门广场的人民英雄纪念碑上镌刻着："由此上溯到一千八百四十年，从那时起，为了反对内外敌人，争取民族独立和人民自由幸福，在历次斗争中牺牲的人民英雄们永垂不朽！"中华民族奋发振兴的历史就是以鸦片战争为起点的。

第三，一场顺应时代的外交升格。1949年新中国成立后，中英之间于1954年建立了代办级外交关系，这不是一种正常的外交关系，被史学家称为"半建交关系"。这是二战后冷战大环境使然，也是由于中国台湾问题上的一些障碍。

直到1972年，国际格局发生了重大变化，中美关系发生了"破冰"，中英关系才迎来了"解冻"。英国承认中国政府关于台湾是中华人民共和国一个省的立场，中英签署了联合公报，将代办级外交关系升格为大使级外交关系，两国关系实现了正常化。这是中英关系的一个重要转折点，开启了两国相互尊重、平等交往的新起点。

2012年正是中英建立大使级外交关系40周年，中英双方举办了不少纪念活动。我在中国驻英国大使馆举办的纪念招待会的讲话中，特意提到了一位英国人，他就是时任英国首相希思先生。他不仅为中英建立大使级外交关系做出了贡献，而且一生中曾经26次访华，致力于中英友好，被中国誉为"人民友好使者"。

牛津学联的史料表明，希思先生曾是这里的书记员和图书管理员。除此之外，我相信他肯定还是这里的一位出色辩手。这里是他的政治摇篮，给他以思想启蒙。

第四，一场具有历史意义的谈判。中英建立了大使级外交关系，但两国关系中还有一桩历史悬案，这就是我前面提到的鸦片战争所遗留下的问题：香港。

摆在中英双方面前的问题是，中国要收回香港，英国要维护在香港的利益。于是两国政府经过多达22轮会谈，1984年在北京签署了关于香港问题的《联合声明》，中国于1997年7月1日对香港恢复行使主权，回归后香港实行"一国两制"。

中英解决香港问题具有里程碑意义。一是扫清了中英间重大历史遗留问题，为两国关系的长期发展进一步奠定了基础。二是为中国实现和平统一创下了先例。按照香港模式，中国和葡萄牙此后顺利解决了澳门问题。三是创下了和平谈判解决国际争端的范例。中英通过和平谈判解决敏感复杂的领土问题，不仅对两国具有深远的现实意义，而且对世界具有重要的现实意义，这应当给个别企图挑战《联合国宪章》宗旨和战后国际秩序、单方采取行动破坏国与国达成的有关和平解决领土争端共识的亚洲国家以深刻启迪。

在这一历史性事件中，牛津的又一位校友以其远见卓识和明智决策，在香港问题的解决上发挥了重要的作用，她就是"铁娘子"撒切尔夫人。

第五，一种新型伙伴关系。世纪之交以来，中国的经济实力、国际地位和作用发生了巨大的变化。中国经过改革开放30多年的励精图治，年均增速达到9.9%，成为世界第二大经济体，创造了世界经济发展史上的新奇迹。中国积极参与国际事务，从过去西方眼中的地区性大国上升为全球性大国，许多国际热点问题和全球性事务的解决离不开中国的参与和支持。

在这样的背景下，中英尽管历史文化、发展阶段和社会制度不同，但两国努力建立了一种超越差异和分歧的互利共赢的新型伙伴关系。1998年，两国将之称为"全面伙伴关系"，2004年又升格为"全面战略伙伴关系"，赋予了其中更多内涵。它建立在两国共同利益基础之上，深刻反映了两国关系的新时代要求。

今天，中英已建立了经济财金对话、战略对话和高级别人文交流机制等双边关系"三大支柱"。双边经贸合作发展迅速，2011年中英货物贸易额近600亿美元，比1972年增长了近200倍。每年，中英有超过100万人次的民众到对方国家旅游、工作、学习，中国成为英国海外留学生最大来源国。两国在国际事务中尽管不是所有问题都持相同观点，但双方保持着密切磋商与协调。两国关系的广度和深度都达到了前所未有的水平。

谈到中英新型伙伴关系，我又不得不提到另一位功不可没的牛津校友，即前首相布莱尔先生，而且据说他当年是牛津学联的活跃分子。在他执政的11年里，中英关系发展可以说是"又快又好"。他高度重视中英关系，专门成立了"对华关系小组"。当然，我们也不应忘了，现任英国首相也是一名牛津校友。

青年朋友们，

刚才我用了"五个一"，将纷繁庞杂的中英关系大致做了一个简化和梳理。2012年正好是马戛尔尼使团赴华220周年，回顾中英220年交往史，我们不难看到这样的轨迹：从陌生到了解，从敌对到友好，从不平等到平等，从竞争到合作，从消极到积极。当然，它不是一条直线，而是一条不断向上的曲线。中英关系并非总是一帆风顺，而是时有起伏，常有波折，但这没有也改变不了两国关系发展的总体趋势。

中国古人说："以史为鉴，可以知兴替。"雨果说："历史是什么：是过去传到将来的回声，是将来对过去的反映。"总结中英关系200多年的历史，我们今天应该得到什么样的启示呢？

我认为，最突出、最重要的启示就是要相互尊重，平等相待。这也是今天中国外交奉行和坚持的一条原则。在中英关系史上，无论是马戛尔尼使华的失败，还是鸦片战争的爆发，都是由于缺乏相互尊重和平等相待；相反，无论是中英外交关系的升格、香港问题的顺利解决，还是中英建立新型伙伴关系，都是由于中英相互尊重和平等相待。可以说，相互尊重和平等相待是中英关系发展的内在之魂。

今天，怎样才能做到相互尊重和平等相待呢？

一是尊重对方的历史、文化、发展阶段和社会制度等基本国情。中国有五千年古老文明史，英国开创了近代工业文明；中国人深受儒家思想影响，英国人则有实用主义传统；英国是近代资本主义的诞生地，是西方发达国家之一，中国实行中国特色社会主义，是最大的发展中国家。这是两国的基本国情，了解是尊重的前提，我们必须了解这样的差异。我们更要尊重差异，尊重对方国家的发展道路和自主选择。只有这样，中英两个历史、文化和社会、政治制度不同的国家才能成为平等的伙伴，才能建立和发展全面战略伙伴关系。

二是尊重对方的利益，特别是核心利益。英国皇家海军军歌《统治吧，不列颠尼亚！》中有一句："英国人永远不会做奴隶。"中国国歌《义勇军进行曲》的第一句就是："起来！不愿做奴隶的人们！"鸦片战争后，中国深受主权沦丧之辱，中华民族遭受了深重的苦难。今天的中国和中国人民，珍爱国家独立和民族自由，视国家主权和领土完整高于一切。在涉及主权和领土等核心利益问题上，中国不容许别人损害和干涉。中英之间曾经有太多这样的历史教训，我们必须避免重蹈覆辙。

牛津校友、英国著名历史学家汤因比曾预言："21世纪将是中国人的世纪。"当然，这句话不能片面理解为21世纪仅属于中国，而是说中国在21世纪将有更大作为。我相信，在中国日益繁荣富强的基础上，中英关系的未来将更加充满机遇。我们应当发展政治上更加互尊互信、经贸上更加互利共赢、文化上更加互知互鉴、国际上更加协调合作的新时期中英新型伙伴关系，造福两国和两国人民。

220年前，乔治三世在致乾隆皇帝的国书中如此写道："现在正是中国和英国这两个伟大和文明的国家传输善意和缔结友谊，从和睦的关系中相互获益的最佳时机。"由于历史条件所限，这样的愿望当时没有成为现实。

今天，在新的时代，中国和英国这两个伟大的国家可以为世界做出许多贡献。我们两国应竭尽所能为建设持久和平的世界这一共同目标而奋斗。

在中英关系的过去，牛津校友起到了举足轻重的作用。在中英关系的未来，牛津学子也一定会大有作为。所以我今天来到你们中间，希望你们顺应时代，承担起使命与责任，与中国的年青一代一道努力，谱写中英关系未来的新篇章。

谢谢！

History Tells a Lot *

President-Elect John Lee,

Young friends,

It is a real pleasure for me to be invited to speak here today.

The Oxford Union is a prestigious debating society, with an unparalleled reputation for bringing international guests and speakers to Oxford and for the cut and thrust of its debate.

So, it is indeed an honour for me to be with you.

Also, I am delighted to have this opportunity to exchange ideas with you young friends here.

This is my second speech at Oxford. Two years ago I was invited to speak about contemporary Chinese foreign policy at the Said Business School. That was a straight forward task as obviously I should know about the subject.

Now back in Oxford, I face a tough challenge.

This is because President Lee has kindly suggested that I choose whatever topic for this speech. This is not an easy choice.

Imagine that you walk into a restaurant. You then ask the chef to cook whatever tastes great. The chef will be at loss for he does not know what kind of food will please your palate.

So I have given some serious thought to how to appeal to your appetite.

In choosing today's topic, I have drawn inspiration from this great university.

Many people ask about what might be the most advantageous degree to study at the

---

* Speech at the Oxford Union. University of Oxford, 9 October 2012.

University of Oxford. Some say philosophy, politics and economics, commonly known as PPE. Some say history.

So I am going to talk about history—the history of China-Britain relations, because I believe history tells a lot.

The relations between China and Britain started over two centuries ago.

It is a long and complicated relationship and has gone through many ups and downs. But in five phrases we can capture the headlines:

- It started with a failed diplomatic mission.
- There was an unjust war.
- Then a well-timed diplomatic upgrading.
- This led to a historic negotiation.
- And finally, a new partnership.

Let me explain them one by one.

First, a failed diplomatic mission.

In 1792, King George III sent a delegation to China. This was known as the Macartney Mission.

It was the first ever diplomatic mission that Britain, and even the entire Western world, had dispatched to China. It was the prelude of official contacts between China and Britain.

The purpose of the Macartney Mission was to launch diplomatic relations between the two countries. The driving motivation of the British was commercial. With rising industrial might, the UK needed new markets. So it was an obvious step to try and open Chinese markets for British products.

Macartney made several requests to the Qing government. One request was the establishment of a permanent British Embassy in China. Another petition was opening some Chinese ports for trade.

Lord Macartney failed to attain his goals. His requests and proposals were declined. Emperor Qianlong wrote in his reply letter to King George III:

"Appointing a representative at my Court is a request contrary to our Imperial Dynastic rules and traditions, and is utterly impracticable."

Emperor Qianlong added:

"Our Imperial virtue has penetrated into every country under heaven. Kings of all nations have offered their richest tributes by land and sea, …and we have no use for your country's manufactures."

Lord Macartney attributed his failure to poor translation.

Of course the best known story about this diplomatic failure was the behavior of Lord Macartney. The court officials of the Emperor made great efforts to brief Lord Macartney about Chinese court etiquette. Despite this advice Lord Macartney refused to drop to his knees when having an audience with Emperor Qianlong.

So was it a failure of communication as Lord Macartney thought?

Some compared this encounter to a dialogue between a blind man and a deaf man.

I think the answer is rather deeper. This was a failure caused by a fundamental clash of ideas. On one side was an established power and on the other was a rising power. There was no mutual respect or trust—a theme I will talk about later.

At that time, Britain was a capitalist country where industrial revolution was forging ahead. It had little knowledge about China at that time which was a closed and agrarian society.

In addition, China was proud of being a "celestial imperial dynasty". At that time China had no interest or motivation to deal with the rapidly ascending Britain. The Chinese leaders did not think there was any need to adapt to the changing world.

Maybe I should also mention the second-in-command of the Macartney Mission. This is Sir George Staunton. Two years before he set out for China, Oxford conferred on him an Honorary Doctorate of Laws.

Let me turn to the second historical headline—an unjust war.

In 1840 a war broke out between China and Britain. This war might be seen as a very minor incident in the British history of external relations. It is known to British people as the first Anglo-Chinese war. It was a war triggered by conflicting trade interests.

But if British history books record this as a minor foot note—it does not excuse the major unjust nature of the war. This was a fight based on the British government defence of the trade in opium smuggling. Even some politicians were appalled by the actions of the British government. In a debate at the House of Commons, a young Tory

MP, William Gladstone, spoke fervently against it. He said:

"I do not know a war more unjust in its origin, a war more calculated to cover this country with permanent disgrace."

This unjust war ended with the defeat of China. Britain imposed an unequal treaty and forced China to concede Hong Kong Island and open five ports for trade. Britain achieved with gunboats what the Macartney Mission failed to secure.

The Opium War has had a deep and long impact on China. It is widely accepted by historians as the beginning of the Chinese contemporary history.

In the 100 years that followed China sank to appalling levels of poverty and chaos. In 1840 China had 30% share of global GDP; by 1940 this had collapsed to under 5%.

Following the Opium War China was plagued by both foreign aggression and civil war. Its sovereignty was violated. Its land was occupied. As a result, the China-Britain relationship for a long time was not on an equal footing.

Every coin has two sides, so does history.

The dire perils triggered by the Opium War helped wake up the Chinese people. They became aware that China must adapt to a changing world. The Industrial Revolution that started in Britain meant that every nation had to change.

After many bitter sufferings Chinese people learned the lesson:

- They started to "open wide their eyes and look around the world".
- They began the search for a way to save and revive the Chinese nation.

It was in this context that a revolution broke in China. The monarchy was overthrown and a republic was born.

- The Chinese people were exposed to European and American modern science and ideas of democracy.
- They then had to fight Japanese aggression for 14 years to win national independence.
- China imported Marxism and established the Communist Party of China and under its leadership founded the People's Republic.

The symbolism of this struggle is at the heart of Tian'anmen Square in Beijing. The inscriptions on the massive Monument to the People's Heroes read:

"Long live the people's heroes over the years since 1840 who had fallen in the fights against internal and external enemies and for the independence of the Chinese nation and happiness of the Chinese people!"

Note the specific reference to 1840—the starting year of the unjust Opium War launched by Britain.

We now reach the third historical headline—a well-timed diplomatic upgrading.

After the founding of the People's Republic in 1949, China and Britain exchanged charges d'affaires in 1954. It was not a normal diplomatic relationship. It was referred to by historians as "half diplomatic relationship". Such a relationship was the product of the Cold War. It was also due to some obstacles caused by the question of Taiwan.

In 1972 great changes took place in the global landscape. A key event was the visit to China by President Nixon.

The visit meant that the thick ice between China and the US was broken. At the same time China-Britain relations were thawing.

Britain acknowledged the position of the Chinese government that Taiwan was a province of the People's Republic of China. The two countries signed a joint communiqué and raised China-Britain relations to ambassadorial level. This normalized China-Britain relations.

This was a vital turning point in Sino-UK ties. It symbolised a fresh start of mutual respect and equal exchanges between the two countries.

This year marks the 40 years since those full diplomatic relations between China and the UK were established. Both sides have hosted many celebrations.

When speaking at the reception hosted by the Chinese Embassy, I particularly mentioned a British leader—the former Prime Minister, Sir Edward Heath.

Sir Edward deserves great credit for his huge role in making China-UK ambassadorial relations a reality. He visited China 26 times in his lifetime. His dedication to China-Britain friendship earned him in China the title "People's Friendship Envoy".

You will know from the records and minutes of your Oxford Union that Sir Edward was both your Secretary and Librarian. In addition, I believe he made his mark as a debater here in the Union. Your Union was the political cradle for him.

We now reach the fourth headline—a historic negotiation.

In spite of the establishment of ambassadorial relations, there was still an outstanding question between the two countries—Hong Kong. This was a question left over from the Opium War that I mentioned earlier.

The thrust of the question was that China wanted Hong Kong back. Britain wanted to maintain its interests in Hong Kong.

After 22 rounds of hard negotiations, the two governments signed in Beijing in 1984 the Joint Declaration over Hong Kong. China resumed the exercise of sovereignty over Hong Kong on 1 July 1997. The principle of One Country, Two Systems was applied in Hong Kong after its return.

The resolution of the Hong Kong question was a major milestone in China-UK relations. It is important in many ways:

- First, it resolved a big historical question that dated back to the Opium War of 1840. It laid the foundation for the long-term growth of our relations.
- Second, it created a model for the Chinese peaceful reunification. After the Hong Kong model, China and Portugal smoothly resolved the Macao question.
- Third, it set a record of settling international disputes through peaceful negotiations.

For two countries like China and Britain, resolving a sensitive and complex territorial question through peaceful negotiation was a remarkable achievement. It has far-reaching historical significance to China and Britain. It is also highly relevant and instructive to the world today.

For example, one Asian country is attempting to challenge the principles of the Charter of the United Nations and post-war international order.

Its unilateral actions have violated the consensus reached between the related countries on peaceful settlement of territorial disputes.

This Asian country should be inspired by the success story created by China and Britain.

In the historic settlement of Hong Kong question, another alumna of Oxford played a prominent role with her wisdom and decisiveness. This was Prime Minister Thatcher, the Iron Lady. I know that she also shared her wisdom here as a guest speaker at your

Oxford Union.

Finally we have the fifth headline—a new type of partnership.

Since the dawn of the new century the world has witnessed extraordinary events in China. The result has brought about great changes in the economic strength, international status and role of China.

Thanks to the hard efforts over the three decades since reform and opening-up, China has surged to be the world's second largest economy. For over three decades China has sustained an annual growth rate of 9.9%. This is an unmatched success that the world economy has ever known.

At the same time China has taken an active part in international affairs.

China has risen from a regional power, as the developed countries used to see it, to a global power.

As a result it is now inconceivable that any major global issue could be resolved without the active participation and support of China.

Against such a backdrop, despite the divergence in history, culture, development stage and social system, our two countries have come remarkably close in our relations. The breakthrough was the establishment of a new type of partnership.

In 1998 China and Britain embarked on a "comprehensive partnership".

In 2004 it was further enriched and elevated to a "comprehensive strategic partnership".

Our relationship is based on our shared interests. This approach answers the call of the age we live in.

Today Sino-UK relations are flourishing. China and Britain have put in place:

- The Economic and Financial Dialogue.
- The Strategic Dialogue.
- The High-Level People-to-People Dialogue.

They are the three pillars of our relations.

Our economic ties are growing fast. In 2011 China-UK bilateral trade in goods totaled nearly 60 billion US dollars. That was 200 times of that in 1972.

Every year more than one million of our people visit each other's country for travel, work or study. China has become the number one source of foreign students in Britain.

Of course our two countries do not see eye to eye with each other on every issue. However, we can resolve issues as we maintain close communication and consultation. Our relationship has never been so deep and extensive.

Talking about our new partnership, I must mention another graduate of Oxford. This is former Prime Minister Tony Blair. I am told he was active in the Oxford Union and like Sir Edward an office holder.

During Tony Blair's 11 years as Prime Minister, development of China-UK relations was both fast and positive. He recognised the strategic significance by establishing his Prime Minister's China Task Force. Of course, we should not forget that the incumbent Prime Minister is also from Oxford.

Young friends,

So far I have given you an overview of the multi-faceted China-Britain relations with five headlines.

This year is the 220th anniversary of the Macartney Mission to China. From 220 years of China-Britain exchanges we witness an upward trajectory that moved:

- From estrangement to understanding.
- From hostility to friendship.
- From rivalry to cooperation.
- And from negative to positive.

It is not a straight line, because our relations went through ups and downs. But this did not, and cannot change the overriding trend of Sino-UK ties.

A very famous ancient Chinese saying is:

"Take history as a mirror and you will understand why dynasties rise and fall."

Coming to Europe, Victor Hugo said:

"What is history? An echo of the past in the future, a reflex from the future on the past."

Both these Chinese and European quotations reflect similar thinking.

So taking a historical view, what lessons can we learn as we take stock of China-Britain relations over the past more than two centuries?

In my view, the most important lesson we should learn is mutual respect and treating each other as equals.

This is also a fundamental principle that China upholds and insists on in its foreign policy.

All unpleasant memories of China-Britain relations show lack of respect and equality. This is the basis of the failure of the Macartney Mission and the tragedy of the Opium War.

All positive progress of our relations were achieved through mutual respect and equality. These are seen in the diplomatic upgrading, the smooth return of Hong Kong and the launch of a new partnership. So we may well conclude that respect and equality is the heart and soul of China-Britain relations.

Then how can China and Britain truly respect each other and treat each other as equals in the world today? I believe it is essential to do the following.

First, respect each other's national realities, such as history, culture, development stage and social system.

There are many differences in the evolution of our two nations:

- China has a history of 5,000 years.
- Britain was the pathfinder of modern industrialisation.
- Confucianism is deep in Chinese people's genes.
- Britons have a tradition of pragmatism.
- Britain is the birthplace of modern capitalism and is a developed Western nation.
- China follows socialism with Chinese characteristics.
- China is the largest developing country.

These are the basic facts of the two countries.

We must be aware of and respect our differences. We should respect each other's development path. We should respect our respective choices.

Only through this kind of respect can China and Britain become equal partners.

Only through this kind of regard can we establish and develop a comprehensive strategic partnership between two countries like China and Britain that differ in history, culture, social and political systems.

The second essential as we move forward is, to respect each other's interests, especially core interests.

You will all be familiar with the famous song *Rule, Britannia!* In one of the verses the song says:

"Britons never, never, never shall be slaves."

It should not surprise that the first line of the Chinese national anthem *March of the Volunteers* says:

"Arise, you people who refuse to be slaves!"

These words reflect how Chinese people refused to accept the humiliation and loss of sovereignty that followed from the Opium War.

Following the Opium War, China had been brought to its knees and the Chinese nation endured untold sufferings. Today's China and Chinese people cherish national independence and freedom. We value sovereignty and territorial integrity more than anything else.

China does not allow violation and interference from anyone on issues that concern the Chinese sovereignty and territorial integrity, because these are our core interests. There were more than enough such historical lessons between China and Britain. We must prevent reoccurrence of such unfortunate incidents.

History is an essential guide. One famous British historian, Arnold Toynbee was also an alumnus of University of Oxford.

Arnold Toynbee predicted that the 21st century would be the Chinese century.

Of course, this should not be interpreted as the 21st century belongs solely to China. Rather it means China will accomplish more in the 21st century.

I am confident that as China increasingly prospers, the future of China-Britain relations will have more opportunities.

We should be committed to a new type of the China-UK partnership I have described. In summary, these are the crucial points to define that relationship:

- Political mutual respect and trust.
- An economic win-win cooperation.
- Reciprocal learning about each others cultures.
- And greater coordination and cooperation in international affairs.

If these goals are realised, then the pattern of history suggests that our two countries and peoples will benefit enormously.

220 years ago, King George III wrote in his letter to Chinese Emperor Qianlong:

"No time can be so propitious for extending the bounds of friendship and benevolence, and for proposing to communicate and receive those benefits which must result from an unreserved and amicable intercourse, between such great and civilized nations as China and Great Britain."

Due to the confines of historical conditions, King George III's wish did not come true.

But in this new era, great nations such as China and Britain have much to offer the world. Both countries should use their immense skills and resources to deliver a common goal. This is the shared objective of creating a sustainable and peaceful world for all humanity.

Oxonians have been critical to the past of China-Britain relations. I do believe you, students of Oxford, also have a huge role to play in this relationship's future. This is why I have joined you here.

I hope my reflections on history may inspire you to follow the spirit of the times and undertake your responsibilities and mission. I hope you will work with the young generation of China to compose new chapters of China-Britain relations.

Thank you!

开启中英全面战略伙伴关系 *

各位记者朋友，

女士们、先生们：

欢迎大家出席今天的记者会。应英国女王伊丽莎白二世陛下邀请，中国国家主席习近平将于10月19日至23日对英国进行国事访问。这是10年来中国国家主席首次对英国进行国事访问，将为中英关系的发展提供历史性机遇。我最近广泛接触了英国王室、政府、议会、工商、智库、高校和媒体等各界人士，真切地感到英国社会各界对习主席此访的热切期盼，衷心期望访问能推动中英关系取得更好发展、收获更大成果。

当前中英双方仍在紧张筹备访问的各项安排，我认为，习主席此次访问有"四大看点"。

一是意义重大。2015年是中英全面战略伙伴关系第二个10年的开局之年，习主席对英国进行国事访问正当时。访问期间，两国领导人将共同为中英关系确定新的定位，树立新的目标，制定新的规划。因此访问具有承前启后、继往开来的重要意义，将成为两国关系新的里程碑。

二是规格超常。我们知道，国事访问是最高规格的访问，英方将为习主席举行传统且盛大的欢迎仪式、国宴和金融城市长晚宴，鸣放103响欢迎礼炮（绿园41响和塔桥62响）。但此次访问在规格上超越以往，有许多特殊

---

* 在为习近平主席对英国国事访问举行的中外记者会上的开场白。2015年10月15日，中国驻英国大使馆。

安排。访问期间，英国王室三代众多成员均将参加接待习主席和彭丽媛女士；习主席将在英国议会发表演讲；卡梅伦首相除正式会谈外，将陪同习主席出席多场在伦敦的活动，并一道去曼彻斯特访问。卡梅伦首相还将与夫人萨曼莎邀请习主席夫妇赴契克斯乡间别墅做客。中方对此访也高度重视，以往中国国家主席出访时通常一访多国，此次习主席是专访英国，即英国是唯一一站，这极为罕见。可以说，此次国事访问堪称一次"超级国事访问"。

三是活动丰富。习主席此访既访首都，也访外地；既看城市，也看乡村；既有传统仪式，也有现代创意展示；既参观英国高科技企业和著名院校，也走访中资电信企业；既结识英国各界新朋友，也不忘为中英关系做出贡献的老朋友；既有许多正式的政治性会见，也有不少轻松的文化体育活动；既出席中英经贸论坛，也参加孔子学院大会。彭丽媛女士的单独活动也将很有特点，她将充分履行联合国教科文组织"促进女童与妇女教育特使"的职责。可以说，访问将亮点不断、精彩纷呈，大家不妨拭目以待。

四是成果丰硕。访问期间，两国政府部门将签署一系列合作协议，进一步促进中英在经贸和人文等领域的合作。两国企业也将有合作大手笔，目前尚不便具体透露，大家尽可期待。

各位记者朋友，

中英都是伟大的国家，历史上都是对人类文明做出重要贡献的国家，今天都是具有全球性影响的大国。两国都面临进一步深化改革、发展经济和改善民生的任务，均致力于通过改革与创新促进增长，都视对方的发展为重大机遇，都对彼此重大发展倡议抱有浓厚兴趣。因此，发展好中英关系符合两国人民的根本利益，也有利于世界的繁荣与和平。

我记得，2014年也在本使馆，也是在这样的记者会上，我曾经不无焦虑地向媒体表示，英国在发展对华关系上已经落在一些欧洲国家之后，亟须迎头赶上。今天，我可以高兴并充满信心地说，英国正在实现赶超，致力于成为中国在西方"最有力的支持者"和"最好的伙伴"。英国正在成为欧洲乃至西方发展对华关系的"领头羊"！

英裔爱尔兰思想家埃德蒙·伯克说："伟人是国家的路标和里程碑。"我认为，伟人也是国家关系的路标和里程碑。让我们共同祝愿习近平主席对英国的"超级国事访问"取得圆满成功，祝这次访问深化中英政治互信，促进共同发展，增进人民友谊，开创中英持久、开放、共赢的全面战略伙伴关系！

  谢谢！

A Comprehensive Strategic Partnership between China and the UK*

Friends from the media,

Ladies and Gentlemen,

Welcome to the press conference at the Chinese Embassy.

At the invitation of Her Majesty The Queen, Chinese President Xi Jinping will pay a state visit to the United Kingdom. This is going to be the first state visit to the UK by a Chinese president in 10 years. It will present a major historic opportunity for China-UK relationship.

I have recently met extensively with people from all walks of life in the UK, including the Buckingham Palace, the UK government, the Parliament, the business community, the academics, universities and media groups. In those meetings, I could clearly feel the enthusiasm and expectations here in Britain with regard to the state visit. It is a shared hope that the state visit will lead to greater progress in the China-UK relationship and will bring impressive outcomes.

Right now, preparations are in full swing both in China and here in the UK. Though I can not, at this moment, give every detail of the programme, I want to share with you four major features of the state visit.

The first is the great significance of the state visit for China-UK relations.

This year marks the beginning of the second decade of China-UK comprehensive strategic partnership. There is nothing more befitting than a state visit in this year.

---

* Opening remarks at the Press Conference on the State Visit by President Xi Jinping. Chinese Embassy, 15 October 2015.

During the visit, President Xi Jinping, together with the British leaders, will give China-UK relations a new position. They will set new goals and draw up new blueprints for the bilateral relations. Therefore, the state visit will be a significant landmark between the past and the future. It will mark a new milestone for the relationship between China and the UK.

The second feature is the extraordinary arrangements for the state visit.

As we all know, a state visit is accorded the highest-level reception here in the UK. As usual, there will be a grand traditional reception for President Xi. These will include:

- The Welcome Ceremony.
- A State Banquet hosted by Her Majesty The Queen.
- A banquet in the City of London at the Guildhall.
- And the honour of a 103 Royal Gun Salute. This involves 41 guns in Green Park and 62 guns at the Tower of London.

But the state visit this time is more than usual. There are a number of "pluses".

President Xi and Madam Peng Liyuan will meet all three generations of the British Royal Family.

President Xi will make a speech at the British Parliament.

In addition to official talks with Prime Minister Cameron, President Xi will be joined by the PM at multiple events in London and during the visit to Manchester.

President Xi and Madam Peng will also visit the PM and Mrs Cameron at Chequers.

The Chinese side likewise attaches great importance to the state visit. In previous overseas visits, the Chinese President usually toured a number of countries on one trip. But this time, it is going to be a one-destination state visit. President Xi's state visit will take him to only one country. That is the United Kingdom. All these facts are pointing to a "super state visit".

The third feature is the rich variety of events during the state visit.

President Xi will visit London and travel out to Manchester.

He will tour the urban area and catch a glimpse of the countryside.

His programme includes both traditional ceremonies and modern creative display, both official talks and meetings, and lighthearted cultural and sports events.

There will be exposures to the UK's high-tech corporation and well-known institution of higher learning as well as a tour of a Chinese telecom business based in the City of London.

He will join the business communities at a China-UK economic and trade forum and attend a conference of Confucius Institutes.

The visit will be a great opportunity to both make friends with people from all walks of life in Britain and renew ties with old friends who have contributed to the China-UK relationship.

The programme for Madam Peng Liyuan is also designed to reflect her responsibility as UNESCO Special Envoy for the Advancement of Girls'and Women's Education.

So, the state visit will be full of highlights and excitements. There will be a great deal for all media to report and reflect upon. Please stay tuned.

The fourth feature is the fruitful outcome of the state visit.

During the state visit, government departments of both countries will sign a number of agreements aimed at furthering China-UK economic, trade, cultural and people-to-people cooperation. The business communities also have plans for major cooperation. The details of those still need to be worked out but we will keep you posted.

Friends from the media,

Both China and the UK are great countries. Both China and the UK had made our contribution to human civilization. Both China and the UK are countries of global influence.

At present, both our countries are tasked with deeper reform, economic growth and better life for the people. As we seek growth through reform and innovation,we regard each other's progress as major opportunities for our respective growth. We find great potential in each other's key development initiatives. A robust China-UK relationship is therefore in the fundamental interest of the people of both countries. It is good for global prosperity and world peace.

Last year, at a similar press conference right here at the Chinese Embassy, I expressed anxiety to the media that the UK was lagging behind some European countries in its relations with China and had some serious catching up to do.

Today, I can happily and confidently say that the UK is coming up from behind, that the UK is committed to becoming the Chinese "strongest supporter" and "best partner" in the West.

In fact, when it comes to developing relations with China, the UK is becoming the leader in Europe and indeed the West.

The Anglo-Irish philosopher Edmund Burke once said, "Great men are the guideposts and landmarks in the states." May I say that great men are also guideposts and landmarks in state-to-state relations.

Let us wish the "super state visit" of President Xi Jinping a complete success.

Let us look forward to deeper political mutual trust, robust common development and closer friendship between China and the UK.

Let us embrace a comprehensive strategic partnership for China-UK relations that is enduring, inclusive and mutually beneficial.

Thank you!

一次"超级国事访问"*

尊敬的英国女王代表胡德子爵，

各位来宾、各位同事：

欢迎大家出席今晚的庆祝招待会。

今天我们在这里欢聚一堂，首先是庆祝习主席此次对英国国事访问取得圆满成功。

习主席此次访英是一次"超级国事访问"，内容丰富，精彩纷呈，打破了一个又一个纪录，创造了一个又一个第一。此次访问可以用三个"超级"来形容，即"超级规格""超级成果""超级影响"。

访问期间，我们共同见证了习主席出席传统盛大的欢迎仪式、女王国宴和金融城市长晚宴；共同见证了习主席与英国王室三代成员友好会见交谈；共同见证了习主席与卡梅伦首相多次会晤并共同出席14场活动，累计15个小时，创下中英领导人交往的纪录；共同见证了习主席在英国议会、金融城、中英工商峰会、孔子学院年会和曼城市政厅发表重要讲话；共同见证了习主席参观中英创意产业展、帝国理工学院、曼彻斯特大学国家石墨烯研究院和国际移动卫星公司等。当然，我们也共同见证了彭丽媛女士访问福提斯米尔中学、皇家音乐学院和曼彻斯特科学与工业博物馆，领略了她的风采和智慧。

---

* 在庆祝习近平主席对英国国事访问圆满成功答谢招待会上的讲话。2015年11月3日，中国驻英国大使馆。

习主席此次访问也是一次取得"超级成果"的合作之旅。中英确立了面向21世纪全球全面战略伙伴关系的新定位。双方签署了13项政府间的非商业合作协议和28项总额约400亿英镑的商业大单,特别是达成了欣克利角C核电项目协议。中方在伦敦发行50亿元的央行票据,并将发行中国以外首只人民币主权债券。双方同意建立"中英创新合作伙伴关系",加强中英科技创新合作。双方宣布建立中英高级别安全对话机制,进一步推进安全执法领域合作。双方就"一带一路"倡议与"英格兰北方经济中心"战略实行了对接。

习主席此次访问还是一次产生"超级影响"的外交之旅。在中国,在英国,甚至在全球,无论是电视、报刊,还是网络,习主席访英都是关注焦点、媒体头条。全球媒体聚焦习主席的访问行程,各方热议中英关系。大家关注中英关系,关注中英商业大单,关注皇家马车,关注契克斯庄园,关注卡兹顿之犁酒吧,关注艾尔啤酒(IPA)、炸鱼和薯条,关注习主席、卡梅伦首相和阿奎罗的自拍合影。有人说,习主席访问就像一部电视连续剧,看了上集想看下集,集集精彩。我觉得,习主席访问更像一部外交大片,立意高远、主题深刻、内涵丰富,立足英国、面向欧洲、辐射全球。

今天我们在这里欢聚一堂,也是共同回顾在过去一年里我们结下的深厚友谊,感谢大家的辛勤付出。为确保访问成功,英国王室、政府、议会、警方和各相关机构在方方面面做出了周到细致以及许多特殊安排。特别是在临近访问的最后几周,我们精心设计,反复磋商,共同踩点,形成了最佳接待方案。在访问过程中,双方相互理解,相互配合,相互支持,确保了访问的顺利、安全和精彩。可以说,访问的成功是你们热情投入的结果,是我们密切合作的结果。在此,我谨向英国同事和朋友们表示衷心感谢。

女士们、先生们,

正如习主席在英国议会演讲时所引用的莎士比亚名言:"凡是过去,皆为序章。"习主席此次历史性访问展现了两国关系发展的广阔美好前景。让我们一道,以访问为新起点,抓住时代机遇,秉承共赢精神,努力落实两国领导人达成的共识,深化中英各领域合作,推动中英面向21世纪全球全面战略伙伴关系不断向前发展。

现在，我提议：

为习近平主席对英国国事访问圆满成功，

为我们的合作与友谊，

干杯！

A "Super State Visit" *

Lord Hood,

Dear guests and colleagues,

A very warm welcome to the Chinese Embassy.

First of all, I wish to thank you all for joining us in marking the success of the state visit by President Xi Jinping.

President Xi's visit can be described as a "super state visit", with three "supers", that is, "super programme", "super outcome" and "super significance".

First, the "super programme." The state visit was full of highlights. It broke many records and created many "firsts":

- There was the highest level of traditional Royal pageantry culminating in Her Majesty's State Banquet and the Lord Mayor's dinner at the Guildhall.
- There were friendly meetings and discussions between the President and three generations of the British Royal Family.
- President Xi and Prime Minister Cameron held a series of important meetings.
- On top of these formal talks, there were 14 events in which President Xi and Prime Minister Cameron had close interactions. They had unprecedented 15 hours together during the state visit.
- President Xi also delivered speeches in the City of London, at the Business Summit, at the Confucius Institute event and in Manchester City Hall.

---

* Remarks at the Reception to Mark the Successful State Visit by President Xi Jinping. Chinese Embassy, 3 November 2015.

- There were also visits to the Creative Industry Show, the Imperial College London, the National Graphene Institute at the University of Manchester and the Inmarsat Company.

Of course, the state visit also saw Madame Peng Liyuan visiting Fortismere, the Royal College of Music and the Science and Industry Museum in Manchester. Her decorum as well as her wisdom shown throughout the visit was an absolute highlight.

Second, the "super outcomes". The state visit was also a journey of cooperation laden with "super outcomes".

During this visit, President Xi and Prime Minister Cameron gave a new definition to the bilateral relationship. They made the commitment that China and the UK "will work together to build a global comprehensive strategic partnership for the 21st century".

That was the key outcome of the state visit.

Other major outcomes include:

- 13 inter-governmental and non-commercial agreements and 28 commercial contracts valued at a grand total of 40 billion pounds, not least Hinkley Point C.
- 5 billion RMB worth of Chinese Central Bank bills to be issued in London. This will be followed by prospective issuance in London of the very first RMB sovereign bond outside China.
- An agreement to establish an innovation cooperation partnership. This will raise the level of China-UK cooperation in tech innovation.
- An announcement on establishing a high-level security dialogue. Our two countries will further enhance security and law-enforcement cooperation.
- Potential cooperation on each other's major initiatives, namely the China's Belt and Road Initiative (BRI) and the UK's Northern Powerhouse.

Now, we come to the third "super". The state visit was a remarkable diplomatic accomplishment with "super significance".

- The state visit made headlines and became the focus of all forms of media. In

China, in the UK and all over the world, on TV, in the papers and on line, every media was covering the visit and commenting on China-UK relations.
- There was enormous interest in every aspect of the state visit:
    * from the China-UK relationship to major commercial contracts,
    * from the Royal Carriages to the meetings at Chequers,
    * from the traditional pub—the Plough at Cadsden, the Indian Pale Ale with fish and chips to the iconic Aguero selfie.
- Someone accurately observed that watching the state visit on TV was like following a drama series—you became glued to the TV screen for more and more. The reason was that every episode was brilliant!
- To me, the state visit was like a "diplomatic blockbuster". It aimed high with a great theme and rich contents. The story took place here in the British Isles. But its impact has been felt far and wide on the Continent and around the globe.

Today, we are gathered here for yet one more reason.

Over the past year, we have worked together closely in preparation for this visit. I wish to take this opportunity to express my sincere thanks to every British colleague and friend present here.

Many of you were involved. There were the Buckingham Palace, the UK government, the British Parliament, the Metropolitan Police and all the institutions and organizations that hosted the President Xi and Madam Peng. All those involved have been working so hard to ensure the success of the state visit. This success came from great attention to details. There have been so many meticulous and exceptional arrangements.

In the week leading up to the state visit, our careful design, in-depth discussions and location recces led to a most satisfactory programme.

During the visit, we appreciated and supported each other's efforts and collaborated well. Your enthusiastic input, plus the close cooperation between our two sides, has been absolutely indispensable in the eventual success of the state visit.

So I wish to say to my British colleagues and friends, from the bottom of my heart,

Thank you very much!

Ladies and Gentlemen,

President Xi quoted Shakespeare in his speech in Parliament. He said:

"What's past is prologue."

The historic state visit has opened up broad and promising prospects for China-UK relations.

The state visit has drawn a fresh starting line for us. We must seize this opportunity and carry on with our win-win spirit.

Let us work hand in hand to implement the agreement of our leaders.

Let us deepen China-UK cooperation in all areas.

Let us make further progress in building a global comprehensive strategic partnership between China and the UK for the 21st century.

I now propose a toast:

To the success of the state visit by President Xi Jinping.

To our continuing cooperation and friendship.

Cheers!

中英关系的"三要三不要"*

尊敬的英国保守党议会中国小组主席克利夫顿-布朗爵士，
尊敬的英国保守党议会中国小组秘书长布拉德肖先生，
尊敬的各位议员，
女士们、先生们：
大家早上好！

很高兴再次出席保守党议会中国小组早餐会。今天是中国农历己亥猪年正月初九，按照中国传统还在"年"里，我谨祝大家猪年吉祥如意！

对于"猪"，中西方文化有不同解读。西方文化大都认为猪懒惰、邋遢，而在中国文化里，猪则象征着财富和幸运。我听说丘吉尔首相曾有一句关于猪的名言："我喜欢猪，狗谄媚，猫轻蔑，而猪不卑不亢。"看来，在西方也有人喜欢猪。这使我感到，对任何事情都不能先入为主，而应多了解、多交流，兼听则明。正是本着这种精神，我今天与各位交流一下对中英经贸合作乃至中英关系的看法。

多年来，中英经贸合作始终是两国关系的"压舱石"和"助推器"。2018年，两国经贸合作有三个特点。

一是双边贸易迈上新台阶。2018年，中英货物贸易额达821亿美元，首次突破800亿美元大关。其中，英国对华出口283.3亿美元，同比增长32.2%。中国是英国在欧盟外第二大贸易伙伴，英国则是中国在欧盟内第三大贸易伙伴。

---

* 在英国保守党议会中国小组早餐会的主旨演讲。2019年2月13日，英国议会大厦。

二是双向投资取得新进展。2018年，英国对华直接投资38.9亿美元，居欧洲之首、全球第五。中国对英直接投资17.1亿美元，同比增长14%。500多家中资企业落户英国，中国在英累计投资超过200亿美元，居欧洲前列。

三是金融合作呈现新亮点。伦敦是中国境外最大离岸人民币交易中心。2018年10月，伦敦人民币和美元日均交易额为730亿美元，首次超过英镑和欧元交易量。中再集团成功收购桥社英国控股公司100%股权。中英机构携手发布《"一带一路"绿色投资原则》，推动中英"一带一路"合作走深走实。

回顾过去一年，中英经贸合作可谓亮点纷呈。展望新的一年，中英经贸合作既有机遇，也有挑战。我始终认为，机遇大于挑战。只要应对得当，我们就能化挑战为机遇，推动双方合作再上新台阶。

那么，中英关系面临什么挑战？我认为，最大的挑战是：英方如何看待中国的发展？是将中国的发展视为机遇，还是挑战，甚至威胁？

出于众所周知的原因，2018年中英关系遭受挫折。近年来，在中英双方努力推动两国关系重归正轨的同时，又有人在渲染"中国威胁论"，鼓吹派英国军舰到南海炫耀武力。联想一个时期以来，一些人炒作所谓中国企业"安全威胁"，要求对华为等中资企业发出"市场禁入令"，这些动向反映出来的是一种冷战思维。

这些日子，我一直在思考一个问题：打造中英面向21世纪的全球全面战略伙伴关系的关键是什么？我认为，关键是"三要三不要"。

首先，要合作共赢，不要冷战思维。冷战已经结束几十年了，但仍有一些人沉浸在历史旧梦中，惯于以意识形态画线，以社会制度论事。以南海为例，当前在中国和东盟国家共同努力下，南海形势持续向好，制定"南海行为准则"磋商驶入快车道，中国与东盟国家之间相互信任不断增强。而个别国家无视中国与东盟国家做出的努力，打着维护"航行自由"的幌子，到南海炫耀武力，侵犯中国主权，破坏地区稳定。如果它们真的关心南海"航行自由"，我要告诉它们：第一，南海航行畅通无阻，每年十万多艘船只在此经过，从未发生任何问题；第二，请尊重中国与有关地区国家为维护南海和平稳定所做出的努力，不再插手南海事务，不再损害地区和平稳定。

再看一下华为。这是一家自主经营的民营企业，不能因其来自中国，创始人是退伍军人，就无端猜测华为受中国政府甚至军方控制，并基于这种猜忌对华为正常经营设置障碍。据我所知，英国有不少议员也是退伍军人，其中有些是我熟知的朋友，我们能说英国议会被英国军方控制吗？真是"欲加之罪，何患无辞"！在全球化深入发展的今天，每个国家都在努力向前奔跑。我们深知，背负历史包袱，干扰威胁他人，并不会让自己跑得更快。只有相互支持，携手合作，共同进步，才能开创人类更加美好的未来。

其次，要开放合作，不要封闭僵化。历史规律表明，只有开放合作才能扩大发展空间。人为设置壁垒，阻碍企业正常合作，这不仅违背时代潮流，不符合商业规律，还会损害自身发展利益。中英都是自由贸易和开放型经济的倡导者和推动者，也是受益者。华为在英经营18年来，不仅自身获得发展，也为英国创造了大量就业岗位和税收，为英国电信产业发展做出积极贡献。过去5年，华为在英投资和采购20亿英镑，创造就业岗位超7500个。未来5年，华为将在英投资和采购30亿英镑，继续助力英国经济社会和信息化发展。在保护主义逆潮涌动的形势下，中英更应坚守融通理念，促进开放合作，共建开放型世界经济。

最后，要"百花齐放"，不要"零和博弈"。在第四次科技革命方兴未艾的大背景下，全球科技产业链、供应链、价值链、创新链高度融合。如果仍以零和博弈、你输我赢的旧思维看待科技创新与合作，必将错失发展机遇。近年来，中国企业通过学习世界先进技术，加强自主研发创新，在一些领域达到世界领先水平，并促进全球技术和相关行业发展。例如，华为电信技术特别是5G（第五代移动通信技术）世界领先，业务遍及全球170个国家和地区，服务近30亿人口，对推进世界电信行业和技术整体进步发挥了积极作用。在新形势下，各国应本着包容的心态，坚持良性竞争和互利合作，共同迎接人类科技创新竞相争艳的春天。

女士们、先生们，

2019年是中英建立代办级外交关系65周年。回首过去65年，正是在保守党执政期间，中英关系实现四次飞跃：中英建立代办级外交关系，升格为大使级外交关系，签署关于香港问题的《联合声明》，构建21世纪全球全面战略伙伴关系。在21世纪即将进入第三个10年的历史时刻，我希望中英双方都珍惜两国关系来之不易的成果，排除各种外部压力和人为干扰，不断增进战略互信，深化务实合作，推动中英关系行稳致远！

谢谢！

Three Choices in China-UK Relations*

Sir Geoffrey,

Secretary Jeremy Bradshaw,

My Lords and MPs,

Ladies and Gentlemen,

Good morning!

It is a real delight to join you again at the Conservative China Group breakfast.

Today is the ninth day of the Year of the Pig. According to Chinese tradition, the festival is not over yet. Let me take this opportunity to wish you a happy and prosperous Year of the Pig!

Pigs have different symbolic meanings in different cultures. In the West, pigs are associated with laziness and sloppiness. In China, pigs symbolise wealth and fortune.

But one westerner by the name of Winston Churchill said, "I like pigs. Dogs look up to us. Cats look down on us. Pigs treat us as equals."

It seems that there are people in the West who like pigs. Our preconceived ideas may be wrong. This shows it is necessary to stay open and exchange ideas with others. Listening to both sides of a story makes people wise.

It is in this spirit that I would like to share with you my views on China-UK business cooperation and our relationship as a whole.

Over the years, China-UK trade and economic cooperation has always been the "ballast" and "propeller" of our bilateral relations. In 2018, we can see three features:

---

* Keynote Speech at the Conservative China Group House of Commons Breakfast. Palace of Westminster, 13 February 2019.

First, bilateral trade reached a new stage.

- In 2018, China-UK trade in goods was 82.1 billion US dollars, exceeding 80 billion US dollars for the first time.
- British export to China reached 28.33 billion US dollars, increasing by 32.2% year on year.
- China remained the second largest trading partner of the UK outside the EU.
- And the UK was the third largest trading partner of China among all the EU members.

Second, two-way investment made new progress.

In 2018, with its direct investment in China totalling 3.89 billion US dollars, the UK is the Chinese fifth largest international investor and number one source of FDI in Europe.

Chinese investment in the UK stood at 1.71 billion US dollars, increasing by 14% over the previous year.

As of today, there are more than 500 Chinese companies in the UK, with a total accumulated investment of more than 20 billion US dollars. This is definitely one of the largest count of Chinese investment in Europe.

Third, financial cooperation produced new highlights.

- London is the world's largest RMB offshore trading centre.
- Last year, RMB did well in London's foreign exchange trading. In October, dollar-yuan turn-over increased to 73 billion US dollars per day, overtaking pound-euro turn-over for the first time.
- China Re completed its 100% equity acquisition of Chaucer.
- China and the UK jointly announced the Green Investment Principles for the Belt and Road Initiative. Our cooperation on the Belt and Road has gone deeper and more substantial.

The past year has seen numerous highlights in China-UK trade and economic cooperation. The new year will bring opportunities as well as challenges.

I always think there are more opportunities than challenges. As long as we address the challenges properly, we can turn them into opportunities and take our cooperation to a new level.

The biggest challenge we now face is this:

How does the UK see the Chinese development? Does the UK see it as an opportunity, a challenge, or even a threat?

As we all know, China-UK relations have encountered some setbacks last year. Both China and the UK are working hard to bring our relations back to the right track. But how could this be possible if someone from the UK government keeps fanning "China threat" and talking about sending a warship to the South China Sea to show off military power?

This strikes the same note as the recent hyping-up of the so-called "security threat" of Chinese companies, and the clamour for a ban on companies such as Huawei. All these noises play the same old tunes of the Cold War mentality.

Recently I have been thinking about this question:

What is the key to building the China-UK global comprehensive strategic partnership for the 21st century?

In answering this question, I believe we should make three crucial choices.

First, we should choose win-win cooperation over the Cold War mentality.

The Cold War was over several decades ago. But still, some people refuse to wake up. Their habit of drawing a line along ideology and social system seems to die hard.

Take the South China Sea for example.

- The situation in the South China Sea has been improving thanks to the concerted efforts of China and ASEAN countries.
- Consultations on the code of conduct in the South China Sea have picked up speed.
- And mutual trust between China and ASEAN countries has been enhanced.

However, certain countries choose to turn a blind eye to the efforts of China and ASEAN countries. They continue to flex their military muscle in the South China Sea under the excuse of "freedom of navigation". They infringed upon the Chinese sovereignty and undermined stability in the region.

If they really care about the "freedom of navigation" in the South China Sea, my advice is as follows.

First, the freedom of navigation in the South China Sea has never been a problem. Every year, hundreds of thousands of merchant vessels pass through the South China Sea safely and unimpededly. There has never been a single case of navigation freedom being affected.

Second, the efforts of China and other regional countries in maintaining peace and stability in the South China Sea should be respected. No more interference in the affairs of the South China Sea and no more damage to peace and stability in the region.

With regard to Huawei, I want to stress that Huawei is an independent, private company. One should not assume that the Chinese government or military has control over Huawei, let alone creating obstacles for Huawei's lawful business operation, just because it is a Chinese company and its founder is a Chinese veteran.

As far as I know, many Lords and MPs are veterans, including some friends of mine. Could we then claim that the UK Parliament is controlled by the British military? Should we really, as the old saying goes, "Give a dog an evil name and hang him?"

Every country wants development and every country is running hard to get ahead. But one cannot run faster by disrupting or threatening others or by carrying historical baggage. In an age of globalisation, we should all work together and support each other in order to achieve common progress and create a brighter future.

Second, we should choose open cooperation over closedness.

History has taught us that open cooperation promises greater development. Attempting to obstruct lawful cooperation between companies goes against the trend of the times and flouts market rules. This would only be counterproductive.

Both China and the UK have upheld, promoted and benefited from free trade and open economy.

Take Huawei for example. Over the past 18 years, the company has benefited from its presence in the British market. At the same time, it has created job opportunities, paid tax and contributed to the development of UK's telecommunications industry.

In the past five years, Huawei has brought 2 billion pounds to Britain through investment and procurement and created over 7,500 jobs. Huawei has also pledged a further 3 billion pounds in investment and procurement in the UK in the coming five years. This will boost the economic and social progress and IT application in this country.

Against surging protectionism, it is all the more important that China and the UK promote connectivity and open cooperation, so as to build an open world economy.

Third, we should choose inclusiveness over zero-sum games.

The fourth scientific and technological revolution is unfolding. The global industrial chain, supply chain, value chain and innovation chain are highly integrated. Anyone who sees the cooperation on science, technology and innovation as a zero-sum game, and who believes that one man's gain is another's loss, would certainly end up missing the development opportunities.

In recent years, Chinese companies have been learning from cutting edge technologies and enhancing their independent research, development and innovation. As a result, they have taken the lead in some areas, and have been working to promote the progress of the relevant technology and industries in the world.

Huawei, for example, has leading telecommunications technology, especially in the area of 5G. It is providing network services for nearly 3 billion people in 170 countries and regions. This has been a positive contribution to the overall progress of the global telecommunications industry and the relevant technology.

Now is the time for countries of the world to uphold inclusiveness, encourage healthy competition and engage in mutually-beneficial cooperation. Together, we can make science, technology and innovation work for everyone in the world.

Ladies and Gentlemen,

This year marks the 65th anniversary of the establishment of China-UK diplomatic relationship at the chargé d'affaires level.

In the past 65 years, it was when the Conservative Party was in office that our two countries achieved four major leaps in China-UK relations, namely:

- The establishment of diplomatic relationship at the chargé d'affaires level.
- The upgrading to ambassadorial diplomatic ties.
- The signing of the Sino-British Joint Declaration on the question of Hong Kong.
- The establishment of a global comprehensive strategic partnership for the 21st

century with China.

As we are about to step into the third decade of the 21st century, I hope that both our two countries could cherish the hard-won momentum in China-UK relations.

We should resist outside interruptions, refrain from creating obstacles and enhance strategic mutual trust and deepen business cooperation. Together we will make China-UK relations more fruitful and sustainable!

Thank you!

在变局中坚守，在合作中共赢 *

尊敬的英国议会跨党派中国小组主席格雷厄姆先生，
尊敬的各位副主席，
尊敬的各位议员，
女士们、先生们：
大家好！

很高兴通过视频连线的方式与大家交流。上次出席议会跨党派中国小组的活动，还是2020年初在议会大厦举行的新春招待会。过去5个月，世界发生了很大变化。新冠疫情持续蔓延，正在深刻改变世界，不仅改变了我们的沟通和见面方式，也给人类带来了前所未有的挑战。

在这个大背景下，英国国内围绕如何看待和处理中英关系，正在展开一场大讨论、大辩论。有人认为，疫情过后，中英关系不会"回到以前"；有人呼吁"重审对华关系"，鼓吹"对华脱钩"，摆脱对华"战略依赖"；甚至还有人提出，要对中国开启"新冷战"。当然，也有不少人认为，中国是"全球化英国"不可或缺的重要伙伴，发展对华关系对英国至关重要。

今天，我想利用这个机会，谈一谈如何认识和理解世界与中英关系的"变"与"不变"，以及如何处理好中英关系。

第一，新冠疫情加速世界百年未有之大变局，给世界带来"四大变化"。

---

* 在英国议会跨党派中国小组座谈会上的主旨演讲。2020年6月23日，中国驻英国大使馆。

一是给人类健康带来严峻挑战。此次疫情是近百年来人类遭遇的影响范围最广的全球性大流行病。当前，疫情已波及210多个国家和地区，累计造成800多万人感染，40多万人丧生。疫情表明，重大传染性疾病仍是人类生命安全和健康的严峻挑战，这种重大公共卫生突发事件不是第一次，也不可能是最后一次，需要各国携手应对。

二是给世界经济带来严重冲击。疫情发生以来，全球生产和需求"双降"，各国人员流动、跨境商贸活动受阻，国际产业链供应链遭重创。国际货币基金组织预计2020年世界经济将萎缩3%，世贸组织预计2020年国际贸易将缩水13%~32%，世界经济可能陷入20世纪大萧条以来最严重衰退。当前，各国复工复产正在逐步推进，但全球经济复苏前路漫漫。

三是给全球治理带来严峻考验。"空前挑战"需要"空前团结"和"空前合作"。无论是应对疫情，还是恢复经济，都应走团结合作之路，都应坚持多边主义。但有的国家却奉行单边主义、保护主义，借疫情搞经济"脱钩"，对别国污名化，甚至鼓吹"新冷战"，严重影响国际抗疫合作，二战后建立的全球治理体系和多边机制正经受严峻考验。

四是国际社会更加深刻认识到人类是命运共同体。疫情使国际社会更加深切感到世界各国命运紧密相连，人类是同舟共济的命运共同体。团结合作是抗击疫情最有力的武器。越是面对困难挑战，越要加强国与国之间的交流合作，在合作中凝聚共识，增强信心。越是面临猜忌疑虑，越要加强文明交流互鉴，从不同文明中汲取力量，促进各种文明共同发展。

面对疫情这一人类重大挑战，选择开放还是封闭，选择合作还是对抗，选择互鉴还是隔阂，选择共赢还是零和，考验了各国的智慧、理性和担当。

第二，面对世界大变局，中英关系的内涵和外延也随之发生深刻变化，但两国关系也有三个"不变"。

一是两国关系的全球性和战略性没有改变。中英都是联合国安理会常任理事国，都是具有全球影响的大国，都肩负着维护世界和平与发展的重任。近年来，中英在联合国、二十国集团、亚洲基础设施投资银行（以下简称亚投行）等框架下开展良好合作，在倡导多边主义、支持自由贸易等方面拥有广泛共同利益,在推动建设开放型世界经济、推进全球治理改革方面共识更加突出。中英还积极引领环境保护、气候变化等国际合作,就两国分别举办COP15(联合国《生物多样性公约》缔约方大会第十五次会议)和COP26(《联合国气候变化框架公约》第二十六次缔约方大会)保持沟通和相互支持。两国还加强在重大国际和地区事务中的沟通协调,推动伊朗核问题、朝核、叙利亚等热点问题的政治解决,为世界注入更多稳定性和确定性。

疫情发生以来,中英加强政策协调和经验交流,积极开展疫苗和药物研发、物资支持和国际抗疫合作。不久前,李克强总理应邀出席英国政府主办的全球疫苗峰会视频会议,并向全球疫苗免疫联盟提供捐助。两国都支持世界卫生组织在全球抗疫中发挥领导作用,都主张帮助发展中国家抗击疫情和恢复经济社会发展,都强调提升疫苗在发展中国家的可及性和可负担性。抗疫合作为中英关系增添了新内涵,两国将共同为维护和促进全球公共卫生安全做出新贡献。

二是两国关系的互补性和互利性没有改变。中英两国经济高度互补,利益深度融合,互利合作不断拓展。英国是中国在欧洲第三大贸易伙伴,中国是英国第三大出口市场,英国是中国在欧洲地区最大投资目的地国。即使在疫情防控期间,中英合作也没有停止脚步,展现出强大的韧性和生命力。2020年3月,我与英国商业、能源和产业战略大臣夏尔马共同出席了中国河北敬业集团收购英国钢铁公司交割仪式。敬业集团不仅保留了当地3200个工作岗位,还承诺未来10年投资12亿英镑实现英钢转型升级。上周,在沪伦通启动一周年之际,中国太平洋保险全球存托凭证在伦敦证券交易所挂牌上市,成为疫情下中英金融合作的新亮点。

中国是最早控制疫情的国家之一,在复工复产方面走在世界前列。不久前闭幕的中国两会再次强调,无论外部环境如何变化,中国都将坚定不移地深化改革开放。中国政府正进一步落实《中华人民共和国外商投资法》,大幅缩减外资准入负面清单,继续推进自由贸易试验区、自由贸易港建设,积极营造内外资企业一视同仁、公平竞争的市场环境。此次疫情也给中国经济加快转型升级带来了机遇,"宅经济"、"云办公"、数字经济、人工智能、医疗健康等领域呈现出巨大的发展活力和潜力。中国有望继续成为世界经济增长的主要发动机。中国经济稳健复苏将给中英经贸合作带来更多机遇，也将有助于英国踏上复苏发展的轨道，积极布局"后脱欧时代"的发展蓝图。

三是两国关系的交融性和互鉴性没有改变。中英历史文化、社会制度、发展阶段不同，但都拥有悠久历史和灿烂文明。近年来，中英在教育、文化、科技、青年、体育、旅游等人文领域交流合作热度空前，不断促进理念沟通、文化融通、民心相通，推动中英友谊薪火相传。双方完全可以用更宽广的胸襟、更宏大的视野，超越文化差异的鸿沟，打破意识形态的藩篱，增进对彼此文明和发展道路的了解和理解，以兼收并蓄的态度深化各领域交流与合作，树立不同背景国家开放包容、交流互鉴的样板。

第三，在"后疫情时代"，中英关系能否实现更大发展？我认为，把握好以下三条原则至关重要。

一是始终坚持相互尊重，平等相待。70年前，英国在西方大国中率先承认中华人民共和国。70年来，双方之间虽然存在一些分歧，但共同利益始终大于分歧，双方没有因分歧越走越远，而是因共同利益越走越近。回首中英关系的发展历程，只要我们平等相待，求同存异，尊重彼此的核心利益和重大关切，中英关系就会向前发展，实现飞跃，反之则会遭遇挫折，甚至倒退。

当前，中英关系中的一个突出问题就是涉港问题。香港已经回归中国23年了，但英国仍有一些人沉浸在殖民时代，还不时对香港事务指手画脚，干涉中国内政。2020年两会期间，中国全国人大审议通过了香港国安法的决定，目前全国人大常委会正在审议相关法案草案。一些人又频频恶言相向，说三道四，中方对此坚决反对。

为什么要审议通过香港国安法？香港回归中国23年来，"一国两制"取得巨大成功，但香港在维护国家安全方面一直处于"不设防"状态，《中华人民共和国香港特别行政区基本法》第23条立法至今无法完成，而且被严重污名化、妖魔化，使香港成为国家安全的"风险"和"漏洞"。特别是2019年的"修例风波"以来，反中乱港势力鼓吹"港独""自决"，从事破坏国家统一、分裂国家的活动，持续制造各种打砸抢烧暴力恐怖事件，严重危害香港社会稳定、经济繁荣和公共安全，严重突破"一国两制"底线，严重危害中国国家安全，使香港面临回归以来最严峻的局面。

维护国家安全是中央政府的首要责任，在任何国家都属于中央事权。在英国，中央政府和英国议会负责英格兰、苏格兰、北爱尔兰、威尔士地区的国家安全事务。英国如此，中国同样如此。中国全国人大依照宪法和《中华人民共和国香港特别行政区基本法》有关规定，以立法形式堵塞香港维护国家安全的风险漏洞，合理合法，势在必行。此次立法针对的是极少数严重危害国家安全的行为和活动，不影响香港的高度自治，不改变香港独立的司法权和终审权，有利于全面准确贯彻"一国两制"，有利于保障香港居民合法权利和自由，有利于保障外国投资者在港正当权益，有利于维护香港法治和营商环境，也有利于巩固各方对"一国两制"和香港发展前景的信心。此次立法得到香港绝大多数民众的拥护，得到汇丰银行、渣打银行、怡和集团、太古集团等企业的支持，也得到世界上很多主持公道正义国家的赞赏和声援。英国在香港有30多万公民、700多家企业，香港保持繁荣稳定不仅符合中国的利益，也符合英国的利益。

我相信，凡是希望香港保持长期繁荣稳定的人、凡是希望"一国两制"行稳致远的人，都会理解和支持香港国安法。我希望，各位议员认清大局和大势，客观、公正、理性地看待香港国安法。

二是始终视彼此为机遇和伙伴，而非威胁和对手。习近平主席指出，"历史将证明，实现中国梦给世界带来的是机遇不是威胁，是和平不是动荡，是进步不是倒退"。中国始终坚持走和平发展道路，致力与包括英国在内的世界各国和平相处，互利合作，共同发展，中国愿意成为"全球化英国"的战略伙伴。

近来，英国国内围绕华为问题有各种声音。有人鼓噪英国政府改变允许华为参与英国5G建设的决定，限制中国对英投资，很多在英中资企业对这一动向表示担忧。华为问题不是一个简单的中国民营企业参加英国5G建设的问题，而是英国如何看待中国的问题，是把中国看作伙伴还是对手，甚至威胁。华为落户英国19年来，对英国经济社会和电信产业发展做出积极贡献，成为中英合作共赢的典范。2012—2017 年，华为在英采购和投资 20 亿英镑，支撑本地就业 2.6 万个。2018 年初，华为承诺其后 5 年在英追加投入 30 亿英镑，迄今已落实 10 亿英镑以上。目前，华为正积极配合英国国家网络安全中心改进其产品和技术的薄弱环节，以更好地协助英国实现 2025 年前 5G 网络全覆盖的目标。华为问题还关系到英国支持自由贸易和开放合作的国际形象，关系到中资企业及其他外资企业对英国信心的问题。我希望，英国政府从本国根本利益和中英关系大局出发，坚持独立判断和自主决策，继续为包括华为在内的在英中资企业提供开放、公平、透明、非歧视的营商环境。

三是始终以平等对话管控分歧，不搞"麦克风外交"。中英之间存在分歧，这很正常，关键是要妥善处理。例如人权问题，一些政客总把人权问题政治化，搞"双重标准"。就人权保障事业而言，中国实现了历史上最快的人权进步。改革开放 40 年来，中国已跃升为世界第二大经济体，7.5 亿人实现脱贫，对全球减贫贡献率超过 70%，人均预期寿命为 77.3 岁，接近发达国家水平。2020 年，中国有信心、有能力克服疫情等各种困难，实现消除绝对贫困、全面建成小康社会的目标。当然，任何国家的人权状况都不是完美无缺的，都需要不断努力改进。但搞"麦克风外交"无助于解决矛盾和分歧。中国愿在平等和相互尊重原则的基础上，以开放、坦诚、包容、合作的态度与各方进行建设性对话，坚决反对充满傲慢与偏见的抹黑和指责。中英之间有人权对话机制，双方应利用好这些渠道，就共同关心的议题开展建设性对话。

各位议员，女士们、先生们，

英国议会跨党派中国小组成立 23 年来，积极推进两国议会对话交流，促进两国各领域合作，为增进中英了解与互信做出了贡献。习近平主席曾说，"封闭的空间只会四处碰壁，开放的道路才会越走越宽"。我衷心希望，议会跨党派中国小组继续做增进对华认知的先行者、中英关系的推动者、中英合作的促进者和中英友好的贡献者。我相信，在双方共同努力下，中英关系在"后疫情时代"将更加强劲，双方合作将更加广阔，两国人民友谊将更加深厚！

谢谢！

Stay Committed to Win-Win Cooperation*

Chairman Richard Graham,

Vice Chairmen,

My Lords and MPs,

Ladies and Gentlemen,

Good morning!

It is a real delight to join you online.

The last APPCG event I attended was Chinese New Year reception at the Palace of Westminster early this year. A lot have happened in the past five months.

The continued spread of COVID-19 is bringing profound changes to the world. This pandemic has not only changed our way of meeting and communicating, but also posed unprecedented challenges to mankind.

Against this background, there have been discussions and debates on the China-UK relationship here in this country. Some people think it could no longer be "business as usual" after the epidemic is over. Some call for a "review" of the relations and "decoupling" so as to make Britain "less strategically dependent" on China. Some even clamour for a "new Cold War" against China.

Of course, the majority still believe that China is an indispensable partner for a "global Britain", and developing relations with China is of critical importance to the UK.

Today, I would like to take this opportunity to share with you my understanding of the world and the China-UK relationship, especially:

---

* Keynote Speech at the APPCG Webinar. Chinese Embassy, 23 June 2020.

- what has changed,
- what has not changed,
- and how to properly handle this important relationship.

COVID-19 has changed the world profoundly in the following four aspects.

First, it has posed grave challenges to global public health.

COVID-19 is the most wide-spread pandemic in the past century. As of today, it has spread to more than 210 countries and regions, infected over 8 million people and claimed over 400,000 lives.

This reminds us that major infectious diseases are still grave challenges to the safety and health of mankind. This is not the first major public health emergency mankind has encountered. It will certainly not be the last. Countries must stand united to fight this battle hand in hand.

Second, COVID-19 has dealt a severe blow to the world economy.

Since the outbreak, global supply and demand have both plunged, international travel and trade have been facing restrictions, and global industrial and supply chains have been under severe strain.

The IMF predicted a 3% contraction in this year's world economy, while the WTO's prediction for international trade is 13%~32% contraction. There is a risk that this might evolve into the most severe recession since the Great Depression of the last century.

Currently many countries are bringing their economies gradually back on track, but an overall recovery for the world economy remains a daunting task.

Third, COVID-19 is a grave test to global governance.

In face of the unprecedented challenges of our times, mankind needs unprecedented solidarity and cooperation. This is true in epidemic response. This is also true for economic recovery. It means countries must uphold multilateralism.

However, some countries are doing the opposite,

- Resorting to unilateralism and protectionism.
- Taking advantage of the pandemic to "decouple" economies.
- Stigmatizing other countries.

- And even clamouring for a "new Cold War".

Such moves severely undermine the joint response to global public health crisis and pose grave challenges to the post-war international governance system and multilateral mechanisms.

Fourth, COVID-19 has reminded the world that all mankind belong to a community with a shared future.

Solidarity and cooperation are the most effective weapons to win the battle against the virus.

The more difficulties and challenges we face, the more we need exchanges and cooperation in order to build up consensus and strengthen confidence.

The more misgivings and doubts we encounter, the more we need mutual learning between different civilisations in order to draw strengths from others and achieve common progress.

In face of the major challenges of COVID-19, we must ask ourselves these questions:

- Do we remain open or hide behind closed doors?
- Do we embrace cooperation or descend to confrontation?
- Do we build bridges or erect walls?
- Do we pursue win-win results or play zero-sum games?

These questions test the wisdom, reason and sense of responsibility of every country in the world.

The world is experiencing profound changes. So is the China-UK relationship. However, I think China-UK ties remain unchanged in the following three aspects.

First, the global and strategic importance of this relationship remains unchanged.

As permanent members of the UN Security Council, China and the UK are both countries with global influence. We both have on our shoulders the important mission of safeguarding world peace and development.

In recent years,

- China and the UK have engaged in sound cooperation within the frameworks of

the UN, the G20 and the Asian Infrastructure Investment Bank (AIIB).
- We have extensive common interests in upholding multilateralism and free trade.
- In particular, we share consensus on building an open world economy and promoting reform in global governance.

China and the UK have played an active and leading role in international cooperation on environmental protection and climate change. We have maintained communication and supported each other in hosting COP15 and COP26 in our respective countries.

Our two countries have also had close communication and coordination on major international and regional issues. We have contributed to the political settlement of hotspots issues such as the Iran nuclear programme, the Korean Peninsula nulear issue and Syria issue. Such efforts have provided more stability and certainty for the world.

Since the outbreak of COVID-19, China and the UK have coordinated our policies and shared experience. We worked with each other on R&D of vaccine and medicines, supported each other with medical supplies and engaged in international cooperation.

Earlier this month, the Chinese Premier Li Keqiang attended the Global Vaccine Summit hosted by the UK government. He announced the Chinese donation to Gavi.

- Both our two countries support the leading role of WHO in the global response to the pandemic.
- Both believe we should help developing countries fight the pandemic and achieve economic recovery and social development.
- Both emphasize greater accessibility and affordability of vaccine in developing countries.

China-UK joint response to COVID-19 adds new contents to our bilateral relationship. There is a great deal our two countries can do together to make new contribution to safeguarding and improving global public health.

Second, the complementarity and win-win nature of the China-UK relationship remains unchanged.

- The economies of our two countries are highly complementary.

- Our interests are deeply intertwined.
- And our mutually-beneficial cooperation has been expanding.

The UK is the third largest trading partner of China in the EU. It is the largest destination for Chinese investment in Europe. China is the third largest export market for the UK.

China-UK cooperation is both vigorous and resilient. Even COVID-19 can not stop us.

In March this year, I attended the event marking the acquisition of British Steel by the Chinese Jingye Group. This deal saved 3,200 jobs for the local community. But that is not all because Jingye also pledged 1.2-billion-pound investment in the next ten years to transform and upgrade British Steel.

Last week, as Shanghai-London Stock Connect marked its first anniversary, China Pacific Insurance Group listed its Global Depository Receipts on the London Stock Exchange. This was a new highlight of China-UK financial cooperation despite the challenge from COVID-19.

China is one of the first countries to have brought COVID-19 under control and restarted the economy.

At the Two Sessions concluded last month, the Chinese government emphasized once again that no matter how the world might change, China will remain committed to deeper reform and further opening-up.

At the moment, the Chinese government is:

- Taking further steps to implement the Foreign Investment Law.
- Shortening the negative list for foreign investment by a large margin.
- Promoting the building of pilot free trade zones and free trade ports.
- And fostering a level-playing field for domestic and foreign businesses.

China is faced with opportunities to accelerate its economic transformation and upgrading. The outbreak of COVID-19 has revealed the enormous vitality and potential of "stay-home economy", "cloud office", digital economy, artificial intelligence, and health care. There is every reason to believe that China will remain a major powerhouse for world economic growth.

The steady recovery of the Chinese economy will create more opportunities for China-UK business cooperation. It will also help the UK realize economic recovery and achieve greater development after Brexit.

Third, the mutual appeal of our cultures and the fact that there is so much we can learn from each other remains unchanged.

China and the UK differ in history, culture, social system and development stage. But our history and culture are both time-honoured and splendid.

Recent years have witnessed close exchanges and cooperation between our two countries in the areas of education, culture, science and technology, youth, sports and tourism. This has enhanced mutual understanding, promoted cultural integration, strengthened the bond between our peoples and will ultimately enable us to carry on China-UK friendship from generation to generation.

Going forward, our two countries could adopt a more inclusive attitude and a broader vision, transcend differences in our cultures, and tear down the ideological fence. We should enhance understanding of each other's culture and development path, deepen exchanges and cooperation in all areas, and become a shining example of open and inclusive exchanges and mutual learning between different civilizations.

Now let me turn to the third part of my speech and explore whether and how we can achieve greater progress in the China-UK relationship when we put the pandemic behind us.

I think the following three principles hold the key to the answer.

The first principle is equality and mutual respect.

70 years ago, the UK was the first major Western country to recognize New China. It is true we had differences throughout the past 70 years. But we have always found more common interests than differences. Our two countries are not driven apart by our differences. On the contrary, we have come closer because of common interests.

A look back at the history of the China-UK relationship tells us that when we treated each other as equals, sought common ground despite differences and respected each other's core interests and major concerns, the China-UK relationship would move forward in leaps and bounds. Otherwise, our relationship would suffer setbacks or even retrogression.

The most prominent challenge we face now is in relation to the Hong Kong Special Administrative Region (SAR). Twenty-three years after Hong Kong's return, some people in this country have yet to bid farewell to the colonial past. They keep making irresponsible remarks about Hong Kong and interfering in the Chinese domestic affairs.

When the Chinese top legislature, the National People's Congress (NPC), adopted the decision at this year's Two Sessions on national security legislation for the Hong Kong SAR, and the draft law is placed under review by the NPC Standing Committee, some people once again made unwarranted and irresponsible remarks to demonize this legislative action. China strongly opposes this.

Why is the national security legislation for the Hong Kong SAR necessary?

In the past 23 years since Hong Kong's return, One Country, Two Systems has achieved tremendous success in the Hong Kong SAR. However, this great city has been "defenseless" in terms of national security. This is caused by severe stigmatization and demonization of Article 23 of the Basic Law, which provides for the making of a national security law for the SAR. As a result, no such law has been enacted, making the SAR a risk and a loophole for national security.

In particular, since the turbulence over the proposed amendment bill in 2019, anti-China elements seeking to disrupt Hong Kong have clamoured for "Hong Kong independence" and "self determination". They have been engaged in separatist activities that threaten national unity and created terror in the city through violence, including beating, smashing, looting and arson.

These activities have gravely undermined the social stability, economic prosperity and public safety in Hong Kong. They have broken the principle of One Country, Two Systems and severely endangered the Chinese national security. They have landed Hong Kong in the gravest situation since Hong Kong's return.

As is in all countries, safeguarding national security is the primary responsibility of the central government and falls within the power of the central government.

Here in the UK, it is the central government and Parliament that are responsible for matters relating to national security in England, Scotland, Northern Ireland and Wales.

In China, it is the same. Therefore, it is within the power of the National People's Congress to plug the loophole that compromises national security in Hong Kong through legislation in accordance with the Constitution and the Basic Law. This is entirely reasonable and lawful. This is something that must be done.

This legislation targets only the few act or activity that gravely jeopardize national security.

- It will not impact the high degree of autonomy in Hong Kong.
- It will not affect Hong Kong's independent judicial power, including the power of final adjudication.
- On the contrary, it will provide better safeguards for the lawful rights and freedoms of the Hong Kong residents.
- It will ensure better protection of the legitimate rights and interests of foreign investors in the city.
- It will guarantee better rule of law and business environment in Hong Kong.
- And it will strengthen people's confidence in One Country, Two Systems, and in Hong Kong's development in the future.

It has already won the support of the majority of the Hong Kong people. Some British businesses, including HSBC, Standard Chartered, Jardine Matheson and Swire Group have expressed their support. And many countries have also upheld justice and expressed their appreciation and support for this legislation.

Hong Kong is home to more than 300,000 British citizens and over 700 British firms. A prosperous and stable Hong Kong is in the interests of both China and the UK.

I believe that everyone who hopes to see long-term prosperity and stability in Hong Kong as well as steady and sustained development of One Country, Two Systems would understand the need for the national security legislation for the Hong Kong SAR and support it.

It is my hope that MPs and Members of the Lords will be able to appreciate the big picture and major trend, and view this legislation from an objective, fair and reasonable perspective.

The second principle is to regard each other as opportunities and partners, rather than threats or rivals.

President Xi Jinping said, "History will demonstrate that the pursuit of the Chinese Dream will bring to the world opportunities rather than threats, peace rather than turmoil, and progress rather than backwardness."

China is committed to peaceful development, pursues peaceful coexistence, mutually-beneficial cooperation and common development with all countries in the world, including the UK, and is ready to be a strategic partner of a "global Britain".

In recent days, there have been many discussions about Huawei and its presence in the UK. Some people urged the UK government to change its decision on allowing Huawei in its 5G development and to impose restrictions on Chinese investment. This is a cause for concern in the Chinese business community in this country.

The question of Huawei is not simply about whether a private company from China is allowed to take part in the UK's 5G development. More importantly, it is about how the UK perceives China. Does it see China as a partner, a rival, or even a threat?

Huawei has been here for 19 years. It has worked for the economic and social progress locally and contributed to the development of the telecommunications sector of this country. It is a good example of win-win cooperation between China and the UK.

From 2012 to 2017, Huawei brought 2 billion pounds into Britain through investment and procurement, and created 26,000 jobs. In early 2018, Huawei pledged a further investment of 3 billion pounds in the UK over the next five years. As of today, over a billion pounds have been put in place.

Huawei is now working with the National Cyber Security Centre (NCSC) to improve the weak links in its products and technology, so as to do a better job in helping the UK realize its goal of full 5G coverage by the year 2025.

The decision on Huawei also matters to the UK's image in the world—whether it remains a supporter of free trade and open cooperation, or not. This will have a very important bearing on the confidence of businesses from China and other countries in the UK.

It is my hope that the UK government will, in light of the fundamental interests of the UK and the big picture of the China-UK relationship, come to an independent judgment and decision, and continue to foster an open, fair, transparent and non-discriminatory environment here in this country for Chinese businesses, including Huawei.

The third principle is to manage differences through equal-footed dialogues rather than "megaphone diplomacy".

It is natural that China and the UK do not always see eye to eye. The key is to deal with the differences in a proper manner.

Take human rights for example. Some politicians have the inclination of politicizing human rights and applying "double standards".

But if they have no bias and take a look at what China has achieved in safeguarding human rights, they would recognize the rapid and tremendous progress in the past 40 years since China started reform and opening-up:

- China has grown to be the world's second largest economy.
- It has lifted 750 million people out of poverty and contributed over 70% of the world's total poverty reduction.
- Life expectancy for average Chinese is 77.3, approaching the level in developed countries.

China has the confidence and capability to overcome COVID-19 and other difficulties, and achieve its goal of eliminating absolute poverty and completing the building of a moderately prosperous society in all aspects this year.

Of course, no country is perfect. There is room for improvement on human rights in every country. There are always differences of views and sometimes even frictions, but the solution of differences can not be found in "megaphone diplomacy".

China stands ready to engage all the relevant parties in constructive dialogues in an open, candid, inclusive and cooperative attitude and on the basis of equality and mutual respect. However, we strongly oppose smears and accusations based on arrogance and bias.

China and the UK should make full use of existing channels, such as the China-UK Human Rights Dialogue, and engage in constructive discussions on issues of common concern.

My Lords and MPs,

Ladies and Gentlemen,

In the past 23 years since its establishment, APPCG has worked hard to promote dialogues and exchanges between the UK Parliament and the Chinese NPC, and to enhance cooperation across the board. You have made significant contribution to better understanding and deeper trust between our two countries.

President Xi Jinping said, "In a closed room, you run into walls and can never get anywhere; but if you open up, the road under your feet will become wider and wider."

It is my sincere hope that APPCG will continue to be a pioneer in enhancing understanding of China in the UK, a supporter for China-UK relations, a promoter of China-UK cooperation and a contributor to China-UK friendship.

I am confident that, with the concerted efforts of both sides, China and the UK will emerge from the pandemic with stronger relationship, broader cooperation and deeper friendship between our peoples.

Thank you!

中英关系的"变"与"不变"*

大家上午好！

欢迎大家出席今天的中外记者会。

2020年年初以来，习近平主席与约翰逊首相两次通电话，就推进中英关系及两国共同抗疫达成重要共识。两国政府各部门认真落实这一重要共识，积极开展多领域合作。中英双方本应珍惜这一良好势头，推动两国关系向前发展，但令人遗憾和痛心的是，近来，中英关系遭遇一系列困难，面临严峻形势。

人们在问：中英关系怎么了？英国媒体也在问：中英关系出现问题的原因何在？是中国变了还是英国变了？今天我就来回答这个问题：中国没有变，变的是英国。中英关系遭遇困难，责任完全在英方。

第一，中方坚定奉行国际关系基本准则没有变。互相尊重主权和领土完整、互不干涉内政和平等互利，是《联合国宪章》确立的国家间关系的基本原则，是国际法与国际关系的基本准则，也是中英关系的基本原则，被写入两国建立大使级外交关系的联合公报。中国从不干涉别国内政，包括英国内政，也决不允许别国干涉中国内政。但是，近期英方却一再违反这些重要原则：在涉港问题上无端指责《中华人民共和国香港特别行政区维护国家安全法》（以下简称香港国安法），改变英国国民（海外）（BNO）政策，暂停与香港移交逃犯协定，粗暴干涉香港事务和中国内政，严重干扰香港稳定与繁荣；

---

* 就中英关系举行中外记者会开场白。2020年7月30日，中国驻英国大使馆。

在涉疆问题上罔顾事实，颠倒黑白，在双边和多边渠道对中国治疆政策大肆抹黑攻击，借所谓新疆人权问题干涉中国内政，严重毒化中英关系氛围。

第二，中方坚持走和平发展道路没有变。走和平发展道路，是中国坚定不移的战略选择和郑重承诺。中国没有侵略扩张的基因，没有也不会输出自己的模式。中国发展是为了让人民过上好日子，而不是要威胁谁、挑战谁、取代谁。历史已经并将继续证明，中国始终是世界和平的建设者、全球发展的贡献者、国际秩序的维护者，中国的发展壮大只能使世界更和平、更稳定、更繁荣。而英国一些政客抱守冷战思维，与英内外反华势力遥相呼应，大肆渲染"中国威胁论"，将中国视为"敌对国家"，扬言要与中国全面"脱钩"，甚至叫嚣要对中国发动"新冷战"。

第三，中方认真履行自身国际义务没有变。2020年是联合国成立75周年，中国是第一个签署《联合国宪章》的国家。中国参加了100多个政府间国际组织，签署了500多个多边条约。中国始终认真履行自身承担的国际责任和义务，从未"退群""毁约"，从不谋求本国利益优先。英方妄称中方出台香港国安法违反《联合声明》，未履行国际义务，这完全是错误的。《联合声明》的核心要义是中国恢复对香港行使主权，而香港国安法正充分体现了中国中央政府对香港的全面管治权。中国政府在《联合声明》中阐述的对港方针政策是中方的政策宣示，既不是对英方的承诺，更不是所谓国际义务，"不履行国际义务"的帽子扣不到中国头上。反倒是英方不履行国际义务，违背自身承诺，改变BNO政策，暂停与香港移交逃犯协定，扰乱香港人心，干扰香港国安法实施，干涉中国内政。

第四，中方致力于发展对英伙伴关系的意愿没有变。2015年习近平主席对英国国事访问期间，中英发表联合宣言，决定构建面向21世纪全球全面战略伙伴关系。中国始终将英国看作伙伴，致力于发展健康稳定的中英关系。正如王毅国务委员兼外长前天与拉布外交大臣通话时指出的那样："对英国而言，中国始终是机遇而不是威胁，是增量而不是减量，是解决方案而不是挑战。"然而，英方近来对华认知和定位发生重大变化，出现严重偏差，"禁用华为"就是最突出例证。这不是英国如何对待一家中国企业的问题，而是关系到英国如何看待中国的问题。英国究竟是把中国看作机遇、伙伴，还是威胁、对手？是把中国看作友好国家，还是敌对或潜在敌对国家？英方领导人多次表示要发展平衡、积极、建设性的中英关系。我们听其言，观其行。

当前，世界百年未有之大变局正向纵深发展。新冠疫情仍在全球肆虐，经济全球化遭遇严重冲击，世界经济陷入深度衰退。面对这样的形势，我们需要一个什么样的中英关系？中英都是联合国安理会常任理事国和二十国集团等国际组织重要成员国，都是具有全球影响的大国，都肩负着维护世界和平、促进发展的重要使命。一个健康稳定发展的中英关系，不仅符合中英两国人民的根本利益，也有利于世界的和平与繁荣。我们有一千个理由把中英关系搞好，没有一条理由把中英关系搞坏。如何搞好中英关系？我认为，做到以下三点至关重要。

一是相互尊重。历史告诉我们，只要国际法和国际关系基本准则得到遵守，中英关系就向前发展；反之则遭遇挫折，甚至倒退。中国尊重英国主权，从未做任何干涉英国内政的事。英方也应以同样态度对待中方，尊重中国主权，停止干涉香港事务和中国内政，避免中英关系受到进一步损害。

二是互利共赢。中英经济互补性强，利益深度融合，双方从彼此合作中都获得了巨大收益，不存在谁更依赖谁、谁多占谁便宜的问题。希望英方不要受个别国家的压力和胁迫，为中国企业提供开放、公平、非歧视的投资环境，重塑中国企业对英国的信心。在"后脱欧时代"和"后疫情时代"，中英在贸易、金融、科技、教育、医疗卫生领域有广阔合作空间，在维护多边主义、促进自由贸易、应对气候变化等全球性挑战等方面拥有广泛共识。英国要打造"全球化英国"，绕不开、离不开中国。与中国"脱钩"，就是与机遇和发展"脱钩"，与未来"脱钩"。

三是求同存异。中英历史文化、社会制度、发展阶段不同，难免存在分歧。70年前，英国在西方大国中第一个承认新中国。70年来，中英本着求同存异的精神，超越意识形态差异，推动中英关系不断向前发展。70年后的今天，中英关系更加丰富、更加深入，不是你输我赢的对手关系，更不是非此即彼的敌对关系，而是平等相待、互利共赢的伙伴关系。我们应当有足够的智慧与能力管控和处理好双方分歧，不让反华势力和冷战分子绑架中英关系。

　　我常说，只有拥有独立自主的外交政策，"不列颠"才是名副其实的"大不列颠"。无论是1950年英国在西方大国中首个承认中华人民共和国，1954年与中国建立代办级外交关系，还是英国选择加入亚投行，与中国构建面向21世纪全球全面战略伙伴关系，英国在关键历史节点都顶住外部压力，做出了正确的战略抉择。现在，中英关系再次处于关键历史节点。我希望，英国政治家和各界有识之士认清国际大势，排除各种干扰，把握时代潮流，做出符合中英两国人民根本利益的战略抉择。

　　谢谢大家！

China-UK Relations: What Has Changed and What Has Not[*]

Good morning!

Welcome to today's press conference.

Since early this year, President Xi Jinping and Prime Minister Boris Johnson have had two telephone conversations, during which they reached important agreements on advancing China-UK relations and enhancing joint response to COVID-19. The departments of the two governments have been working hard to implement these agreements and carry out cooperation in various areas.

This was a positive momentum in the China-UK relationship that should be cherished so that further progress could be achieved. To our regret however, this relationship has recently run into a series of difficulties and faced a grave situation.

People are asking: What is happening to the China-UK relationship? The British media are also asking: What has caused the current difficulties in the China-UK relationship? Has China changed or has the UK changed?

Today, I am going to give you my answer to these questions. My answer is loud and clear: China has not changed. It is the UK that has changed. The UK side should take full responsibility for the current difficulties in the China-UK relationship.

First, the Chinese determination to follow the basic norms governing international relations has not changed.

These basic norms include:

---

[*] Opening Remarks at the Press Conference on the China-UK Relationship. Chinese Embassy, 30 July 2020.

- Mutual respect for each other's sovereignty and territorial integrity.
- Non-interference in each other's internal affairs.
- Equality.
- And mutual benefit.

These are the fundamental principles that are enshrined in the UN Charter. They are the basic norms of the international law and state-to-state relations. They are also the basic guidelines that have been written into the joint communiqué of China and the UK on exchange of ambassadors and hence form the bedrock for the China-UK relationship.

China has never interfered in the internal affairs of other countries, including the UK, and we ask the same from other countries.

Recently, however, the above-mentioned important principles have been violated time and again.

On Hong Kong:

There has been blatant interference from the UK in Hong Kong affairs, which are internal affairs of China, including:

- groundless accusations against the National Security Law for the Hong Kong SAR,
- change to the policy involving BNO passport holders,
- and suspension of the surrender of fugitive offenders agreement with Hong Kong.

These moves have severely disrupted the stability and prosperity in Hong Kong.

On Xinjiang:

- The UK disregarded the facts.
- Confused right and wrong.
- Flung slanders recklessly at the Chinese Xinjiang-related policies.
- And interfered in the Chinese internal affairs by raising the so-called "human rights issue" in Xinjiang, bilaterally and multilaterally.

These actions have seriously poisoned the atmosphere of the China-UK relationship.

Second, the Chinese commitment to the path of peaceful development has not changed.

Pursuing peaceful development is the unwavering strategic choice and solemn pledge of China. China has never invaded other countries or sought expansion. China has never and will not export its system or model. China seeks development because we want better life for our people. We do not want to threaten, challenge or replace anyone.

History has proved and will continue to prove that China is always a defender of world peace, a contributor to global development and an upholder of international order. A stronger China will make the world a more peaceful, stable and prosperous place.

However, some British politicians cling to the Cold War mentality and echo the remarks of anti-China forces in and outside the UK. They

- Play up the so-called "China threat".
- See China as a "hostile state".
- Threaten a "complete decoupling" from China.
- And even clamour for a "new Cold War" against China.

Third, the Chinese resolve to fulfill its international obligations has not changed.

This year marks the 75th anniversary of the founding of the United Nations. China was the first country to put its signature on the UN Charter. It is now a member of more than 100 inter-governmental international organisations and has signed over 500 multilateral treaties.

- It has faithfully fulfilled its international responsibilities and obligations.
- It has never withdrawn from international organisations or treaties.
- Nor does it believe in "us first" at the expense of others.

It is completely wrong to see the National Security Law for the Hong Kong SAR as a violation of the Sino-British Joint Declaration or a failure to honour international obligations.

The core content of the Joint Declaration is about the Chinese resumption of exercise of sovereignty over Hong Kong. The National Security Law for the Hong Kong SAR fully embodies the comprehensive jurisdiction of the central government of

China over Hong Kong.

The policies regarding Hong Kong laid out in the Joint Declaration were proposed by China on our own initiative. They are not the Chinese commitments to the UK or international obligations. The label of "failure to fulfill international obligations" should not be stuck on China.

It is the UK side that has failed to fulfill its international obligations and went against its own pledges by changing the policy on BNO passport holders and suspending the surrender of fugitive offenders agreement with Hong Kong to create public confusion in Hong Kong, disrupt the implementation of the National Security Law and interfere in the Chinese internal affairs.

Fourth, the Chinese willingness to develop partnership with the UK has not changed.

During President Xi Jinping's state visit to the UK in 2015, China and the UK issued a joint declaration on building a global comprehensive strategic partnership for the 21st century.

China has always seen the UK as a partner and it has been committed to developing a sound and stable relationship with the UK. As State Councilor and Foreign Minister Wang Yi said two days ago in his telephone conversation with Foreign Secretary Dominic Raab, for the UK, China is an opportunity rather than a threat, a factor for growth rather than a cause for decline, a solution rather than a challenge or a risk. However, there have been major changes and serious deviations in the UK's perception and definition of China. This is particularly evidenced by the recent ban on Huawei.

The issue of Huawei is not about how the UK sees and deals with a Chinese company. It is about how the UK sees and deals with China. Does it see China as an opportunity and a partner, or a threat and a rival? Does it see China as a friendly country, or a "hostile" or "potentially hostile" state?

The UK leaders have said on many occasions that they want to build a balanced, positive and constructive China-UK relationship. We hope they will match their words with actions.

The world is undergoing increasingly profound changes unseen in a century. COVID-19 is still ravaging, dealing a heavy blow to economic globalization and resulting in a deep recession of the world economy. What kind of China-UK relationship do we need in face of such a situation?

China and the UK are both permanent members of the UN Security Council and important members of the G20 and other international organizations. Both are countries of global influence. Both shoulder the important mission of safeguarding world peace and promoting development.

A sound and stable China-UK relationship is not only in the fundamental interests of the peoples of the two countries, but also conducive to world peace and prosperity. We have a thousand reasons to make this relationship successful, and not one reason to let it fail.

How can we make it successful? I think it is critically important to follow three principles.

The first principle is: Respect each other.

History tells us that when international law and the basic norms governing international relations are observed, the China-UK relationship will move forward; otherwise, it will suffer setbacks or even retrogression.

China respects the UK's sovereignty and has never interfered in the UK's internal affairs. It is important that the UK do the same, namely, respect the Chinese sovereignty and stop interfering in Hong Kong affairs, which are the Chinese internal affairs, so as to avoid further harm to the China-UK relationship.

The second principle is: Engage in mutually-beneficial cooperation.

China and the UK have highly complementary economies and deeply integrated interests. The two sides have both benefited tremendously from cooperation. Such mutual benefit should not be gauged by an over-simplified comparison of who is more dependent on the other or who has been "taken advantage of".

It is our hope that the UK would resist the pressure and coercion of a certain country, and provide an open, fair and non-discriminatory environment for Chinese investment, so as to bring back the confidence of Chinese businesses in the UK.

China and the UK already share broad consensus on safeguarding multilateralism, promoting free trade and addressing global challenges such as climate change. When Brexit is completed and COVID-19 is over, there will be unlimited prospects for China-UK cooperation in the areas of trade, financial services, science and technology, education and health care.

It is hard to imagine a "global Britain" that bypasses or excludes China. "Decoupling" from China means decoupling from opportunities, decoupling from growth, and decoupling from the future.

The third principle is: Seek common ground despite differences.

China and the UK differ in history, culture, social system and development stage. It is natural that we do not always see eye to eye.

70 years ago, the UK was the first major Western country to recognize New China. For the past 70 years, China and the UK have found common ground despite differences and went beyond ideological differences to achieve continuous progress in their bilateral relationship.

Today, after 70 years, this relationship has been more substantial and profound. It is not a relationship between rivals, where one side's gain is the other's loss. Still less is it a relationship of "either-or" that exists between hostile states. The China-UK relationship is one of partnership, which is defined by equal treatment and mutual benefit.

China and the UK should have enough wisdom and capability to manage and deal with differences, rather than allowing anti-China forces and "Cold-War warriors" to "hijack" the China-UK relationship.

I often say "Great Britain" cannot be "great" without independent foreign policies. The UK has withstood the pressure from others and made the right strategic choices at many critical historical junctures,

- from becoming the first major Western country to recognize the People's Republic of China in 1950, to establishing diplomatic relationship with China at the chargé d'affaires level in 1954;
- from taking part in the Asian Infrastructure Investment Bank to building a global comprehensive strategic partnership for the 21st century with China.

Now, the China-UK relationship is once again standing at a critical historical juncture. It is my hope that political leaders and visionary people from all sectors in the UK would keep in mind the big picture of the international trend, prevent various disruptions and make the strategic choice that serves the fundamental interests of the peoples of our two countries.

Thank you!

精诚如一，善始令终 *

尊敬的英国外交发展部总司长贝茨女士，

尊敬的各位议员，

尊敬的各位使节，

女士们、先生们、朋友们：

大家上午好！

感谢大家出席我和我的夫人胡平华女士的线上离任招待会。2009年12月，我被任命为新中国第11任驻英国大使。2010年2月，我抵英履职。在英国工作生活的11年，是我47年外交生涯中驻外时间最长的一次，也是最后一次。我有幸成为中英关系史上任期最长的中国驻英使节和中国历史上任职时间最长的驻外大使。我对此深感荣幸，也倍感珍惜。

这11年是中国和世界发生巨大变化的11年。正如习近平主席所说，世界正经历百年未有之大变局。11年来，我见证了中国发展实现历史性跨越、中国特色社会主义进入新时代，见证了中国与世界的关系发生历史性变化，也见证了中英关系历经波澜起伏。11年来，我经历英国4次大选、2次公投，目睹了英国"脱欧"全过程和"全球化英国"再启程，有幸与英国4任首相和6任外交大臣共事。我遍访英国各地，北至最北端的设得兰群岛的耶尔岛，南至英吉利海峡诸岛，从英格兰到苏格兰，从北爱尔兰到威尔士，从皇家属地到海外领地，我广泛接触英国各界人士，积极推进中英各领域合作，发表

---

* 在离任招待会上的讲话。2021年1月25日，中国驻英国大使馆。

演讲 700 余场，在主流报刊撰文 170 多篇，接受主流媒体采访 170 多次。

习近平主席说，"不忘初心，方得始终"。11 年前，我在履新后不久接受英国《外交官》杂志采访时，曾用"IDEA"一词来概括自己作为驻英大使的使命："I"代表利益（interests），即扩大中英共同利益；"D"代表对话（dialogue），即对话永远好于对抗；"E"代表探索（exploration），即探索合作新领域；"A"代表互谅（accommodation），即相互尊重、互谅互让。11 年来，我始终牢记使命，锐意进取，与英国各界人士一道推动中英关系不断向前发展。

第一，中英共同利益的"蛋糕"越做越大。11 年来，中英双边货物贸易额翻了近一番，英国对华出口增长约 20 倍，中国成为英国第三大货物出口市场；中国对英投资增长约 20 倍，英国成为中国在欧洲第二大投资目的地国，欣克利角 C 核电站作为中国在欧洲最大单笔投资，成为中英合作旗舰项目；中英金融合作开创诸多"第一"：英国第一个发行人民币主权债券，第一个申请加入亚投行，中国在伦敦发行中国境外第一笔人民币主权债券；伦敦成为世界第一大人民币离岸交易中心和第二大人民币离岸清算中心，人民币清算量超过 50 万亿元；沪伦通正式开通，多家中资企业在伦敦证券交易所上市，开中国与境外资本市场互联互通先河；中英"一带一路"合作方兴未艾，双方签署第三方市场合作协议，共同致力于推进"一带一路"高质量发展。

第二，中英高层对话机制更加丰富。两国领导人保持沟通和交往，为中英关系发展不断注入新动力。11 年来，中英举行了 5 次总理会晤、5 次战略对话、8 次经济财金对话，还开启了两国高级别人文交流机制和高级别安全对话。最令我记忆深刻的是，2015 年习近平主席对英国进行了具有历史性、里程碑意义的"超级国事访问"，在中英关系史上留下了浓墨重彩的一笔。

第三，中英国际协作探索广阔领域。面对国际形势风云变幻，中英在联合国、二十国集团等国际组织框架下加强协作，在支持多边主义和自由贸易、反对单边主义和保护主义、携手应对气候变化等全球性挑战方面共识更加突出，在国际和地区热点问题上保持沟通协调。近年来，中英积极推进气候变化和绿色发展合作。2021年，中英将分别举办COP15和COP26，双方正加强沟通协调，确保两场大会相得益彰、协同增效，为推进中英气变合作、促进绿色发展、引领全球环境治理注入动力。

第四，中英互尊互信互谅任重道远。在中英各界人士共同努力下，两国相互了解和认知不断加深，民意基础逐步扩大。11年来，中英年度人员往来数量翻了一番，达200万人次；在英中国留学生数量增长一倍多，达22万人。英国已成为中国学生留学的首选地，两国文化、科技、创新交流合作成果丰硕，英国成为第一个与中国签署科技创新合作战略的国家。新冠疫情暴发以来，两国人民守望相助、共克时艰的友好情谊令人感动。

诚然，中英政治制度、发展阶段、历史文化不同，在一些问题上难免存在分歧。11年来，中英关系也并非一帆风顺。但回首中英关系发展的历史，我们有理由相信，只要相互尊重、平等相待、遵守国际法和国际关系基本准则，中英关系就能超越分歧，沿着正确轨道向前发展。当前，百年变局与世纪疫情相互激荡，国际格局深刻调整，世界面临合作与对抗、对话与分裂、开放与封闭的选择。在这样的形势下，中英作为具有全球影响的大国，肩负着维护世界和平与发展的重任。我衷心希望，中英双方能着眼大局、顺时应势、相向而行，推动两国关系健康稳定发展，更好地造福中英两国人民和世界人民。

女士们、先生们、朋友们，

在即将离任回国之际，我收到许多英国朋友热情洋溢的来信，大家对我任内推动中英交流合作给予积极评价，对我、平华及家人致以美好祝福，令我深受感动。11年来与中英两国朋友们共话友谊、共促合作的一幅幅美好画卷，不时浮现在我的眼前，它们将成为我最宝贵、最温馨的回忆。在此，我谨向所有关心与支持中国发展和中英友好的朋友们、向所有为我履职提供支持和帮助的朋友们，表示最诚挚的谢意！

我还要感谢中国驻英国大使馆的同事们。11年来，我先后与6位公使兼首席馆员、数百名外交官及工作人员共事。他们是中国外交队伍的杰出代表，个个都是好样的。正是因为有他们的敬业精神和高效工作，我才能有所作为。

最后，我要感谢我的夫人胡平华。她的理解和支持是我永恒的动力，也是我成功的秘密。现在我请她给大家讲几句话。（胡平华女士讲话内容略。）

女士们、先生们、朋友们，

莎士比亚说，"欢迎是永远含笑的，告别总是带着叹息"。离别时分，我心有不舍，但也深感欣慰。过去11年，为了中国外交和中英关系，我精诚如一，不辱使命，无愧于心，善始令终。我衷心祝愿中英友谊地久天长，祝愿中英合作走深走实，祝愿中英关系行稳致远。再过17天，就是中国农历牛年春节。祝愿各位朋友牛年吉祥、身体健康、阖家幸福、诸事顺遂！

谢谢大家！

Serve with Sincerity All the Way through*

Director General Bates,

My Lords and MPs,

Ambassadors,

Ladies and Gentlemen,

Dear Friends,

Good morning!

Thank you for joining me and my wife Hu Pinghua at our Farewell Reception online. In December 2009, I was appointed the eleventh Chinese Ambassador to the UK. In February 2010, I arrived in London to take up my post.

Now I have been working and living in the UK for 11 years. This is the longest and last tour of my diplomatic career of 47 years.

It has been an honour to be the longest-serving Chinese Ambassador both in the history of China-UK relations and of all Chinese ambassadors of all time. I will cherish the memory deeply for the rest of my life.

These 11 years have seen tremendous changes in both China and the world. As President Xi Jinping said, "the world is experiencing profound changes unseen in a century."

In these 11 years, I have witnessed:

- Historic leaps in the Chinese development.
- A new era for socialism with Chinese characteristics.
- Historic changes in the relations between China and the rest of the world.

---

* Speech at the Farewell Reception. Chinese Embassy, 25 January 2021.

- And the ups and downs, and twists and turns in China-UK relations.

Here in the UK, I have witnessed four general elections and two referendums. I have observed the entire process of the UK leaving the EU and embarking on the journey of building a "global Britain". And I have had the honour of working with, among others, four prime ministers and six foreign secretaries.

I have been to all corners of the UK, from Yell of Shetland Islands in the north to the Channel Islands in the south, from England to Scotland, from Northern Ireland to Wales, and from the Crown dependencies to overseas territories.

I have worked with people from all walks of life in this country to advance China-UK cooperation across the board. Altogether I have made over 700 speeches, contributed more than 170 articles to mainstream newspapers and had over 170 interviews with mainstream media.

As President Xi Jinping said, "if you never forget why you started, you can accomplish your mission."

At an interview with the British magazine *Diplomat* 11 years ago upon arrival, I used the acronym "IDEA" to summarize my missions as Chinese Ambassador to the UK:

- I is for "interests": I will work to expand the common interests of China and the UK.
- D is for "dialogue": I will promote dialogue, which is always better than confrontation.
- E is for "exploration": I will provide facilitation for our two sides to explore new areas for cooperation.
- And A is for "accommodation": I will highlight the principles of mutual respect, understanding and accommodation in our bilateral relations.

For the past 11 years, I have kept these missions in mind and worked tirelessly with people from all sectors in the UK to bring China-UK relations forward.

First, our common interests have grown. The pie is getting bigger and bigger.

In the past 11 years, China-UK bilateral trade in goods almost doubled, with British export to China increasing by about 20 times, making China the third largest market for British export of goods.

Chinese investment in the UK has surged by about 20 times. The UK is now the second largest destination in Europe for Chinese investment. Hinkley Point C nuclear power station has been the largest investment from China in Europe and become a flagship project of China-UK cooperation.

There have been many "firsts" in China-UK financial cooperation. The UK was the first major Western country to issue RMB sovereign bond and to join the Asian Infrastructure Investment Bank. London also witnessed the issuance of the first Chinese RMB sovereign bond outside China.

London is now the world's largest offshore RMB exchange centre and the second largest offshore RMB clearing centre. The total clearing volume has exceeded 50 trillion RMB yuan.

The Shanghai-London Stock Connect was officially launched, connecting for the first time the Chinese capital market with a foreign one, and enabling many Chinese companies to benefit from London's world-class financial services.

China and the UK are also committed to working together to promote the high quality development of the Belt and Road Initiative and we have signed an agreement on cooperation in third markets.

Second, China and the UK have more dialogue mechanisms for exchanging views at the top level.

Leaders of our two countries have maintained communication and exchanges and this provides driving forces for the growth of China-UK relations.

In the past 11 years, China and the UK have held 5 sessions of the Prime Minister's Meeting, 5 sessions of the Strategic Dialogue, and 8 sessions of the Economic and Financial Dialogue. Our two sides also launched the High-Level People-to-People Dialogue and the Security Dialogue.

The definite highlight of these exchanges was President Xi Jinping's "super state visit" to the UK in 2015. This milestone event bore historic significance, and left an indelible mark in the history of China-UK relations.

Third, China and the UK have explored broader areas for international coordination.

In face of the ever-changing international situation, China and the UK have enhanced coordination under the framework of various international organisations, such as the UN and the G20.

We share growing consensus in supporting multilateralism and free trade, opposing unilateralism and protectionism and addressing global challenges such as climate change. We have also maintained communication and coordination on international and regional hotspot issues.

In recent years, our two countries have worked vigorously to promote cooperation on climate response and green development. Later this year, China and the UK will host COP15 and COP26 respectively. Our two sides are working on synergy between the two conferences to make them successful so as to enhance cooperation on climate response, promote green development and take the lead in global governance on the environment.

Fourth, China and the UK have enhanced mutual respect, trust and accommodation but daunting tasks still remain.

Thanks to the concerted efforts of people from all walks of life in both countries, China and the UK have deepened mutual understanding and cemented public support for bilateral relations.

In the past 11 years, annual mutual visits between our two countries have doubled, reaching two million. The number of Chinese students in the UK also doubled, reaching 220,000. The UK has become the top destination for Chinese students who want to study overseas.

Fruitful results have been achieved in exchanges and cooperation in areas of culture, science and technology, and innovation. The UK was the first country to sign the joint strategy for Science, technology and innovation cooperation with China.

Since the outbreak of COVID-19, the peoples of our two countries have come to each other's aid and tackled the difficulties together. There have been numerous touching moments.

China and the UK differ in political system, development stage, history and culture. It is natural that we do not always see eye to eye. The China-UK relationship has not always been smooth sailing in the past 11 years. But the history of China-UK relations tells us that when the principles of mutual respect and equality are followed, and when international law and the basic norms governing state-to-state relations are observed, the China-UK relationship will transcend differences and move forward along the right track.

At the moment, the worst pandemic in a hundred years is ravaging the world, precipitating the profound changes unseen in a century and bringing deep adjustments to the international landscape. The world is facing an important choice between cooperation and confrontation, between dialogue and division and between openness and closedness.

Against such a backdrop, China and the UK, as major countries of global influence, shoulder the important mission of safeguarding world peace and development. I sincerely hope that China and the UK will see the big picture, follow the megatrend and work with each other in the same direction. A sound and stable China-UK relationship will benefit the people of both countries and beyond.

Ladies and Gentlemen,

Dear Friends,

As I am about to leave the UK, I have received warm letters from many British friends. I thank you for your recognition of my work in promoting China-UK exchanges and cooperation. I also appreciate your best wishes to me, Pinghua and my family. I am deeply touched.

Many beautiful moments keep coming back. They remind me of the work I have done for better China-UK relations and the friends I have made and worked together toward this goal. They will be my sweetest and most deeply cherished memories.

I would like to express my most sincere thanks to all the friends who have cared for and supported the Chinese development and China-UK friendship, and who have provided support and assistance to me in my work!

My thanks also go to my colleagues in the Chinese Embassy in the UK. Over the past 11 years, I have worked with six deputy heads of mission, and hundreds of diplomats and staff. They represent the best of the Chinese diplomatic team. Each one of them is remarkable. I would not have achieved anything without their dedication and efficiency.

Last but not least, I would like to say a big "thank you" to my wife Hu Pinghua. Her understanding and support are my source of strength. If I had achieved anything, she would be the secret to the success. Now I would like to invite her to make a few remarks.

(Madame Hu made a few remarks.)

Ladies and Gentlemen,

Shakespeare said, "Welcome ever smiles, and farewell goes out sighing." I am reluctant to say farewell. But at the same time, I am pleased that I have accomplished my mission, served my country and worked for China-UK relations with all my heart from the beginning to the end.

It is my sincere hope that the China-UK friendship will last forever, China-UK cooperation will become deeper and wider, and China-UK relations will go steady and go far.

In 17 days, we will celebrate the Chinese New Year and ring in the Year of the Ox. I wish everyone online a happy, healthy and prosperous Year of the Ox!

Thank you!

第二章　政党议会交流
PART Ⅱ　Party and Parliamentary Exchanges

党际交往和议会交流是中英关系的重要组成部分。使英期间，我积极推动和参与政党外交与议会交流，多次参加保守党、工党和自民党三大党年会，并在年会期间举办"中国论坛"。我还广泛接触英国各地方政党，包括苏格兰民族党和北爱尔兰民主统一党，努力增进英国各党派对中国的了解。英国议会跨党派中国小组新春招待会是我每年必出席的活动，也是我发表年度首篇演讲的场所。英国议会各党派举办的早餐会、午餐会和各种座谈会，我也是常客。还有各政党春节期间举行的庆祝活动，我都是有请必到，甚至不请也到。我经常为各政党和议会举办一些活动，包括主动请缨到议会发表演讲。

本章收录了我的3篇演讲，其中两篇分别是在出席英国保守党和工党年会期间发表的，一篇发表在2019年1月英国议会跨党派中国小组新春招待会上，这也是我最后一次在英国议会大厦发表演讲。后来出于疫情的原因，我和议员们的交流都是在线上进行的。

Inter-party exchanges and parliamentary exchanges are important components of China-UK relations. During my tenure in the UK, I actively promoted and participated in party diplomacy and parliamentary exchanges, attending annual conferences of the Conservative Party, the Labour Party, and the Liberal Democrats many times, and hosted the "China Forum" during these conferences. I also extensively engaged with other political parties across the UK, including the Scottish National Party and the Democratic Unionist Party of Northern Ireland, striving to enhance the understanding of China among various British parties. The annual Chinese New Year reception hosted by the All-Party Parliamentary China Group was an event I never missed. It had been the venue for my first speech of the year. I was also a regular at breakfast meetings, luncheon discussions, and various seminars organized by different parties in the UK Parliament. Additionally, I attended all the events held by various political parties marking the Chinese New Year, with or without invitation. I often hosted events for political parties and members of parliament, and offered to give speeches at the Parliament.

This chapter includes 3 of my speeches, 2 of which were delivered at the annual conferences of the Conservative Party and the Labour Party respectively, and 1 at the Chinese New Year reception hosted by the All-Party Parliamentary China Group in January 2019, which was also my last speech at the UK Parliament. After that, due to the pandemic, my interactions with MPs were conducted online.

为什么要深化中英伙伴关系 *

尊敬的英国前副首相普雷斯科特勋爵,
尊敬的影阁财政部首席大臣利亚姆·伯恩议员,
尊敬的英国议会跨党派中国小组主席马克·亨德里克议员,
女士们、先生们:

欢迎大家出席"中国论坛"。这是我首次在工党年会期间举办"中国论坛",见到各位新老朋友感到十分高兴。

首先,我愿借此机会祝贺工党大会前天选出了新的工党领袖,我已向埃德·米利班德先生表示了热烈祝贺。

我是2010年2月底来到英国担任中国驻英国大使的,我来了以后经常说的一句话就是:在工党执政以来的13年里,中英关系取得了长足发展。今天,我们不妨来看看中英关系到底取得了哪些发展,发生了什么样的变化。

第一,两国关系的内涵更加充实。2004年,两国政府将双边关系明确定位为全面战略伙伴关系,这表明中英不是竞争对手,而是合作伙伴。两国开展的合作具有全方位、宽领域的特点。

政治上,双方高层互访频繁,工党政府与中方建立了两国高层定期互访、战略对话和经济财金对话等机制,目前这些都被联合政府继承和沿用。

经贸上,1997年中英双边货物贸易额仅58亿美元,而2008年达到了456亿美元,增加了近7倍,2010年有望再创纪录。

---

* 在英国工党秋季年会"中国论坛"上的讲话。2010年9月27日,曼彻斯特雷迪森酒店。

教育上，在英中国留学生人数已超过 10 万，在华的英国留学生也有 3000 多人。

文化上，中英知名演出团体几乎都已到对方国家进行了演出，特别是 2010 年上海世博会期间，英国多个知名交响乐队、芭蕾舞团集中访华，为中国观众上演了一场文化大餐。最近根据简·奥斯汀小说制作的 BBC（英国广播公司）广播剧正在中国热播。

人员往来上，2009 年中国来英人数达到史无前例的 54.4 万，其中仅来自中国的旅游观光客就有 12.5 万人。

第二，两国对彼此的看法更加理性。中国早已抛开了意识形态思维来看英国。今天中国民众提到英国，首先想到的就是英国发达的经济金融、优质的教育资源、丰富的文化思想和重要的国际影响，当然还有高水平的英超联赛。

英国也在重新认识中国。最近布莱尔先生在其新书《旅程：布莱尔回忆录》中多次写到中国。比如，他认为中国再也不是神秘不可知的，中国正以非凡的速度实行对外开放；中国致力于战胜发展进程中的挑战，同时再也不走回头路；中国的发展对英国是机遇，英国应当以信心而不是恐惧来面对。我认为，他对中国的这些中肯看法在工党及英国社会具有一定代表性。

第三，两国关系具备了更加良好的政治环境。1997 年，中英顺利实现了香港政权交接，消除了两国关系中一大障碍。2008 年，英国调整了延续百年的西藏问题立场，承认西藏是中国的一部分，搬掉了中英关系发展道路上的另一块绊脚石。在人权问题上，中英双方也坚持采取对话而不是对抗的方式，加强沟通，增进了解，深入对话化解分歧。可以说，当前中英两国没有根本利害冲突，既没有突出历史遗留问题，也没有重大现实分歧干扰。

过去十几年来，中英关系取得的长足发展同英国工党的战略远见和大力推动密不可分，我们高度赞赏工党政府为中英关系的长期持续发展打下的坚实基础。如今，工党虽然在野，但是我相信，工党同样能为中英关系发展做出新的贡献。

今天论坛的主题是"为什么要深化中英伙伴关系？"我认为主要有"三个需要"。

一是两国共同发展的需要。当前，中英两国都面临着促进经济增长的严峻挑战。中国虽然成为世界第二大经济体，但仍是发展中国家，人均GDP只有3700美元，还排在百位之后。最近，我在《泰晤士报》上专门撰写了一篇文章，谈到这个问题。同时，中国亟须调整经济结构，转变经济发展方式。

英国经济虽然已走出衰退，但还面临着实现可持续增长的任务。后金融危机时代，中英仍然需要同舟共济。从双方合作潜力看，英国已进入后工业时代，中国还处于工业化中期，因而两国经济互补性强，利益契合点多。英国有飞机、汽车等先进制造业，金融、信息、航运、咨询等高端服务业，节能、环保、低碳等高新技术，中国有充足的劳动力资源、完备的工业体系、强大的制造能力和广阔的产品市场，中英之间合作互补性强，潜力巨大，前景广阔。

二是共同国际责任的需要。当前，国际形势错综复杂，和平与发展仍是世界的主题，但各种传统安全威胁和非传统安全挑战相互叠加，世界仍很不太平。中英作为联合国安理会常任理事国和有重要影响的大国，在维护世界和平、促进共同发展方面肩负着重要责任，两国关系的全球性和战略性日益突出。双方应当携手合作，共同致力于防止地区冲突，促进多边主义，应对气候变化，捍卫自由贸易体系，推动国际金融体系改革及维护核不扩散体系。

三是相互学习借鉴的需要。阳光有七种颜色，世界是五彩缤纷的。中英两国都具有悠久的历史和丰富的文化，只有相互学习，取长补短，才能共同进步。

正如英国著名剧作家萧伯纳所说："你有一个苹果，我有一个苹果，互相交换，我们每人只有一个苹果；你有一种思想，我有一种思想，互相交换，我们每人有两种思想。"两年前，北京奥运会的成功举办，很大程度上改变了许多英国人对中国的看法，因为他们看到了一个开放、自信的中国。现在，上海世博会又成为中英增进了解和交流的一个重要平台。两年后，我相信，伦敦奥运会将会使中国民众更好地了解英国。

56年前,贵党领袖艾德礼率代表团访华,表示希望从中国带回"友谊与和平"。今天,一种强有力的中英关系带给两国人民的不仅是友谊与和平,更是发展和繁荣。

让我们一起为加强中英全面战略伙伴关系而携手努力,缔造共同繁荣的美好明天。

谢谢!

Why China and the UK Need a Stronger Partnership*

Lord Prescott,

Mr Liam Byrne,

Mr Mark Hendrick,

Ladies and Gentlemen,

It is my great pleasure to welcome friends both old and new to the China Forum. This is the first China Forum I have hosted during a Labour Party Conference.

I wish to take this opportunity to congratulate you on the election of your new leader. I have offered my warm congratulations to Mr Ed Miliband.

Since I came to London as the Chinese Ambassador at the end of February, I have been telling friends that China-UK relations have come a long way during the 13 years of the Labour government.

Firstly, our relations have become more substantive. In 2004, the two governments defined the bilateral relationship as comprehensive strategic partnership instead of rivalry. And cooperation has since expanded across a wider range of areas.

Politically, the two sides have enjoyed regular high-level exchanges, through the annual Prime Ministers' visit, the Strategic Dialogue and the Economic and Financial Dialogue. All these have been and will be continued under the coalition government.

In economics and trade, we have seen a surge in trade, from 5.8 billion US dollars in 1997 to 45.6 billion US dollars in 2008, up nearly 7 times, with the trend expected to

---

* Speech at the China Forum of the Labour Party Conference. Radisson Hotel, Manchester, 27 September 2010.

continue this year.

On the educational front, over 100 thousand Chinese students are studying here in the UK, and over 3,000 British students are studying back in China.

Culturally, we have seen exchange of performances by almost every famous Chinese and British art group. This has been spotlighted by a number of British symphony orchestras and ballet troupes performing during the Shanghai World Expo. And the BBC radio programme based on Jane Austin's novels has proved to be popular in China. In 2009, a record high of 544 thousand Chinese visited Britain, which included 125 thousand tourists from China.

Secondly, our two countries have learnt to see each other in a more rational light. China has long stopped drawing ideological line when it views Britain. Now the most common views held in China about Britain are that it is an advanced economy with the world's leading financial sector; it is an excellent education provider, a source of splendid culture, creative ideas and is a major international influence. These are of course secondary to the fact that it is the country that has the Premier League.

The UK is also developing a new understanding of China. Tony Blair mentions China many times in his new book *A Journey*, observing that China is no longer "a mystery". Instead, it is "opening up at an extraordinary rate" and he believed that Britain should approach China "with confidence, not fear". I trust what he thinks of China is fairly representative of the views of the Labour Party and the British public.

Thirdly, our relations are now blessed with a more enabling political environment. The smooth hand-over of Hong Kong in 1997 removed an obstacle in our relations. And in 2008, Britain readjusted its century-old position on Xizang, by recognising it as part of China. These have cleared the way for sound China-UK relations. On the issue of human rights, the two sides have also chosen dialogue over confrontation to enhance mutual understanding and defuse differences.

The progress we have made in the past decade would not have been possible without the vision and efforts of the Labour Party. We highly commend the solid foundation the Labour Party has laid for long-term growth in our relations. I am confident that your Party will continue to contribute to this relationship whether you are in government or in opposition.

The theme of this forum is "Why China and Britain need a stronger partnership?" I think our stronger partnership will meet the following three needs.

Firstly, we both need development. And this is a serious challenge for both of us, as our economies grow. Although being the second largest economy, China is still a developing country: With a per capita GDP of merely 3,700 US dollars, ranking behind 100 other countries. I addressed these issues in a recent article for *The Times*. China urgently needs to restructure its economy and upgrade its economic growth pattern.

The UK has put the recession behind it, but it still needs to achieve sustainable growth. China and the UK need to work closely in the post-crisis era, as our cooperation holds the greatest promise, given our strong economic complementarity. A post-industrial UK's strengths lie in advanced manufacturing such as aeroplane and automobile, high-end service industries such as financial and consulting services, and the new high-tech industries, of energy conservation, environmental protection and low-carbon technologies. China, on the other hand, is in the process of industrialisation with a large labour force, a strong manufacturing sector and a vast consumer market.

Secondly, as two permanent members of the UN Security Council and major countries of influence we need to shoulder common responsibilities in international affairs. In the current complex international situation, we must continue to be alert to the threats that still endanger world peace. And we should work together to prevent regional conflicts and advance multilateralism. In this way we can effectively respond to climate change and safeguard free trade, whilst pressing ahead with the reform of the international financial system and upholding nuclear non-proliferation.

Thirdly, we need to draw upon each other's strength. Just as sunlight has seven colours, our world is full of diversity. As two countries, each with a time-honoured history and splendid culture, we need to learn from each other and progress together.

As the famous playwright George Bernard Shaw said, "If you have an apple and I have an apple and we exchange these apples, then you and I will still each have one apple. But if you have an idea and I have an idea and we exchange these ideas, then each of us will have two ideas." The success of the Beijing Olympics two years ago has largely changed the way many Britons view China, as they saw an open and confident country. The ongoing Shanghai World Expo is now offering another chance to boost our mutual understanding and interaction. And I am sure that the 2012 London

Olympics will widen the Chinese people's view about this country.

56 years ago, Earl Attlee, the then Labour Party leader, led a delegation to China in the hope of bringing back "friendship and peace". Today, a strong China-UK partnership not only means friendship and peace for our peoples, but also development and prosperity.

Let us continue to strengthen the comprehensive strategic partnership and build a better future of common prosperity.

Thank you!

勇于开拓，积极进取 *

尊敬的文化、奥运、媒体和体育大臣亨特阁下，
尊敬的外交大臣议会事务私人秘书基思·辛普森议员，
尊敬的保守党国际事务主席克利福德·布朗议员，
各位保守党朋友：

欢迎大家出席今天的"中国论坛"活动。这是保守党时隔13年重新成为执政党后首次举行年会。英国是世界上最早产生政党的国家，英国保守党是世界上历史最长的政党。有人说：了解了保守党的历史，就是了解了英国历史。此言不虚。我很高兴借助保守党秋季年会这个机会，与大家进行交流，进一步了解保守党；也希望你们通过"中国论坛"活动，进一步了解中国。

说起保守党与中国的关系，我们过去经常用三句话来赞赏保守党对中英关系的历史性贡献：一是在20世纪50年代，丘吉尔二度任首相时期，两国建立了代办级外交关系；二是在70年代，希思首相时期，中英建立了大使级外交关系；三是在80年代，撒切尔夫人首相时期，中英签署了《联合声明》，扫清了两国关系中的一大障碍。正是这三大贡献，实现了中英关系历史上的"三级跳"。

现在，保守党再度成为执政党，我们期待着保守党为中英关系的发展做出新的贡献。当前，我们该如何看待和发展中英关系？这是本次论坛的主

---

* 在英国保守党秋季年会"中国论坛"上的讲话。2010年10月5日，伯明翰国际会议中心。

题，我愿与大家进行探讨。我想用"三个A"来概括我的看法和建议。

第一个A是期待（anticipation），即中英双方都有进一步深化两国关系的期待。英国联合政府在执政协议中明确提出要与中国发展"更紧密的关系"；卡梅伦首相在与中国领导人会晤和通电话时也明确表示愿进一步提升中英关系；黑格外交大臣2010年7月访华时，提出中英要发展"促进经济增长的伙伴关系"。英国政府希望能扩大对华出口，吸引更多的中国投资、留学生和旅游者，共同促进世界经济的可持续复苏。

同样，中方也始终视英国为重要伙伴，希望两国增强政治互信，扩大经贸、教育和文化等领域的务实合作，加强在国际事务中的磋商与协调，使两国关系"百尺竿头，更进一步"，更好地造福两国和世界人民。

第二个A是有利条件（advantage），即发展中英关系存在许多有利条件，具备良好基础。

一是，政治上两国没有根本利害冲突，没有突出的障碍。香港已经回归中国13年，"一国两制"运行良好。英国政府也明确承认西藏是中国的一部分。曾长期影响两国关系的这两个障碍被清除。

二是，中英间具有良好的沟通渠道。两国建立了领导人定期互访、战略对话、经济财金对话的高层沟通机制，同时建立了经贸联委会、科技创新合作联委会、教育部长年度会晤、人权对话等各领域的对话和磋商机制，充分探讨合作，有效化解分歧。

三是，两国经济上存在很强互补性。英国是发达国家中的大国，中国则是最大的发展中国家，尽管取得了很大成就，但人均GDP水平还很低，仅相当于英国的1/10，还有1.5亿人尚未摆脱贫困，中国城乡区域发展很不平衡。中英发展阶段不同，两国经济各有特色。中国的制造业具有强大的竞争力，英国则在金融服务业、高端制造业、创意产业等方面世界领先，双方合作具有广阔空间。

四是，中英教育、文化等领域的合作势头令人鼓舞。在英的中国留学生人数已超过10万，在华的英国留学生也有3000多人。中国有4亿多人在学英语，许多英语学习者都对英国文化非常感兴趣，希望来英语的发源地"朝圣"。2009 年，仅中国来英旅游者就有 12.5 万人。上海世博会成为中英交流合作的大舞台，英国馆充分展现了英国的设计与创意，获得中国媒体和观众高度评价。

第三个 A 是行动（action）。"千里之行，始于足下。"仅有意愿和有利条件，没有实际行动，则只能在原地踏步。进一步发展中英关系，我认为关键要在以下五个方面采取行动。

一是在政治上增强互信。政治信任既是全面合作的前提，也是两国关系可持续发展的保障。中英不是竞争对手，而是合作伙伴。当前，双方应抓住卡梅伦首相将于 2010 年晚些时候对中国进行首次正式访问这一机遇，进一步强化两国战略伙伴关系。

二是在经贸上找准重点。双方要推动两国标志性合作项目，深化两国经贸合作；要便利两国中小企业交流，积极提供信息服务，扩大经贸合作面；要坚持自由贸易原则，坚持反对保护主义，推动多哈回合谈判早日取得进展。

三是在人文上促进了解。双方要继续加强文化交流，特别是应举办影响大、水平高的活动，形成声势，扩大受众。双方应借助教育合作、青年交流等方式，增进两国青年友好，培养一代人甚至未来几代人的友谊。中方欢迎更多英国年轻人到中国留学。我们也将继续支持在英办好孔子学院和孔子课堂，使它们成为增进了解、促进友好的窗口。

四是在国际上加强协调。中英作为联合国安理会常任理事国和有重要影响的大国，在维护世界和平、促进全球繁荣方面肩负着重要责任，也有着共同利益。双方应当携手合作，共同致力于防止地区冲突、促进多边主义、应对气候变化、推动国际金融体系改革及维护核不扩散体系。

五是在分歧问题上坚持对话。中英社会制度、发展阶段、文化传统不同，在一些问题上存在分歧是正常的，但中英之间的共同利益远大于分歧。丘吉尔说："站起来说话需要勇气，坐下倾听同样需要勇气。"当出现分歧时，我们需要有勇气去倾听和协商，更需要有智慧去缩小分歧，扩大共识。

各位朋友，我到任英国半年多以来，发现"保守"是一个很让人回味的英文单词，尽管我翻遍了字典，包括我最近出席发行仪式的最新版《牛津英汉汉英辞典》，都没有找到一个令我满意的解释。因为"保守"这个词在英国，代表的不一定是墨守成规、不思革新，而是注重传统与稳健，主张变革与进步。一个最明显的例子就是，保守党并不"保守"。当前，中英关系正站在一个新的起点上，我希望保守党在发展中英关系上同样"不拘保守"，勇于开拓，积极进取，与中方共同努力，推动中英关系朝着友好合作、互利共赢的方向不断迈进。

谢谢大家！

Make a Creative and Bold Effort[*]

Mr Jeremy Hunt,
Mr Keith Simpson,
Mr Clifford Brown,
Friends from the Conservative Party,

May I warmly welcome you to the China Forum.

I am very pleased to attend the Conservative Party Conference. I congratulate your Party on your return to power after 13 years.

The UK was the birthplace of political parties, with the Tory Party being the first. So, I think it is fair to say that if you know the history of the Conservative Party, you know the history of modern Britain.

I am glad to have this opportunity to learn more about your party. I also hope that you will get a better understanding about China through today's event.

The Conservative Party has made three historic contributions to China-UK relations.

In the 1950s, during Sir Winston Churchill's administration, Britain established diplomatic relationship with the People's Republic at the chargé d'affaires level.

Then in the 1970s Prime Minister Sir Edward Heath established full diplomatic relations at the ambassadorial level with China.

Finally in the 1980s when Lady Thatcher was Prime Minister, the two countries signed the Joint Declaration on Hong Kong, removing a major obstacle to China-UK relations.

---

[*] Remarks at the China Forum of the Conservative Party Conference. International Convention Centre, Birmingham, 5 October 2010.

Now with the Conservative Party back in government, we do hope that it will make new contributions to our relations. And I would like to share with you my thoughts on how we can build a stronger China-UK partnership, which is the theme of today's forum.

I have summed up my thoughts in 3 As: Anticipations, Advantages and Actions.

First, Anticipations.

There is a shared anticipation between China and the UK for a closer relationship. The coalition government has made it clear that it seeks closer ties with China, when Prime Minister Cameron expressed his desire to further the China-UK relationship, during his recent meetings and phone calls with Chinese leaders.

Foreign Secretary Hague also proposed the "partnership for growth" during his July visit to China. It is clear that the UK is also keen to expand exports to China, whilst bringing in more Chinese investors, students and tourists, in support of a sustainable global recovery.

For China, the UK has always been an important partner. We want to enhance mutual trust and expand cooperation across trade, education and culture, as well as strengthening ties with the UK on international affairs. This will not only promote our relationship, but will also benefit the interests of the people around the world.

Second, Advantages.

There are many advantages for the growth of the China-UK relationship.

Firstly, we have no fundamental conflict of interests politically. The One Country, Two Systems has been functioning smoothly in Hong Kong since its return to China 13 years ago. And the UK government adjusted its century-old policy on Xizang by recognising it as part of China. These two long-time obstacles to China-UK relations are now things of the past.

Secondly, we already have effective mechanisms for dialogue, in the annual Prime Ministers' visits, the Economic and Financial and the Strategic Dialogues.

We also have consultation groups across a wide range of areas including trade, technology, education and human rights. These arrangements have allowed us to fully explore possibilities for cooperation and narrow our differences.

Thirdly, we have much to offer each other economically. The UK is a major developed country. China is the largest developing country. But despite the tremendous progress China has made, its per capita GDP remains low, at only one tenth of that of the UK.

With 150 million people in China still living in poverty and the challenges of unbalanced economic development across our industrialised and rural landscape, we still have a long way to go.

Given our different stages of development, our two economies each have unique strengths. China is highly competitive in manufacturing, whilst the UK leads the world in financial services, high-end manufacturing and the creative industries. This has opened up enormous prospects for our future cooperation.

Fourthly, our cooperation in education, culture and other fields is thriving.

With over 100 thousand Chinese students now in the UK, and more than 3 thousand British students are studying in China.

Over 400 million people are learning English in China, and many of them have developed a keen interest in British culture and visited the UK. Last year, 125 thousand Chinese tourists visited the UK.

This year, the Shanghai World Expo has provided another exciting stage for exchanges and cooperation between our two countries. The UK national pavilion, with designs and creativity unique to Britain, has won the hearts and minds of many Chinese visitors and the Chinese media.

Finally, Actions.

As a Chinese saying goes, "A thousand-mile journey starts with the first step." I believe a stronger China-UK relationship calls for actions in the following 5 areas.

Politically, we should strengthen mutual trust at governmental level. China and Britain are partners, not rivals.

This is not only crucial to our cooperation, but is also a guarantee for sustainable growth of bilateral relations.

And we have an unusual opportunity on hand to further cement our strategic partnership by ensuring the success of Prime Minster Cameron's first official visit to China next month.

Economically, we should deepen our cooperation in trade and investment, identify priorities and promote flagship projects.

We should assist exchanges between our small and medium-sized enterprises, and provide the information and services they need.

We must also uphold the principle of free trade, reject protectionism and work for the early conclusion of the Doha Round negotiations.

Culturally, we must also improve the understanding between our peoples. People-to-people and cultural exchanges should be further expanded, as we need to foster friendship amongst our young people. China hopes to see more British students studying in China and we will continue to support the Confucius Institutes and Confucius Classrooms in the UK.

Internationally, we need to strengthen our cooperation and coordination. As two permanent members of the UN Security Council and countries of major influence, we share common interests and important responsibilities in upholding world peace.

Working together, we can help resolve regional conflicts, advance multilateralism and safeguard the non-proliferation regime, as well as addressing climate change and promoting the reform of the international financial system.

Lastly, we should engage each other through candid dialogue. Given our different social systems, levels of development and cultural traditions, it is only natural that our views differ on certain issues.

But our common interests far outweigh our differences. As Sir Winston Churchill said, "Courage is what it takes to stand up and speak; courage is also what it takes to sit down and listen." We need the courage to listen and talk when differences occur. We need the wisdom even more to bridge our differences and widen our common understanding.

I have been to this country for over seven months. And I still found the word "conservative" to be a bit difficult to grasp. When I looked it up in all of my dictionaries, even the recently launched the *Oxford Chinese Dictionary*, I could still not find a satisfactory explanation.

In this country, "conservative" doesn't mean upholding the status quo or opposing change. On the contrary, it represents the best of this country's traditions, discretion and a call for progress.

Maybe the Conservative Party itself best embodies the meanings of the word.

As we now stand at a new starting point in China-UK relations, I do hope that the Conservative Party will stay true to what "conservative" stands for and make a creative and bold effort for a friendly, cooperative and mutually beneficial China-UK relationship.

Thank you!

聚同化异，淬炼真金 *

尊敬的英国外交大臣亨特阁下，
尊敬的英国议会跨党派中国小组主席格雷厄姆先生，
尊敬的英中贸协主席沙逊勋爵，
尊敬的各位议员，
女士们、先生们：
大家晚上好！

今天是中国农历腊月二十三，俗称"小年"。按照中国传统，这是"过年"筹备的开始，蕴含着辞旧迎新、迎祥纳福的美好愿望，寓意着新年要有新气象。

很高兴在这个吉祥的日子，第九次出席英国议会跨党派中国小组新春招待会，与大家共同迎接猪年的到来。在中国文化里，猪象征多福多财、幸运美好。2019年我们将庆祝新中国成立70周年，也将迎来中英建立代办级外交关系65周年。我衷心希望，中英关系在这样一个特殊的年份取得新进展，结出新成果。

回首过去65年，中英关系栉风沐雨，实现了"四次飞跃"。

一是冲破意识形态藩篱，建立代办级外交关系。1950年1月，中华人民共和国刚刚成立3个月，英国在西方大国中率先承认新中国，两国于1954年6月17日建立了代办级外交关系。

---

* 在英国议会跨党派中国小组新春招待会上的讲话。2019年1月28日，英国议会大厦。

二是奠定相互尊重基石，建立大使级外交关系。1972年，英方承认台湾是中华人民共和国的一个省，两国于3月13日正式建立大使级外交关系。

三是扫清历史遗留障碍，成功解决香港问题。1997年7月1日香港顺利回归祖国，不仅使中英关系卸下历史包袱，也为通过外交谈判解决国际争端和历史遗留问题树立了典范。

四是勾勒携手共进蓝图，开启中英全面战略伙伴关系。中英先后建立全面伙伴关系、全面战略伙伴关系、面向21世纪的全球全面战略伙伴关系。

中英关系65年的发展历程表明，只要我们尊重彼此核心利益和重大关切，平等相待，求同存异，中英关系就会向前发展，实现飞跃；反之，则遭受挫折，停滞不前，甚至倒退。

当前，世界正经历百年未有之大变局，中国与世界的关系发生了历史性变化。这对中英关系意味着什么？如何在大变局中推动两国关系迎接新机遇，化解新挑战，更好地造福两国人民？这是我一直思考的问题，我想这也是各位经常讨论的问题。我的答案是，关键要做到坚守"三个精神"。

一是坚守担当精神，始终致力促进全人类福祉。中英都是具有全球视野和影响的大国，两国都主张多边主义，维护国际规则和秩序，推动完善全球治理体系。中英作为负责任大国，应充分展现大国担当，积极发挥引领作用，共同维护以规则为基础的国际体系，推动构建新型国际关系和人类命运共同体，为人类和平与繁荣做出更大贡献。

二是坚守合作精神，始终坚持互利共赢。中英都是自由贸易和开放经济的支持者、践行者和受益者。双方应坚持开放合作，共同捍卫开放经济，反对各种形式的保护主义，携手推动经济全球化朝着更加开放、包容、普惠、平衡、共赢的方向发展。应排除各种压力和干扰，避免人为制造障碍，为两国企业打造公平、透明、非歧视性的营商环境。应不断提升两国"一带一路"合作水平，秉持共商共建共享精神，共同促进高质量、高标准、高水平的"一带一路"建设。2019年中国将召开第二届"一带一路"国际合作高峰论坛和第二届中国国际进口博览会，我们欢迎英方积极参与。

三是坚守包容精神，始终客观理性处理分歧。中英社会制度、历史文化、发展阶段不同，难免在一些问题上发生误解和分歧。关键在于双方应视彼此发展为机遇，而非挑战，更非威胁，双方应尊重彼此主权、安全、发展利益，不做损害对方核心利益和破坏战略互信的事。我相信，只要双方坚持相互尊重，平等相待，加强战略沟通，增进政治互信，妥善处理分歧，就能使中英关系这艘大船始终保持正确航向。

女士们、先生们，

两千多年前，中国思想家史伯说过，"和实生物，同则不继"。2018年，英国议会跨党派中国小组组团访华，为增进双方相互了解、推进两国议会交流与合作做出了不懈努力。展望新的一年，我们期待与议会跨党派中国小组及各方有识之士携手共进，推动中英议会交流再上新台阶，推动中英各领域合作取得新进展。

最后，祝愿大家猪年好运，诸事顺遂！

谢谢大家！

Build Common Ground for China-UK Relations[*]

Secretary Jeremy Hunt,

Chairman Richard Graham,

Lord Sassoon,

My Lords and MPs,

Ladies and Gentlemen,

Good evening!

Today is the 23rd day of the last month of the Year of the Dog, according to Chinese lunar calendar. It is known as "Xiao Nian", or "Minor Chinese New Year". In Chinese tradition, this is the day to start preparations for the Chinese New Year. On this day, people could begin to say goodbye to the old year and start making best wishes for the new year.

This is the ninth time that I have attended the APPCG Chinese New Year Reception. It is a real delight to join you on this auspicious day to celebrate the Year of the Pig.

In the Chinese culture, pigs symbolise happiness and good fortune. In the Year of the Pig, China will celebrate the 70th anniversary of the founding of the People's Republic; China and the UK will celebrate the 65th anniversary of the establishment of our diplomatic relationship at the level of chargé d'affaires.

I sincerely hope that, in this special year, the China-UK relations will make new progress and achieve new outcomes.

---

[*] Remarks at the APPCG Chinese New Year Reception. Palace of Westminster, 28 January 2019.

In the past 65 years, despite all the twists and turns, the China-UK relationship has achieved four major leaps forward.

The first leap was the establishment of diplomatic relationship at the level of chargé d'affaires. This was a leap over ideological barriers.

The UK recognised the People's Republic of China in January 1950, only three months after the founding of New China. It was the first major Western country to do so. Then on 17 June 1954, our two countries established diplomatic relationship at the level of chargé d'affaires.

The second leap was the establishment of ambassadorial diplomatic relationship on the basis of mutual respect.

This was officially announced on 13 March 1972, following UK's recognition that Taiwan is a province of the People's Republic of China.

The third leap was the settlement of the Hong Kong question, which removed the obstacles left over from history.

The return of Hong Kong to the motherland on 1 July 1997 cleared the historical obstacles to closer China-UK relations. It also set a fine example of resolving historical issues and international disputes through diplomatic negotiations.

The fourth leap unleashed the potential of our bilateral relations for greater progress.

- We started with "comprehensive partnership",
- and moved on to "comprehensive strategic partnership".
- That was followed by the "global comprehensive strategic partnership for the 21st century".

The message of the past 65 years is loud and clear.

As long as China and the UK respect each other's core interests and major concerns, treat each other as equals and seek common grounds, the China-UK relationship will make progress and develop by leaps and bounds. Otherwise, our relations would suffer setbacks, stall or even retrogress.

Today, the world is undergoing profound changes unseen in a century. So is the Chinese relationship with the rest of the world. What does this mean to China-UK relations?

In face of these changes, what shall we do if we want to embrace the new opportunities, address the new challenges and deliver more benefits to our people?

These are the questions that I have been thinking about quite a lot. I am sure they also feature quite often in your discussions. My answers to these questions are: Take responsibility, engage in cooperation and embrace inclusiveness.

First, we should hold fast to our responsibility and work for the benefits of all mankind.

China and the UK are both countries with a global vision and global influence. We both support multilateralism, uphold international rules and order, and stand for improving the global governance system.

As responsible major countries, China and the UK should take a leading role and work together to:

- Uphold the rule-based international system.
- Build a new type of international relations and a community with a shared future for mankind.
- And make greater contribution to world peace and prosperity.

Second, we should stay committed to cooperation and work for win-win results.

Both China and the UK have supported, practiced and benefited from free trade and open economy. Therefore, we have every reason to stay committed to open cooperation, safeguard open economy and oppose protectionism of all forms. When China and the UK join hands, we could make economic globalisation more open, inclusive and balanced.

It is also important that we resist pressure and interruptions, refrain from creating obstacles and foster a fair, transparent and non-discriminatory business environment for companies of our two countries.

On the Belt and Road Initiative, we should improve our cooperation under the principles of extensive consultation, joint contribution and shared benefits. We should work to ensure higher quality and higher standards at a higher level in BRI development.

This year, China will host the second Belt and Road Forum for International Cooperation and the second International Import Expo. We welcome friends from all cross the UK to these events.

Third, we should adhere to an inclusive approach and deal with differences in an objective and reasonable manner.

China and the UK differ in social system, history, cultural heritage and development stage. It is natural that we do not see eye to eye on every issue. But it is important that we see each other's development as an opportunity rather than a challenge, still less a threat.

We should respect each other's sovereignty, security and right to development. We should do nothing to undermine each other's core interests and weaken strategic mutual trust.

I am confident that as long as our two countries treat each other with respect and on an equal footing, as long as we enhance strategic communication, deepen political trust and address differences properly, we will steer the giant ship of China-UK relations in the right direction.

Ladies and Gentlemen,

More than 2,000 years ago, Chinese philosopher Shi Bo said, "Harmony invigorates life while uniformity stifles vitality."

In 2018, APPCG made valuable contribution to enhancing mutual understanding and deepening parliamentary cooperation between our two countries.

In the new year, we look forward to working together with APPCG and people from all walks of life here in the UK. I am sure we will take China-UK parliamentary exchanges to a new level, achieve new progress in our cooperation across the board.

In conclusion, I wish everyone a happy and prosperous Year of the Pig!

Thank you!

2010 年 5 月 26 日
在白金汉宫向英国女王伊丽莎白二世递交国书。女王生前曾接受 12 位中国大使递交国书，刘晓明是最后一位当面向她递交国书的中国大使。

●2010 年 5 月 26 日
向英国女王伊丽莎白二世递交国书后，与夫人胡平华乘坐英国皇家马车离开白金汉宫。

●2012 年 2 月 6 日
在伦敦"金融城之周"活动上发表主旨演讲：《深化合作，互利共赢》

2012 年 5 月 29 日
在英国杜伦大学发表演讲:《我们需要什么样的中英关系》

2012 年 5 月 1 日
在英国市场营销集团晚宴上发表演讲:《中英经贸合作"三问"》

2012 年 10 月 9 日
在牛津大学学联发表演讲：《以史为鉴，可以知兴替》

2013 年 12 月 18 日
在英国工商界联合举办的演讲会上发表主旨演讲：《中国发展新动力，中英合作新机遇》

2014年10月9日
出席"走进江苏"人文经贸交流活动开幕式并致辞：《走在中英关系前列的江苏》

2014年10月21日
出席英国政府发行30亿元人民币主权债券上市交易仪式并发表讲话：《人民币国际化在英国迈出坚实步伐》

2015 年 6 月 8 日
在中国驻贝尔法斯特总领馆开馆仪式上发表讲话：《拉起风箱，打出真铁》

2015 年 11 月 3 日
在庆祝习近平主席对英国国事访问圆满成功答谢招待会上发表讲话：《一次"超级国事访问"》

● **2016年5月19日**

在英国关于抗生素耐药性问题研究报告发布会上发表讲话：《凡事预则立，不预则废》

● **2016年6月8日**

出席中国政府发行人民币主权债券上市仪式并发表讲话：《硕果累累，精彩无限》

2016年10月11日

在汇丰中国与人民币论坛上发表主旨演讲：《共同塑造中英金融合作的美好未来》

2017年6月14日

在中国（广东）–英国经贸合作交流会上发表讲话：《敢为人先，务实进取，再谱合作新篇章》

第三章　经贸关系
PART Ⅲ　Economic and Trade Relations

英国是我国在欧洲的第三大贸易伙伴、第二大投资目的地和外资来源地,我国是英国在亚洲的最大贸易伙伴。我担任驻英大使11年间,正是中英经贸关系发展最快的时期。2010—2020年,中英双边货物贸易额从501亿美元增至924亿美元,翻了将近一番,英国对华出口增长约20倍。两国双向投资增长强劲,英国对华投资近300亿美元,我国对英国投资超过200亿美元,增长约20倍。目前有800多家中资企业落户英国,两国经贸合作呈多样化发展趋势。

本章收录了我的9篇演讲,从中可以看到中英经贸关系的发展历程。即使在中英政治关系遇到困难时,两国工商界对发展中英经贸关系的热情依旧未减。中英互利合作给两国人民带来了实实在在的益处,经贸合作成为两国关系的"压舱石"和"稳定器"。

The UK is China's third-largest trading partner, second-largest investment destination and second-largest source of foreign investment in Europe. China is the UK's largest trading partner in Asia. During my 11 years as the Chinese Ambassador to the UK, China-UK economic and trade relations developed at the fastest pace. From 2010 to 2020, the bilateral trade volume in goods between China and the UK nearly doubled from 50.1 billion US dollars to 92.4 billion US dollars, with the UK exports to China increasing by about 20 times. Two-way investment grew strongly, with the UK investment in China nearing 30 billion US dollars and Chinese investment in the UK exceeding 20 billion US dollars, increasing by about 20 times. Currently, more than 800 Chinese enterprises are established in the UK, and China-UK economic and trade cooperation is diversifying.

This chapter includes 9 of my speeches, which offer a glimpse into the development of China-UK economic and trade relations. Even when political relations between China and the UK encountered difficulties, the enthusiasm of the business communities in both countries for developing China-UK economic and trade relations remained undiminished. China-UK mutually beneficial cooperation has brought tangible benefits to the people of both countries, making economic and trade cooperation the ballast and stabilizer of bilateral relations.

中英互利合作新机遇 *

尊敬的埃文斯副议长，
尊敬的格雷厄姆主席，
各位保守党议员，
女士们、先生们：

两年前我刚履新不久，就参加了英国议会保守党中国小组为我举行的欢迎早餐会。2011年底，我曾与小组部分成员共进午餐。格雷厄姆主席希望我今早专门谈谈两国经贸合作前景，我乐意就此与大家进行交流。

在我们进入经贸主题前，我愿首先介绍一下两国关系总体发展状况，因为这是两国经贸合作的重要条件和基础。

2012年是中英两国建立大使级外交关系40周年。1972年在保守党领袖希思担任首相期间，中英建立了大使级外交关系。事实上，我们两国的关系可以追溯到更早。1954年，在丘吉尔担任首相期间，中英互派代办。这两件大事充分说明了保守党政治家们的远见卓识。

中国人常说"四十不惑"，因为人到40岁，心智比较成熟。国家关系也是一样，经过了40年的曲折历程，中英顺利解决了香港问题，建立了全面战略伙伴关系，两国关系日渐稳定、成熟。两国间建立了总理年度会晤机制，又建立了经济财金对话、战略对话和高级别人文交流机制这"三大支柱"，其中，高级别人文交流机制在上周刘延东国务委员访英时刚刚启动。

---

* 在英国议会保守党中国小组早餐会上的演讲。2012年4月24日，英国议会。

两国在国际事务中共同利益不断增加，双方在世界经济治理、国际安全事务、核不扩散等领域的协调和磋商越来越密切。两国人民之间的往来空前频繁，每年近百万旅行者、几万名留学生、数百场文化交流活动，以及几十所孔子学院和孔子课堂，使两国人民之间的了解与友谊日益深化。

可以说，中英关系正站在新的起点，面临新的发展机遇。这也正是两国经贸合作不断迈上新台阶的大背景。2011年，中英双边货物贸易额是587亿美元，同比增长28.8%。在英国前15大出口目的国中，英国对华出口增长最快。两国正朝着2015年双边货物贸易额突破1000亿美元的目标迈进。

近年来，英国对华投资一直在欧盟内处于领先地位，同时，中国对英投资加速增长，双向投资格局正在形成。2009年底，中国对英非金融类投资额累计6.2亿美元，到2011年，这个数字增加到23亿美元，其中仅2011年的新增额就达11.3亿美元，呈倍数增长。上汽投资的MG汽车英国有限公司首创"英国设计、中国制造、英国组装"模式，既振兴了英国百年品牌，又为当地创造了400多个就业岗位。

我来英两年多，先后赴苏格兰、威尔士、英格兰中部、西北部和东北部等地区深入考察，了解英国企业的看家本领。我曾在许多论坛、会议上全面介绍中英经济的互补优势。我也在英国的全国性和地方报纸上分别发表了十多篇文章，推介两国互利合作。

我认为，中英经济结构上有互补性，产业各有优势，相互投资条件良好，双方合作潜力巨大。当前，中英双方应抓住以下五大机遇。

第一，技术贸易与研发合作的机遇。中国正在进行经济结构调整和产业升级，需要大量进口高端设备和先进技术。英国可发挥在可再生能源、生物医药等产业的优势，扩大对华高技术产品出口。中国目前正加大科技创新力度，同时资金较为充裕，也愿与国外积极开展联合研发，共享合作成果。希望更多的英国企业和大学利用自身研发优势，与中方共同设立研发中心或开展具体项目的研发合作。

第二，扩大双向投资的机遇。中国欢迎英国企业到中国投资现代服务业、绿色产业和高端制造业，并积极投资中国的西北部地区和东北老工业基地。同时，中国将继续鼓励企业到英国投资兴业。英国欢迎中国企业投资其基础设施，这在西方大国中是为数不多的。2012年新年伊始，双方基础设施合作就实现了"开门红"，中投公司投资收购了泰晤士水务公司8.68%的股份，交易金额市场估计约12亿英镑。仅此一笔交易所涉金额就超过了2011年中国对英投资的总额。

我听说，路虎公司计划在中国投资设厂，如果属实的话，那么这又将创造一种新合作模式，即"第三国资本、英国品牌和技术、中国生产和销售"的三方合作模式。

第三，深化金融合作的机遇。金融是英国的经济支柱，伦敦是世界第一大金融中心，中国也正在大力发展金融业，为实体经济发展提供更坚实的支撑。据我所知，汇丰银行是最大的在华外资银行，并计划进一步完善在华战略布局，将分支机构数量增至800家。与此同时，中国五大商业银行"工农中建交"都在伦敦设立了子公司，业务种类不断增加。就在昨晚，我出席了中国工商银行的乔迁仪式。

当前，人民币国际化进程不断加快，伦敦有意成为人民币离岸业务中心，中英金融合作面临新突破。就在4月18日，伦敦金融城举行了伦敦人民币业务中心建设计划启动仪式。同日，汇丰银行在伦敦证券交易所发行了三年期人民币债券。原来预计发售10亿元人民币，但市场热情远超过预期，最终发售20亿元人民币。这是伦敦向成为人民币离岸业务中心迈出的重要一步，也是人民币国际化进程向前推进的重要一步。

第四，加强中小企业合作的机遇。加强中小企业合作是中英两国经贸合作的一个重要方面。英国不少中小企业技术独特，产品科技含量丰富，与中国企业和市场的互补性强。我本人就参观过不少这样的中小企业。我们愿与英方共同为双方中小企业合作进一步创造有利条件，帮助它们共同成长。

第五，推进文化创意产业合作的机遇。文化创意产业具有高附加值、低碳环保的基本特征，还具有创造大量就业岗位的优势，属于高增长、高利润的新兴产业。中国要从低端制造业走向高端制造业，从以制造业为主逐步走向高端服务业，实现从"中国制造"到"中国创造"的转型，就必须大力发展文化创意产业。近年来，中国文化创意产业增加值的增速每年都在17%以上，高于GDP的增速，成为转变经济发展方式的重要着力点。而英国是世界公认的文化创意产业大国，"创意产业"这个概念最早就是英国提出的。目前，创意产业占英国GDP的7%左右，对经济的贡献率同金融服务业旗鼓相当，是英国经济中最具活力的部分。中英加强文化创意产业合作符合两国发展战略，市场潜力巨大，是两国未来经贸合作的新增长点。

各位保守党议员，

与我两年前参加贵小组的早餐会时不同，保守党现在已是英国的执政党，所以你们的影响力也今非昔比。我衷心希望你们发挥积极影响和作用，为中英开展互利合作做出新贡献。

谢谢！

New Opportunities for Mutually Beneficial Cooperation between China and the UK*

Deputy Speaker Evans,

Chairman Richard Graham,

MPs from the Conservative Party,

Ladies and Gentlemen,

It is a real pleasure for me to attend this breakfast meeting.

I have warm memories from two years ago of the first breakfast that was kindly hosted for me by the Conservative Party China Group.

I was delighted late last year to repay this kindness with a lunch for some of you at my Embassy.

I regard these meetings as most valuable to our better mutual understanding.

Chairman Graham has suggested a topic for me to talk about today. The theme is the future of China-UK economic cooperation. This is a most important topic so I am very glad to share with you my views.

We all know that a sound bilateral relationship is essential for the growth of economic ties. This is why I propose to start by giving a quick overview of China-UK bilateral relationship as a whole. Then our economic cooperation can be understood most clearly.

This year marks 40 years of full diplomatic relations between China and the UK. By "full diplomatic relations", we are talking about the ambassadorial ties built in

---

* Speech at the Breakfast Meeting Hosted by Conservative Party China Group. House of Commons, 24 April 2012.

1972, presided over by Prime Minister Edward Heath. And the fact is, this China-UK partnership went back to a much earlier time. That was when we exchanged chargé d'affaires in 1954 under the premiership of Sir Winston Churchill. And both these two milestones saw vision and leadership provided by Conservative statesmen.

Today, our 40-year ambassadorial relationship has come into a stage that can be best described by a Chinese saying:

" One no longer has doubts or misgivings at the age of 40."

This means that a man of 40 years old is sensible and mature. So is a 40-year old bilateral relationship.

Looking back there have been many challenges in our relations during those 40 years. But there have been outstanding successes. One highlight was the successful resolution of the question of Hong Kong. Another was the creation of a comprehensive strategic partnership.

Bolstering the mature and stable relations are three important mechanisms:

- Prime Minister's Annual Meeting.
- The Economic and Financial Dialogue.
- And the Strategic Dialogue.

The High-Level People-to-People Dialogue Mechanism was newly launched last week. This was during State Councilor Madame Liu Yandong's visit to the UK.

At the global level, our two countries now share growing common interests in international affairs. We have developed ever closer coordination and consultation. The key areas are in world economic governance, global security and non-proliferation.

Contacts between our peoples have never been more frequent. Every year, more than one million tourists travel between our two countries. Hundreds of cultural exchange programmes are held. On top of that, the UK hosts tens of thousands of Chinese students and dozens of Confucius Institutes and Confucius Classrooms. All these have deepened understanding and friendship between our peoples.

These strong and dynamic bilateral relationships have created a broad foundation for our commercial exchanges. In turn this has greatly boosted China-UK economic ties. I will give you some figures:

- In 2011, our bilateral trade was 58.7 billion US dollars.
- That was an increase of 28.8% year-on-year.
- Among the UK's top 15 export markets, China is the fastest growing one.
- We have set the goal of raising bilateral trade to 100 billion US dollars by 2015. I believe we are on track to reach that target.

Another measure of economic relations is two-way investment. The UK has been a leader of the EU members in terms of investing in China. More importantly, Chinese investment in the UK is growing more rapidly. The statistics are impressive:

- By the end of 2009, the Chinese non-financial investment in the UK had totaled 620 million US dollars.
- By 2011, it surged to 2.3 billion US dollars.
- This means the year 2011 alone saw 1.13 billion US dollars of Chinese investment in this country.

Let me also highlight the progress in the manufacturing sector. MG Motors UK is now owned by Shanghai Automotive Industry Corporation (SAIC). Investments by SAIC have created a new business model: "designed in the UK, manufactured in China and assembled in the UK." This innovation revived a famous British brand and set it on a path to renewed strength. It also created more than 400 local jobs.

Since I came to Britain two years ago, I have traveled across the country. Through this I have gained a better understanding of the strengths of British companies. I have used this knowledge to communicate the complementarities of our economies. I have done this through many speeches, TV and radio interviews and publication of numerous articles in British national and local newspapers.

I have brought together my knowledge of the Chinese and British economies to promote my belief that China-UK economic cooperation has great potential. To fulfill the potential, we need to seize opportunities in the following aspects.

First, the opportunity for trade in technology and joint R&D. China is restructuring its economy and upgrading its industries. We need to import sophisticated equipments and advanced technologies in great quantities. For example, the UK is a world leader in renewable energy and bio-medicine. I encourage the UK to sell more high-tech products to China.

China gives top priority to technological innovation and has adequate funds available. We are happy to conduct joint research with foreign countries and share the results. I hope more British companies and universities will cooperate with Chinese partners in setting up joint R&D centres or specific research projects.

Second, the opportunity for two-way investment. China welcomes British companies to make investments in the Chinese modern services sector, green industry and high-end manufacturing. We particularly welcome British investment in the Chinese Northeast and Northwest.

Meanwhile, China will continue to encourage Chinese companies to invest in the UK. The UK is one of the few Western countries opening its infrastructure to Chinese investment.

Our cooperation in this regard has kicked off with a good start early this year. The China Investment Corporation bought 8.68% of Thames Water with an estimated market price of 1.2 billion British pounds. This one transaction alone is more than the total Chinese investment in the UK last year.

And recently, I heard Land Rover planned to open a facility in China. If so, that will create a new and positive business model. This will combine capital from a third country with a great British brand and technology; in turn the vehicles will be produced and sold in China.

Third, the opportunity for financial cooperation. Finance is a pillar of the British economy. London is the number one financial hub of the world. China is also making an all-out effort to develop its financial sector. Progress towards sound and dynamic financial sectors and exchanges will certainly boost growth of the real economy.

This financial dialogue and exchange is happening. As far as I know, HSBC is the largest foreign bank in China. HSBC plans to increase the number of its offices in China to 800. In the UK, all of the top five Chinese commercial banks have opened branches in London. These five banks are:

- Industrial and Commercial Bank of China.
- Agricultural Bank of China.

- Bank of China.
- China Construction Bank.
- And Bank of Communications.

Yesterday evening, I attended the launching ceremony of ICBC London new office. The fact is for all of these Chinese banks, we have seen their business rapidly growing in the UK.

Another example of financial potential is with the international advance of the Chinese currency. China has quickened the steps to internationalize its currency, the RMB. London has expressed its ambition to become an offshore centre for RMB settlement.

In fact London is already on track to this goal. On 18th April, the City of London officially launched its programme aimed to become an offshore centre for RMB trading. On the same day, HSBC issued its inaugural 2-billion 3-year international RMB bonds. The original plan was to issue 1 billion RMB. Yet the immense interest and great demand from the markets raised the sum to 2 billion. This trade broke new ground by being the first of its type to specifically target distribution to European investors. It was a major step forward towards London's goal of becoming an offshore center for RMB trading. It was also a marked progress of RMB internationalization.

All these developments I have highlighted undoubtedly hold out great prospects for China-UK financial cooperation.

The fourth opportunity for increasing our economic ties is to strengthen SME cooperation. SME cooperation is an important part of our economic links. Many British SMEs have specialty products and technologies popular in the Chinese markets. I myself visited some of them. We stand ready to facilitate cooperation between our SMEs and help them grow together.

Last but not least, we face great opportunities in cultural cooperation, in particular creative industries.

Creative industries are high value-added and environment-friendly. They not only generate huge profits but also create many jobs. More importantly, they are emerging industries and have great potential.

China wants to move up the value chain of manufacturing. Our goal is to turn from a production base into a design centre. To achieve this, we need to press ahead with creative industries.

In recent years, the value-added of the Chinese creative industries has grown at an annual rate of more than 17%. This growth rate is higher than that of the Chinese GDP. In summary, creative industries have become an important area of growth as China transforms its economy.

Another reason that I believe we face great opportunities in this area is that the UK is the birthplace and a recognized world leader of creative industries.

Creative industries now contribute around 7% of British GDP. This gives them an equally important position in the British economy as the financial sector. Moreover, it is the most dynamic sector of the British economy.

As I suggested, our cooperation in creative industries face great potential. It also serves our development plans. I believe it will become a new highlight in our future economic cooperation.

Friends from the Conservative Party, much has happened since our first breakfast two years ago. What makes today's breakfast different from the one two years ago is the Conservative Party is in power! This means you have a much bigger means to influence events. I hope you will agree with the ideas I have proposed this morning. In turn I hope you can use your power to help drive forward ever closer economic ties and play a bigger part in promoting win-win cooperation between China and the UK.

Thank you!

中英经贸合作"三问"*

尊敬的市场营销集团主席拉斯·肖先生，

女士们、先生们：

很高兴参加英国市场营销集团举办的晚宴，与在座各位英国商界精英就中英经贸合作进行交流。

事实上，我最近一周就这一主题已经做了两场演讲。第一场是我在保守党议会中国小组早餐会上讲了中英互利合作的新机遇。第二场是在亚洲之家，我从三个角度分析了中国的对外投资，包括对英投资。今天是第三场，我想换一个角度，具体谈谈当前中英经贸合作中大家可能比较关注的三个问题。

第一个问题：英国如何扩大对华出口？

众所周知，为促进经济增长，英国联合政府将扩大对中国等新兴经济体的出口作为政策优先目标。目前这一政策效果初显，2011年英国对华出口增长了28.8%。但不可忽视的是，尽管增幅很大，2011年英国对华出口额只有146亿美元，仅占英国出口总额的3.1%。你们经常听到的一句话是：英国对金砖五国的出口总额还不及英国对爱尔兰的出口额。显然，区区146亿美元与中国和英国——世界第二和第七大经济体的经济规模很不相称。英国对华出口前十大类商品在中国进口市场中所占份额全部远低于德国。英国对华出口潜力有待进一步挖掘。

我个人认为，英国对华出口今后应在三方面加大力度。

---

* 在英国市场营销集团晚宴上的演讲。2012年5月1日，伦敦克拉里奇酒店。

一是扩大高端产品出口。中国转变经济发展方式的一项重要措施就是扩大消费，国内消费市场增长迅速。从 2011 年到 2015 年的"十二五"规划这 5 年，中国进口规模的保守数字是超过 8 万亿美元，乐观一点有望达到 10 万亿美元。英国要与其他国家分享中国这巨大的市场，就必须在品牌、设计、技术上做足功夫。比如，英国需向法国人、德国人学习，加大品牌和产品推广。法国的路易威登在中国的知名度远大于英国的博柏利；法国红酒在中国的销量也远远超过苏格兰威士忌，尽管苏格兰威士忌 2011 年在华销售创下了历史最好成绩；汽车方面，德国的"宝马"在中国的名气也远大于英国的"路虎"，尽管在中国文化中"虎"的声威要远远超过"马"。

二是扩大技术贸易出口。中国转变发展方式的另一途径是实现经济结构调整，进行产业升级，提高制造业的技术含量和产品附加值。英国是世界第二大科技强国，技术发明和产业创新层出不穷，但囿于市场和产业构成，有些技术在英国无用武之地，或者很难实现价值最大化。比如，英国在可再生能源、低碳经济、环保领域的许多技术，如果运用到中国就能产生巨大的经济和社会效益。在高技术出口方面，英国目前在欧盟中仅列第五，排在德国、法国、意大利和瑞典之后。英国不应再这样"保守"下去，而应解放思想，跟上时代。

三是扩大文化创意产业出口。英国是世界公认的文化创意产业大国，创意产业占英国经济的贡献率高达 7%，同金融服务业平分秋色，是英国经济中最活跃的部分。中国要实现从"中国制造"到"中国创造"的转型，就必须大力发展文化创意产业。近年来，中国文化创意产业增加值的年增速在 17% 以上，高于 GDP 增速，成为转变经济发展方式的重要着力点。中英同作为文化大国，文化上互不排斥；中英同作为经济大国，经济上结构互补。因此，两国加强文化创意产业合作具有良好的基础，市场潜力巨大，将是两国未来经贸合作的新增长点。

第二个问题：英国如何进一步吸引中国投资？

英国朋友经常向我表示，英国是西方对中国投资最为开放的国家之一，特别是欢迎中国投资英国基础设施。目前，中国对英非金融直接投资总额约

40亿美元。说实话，这一数字尽管比2011年翻了近一番，但仍然令人难以满足，因为预计"十二五"期间，中国对外投资额将超过5000亿美元。

英国如何在这5000亿美元中获取更大份额，我认为同样要做到三点。

一是做好政策和法律服务。英国是发达国家，法律体系完善，但同时带来的问题是，法律法规繁复，对企业在劳工、安全、财务上的要求非常严格，这会"吓退"相当一部分不熟悉英国制度的中国投资者。所以，英国不仅要在政策上欢迎中国投资，也要做好投资配套服务工作，消除中国投资者的担忧，并且在中国企业因不了解、不熟悉英国的法规而出现一些失误时，要宽容大度。

二要拓宽投资方式。传统的中国企业在英国投资设立分公司、子公司固然是一种投资方式，但这种方式投资周期长、见效慢，也存在一定的法律、管理和人才风险。所以，中国企业目前更多转向了参股和并购。比如，2012年初中投公司投资泰晤士水务公司就采取了参股形式。同样是2012年初，华为公司则是全资收购了英国集成光电器件公司。

三要降低投资门槛。中国企业目前来英投资普遍反映的一个障碍是签证问题。如同外国在华企业一样，中国企业来英投资不可能都用当地雇员，特别是一些大型国有企业，总是需要从总部派驻一些工作人员。但英国政府在签证上设置了不少门槛，如语言能力和最低薪资要求，影响了中国企业人员正常轮换。所以，英方需要为中方企业人员往来提供便利。

第三个问题：伦敦如何才能成为人民币离岸中心？

在2011年9月的第四次中英经济财金对话中，奥斯本财政大臣首次向中方提出了伦敦成为人民币离岸中心的设想。2012年1月，奥斯本访问中国香港时，英国财政部和香港金融管理局签署了相关合作协议。4月，伦敦金融城联合全球五大银行设立了工作组，以推动伦敦成为人民币离岸服务和交易中心。同样在4月，汇丰银行首次在伦敦发行了人民币债券。原计划发行10亿元人民币，可市场反应出奇热烈，结果发行了20亿元人民币。可以说，英方对伦敦成为人民币离岸中心是志在必得。

从长远看，人民币国际化并成为全球主要国际货币是必然趋势，人民币国际化要依靠开放境内市场，同时必须发展离岸市场。目前中国香港、新加坡和伦敦等地都在竞争人民币离岸中心。

伦敦建立人民币离岸中心，我认为对中英双方来说是互利共赢的一件大好事，将为中英贸易、金融、投资等领域合作注入新活力，打开新局面。

伦敦建立人民币离岸中心具有一些先天性优势。伦敦是世界第一大金融中心，又是全球最大的外汇市场。伦敦资本市场开放度高，金融机构林立，法规监管健全，基础设施完善。伦敦与中国香港在金融上既具有历史联系，又在时间上可形成对接。

但不可否认，伦敦也有一些不利条件。

一是人民币存量问题。据伦敦金融城的最新报告，伦敦人民币客户存款及银行同业存款总额 2011 年超过 1090 亿元人民币，其中客户存款为 350 亿元人民币，人民币资金池初步形成，但与中国香港相比，相差仍较悬殊。比如，截至 2011 年 12 月，香港人民币客户存款总额高达 5890 亿元。

二是人民币供给问题。人民币尚未实现可自由兑换，同时中英双方目前尚未签署货币互换协议，因此，近期很难有大量人民币流入英国。

三是人民币需求问题。英国企业对人民币的接受程度还不高，特别是在贸易结算方面，很少有企业愿意使用人民币。虽然一些金融机构对人民币感兴趣，但它们或是押宝人民币升值，或是为了融资方便，并非真实需求。

四是人民币结算系统问题。这一问题本身是技术问题，但建设、运行和完善也需要时日。

总之，伦敦建立人民币离岸中心是好事，但中国俗话说，"好事多磨"，伦敦既需要努力克服目前的短板，同时也需要面对世界其他金融中心的挑战。

以上就是我对当前中英经贸关系中三个突出问题的一些思考。我相信，未来中英经贸合作机遇无限、空间广阔，希望各位企业家抓住机遇，大胆开拓。

谢谢！

Three Questions on China-UK Economic Cooperation*

Chairman Russ Shaw,

Ladies and Gentlemen,

I am delighted to attend this dinner hosted by the Marketing Group of Great Britain.

It is always a pleasure for me to have an opportunity to exchange ideas with British business leaders. Today, I much appreciate the invitation to talk with you about China-UK economic cooperation.

This is such an important theme that I have recently made two speeches on this topic. The first was to the Conservative Party China Group in the House of Commons. In that speech I talked about opportunities for business with China in the years ahead.

At the Asia House yesterday evening, I analyzed Chinese overseas investments from three perspectives including Chinese investment here in the UK.

My speech tonight will cover new areas, even though this will be my third speech in one week on the same theme. This evening I will approach China-UK economic cooperation from another angle. My aim is to build understanding on three questions.

The first question is how to expand British exports to China?

As you know, boosting growth is a core objective of the UK coalition government. As part of the plan top priority has been given to expanding exports to China and other emerging economies. This policy effort is paying off.

British exports to China increased 28.8% last year. Despite the high rate, the volume

---

* Speech at the Dinner of the Marketing Group of Great Britain. Claridge's Hotel, London, 1 May 2012.

was just 14.6 billion US dollars. It made up only 3.1% of total British exports.

I say "just" 14.6 billion US dollars as comparison with other export markets strongly highlights the potential of boosting China-UK economic cooperation.

You may be familiar with one comparison with the BRICS countries—Brazil, Russia, India, China and South Africa. The UK's total exports to all the BRICS countries is not as much as Britain exports to Ireland.

Another way to look at the potential is this. In terms of economic size China ranks second and Britain is seventh. Clearly, the figure of 14.6 billion US dollars is disproportionate, and points to the immense potential for increasing trade.

Analysis of the top ten British export products to China show only a modest share in the Chinese market. China buys a lot more of these products from Germany. Again this comparison shows great potential.

So how to increase British exports to China? I personally suggest the UK step up efforts in the following three areas.

First, export more high-end products to China.

Significant opportunities lie in the economic strategy that the government has set out. An important part of the Chinese effort to shift its growth model is to boost consumption, in particular consumer spending. In the 12th Five-Year Plan period, which is between 2011 and 2015, the Chinese imports are expected to reach 8 trillion US dollars. Some bold analysts have even put it at 10 trillion US dollars.

Britain will have to compete with other countries in this huge marketplace. To win the competition, you need to outdo others in branding, design and technology. Maybe I am being too frank, but Britain needs to learn from France and Germany in marketing and product promotion. Here are some examples:

- Louis Vuitton, or LV, is much more famous in China than Burberry.
- The sales of Scotch whisky in China hit a record high last year. But sales of French wine are way ahead of whisky.
- Branding is key in China. BMW is translated as "precious horse" in Chinese and Land Rover as "tiger on land". Though in Chinese culture, the tiger is much more powerful than the horse, BMW is hugely more popular in China than Land Rover.

Second, export more technologies to China. Another way of restructuring the

Chinese economy is industrial upgrading. With advanced technologies, China will be able to move up the value chain.

The UK is a world leader in science and technology. But there are constraints in the UK to exploit these strengths with a population of 60 million. China with a population of 1,300 million could make some British technologies much easier to commercialize. For example, Britain has developed many technologies in renewable energy, low carbon economy and environmental protection. They will generate huge economic and social benefits if used in China.

In terms of high-tech exports to China, Britain comes fifth among the EU members after Germany, France, Italy and Sweden. Perhaps this ranking suggests Britain is being too "conservative" with the international exploitation of its strengths in science and technology. The opportunities are there in China but success needs open minds and keeping pace with the changing times.

Third, the UK needs to export more products of creative industries to China. The creative industries are a specialty of Britain. They contribute to 7% of the British economy. That is as much as the financial sector. Creative Industries are a most dynamic sector and will be a great global growth area in this century.

China wants to turn itself from a production base into a design centre. To achieve this goal, it needs to develop creative industries with a powerful momentum. In recent years, the value-added from creative industries in China has grown at an annual rate of over 17%. That is much higher than that of the Chinese GDP. The creative industries have become a major source of growth for China.

Both China and Britain have great pride in their distinctive cultures. Our economies have a lot to offer each other. So cooperation in culture and creative industries between us is blessed with a solid foundation and great potential. It will become another highlight of our economic cooperation.

Let me now turn to the second question I want to address this evening. This is how Britain can attract more Chinese investment.

My British friends often tell me that the UK is one of the Western countries most open to Chinese investment. One sector in particular is the UK infrastructure.

Currently, Chinese non-financial investment in the UK totals around 4 billion US dollars. I must say that though this figure is almost double that of last year, it is far from gratifying. The reason is during the 12th Five-Year Plan period, the Chinese total outbound investments will pass 500 billion US dollars.

So how is Britain to get a bigger share of this outward investment pie? I have the following suggestions for you.

First, on policy and legal services. These need to be high quality but simple and clear. Britain has a sophisticated legal system. At the same time, it is very complicated. British law has rigorous requirements for companies in benefits, safety and finance. This will discourage many Chinese investors not familiar with British system.

So Britain needs to attract Chinese investors through welcoming policies and support for solving practical problems with quality services on the ground. In very few cases, Chinese investors may slip up because they are new in this country. As the host, Britain should be understanding and tolerant.

Second, diversify the means of investment. A traditional way of Chinese investment in Britain is to set up branches or subsidiaries here. But it has some drawbacks:

- It is slow.
- It takes a long time to get returns.
- It has legal and management risks.

That is why Chinese companies are now more interested in joint share holding and merger and acquisition. For example:

- Earlier this year, China Investment Corporation bought stake in Thames Water.
- Also this year, the Chinese Huawei completely acquired CIP.

Third, lower the threshold. A wide concern of Chinese companies making investment here are visa applications. It is impossible for Chinese companies here to recruit only British people. Flexibility is needed as Chinese business in the UK will always need some foreign employees.

The issues of visas is a challenge for some Chinese state owned enterprises or SOE's. They need to bring some staff from headquarters in China. The British government has laid many restrictions on visas, such as English language proficiency and minimum wages. These restrictions have affected the SOE HR policies and internal transfers. My point is Britain needs to facilitate travel of Chinese company staff to optimise success in economic cooperation.

The UK has great strengths in financial services. This leads to the third question for this evening: How can London become an offshore centre for RMB trading?

There have been four important developments for RMB trading in recent months:

- In the fourth China-UK Economic and Financial Dialogue last September, Chancellor Osborne set out his proposal of making London a RMB centre in the West.
- In January this year when Chancellor Osborne visited Hong Kong, Her Majesty's Treasury and the Hong Kong Monetary Authority signed an agreement.
- Last month, the City of London launched the initiative to strengthen London's position as a hub for international RMB business in the West. The current members are Bank of China, Barclays, Deutsche Bank, HSBC and Standard Chartered.
- Also last month, HSBC issued RMB bonds in London for the first time. The original plan was to issue 1 billion RMB. Yet, the immense interest and great demand from the markets raised the sum to 2 billion RMB.

In the long run, RMB internationalization is a must. Progress in this regard depends on both domestic and offshore markets. Hong Kong, Singapore and London are vying for this position.

London as an offshore RMB centre is a win-win for China and the UK. It will open a new dimension for our cooperation in trade, finance and investment.

So can London beat other competitors? Let me give you an overview of its strengths and weaknesses.

London has some natural advantages:

- It is the leading global financial centre.
- It is the world's largest forex market.
- It boasts many prestigious financial institutions.

- It is known for sound regulation and developed infrastructure.
- It has historical links with Hong Kong.
- And it has a time zone advantage.

If these are London's assets, then I will point out to you its liabilities:

- On RMB deposits. The latest City report shows that the total amount of London customer, institutional and inter bank RMB deposits is in excess of 109 billion yuan. Customer deposits has reached 35 billion yuan. This indicates that a pool of RMB liquidity is being established. But compared with Hong Kong, it still has a big gap to close. By December last year, Hong Kong's customer RMB deposits had totaled 589 billion yuan.
- On RMB supply. RMB is not fully convertible yet. China and the UK have no currency swap agreement. So Britain can not expect to see large RMB inflows in the near future.
- On RMB demand. British companies are not very receptive to RMB. Some financial institutions are interested in RMB either for hedging or for financing. That is not real demand.
- On RMB settlement system. This is a technical problem. It takes time for the system to be built, tested and improved.

London has great potential to become a centre for international RMB business. Yet as a Chinese saying goes:

"The road to happiness is not lacking in setbacks."

So, London needs to overcome the current shortcomings and meet the challenges from other financial centres.

These are some of my thoughts on the three issues that currently stand out in our economic ties.

In conclusion, I am confident that China-UK economic cooperation enjoy boundless opportunities and broad prospects. I do hope all of you will seize the opportunities and achieve greater success.

Thank you!

从儒家经典看中英经贸合作 *

女士们、先生们：

很高兴出席 D Group 举办的午宴，并与各位英国企业家朋友交流。

D Group 是世界知名的商务咨询公关公司，其 23 个分支机构活跃在全球各地。在过去的 20 年里，D Group 成员建立起一个庞大的全球商务网络，并且许多成员都与中国有业务联系。

主持人克莱恩先生告诉我，你们希望我就中英如何构建更加紧密的经贸联系谈一些看法。在我看来，这个题目包含两层含义。

第一层含义，中英经贸联系已经非常紧密。2011 年中英双边贸易额近 600 亿美元，中国是仅次于欧盟、美国的英国第三大贸易伙伴。英国对华直接投资累计超过 100 亿英镑，在欧盟位居第二。同时，英国成为中国增长最快的海外投资市场之一。

第二层含义，中英经贸合作还需要更加紧密。2011 年英国对华出口额达 146 亿美元，但这仅占英国出口总额的 3.1%，低于英国对爱尔兰的出口额，这与中国全球第二大进口市场和英国第四大贸易国的地位很不相称。英国对华出口前十大类商品，在中国进口市场中所占份额全都远低于德国。中国对英国投资虽然增速较快，但目前还在起步阶段。中英经贸合作还有很大发展潜力。

那么，如何发展更紧密的中英经贸合作呢？我想从西方最熟悉的一位中

---

* 在英国工商业组织 D Group 的演讲。2012 年 9 月 28 日，英国工商业组织 D Group 总部。

国古代名人——孔子说起。孔子虽然不是商人，但他及其后人创立的儒家思想具有普适性，不仅是做人处世的哲学，也是治国经商的法宝。比如，孔子的一位弟子（子贡）当时就成了中国最成功的商人，亚洲的不少著名企业在发展过程中也从儒家思想中吸取了其精华。今天，我愿借儒家经典中的三句话来谈谈如何拓展中英经贸合作。

第一句话："天时不如地利，地利不如人和。"当前，中英经贸合作可谓占天时，居地利。首先，中英关系经过自建立大使级外交关系以来40年的积累，目前正站在新的起点，两国深化经贸合作是大势所趋、恰逢其时。其次，英国是全球金融、信息、物流的中心枢纽，拥有自由开放的经营和投资环境，中国企业纷纷把英国作为辐射欧洲、开拓全球的重要基地。

如何将中英天时、地利方面的优势最大化呢？这就需要"人和"，也就是良好的政治关系和社会舆论环境。近十几年来，中英经贸合作呈现强劲增长趋势，这不是巧合，而是因为两国战略互信增强，民众相互了解加深，改善了两国经贸合作的氛围。但是，中英经贸合作要竿头日进，目前并非没有阻力，没有噪声。例如，英国媒体经常炒作华为公司的所谓"军方背景"，仅仅因为该公司总裁是一位退伍军人。可见，今天一些人的脑袋里还装着"冷战思维"，一些人总是热衷炒作各种版本的"中国威胁论"，喜欢戴着有色眼镜看中国，这种舆论有百害而无一利。我希望在座的各位企业家，能客观、理性地看待中英互利合作，积极向民众、媒体表达意见和看法，努力创造和维护双方合作所需的"人和"。

第二句话："凡事预则立，不预则废。"扩大和深化中英经贸合作，并非一时之事，而是长久之计，这就必须找准目标，确立重点，做好规划。比如，2011年中英两国政府召开了基础设施投资大会，建立了工作组，将基础设施投资作为双方的重点合作领域。正是由于这样的"预"，短短一年不到，就取得了明显的成果。中投公司年初收购了泰晤士水务公司部分股权，一举超过2011年中国对英投资总额；光明食品集团收购英国维他麦企业60%的股份，这是中国食品行业最大宗的海外收购；中石化收购了加拿大塔利斯曼能源公司英国子公司49%的股份。上周加拿大法院批准了中海油收购尼克森公司，而该公司总产量的 1/2 来自北海油田。也是在上周，华为公司宣布将在英国进行 13 亿英镑的投资和采购，在未来 5 年内为当地创造至少 700 个工作岗位。可以说，2012 年是"中国对英投资年"。

中英经济结构互补，双方各有优势，类似基础设施这样的合作领域相信还有不少，双方应该努力挖掘，加强谋划，共同推动。

第三句话："知者不惑，勇者不惧。"中国是全球第二大市场，也是对外投资增速最快的国家。中国的"十二五"规划表明，2011—2015 年，中国进口规模将达 8 万亿~10 万亿美元，对外投资将超过 5000 亿美元。中国是全球出境旅游人数增速较快的国家，2011 年出境旅游对世界旅游市场的贡献率达 7.2%。伦敦奥运会期间，据说中国游客的人均消费比阿联酋游客还高 10%。英国企业必须抓住中国市场提供的巨大机遇。

但是我有一种感觉，目前英国政府面对中国很"纠结"，既想扩大合作，又顾虑重重，因而各部门政策有时左右矛盾，相互掣肘。比如，英国商务部门大力吸引中国投资者来英考察洽谈，文化旅游部门希望英国能迎来与法国同样多的中国游客和消费者，而不是目前的仅为法国的 1/8，但是英国内政部门的政策是严防"非法移民"，在签证上制定了繁文缛节，难怪最近英国媒体引用英国驻华大使的话说，"英国面临着一种风险，那就是将自己在中国的形象塑造成'不列颠堡垒'"。例如，要求中国签证申请者填写长达十几页的表格，申报个人、家庭的各种隐私，提交财产证明，而且必须亲自到仅设于中国几个大城市的签证中心去按指纹。这种不合理的待遇，我听到过不少中国企业家和游客的抱怨，我也不知道英国公民出国时是否遇到过，但我清楚的是，英国游客申请中国签证的过程简单便捷，只需花几分钟填写两页纸的表格。我认为，孰轻孰重，孰利孰害，英国政府必须认真考量，做出抉择。

同样，我感到英国企业在对华合作上还有犹豫，显得比较保守。中国正在实现经济转型，需要引进一些技术来进行产业升级。英国是世界第二大科技强国，但在高技术对华出口方面，在欧盟中却排在德国、法国、意大利和瑞典之后。英国企业总是有这样或那样的担心。事实上，有些可再生能源、低碳经济和环保领域的技术囿于英国的市场规模和产业构成，在英国无多大用武之地，或者很难实现价值最大化，但如果运用到中国就能产生巨大的经济和社会效益。有些信息领域的技术，如果不能立即投入商业化，则很快就会落伍，只有实现研发和制造的迅速结合，才能获得新资金注入以继续从事研发，从而进一步扩大效益。我希望英国企业家更加大胆、果断一些，"该出手时就出手"。

各位企业家朋友，

中英经贸关系的良性发展离不开国际经济大环境，特别是与欧洲的经济走向密切相关。不久前，中国总理温家宝赴欧出席了第十五次中欧领导人会晤，双方在经贸等领域达成了许多共识，取得了重要成果。会晤再次表明了中国愿积极帮助欧盟应对债务危机，促进中欧经济共同增长。我相信，欧洲经济形势的趋稳向好，中欧经贸关系的稳定发展，将为中英经贸合作提供有益的环境和有效的动力。

我今天借儒家思想中的三句话，谈了中英经贸合作中的合作成果、存在的问题和努力的方向。我认为，只要中英双方抓住机遇，大胆开拓，正视挑战，积极应对，两国经贸合作成果可期，前景看好。

谢谢！

Confucius Wisdom and China-UK Economic Ties *

Ladies and Gentlemen,

It is a real pleasure for me to join you at this lunch.

I have learned the D Group is a leading business networking entity. It is active in 23 locations around the world. Over the past 20 years members of the D Group have evolved an influential global business development network. Many of them are associated with China.

The D Group is clearly global in its thinking. But it is headquartered in London and I am Chinese Ambassador in the UK. So, I am delighted to respond to the theme proposed by Mr Craine: How to build closer economic ties between China and Britain?

I believe this topic has two implications.

First, economic ties between China and the UK are already very close. Examples are many:

- Last year our bilateral trade neared 60 billion US dollars.
- China was the UK's third largest trading partner only after the European Union and the United States.
- The UK's direct investment in China amounted to more than 10 billion pounds. This made Britain the second biggest investor in China among EU members.
- Moreover, Britain has become one of the fastest growing markets for the Chinese

---

* Speech at the Lunch with the D Group. The Headquarters of the D Group, 28 September 2012.

outbound investments.

Second, this topic implies that China-UK economic cooperation needs to be even closer. Let me explain to you why:

- British exports to China last year had a value of 14.6 billion US dollars. But it only accounted for 3.1% of Britain's total exports.
- That 3.1% was even less than Britain's exports to Ireland.
- This China-UK export share is far too modest!
- The reason is very simple. China is the world's second largest importer and Britain the fourth largest trading nation.

Let me give you some further indicators about the potential for increased trade and economic ties:

- The market shares of the top ten British export products in China are way below the market shares of Germany in China.
- Chinese investment in Britain is growing rapidly, yet it is still in the initial stage.
- The result is that great potential in China-UK economic cooperation remains untapped.

Then how can we develop closer economic cooperation between our two countries?

My answer may surprise you. I believe we should draw inspirations from the wisdom of Confucius.

Confucius is the Chinese philosopher who is best known to the Western world. In very simple terms, the philosophy of Confucianism is about conducting oneself in society.

Confucius was not a businessman. But his philosophy has proved also applicable to statecraft and business management. For instance, one disciple of Confucius became the most successful businessman in China. Many modern Asian business leaders have benefited a lot from Confucianism in their careers.

I want to use three quotations from Confucianist classics to explain to you my thoughts on expanding China-UK economic cooperation.

The first quotation is:

"Opportune time is not as helpful as favourable geographical position; favourable geographical position is not as important as harmonious relationship."

At present, China-UK economic cooperation is blessed with both opportune time and favourable geographical position.

After past four decades of efforts since the inception of full diplomatic relations, our bilateral ties have come to a new starting point. Deepening economic cooperation between China and Britain is an overriding trend. It is a logical choice at a right time.

In terms of geographical position, Britain is reputed as a global hub of finance, information, logistics, creativity and innovation. In addition the UK boasts an open and free environment for business and investment. Little surprise then that Chinese companies consider Britain an important base for reaching out to the European continent and the world.

What we should do is to maximize these advantages, and this is where a harmonious relationship can make a huge difference. A harmonious relationship between two countries is composed of, among others, a sound political relationship and an enabling public opinion.

In the recent decade, China-UK economic cooperation has showed dynamic growth. This is by no means a coincidence. It is because of the following reasons:

- Enhanced strategic mutual trust of the two countries.
- Increased mutual understanding of the two peoples.
- And an improved overall environment.

However, further growth of China-UK economic cooperation is not without resistance. Some negative noises are continuously being heard.

For example, British media often kick up a fuss about the so-called "military background" of a Chinese company Huawei. The only reason is the president of this company is a veteran. This shows that some people's minds are still trapped in Cold War mentality. They are bent on creating all kinds of theories of "China threat." Some of them have a myopic or blind view of China. Such closed mind-sets and biased opinion are nothing but harmful.

I hope the business leaders present here will see China-UK win-win cooperation in an objective and reasonable light. I hope you will actively communicate your message to British public and media and foster a harmonious relationship.

The second quotation from Confucian classics is:

"Pre-planning ensures success, unpreparedness spells failure."

Expanding and deepening China-UK economic cooperation is not an easy task. It can be a long job.

We need to identify targets and priorities and plan carefully. For example, our two governments sponsored a conference last year on infrastructure investment. A working group was set up at the conference to prioritize our cooperation in infrastructure.

In less than one year such planning has appreciably paid off. Here are some facts and figures:

- Early this year China Investment Corporation purchased some shares of Thames Water. This purchase alone already passed the total Chinese investment in Britain last year.
- Sinopec (China Petrochemical Corporation) acquired 49% of the Canadian based Talisman Energy's assets in the UK.
- Last week the Canadian court approved China National Offshore Corporation's takeover of Nexen oil company. The production in North Sea account for half of its total output.
- Also last week, the Chinese Huawei announced its investment and procurement package of 1.3 billion pounds in the UK. This package will in the coming five years create at least 700 local jobs.
- There is also significant progress in other business sectors.
- For example, the Chinese Bright Food bought 60% of Weetabix shares. This is the largest ever single overseas investment by the Chinese food industry.
- So this is a year of rapid advance of Chinese investment in the UK.

Chinese and British economies have a great deal to offer each other. I have no doubt that there are more win-win cooperation areas like infrastructure. Both sides should tap into the potential, strengthen planning and work together for more success stories.

The third Confucian quotation I want to give is:

"The wise have no doubts. The brave have no fears."

British business leaders certainly do not lack courage! Many are wise but the low levels of trade indicate they lack knowledge of business opportunities with China. These are key points they need to know:

- China is the world's second largest market.
- There is a clear road map for British business to follow in the Chinese 12th Five-Year Plan. It provides excellent strategic indicators.
- The latest plan covers the five years from 2011 to 2015.
- The plan estimates the Chinese imports will reach 8~10 trillion US dollars.
- China is also the fastest growing source of outbound investment.
- The plan indicates that outbound investment will top 500 billion US dollars.
- The number of Chinese outbound tourists is growing fast.
- Last year China contributed 7.2% to global tourism markets.
- Records show that during the London Olympics average spending of Chinese tourists was 10% higher than that of those from the UAE.
- In summary, British businesses must seize such enormous opportunities linked to the Chinese market.

However, my observation shows that the British Government agencies give the impression of a somewhat "love-hate" feeling towards China.

On the positive side, the UK wants to expand cooperation with China. Then there are negative messages expressed through worries and concerns.

The result is that the policies of different government departments sometimes conflict with each other. Some are even self-defeating. Here are some examples.

The Department for Business, Innovation and Skills is working hard to attract more Chinese investors. The cultural and tourist authorities stress the aim that Britain will receive as many tourists and consumers from China as from France. Currently France attracts eight times more Chinese tourists than the UK.

But the policy of some UK government offices gives a very different signal; their message is to strictly prevent "illegal immigrants". In turn, the UK Borders Agency enforces very complicated and time-consuming rules for visa applications. Little wonder that the British Ambassador in China was recently quoted in the British media on this issue; he indicated that the UK runs the risk of creating an image in China of "Fortress Britain".

This image presents itself in the UK visa application process:

- The rules ask Chinese applicants to fill a form as long as a dozen pages, declare individual and family privacy and provide proof of income.
- Applicants also have to leave their fingerprints at the designated visa centers that only exist in very few big Chinese cities.
- I have heard a lot of complaints from Chinese businessmen and tourists about such obviously unreasonable treatment.
- I have no idea whether British citizens will have to go through the same if they are traveling abroad.
- Certainly in the case of China the process is simple and fast for the UK tourists applying for a visa. It takes a matter of minutes to fill out a simple two-page form.
- In summary, I would suggest that the British government weigh and balance the opportunity costs and make the right choice.

Likewise, I feel some British businesses also reveal misgivings about cooperation with China and seem to be rather conservative. Overall, I sense that this is due to lack of knowledge of the reality of China today.

China is transforming its economic growth pattern. It needs to import some technologies for industrial upgrading. Britain ranks the second in the world in terms of a technology reservoir. Yet when it comes to high tech export to China from the EU members, the UK comes after Germany, France, Italy and Sweden.

Let me describe examples of the potential of some technologies where Britain is really strong. This is in the area of "new energy" technology.

The UK has great strengths in renewable energy, low carbon developments and the environmental sectors. These do not have a big role to play in Britain due to the small market size and the current industrial mix. Or you could say their value can hardly be maximized.

But once introduced to China, these "new energy" technologies will generate huge economic and social returns.

In other areas such as information technologies, if not commercialized immediately, they will soon become outdated. Only quick and efficient combination of R&D and commercialization will help get new capital for continued R&D and make more profits. I do hope British business leaders will be more decisive and bold. I hope you will "strike while the iron is hot".

Friends from the British business sector,

Sound development of China-UK economic ties cannot be isolated from the overall global economic landscape. There are particular close links related to the trajectory of the European economy.

Recently, Chinese Premier Wen Jiabao attended the 15th China-EU Summit in Brussels. The two sides reached broad agreement in the economic field and achieved important outcomes.

The meeting in Brussels once again sent out clear signals:

- China stands ready to help the EU cope with the debt and financial crisis.
- China wants to promote growth of both Chinese and European economies.

I am convinced that the more stable the European economy, the better China-EU economic ties. Steady growth of China-EU economic relations will provide a favourable environment and strong driving force for China-UK economic cooperation.

Today I have made three quotations from Confucianist thoughts. My aim was to help express my views on the achievements, problems and future direction of China-UK economic cooperation.

I have no doubt that as long as both China and the UK seize the opportunities, take bold action and rise up to challenges, our economic cooperation will have a bright future.

Thank you!

中国发展新动力，中英合作新机遇 *

尊敬的豪威尔勋爵，

尊敬的英中协会主席彼得·巴蒂先生，

女士们、先生们、朋友们：

今天，我很高兴出席英中贸协、四十八家集团、英中协会和毕马威会计师事务所联合举办的演讲会，我愿利用这个机会向四个组织的成员介绍中共十八届三中全会通过的《中共中央关于全面深化改革若干重大问题的决定》（以下简称《决定》）及其对中英关系的意义。在座的各位长期关心和支持中国发展、积极参与中英各领域合作，我在此向你们致以崇高的敬意。

11月，在《决定》公布不久，我在伦敦改革俱乐部做了一场演讲，强调《决定》体现了中国继续改革的坚定决心、顶层设计和总体部署，由于"决心""设计""部署"这三个英文单词的首字母正好是三个"D"，所以我称之为"3D立体解读"。最近，我回国参加接待卡梅伦首相访华，亲耳聆听了习近平主席、李克强总理和张德江委员长向卡梅伦首相介绍中共十八届三中全会《决定》的主要内容，感到深受启发、获益匪浅。今天，我愿结合我的新认识、新体会对《决定》做进一步解读。

中共十八届三中全会的《决定》是中国今后改革开放的纲领性文件，是全面深化改革的总部署、总动员，我认为读懂《决定》的关键是要准确理解

---

* 在英国英中贸协、四十八家集团、英中协会和毕马威会计师事务所联合举办的演讲会上的主旨演讲。2013年12月18日，伦敦毕马威会计师事务所。

"全面"和"深化"的含义。

何谓"全面"？我认为就是改革目标清晰，内容全面，重点突出，大小兼顾。

从改革总目标看，《决定》明确指出是完善和发展中国特色社会主义制度，推进国家治理体系和治理能力现代化。改革不是局限于一个领域、一个方面，而是着眼全局，强调改革的系统性、整体性、协同性，要求改革相互促进、良性互动，整体推进、重点突破，形成改革的强大合力。

从具体改革目标看，《决定》坚持"五位一体"，要求加快发展社会主义市场经济、民主政治、先进文化、和谐社会和生态文明，同时《决定》也特意包括了国防建设和党的制度建设。针对这7个方面，提出每个领域各个特定的主线和方向。正是因为《决定》针对中国发展面临的一系列突出矛盾和问题，积极回应社会各方面对改革的呼声和期盼，因而涵盖了15个领域、55个重大改革任务、300多条重大改革措施，内容之广、力度之大均前所未有。

改革既强调全面，同时突出重点。经济体制改革是改革的重点，15个领域中，经济领域的任务占了所有改革任务的近一半。这主要是考虑当前中国存在的问题根本上说还是发展问题，推进经济持续健康发展是党和国家的首要任务。经济改革成功了，就能对其他领域改革起到"火车头"牵引作用。

改革既重视宏观，也关注微观。比如，改革既有健全宏观调控体系等完全属于政府层面的"大任务"，也有高考不分文理科等与百姓密切相关的政策细节。

何谓"深化"？此次改革建立在中国过去35年改革的基础上，是一次改革的再探索、再突破。当前，中国发展进入新阶段，改革进入深水区和攻坚期，按照习近平主席的生动比喻，就是"好吃的肉都吃掉了，剩下的是难啃的硬骨头"。所以《决定》强调最大限度调动一切积极因素，敢于啃硬骨头，敢于涉险滩，以更大决心冲破思想观念的束缚，突破利益固化的樊篱。

深化改革，首先是思想观念的突破和创新。比如，《决定》首次提出使市场在资源配置中起决定性作用，并按照这个要求，提出了经济领域众多新的重大改革措施。这是一个重大理论突破，是中国改革开放历史进程中具有里程碑意义的创新和发展。改革开放以前，中国实行的是高度集中的计划经济体制，否定和排斥市场作用；中国实行改革开放后，我们逐渐认识到社会主义也有市场，计划和市场都是经济手段，后来又进一步明确提出市场对资源配置起基础性作用。现在，中国将处理好政府和市场的关系作为经济体制改革的核心问题，使市场在资源配置中起决定性作用和更好地发挥政府作用，着力解决市场体系不完善、政府干预过多和监管不到位问题。我认为这是解放思想、正本清源之举，将有利于最大限度激发各类市场主体创业、创新活力，加快中国经济转型升级，建设高效廉洁的服务型政府及构建开放型经济新体制。当然，市场起决定性作用，绝不是弱化和否定政府的作用。《决定》清晰界定了政府职能和作用，就是宏观调控、公共服务、市场监管、社会管理和环境保护。

深化改革，要从体制机制上着手。比如，《决定》要求深化财税体制改革。我们现行的财税体制已经不完全适应合理划分中央和地方事权、完善国家治理的客观要求，不完全适应转变经济发展方式、促进经济社会持续健康发展的现实需要。因此《决定》提出，要改进预算管理制度，完善税收制度，建立事权和支出责任相适应的制度等。比如，适当加强中央事权和支出责任，国防、外交、国家安全、关系全国统一市场规则和管理等作为中央事权；部分社会保障、跨区域重大项目建设维护等作为中央和地方共同事权，逐步理顺事权关系；区域性公共服务作为地方事权。中央和地方按照事权划分相应承担和分担支出责任，能更好地发挥中央和地方两个积极性。

再比如在人民群众关心的社会保障制度改革上，《决定》明确提出建立更加公平可持续的社会保障制度。针对民众普遍关心的"养老保险双轨制"，《决定》要求推进机关事业单位养老保险制度改革。针对中国人口结构、城乡二元结构的显著变化，《决定》还要求整合城乡居民基本养老保险制度、基本医疗保险制度，并提出要研究制定渐进式延迟法定退休年龄政策。

可以说，中共十八届三中全会描绘了全面深化改革的新蓝图、新目标，为中国的未来发展释放了改革新红利，增添了新动力，为实现"中国梦"奠定了坚实的理论基础和制度保障。

朋友们，

中共十八届三中全会不仅是中国未来发展的新动力，它也为中英关系发展提供了合作新机遇。这是中英两国领导人的一致共识，也是成果逐步显现的客观事实。

我认为《决定》为中英合作提供了"十大新机遇"。

一是市场准入新机遇。《决定》要求实行统一的市场准入制度，在制定负面清单基础上，各类市场主体可依法平等进入清单之外领域，并明确表示将探索对外商投资实行准入前国民待遇加负面清单的管理模式。《决定》更进一步明确要推进金融、教育、文化、医疗等服务业领域有序开放，放开育幼养老、建筑设计、会计审计、商贸物流、电子商务等服务业领域外资准入限制，进一步放开一般制造业。可以说，中国的市场将更加开放、公平和透明。

二是双向投资新机遇。《决定》要求统一内外资法律法规，保持外资政策稳定、透明、可预期。《决定》也指出要深化投资体制改革，扩大企业及个人对外投资，确立企业及个人对外投资主体地位，允许发挥自身优势到境外开展投资合作，允许创新方式走出去开展绿地投资、并购投资、证券投资、联合投资等，加快同有关国家和地区商签投资协定。我相信，中英双向投资将迎来新一轮高潮。

三是自贸协定新机遇。《决定》提出加快自由贸易区建设，改革市场准入、海关监管、检验检疫等管理体制，加快环境保护、投资保护、政府采购、电子商务等新议题谈判，形成面向全球的高标准自由贸易区网络。中国和欧盟互为最大贸易伙伴，卡梅伦首相此次访华明确表示将推动欧盟与中国商签自贸协定，我们对此表示赞赏，希望中英双方以卡梅伦访华为契机，尽早启动有关磋商，加强在自贸领域的协调与配合，共同推动早日签署中欧自贸协定。

四是金融合作新机遇。《决定》表示中国将完善金融市场体系，扩大金融业对外开放；鼓励金融创新，丰富金融市场层次和产品；推动资本市场双向开放，有序提高跨境资本和金融交易可兑换程度，加快实现人民币资本项目可兑换。相信借助中共十八届三中全会的东风，伦敦建设人民币离岸中心的进程将进一步加快，两国金融企业也将在对方国家获得更大发展。

五是科技创新合作新机遇。《决定》提出深化科技体制改革，建立产学研协同创新机制，强化企业在技术创新中的主体地位，建设国家创新体系。《决定》特别提到要加强知识产权运用和保护，健全技术创新激励机制，探索建立知识产权法院。此次卡梅伦首相访华期间，中英共同签署了建立总额为2亿英镑的中英联合科学创新基金的谅解合作备忘录，支持两国企业、科研机构合作研发。关于知识产权保护问题，李克强总理向卡梅伦首相明确表示，中国经济转型升级已到了关键时期，科技创新对经济转型升级至关重要，但如果不保护知识产权，就不能调动社会和企业科技创新的积极性，因此中国政府最近决定，向社会公开知识产权侵权行政处罚案件，让侵犯知识产权的企业或个人付出高昂甚至无法承受的代价。这充分体现了中国政府保护知识产权的坚定决心并将采取切实行动。

六是消费能力提升新机遇。《决定》提出合理有序的收入分配格局，增加低收入者收入，扩大中等收入者比重，努力缩小城乡、区域、行业收入分配差距，逐步形成橄榄型分配格局。这意味着中国民众的收入水平将普遍提高，购买进口优质产品、海外旅游和消费的能力将进一步增强。

七是中西部发展新机遇。《决定》提出扩大内陆沿边开放，推动内陆贸易、投资、技术创新协调发展；创新加工贸易模式，形成有利于推动内陆产业集群发展的体制机制；支持内陆城市增开国际客货运航线，发展多式联运。英方对此可谓"捷足先登"，不久前开通了伦敦—成都直航，又即将在武汉设立总领馆。我此次陪同卡梅伦首相访问了成都，目睹了中国中西部地区的发展速度和规模，也真切地感到中英今后合作的广阔空间。

八是人文交流合作新机遇。《决定》要求提高文化开放水平，扩大对外文化交流，培育外向型文化企业，支持中国文化企业到境外开拓市场，鼓励社会组织、中资机构等参与孔子学院和海外文化中心建设并承担人文交流项目，积极吸收借鉴国外一切优秀文化成果，引进人才、技术和经营管理经验。我相信，这将为中英人文交流注入新活力、新力量。就在本月，中英两国新签署了未来五年文化交流计划，推动全方位文化交流。

九是城镇化合作机遇。《决定》提出坚持走新型城镇化道路，推进以人为核心的城镇化，推动大中小城市和小城镇协调发展、产业和城镇融合发展，优化城市空间结构和管理格局。英国既有老工业城市转型复兴的成功经验，也不乏小城镇生态宜居的良好范例，在城市规划方面也有着成熟完备的规章制度，中英在城镇化领域的交流与合作潜力巨大。

十是医疗卫生合作新机遇。《决定》指出要推进医疗保障、医疗服务、公共卫生、药品供应、监管体制综合改革。此次卡梅伦首相访华时，中英双方卫生主管部门签署了卫生合作备忘录，其目的就是要加大合作力度，提升中国的医疗水平。此外，双方还商签了4个医疗卫生商务合同，总值逾1.5亿英镑。这说明，医疗卫生领域将是中英合作的新增长点。

女士们、先生们，

中共十八届三中全会标志着中国的发展站在新起点上，与此同时，此次中英领导人会晤也标志着中英关系开启了新航程。中国有句古语："来而不可失者，时也；蹈而不可失者，机也。"希望英国社会各界的朋友们，不失时机，抓住机遇，积极开拓与中国各领域的交流与合作，与中国的全面深化改革深度融合，在中国的持续不断发展中互利共赢。让我们共同努力，一道开创共同构建中英关系更加美好的明天。

谢谢！

New Driving Force for China's Development, New Opportunities for China-UK Cooperation[*]

Lord Howell,

Chairman Peter Batey,

Ladies and Gentlemen,

Dear Friends,

I want to thank the China-Britain Business Council, the 48 Group Club, the Great Britain-China Centre and KPMG for organizing this event.

All your organizations have long been friends of China, supporters of the Chinese development and active players in China-UK cooperation. I salute you for your contribution to China-UK relations!

Given your keen interest in China, I am sure you have read about an "important meeting" in China not long ago! This was, of course, the Third Plenum of the 18th Central Committee of the Communist Party of China.

The Third Plenum produced a document titled The Decision of the CPC Central Committee on Major Issues Concerning Comprehensively Deepening Reform and Opening-Up. For convenience I will refer to this document as The Decision.

Last month soon after the publication of The Decision, I was invited to give a speech at the Reform Club. In that speech I stressed that The Decision demonstrated the Chinese

---

[*] Speech at the Seminar on the Third Plenum organized by the China-Britain Business Council, the 48 Group Club, the Great Britain-China Centre and KPMG. KPMG Building, 18 December 2013.

strong determination, top-down design and overall deployment in continuing reform.

It happens that determination, design and deployment all start with the letter D. In turn, that enables what I call a "3D", or three dimensional analysis of The Decision.

Most recently, I went back to China to accompany Prime Minister David Cameron on his visit.

I was greatly inspired by President Xi Jinping, Premier Li Keqiang and NPC Chairman Zhang Dejiang after listening to their comments on The Decision in meetings with Prime Minister David Cameron. As a result I would like to take this opportunity to share with you my understanding of the importance of The Decision and its implications for China-UK relations.

The Decision is a prospectus of the Chinese future reform and opening-up. It is a master plan for comprehensively deepening reform. In my view, the key to grasp The Decision is to understand the meaning of "comprehensively" and "deepening".

"Comprehensively" means the reform is clear in aim and extensive in content. While sorting out priorities, The Decision is both general and specific.

The Decision states clearly the general goal:

- This is to improve and develop a socialist system with Chinese characteristics.
- And modernize government systems and governance capacity.

The Chinese reform will not be limited to one field or one aspect. Instead, The Decision is a panorama of systemic, integrated and synchronized reforms. It requires reform measures to be mutually enhancing and facilitating. Such a synergy will help achieve breakthroughs in key areas while ensuring overall progress.

In terms of specific targets, The Decision is a five-in-one guideline. It aims to:

- Gear up the development of the socialist market economy.
- Advance democracy.
- Promote cultural development.
- Build a harmonious society.
- And protect the environment.

It also covers national defense and institutional building of the Party.

Pointing out the reform direction for each of these seven aspects and answering the call for reform from various social sectors, The Decision has set out more than 300 reform measures to achieve 55 main tasks in 15 areas. The magnitude of the reform is without precedent.

The reforms will be both sweeping and focused.

Economic reform is the centre piece. Economic reform measures account for over half of all the tasks. This is because problems facing China now all point to development. Ensuring sustainable and healthy economic development is a top priority for China. Successful economic reform will become the locomotive driving forward reform in other sectors.

The reforms cover both big and smaller issues. On the large size, examples are improving macro-control which mainly concerns the government. At the other end of the scale there are matters of immediate concern to every household, such as stopping the division of science and humanities in the national college entrance examination.

Let me now turn to the definition of "deepening" reform.

The reforms laid out in The Decision are built on the Chinese reform in the past 35 years. "Deepening" means a further exploration and new breakthrough.

At present, the Chinese reform has entered the "deep water".

As President Xi Jinping metaphorically said:

"All the tender meat has been eaten up. What's left now are hard bones."

Therefore, The Decision states that the government will mobilize all resources to meet the challenges and take on the difficulties. We will discard outdated mindsets and break vested interests.

China needs to be bold in thinking to deepen reform.

For example, The Decision has for the first time made clear that the market will play a decisive role in resources allocation. The Decision sets out a raft of major economic reform measures in line with this principle. This is a monumental and historical breakthrough in theory in the course of the Chinese reform and opening-up.

As you all know prior to reform and opening-up, China practiced a planned economy that was highly centralized. The role of the market was denied and suppressed. In the early days of reform and opening-up, China realized that the market is compatible with socialism. Both planning and the market are means to grow an economy. We then went on to confirm that the market played a basic role in allocating resources.

Now, China is focusing on properly handling the relationship between the government and the market, which is the crux of economic reform. This means China will both let the market play a decisive role in resources allocation and better play the role of the government. We will improve the market system, reduce government intervention and address inadequate regulation.

I believe this approach will inspire open thinking. It will tackle the issues holding back the advance of China at the root:

- This will unleash the potential and originality of all market players.
- It will speed up the Chinese economic transformation and upgrading.
- It will build an efficient and clean government that truly serves the people.
- Above all, it will help foster a new and open economy.

Of course, the decisive role of the market does not mean that the role of the government will be weakened or negated. The Decision clearly defined the function and role of the government:

- Macro-control.
- Public services.
- Market regulation.
- Social management.
- And environmental protection.

To deepen reform, we need to start from systems and institutions.

For example, the reform of fiscal and taxation system:

- The current system is inconsistent with the changed division of powers between the central and local governments.
- It is inadequate to meet the requirements for better governance.
- It is incompatible to the needs of economic transformation and promoting

sustainable and healthy economic and social development.

Therefore, The Decision says the following:

- China should improve its budget management system.
- Improve its taxation regime.
- And put in place a system corresponding to the division of administrative power and financial power.

The result is to give the central government more administrative powers and financial responsibilities. That means the following will all be the responsibility of the central government:

- National defense.
- Foreign affairs.
- National security.
- And national rules on market regulation.

Other sectors will be shared between the central and local governments. These will include:

- Social security.
- And construction and maintenance of large cross-regional projects.

Regional public services will be in the portfolio of local governments.
This clearer and more reasonable division of administrative and financial powers will win the support of both central and local governments.
In China the general public care most about social security reform. In this area The Decision stresses the need to establish a fairer and more sustainable social security system. The pension schemes of government institutions will be reformed. The aim is to address public concerns over "dual track" pension schemes. Moreover, basic old age insurance and medical care for urban and rural population will be integrated. There will

also be a gradual extension of the retirement age.

So, we have every reason to conclude that the Third Plenum has drawn up a new blueprint for China. The Decision has set out new targets for comprehensively deepening reform in China.

Through reform, The Decision has unleashed the potential and added a new driving force for the Chinese future growth. It has also laid a solid theoretical and institutional foundation for the realization of the Chinese Dream.

Dear Friends,

The Third Plenum is not only a new powerhouse for the Chinese future development. It also creates new opportunities for China-UK cooperation. This is the consensus of the leaders of our two countries. The opportunities are clear to see.

Specifically, I believe The Decision has opened ten new opportunities for China-UK cooperation.

First, market access.

The Decision provides for uniform market access. On the basis of the "negative list", all market players have equal access to sectors out of the list in accordance with law. An approach that combines pre-establishment national treatment and "negatives" will be adopted towards foreign investments.

The Decision further clarifies that China will open up in an orderly manner these sectors:

- Finance.
- Education.
- Culture.
- Medical care and other services sectors.

China will lift restrictions on foreign investments in these areas:

- Child care.
- Old age support.
- Construction design.
- Accounting and auditing.

- And logistics and e-commerce.

The general manufacturing sector will also be further opened up. In a word, the Chinese market will be more open, fair and transparent.

Second, two-way investment.

The Decision aims to harmonize laws governing foreign and domestic investments. The changes will aim to maintain a stable, transparent and predictable policy environment for foreign investment.

The Decision also underlines the need to deepen reform in the investment system in the following way:

- Expand outbound corporate and individual investments.
- Recognize their status as investors.
- Allow and encourage innovative outbound investments such as green land investment, mergers and acquisition, securities and joint investment, etc.

On top of these legal changes, China will negotiate and sign investment agreements with countries and regions concerned. Without doubt, there will be a new wave of mutual investment between China and the UK.

Third, free trade agreements.

The Decision says China will accelerate development of free trade zones. This will lead to:

- Reform of rules of market access.
- And revised customs, inspection and quarantine regulations.

There will be a speeding up of negotiations on these new topics:

- Environmental protection.
- Investment protection.
- Government procurement.
- E-commerce.

All these are intended to build a network of high quality free trade zones reaching out to the whole world.

China and the EU are the largest trading partners to one another. We appreciate Prime Minister David Cameron's statement on his China visit that he will help push through a China-EU free trade agreement.

We hope that our two countries will use Prime Minister Cameron's visit as an opportunity to start related consultations at an early date, increase coordination in backing free trade and working together to pull off the plan.

Fourth, financial cooperation.

According to The Decision China will take steps to:

- Improve the financial market system.
- Further open up the financial sector.
- Encourage financial innovation.
- Build a multi-tiered financial market.
- Introduce more financial products.
- Work for mutual openness of capital markets.
- Increase the convertibility of cross-border capital and financial transactions.
- And make the RMB convertible under capital account.

I believe with the impetus of the Third Plenum, London will take faster steps in becoming an offshore centre for RMB business. This means our financial corporations will benefit more from increased business and exchange.

Fifth, innovation in science and technology.

The Decision aims to deepen reform in science and technology system, set up innovation models that join the industry, universities and research institutions, foreground enterprises in technological innovation and build a national innovation system. In particular, it stresses:

- Strengthening the use and protection of intellectual property rights.
- Improving the incentive measures for scientific innovation.
- And exploring setting up an IPR court.

During Prime Minister Cameron's visit, China and the UK signed the MOU on a 200 million pounds innovation fund. The objective is to support joint R&D projects of our companies and scientific research institutions.

On IPR protection, Premier Li Keqiang made clear to Prime Minister Cameron that the Chinese economic transformation has come to a critical juncture. Scientific innovation is essential to economic transformation and upgrading.

But in the absence of effective IPR protection, it will be a serious challenge to motivate enthusiasm for innovation from our universities or businesses.

Following this trend, the Chinese government has recently decided to disclose penalties administered to all cases of IPR infringement to make the cost of wrong-doing heavy and unaffordable for infringing companies and individuals. This fully demonstrates the firm resolve and credible actions of the Chinese government to protect IPR.

Sixth, stronger spending ability.

The Decision aims at reasonable and orderly incomes distribution. China will increase the income of low earners. In turn this will enlarge the middle class and so bridge the income gap between rural and urban areas. The same policies will aim to reduce income differentials between regions and between different sectors. This means all Chinese will have more money to spend on quality imports, overseas traveling and shopping.

Seventh, development of central and western China.

The Decision calls for further opening-up of border areas in the Chinese hinterland. The objective is to promote coordinated development in trade, investment and technological innovation in these areas.

China will innovate models of processing trade. It will create institutions that help form industrial clusters in the western parts of China. It will support more cargo flights to and from interior cities.

In fact Britain has taken a very visionary step by opening direct flights between London and Chengdu. Britain will also soon open a consulate-general in Wuhan. While accompanying Prime Minister David Cameron on his visit to Chengdu, I witnessed the speed and scale of development in the Chinese western regions. I also felt strongly the ample space for future China-UK cooperation this provides.

Eighth, cultural and people-to-people exchanges.

The Decision says China will increase openness in the cultural sector. The effect will be to:

- Broaden cultural exchanges with foreign countries.
- Foster export-oriented businesses in the cultural sector and support their efforts to explore overseas markets.
- Encourage social organizations and Chinese companies to take part in programmes like the Confucius Institutes, Chinese Culture Centers, and to undertake cultural exchange projects.
- And to draw on the finest of foreign cultures, attracting talent, technologies and expertise.

I believe all these will inject new dynamism into the China-UK cultural and people-to-people exchanges. Just this month, China and the UK have signed the agreement on cultural exchanges for the coming five years.

Ninth, urbanization.

The Decision reiterates that China should pioneer a new path of urbanization that puts people first. It means we will:

- Promote coordinated development of cities and towns of different sizes.
- Strike a balance between industrial and urban development.
- And improve urban planning and management.

Britain has a wealth of experience in reviving old industrial cities and developing eco-friendly small towns. You also have mature institutions and regimes in urban planning. For all these reasons, China and the UK have great cooperation potential in urbanization.

Tenth, medical and health care.

The Decision confirms that China will advance important reforms in these areas:

- Medical insurance.
- Medical care.

- Public health.
- Pharmaceuticals.
- And medical regulation.

During Prime Minister Cameron's China visit, health authorities of our two countries signed an MOU on health cooperation. It is aimed to strengthen bilateral cooperation in health sector and boost the quality of the Chinese medical care. Moreover, the two sides also signed four commercial contracts on medical business with a combined value of over 150 million pounds. This shows that medical and health care cooperation will be a new growth area in China-UK cooperation.

Ladies and Gentlemen,

The Third Plenum marks a new starting point for China.

At the same time, the meeting of our national leaders marked the beginning of a new voyage of the China-UK relationship.

As an old Chinese saying goes:

"An opportune moment shall not be missed; a good opportunity shall not be wasted."

I hope our British friends, whatever sector you are from, will not miss the moment or waste the opportunity.

I hope you will actively expand exchanges and cooperation with China in all fields.

There are immense mutual gains if you ride on the train of the Chinese comprehensively deepening reform.

I am sure both countries will enjoy win-win from the Chinese continuous growth.

Let us work together for a better future of China-UK relations.

Thank you!

沉舟侧畔千帆过，病树前头万木春*

女士们、先生们，

很高兴出席 Pi Capital 公司和汉普集团共同举办的晚餐会。

五个多月前，主办方邀请我演讲，主题是关于中英关系，但在过去近三周时间里，论影响可能没有比英国公投"脱欧"更大的事件了。所以我认为还是有必要先从英国公投"脱欧"讲起。

英国公投"脱欧"，有人说这是"地震"，引发英国、欧洲和世界强烈震动，至今余波未息；也有人说是"黑天鹅"事件，因为市场始料不及，短期出现剧烈波动；还有人说是"革命"，因为它是民众反精英、反体制思潮的爆发，民众的力量战胜了体制的力量。

过去的三周，正如列宁所说："有时候几十年里什么都没发生，有时候几周里发生了几十年的大事。"我似乎看到了《纸牌屋》、《是，大臣》和《是，首相》，也看到了"买家的懊悔"，我不知道是否还会看到"无休止的公投"。

不管如何，公投"脱欧"后，英国政坛将如何重组？未来的英欧关系会怎么样？对欧盟发展和国际格局会产生什么样的影响？这些都是大家关注的问题，我现在听到最多的回答是："存在巨大不确定性。"尽管面临这么多的不确定性，自英国公投"脱欧"以来，我一直在传递"确定的"信息，那就是中方将继续致力于推进中英全面战略伙伴关系。

---

* 在英国工商界晚餐会上的演讲。2016 年 7 月 12 日，伦敦克拉里奇酒店。

正如习近平主席和李克强总理近期分别指出的，我们尊重英国人民的选择，希望看到一个稳定、繁荣的英国和欧盟。我们将继续致力于维护和发展好中英关系和中欧关系，也希望英欧通过协商谈判早日达成互惠共赢的安排。

因此，无论英国是留在欧盟还是离开欧盟，我们将一如既往地从战略高度和长远角度看待和发展中英关系，将一如既往地从开放包容、互利共赢出发深化和拓展两国各领域合作。

俗话说，孤掌难鸣。我们也希望，无论英国内政如何变化，无论英国对外关系如何调整，英国政府都将与中方相向而行，奉行积极、开放、务实的对华政策，继续将对华关系作为英国外交的优先方向。

当前，中国企业开展对英合作没有受到影响。6月25日，就在公投后两天，中国海南航空公司旗下天津航空正式开通了天津—重庆—伦敦往返航班。6月28日，就在公投后五天，华为公司承诺在英投资13亿英镑的计划将继续进行。这是中国企业对英国投下的信任票。很多中国企业告诉我，它们在英投资，既由于英国是面向欧洲的桥头堡，更由于英国是世界第五大经济体，本身经济体量大、市场容量大，同时市场开放透明、服务完善。

关于两国经贸关系未来，我认为中英双方应继续致力于以下四点。

一是扩大贸易与投资。希望英方继续欢迎中国企业投资，推进落实欣克利角C核电项目等各方已达成原则性协议的合作，双方还应探讨建立更高水平的双边贸易和投资安排。

二是加强金融合作。我们重视伦敦国际金融中心地位，将继续支持伦敦人民币离岸中心建设，推进两国绿色金融合作，支持更多中资银行进入英国市场，也希望英方能与欧盟做出互惠的金融服务安排。

三是深化两国发展战略对接。希望两国企业更深入地参与"一带一路"、中国"长江经济带"、英方基础设施建设升级改造计划、"英格兰北方经济中心"等发展战略和计划，充分发挥各自的技术、创新和资金等优势，开展更多的基础设施建设、并购融资和国际产能合作。

四是携手促进世界经济的繁荣与增长。我们应共同推进全球经济金融治理体系改革，促进多边贸易体系发展，坚持反对贸易保护主义。中方期待着与英方继续共同努力，推动二十国集团领导人杭州峰会取得丰硕成果。

女士们、先生们，

正如我一开始所言，英国公投"脱欧"的后果带来不确定性，包括世界经济的不确定性进一步上升。中国既致力于在国际上推动各国共同应对挑战、提振信心，共同营造稳定的国际环境，寻求治本之策，也努力以自身的经济稳步增长，为世界经济的繁荣与稳定提供有力支撑。

2016年以来，中国政府继续大力推进结构性改革，着力培育新动能，经济运行总体平稳、稳中有进。一季度经济增长6.7%，二季度继续保持稳定增长。工业企业效益回稳提升，服务业较快发展，市场销售平稳增长，居民消费价格指数基本稳定，工业生产者出厂价格指数降幅收窄，就业保持稳定。我们也认识到，中国经济正处在调整转型时期，经济稳定运行的基础还不牢固，下行压力仍然较大，短期内难免有波动起伏，但我们有足够的政策工具保持经济运行在合理区间，有充分的能力防范系统性、区域性风险，有信心实现经济社会发展主要预期目标。为此，中国将做到以下五点。

一是中国将保持宏观政策连续性和稳定性，继续创新宏观调控方式，加力增效实施积极的财政政策，灵活适度实施稳健的货币政策，把资源更多引向有利于促进转型升级等新经济的领域。

二是中国将继续落实创新、协调、绿色、开放、共享的新发展理念，在适度扩大总需求的同时，坚定不移推进供给侧结构性改革，抓好去产能、去库存、去杠杆、降成本、补短板，使中国经济保持中高速增长，迈向中高端水平。

三是中国将继续以创新引领经济转型升级，深入实施创新驱动发展战略，发展新经济，培育新动能，着力推动大众创业、万众创新，发展共享经济和众创经济，培育新的经济增长点。

四是中国政府将继续以全面深化改革推动经济转型升级，推进简政放权，淘汰严重过剩产能，协同推进财税、金融、国企、市场准入等重点领域改革，释放经济发展的更大活力。

五是中国政府将继续以开放助推经济转型升级，提高开放型经济水平，扩大服务业和一般制造业开放，营造更加公平、透明、可预期的投资环境。

总之，正如习近平主席上周在经济形势专家座谈会上指出的那样，中国经济发展长期向好的基本面没有变，经济韧性好、潜力足、回旋余地大的基本特征没有变，经济持续增长的良好支撑基础和条件没有变，经济结构调整优化的前进态势没有变。据毕马威会计师事务所近期对全球1200多位企业高管的调查，企业家们仍然认为中国是最具增长潜力的市场，对中国未来充满信心。

女士们、先生们，

中国古诗说："沉舟侧畔千帆过，病树前头万木春。"机遇总是与挑战并存的，历史的车轮总是向前的，只要我们充满信心，前途就会一片光明。让我们一道把握机遇，应对挑战，共同驾驭中英经贸合作这艘巨轮，乘风破浪，驶向更加光明美好的未来。

谢谢！

Hard Times Will Not Stop the Wheel of History*

Ladies and Gentlemen,

It gives me great pleasure to join you for this dinner co-hosted by Pi Capital and Hampton Group.

The invitation to tonight's event came to me five months ago. It was for me to talk about China-UK relations.

But given the events that have unfolded in the UK over the past three weeks, I feel sure you will agree with me on talking from a different perspective—the Brexit. The result of the Brexit in the UK may prove to have a profound impact and global significance.

- Some people call Brexit an "earthquake". It is sending a shock wave across the UK, Europe and the world. Indeed, almost daily, the aftershocks are still being felt.
- Some consider it a "black swan event". It has caught the markets by surprise and given rise to short-term, drastic convulsions.
- Some also equate it to a "revolution" driven by an outbreak of anti-elite and anti-establishment sentiment.
- They suggest it is a "triumph" of the people over the system.

---

* Speech at the Dinner Co-hosted by Pi Capital and Hampton Group. Claridges Hotel, London, 12 July 2016.

That reminds me of a quote from Vladimir Ilyich Lenin.

"There are decades where nothing happens; and there are weeks where decades happen."

There can be no better characterisation than these words of what happened during the past three weeks. Many have reflected that fictional politics suddenly came alive:

- It felt like watching the famous TV series *House of Cards*, *Yes, Minister* and *Yes, Prime Minister*.
- We already see signs of "buyer's remorse". I wonder if there is going to be a clamour for "neverendum."

As days pass harsh realities are coming into sharper and sharper focus. Above all is the great uncertainty and the need to answer a string of questions:

- How will British politics evolve?
- What will be the future of Britain-Europe relations?
- What impact will the referendum outcome have on the EU?
- How will it reshape the architecture of global relations?

Many people are asking these and many other questions. I also listen very carefully to others who answer these questions.

The clear consensus amongst the answers I have heard so far is—"huge uncertainties".

But since the referendum, I have been busy spreading "certainties". That is, China will remain committed to the the comprehensive strategic partnership for China-UK relations.

As President Xi Jinping and Premier Li Keqiang said recently:

- China respects the choice of the British people.
- We would like to see a stable and prosperous EU and a stable and prosperous Britain.
- China will stay committed to growing stronger ties with the UK and the EU.
- China hopes that the UK and the EU will consult and negotiate and reach an

early, win-win arrangement on a reciprocal basis.

Whether the UK is in the EU or not, China will take a strategic and long-term perspective when it comes to our bilateral relations. And China will continue to deepen and expand our win-win cooperation across the board in the spirit of openness and inclusiveness.

However it takes two to tango:

- There will be changes within British politics. But we hope the UK government will continue to work with China.
- We wish that the UK stay committed to its active, open and pragmatic China policy.
- And we also hope that, regardless of any foreign policy adjustments in the UK, advancing ties with China will always be a priority in Britain's external relations.

Let me turn from politics to business. So far, business cooperation between our two countries has not been affected. On 25th June, just two days after the referendum, a Chinese company made a new move. Tianjin Airlines, a subsidiary of the Chinese Hainan Airlines Group, opened a direct flight route connecting Tianjin, Chongqing and London. On 28th June, five days after the referendum, Huawei UK went ahead with its 1.3 billion-pound investment as planned.

These are votes of confidence from Chinese businesses. Many Chinese entrepreneurs have told me that their decisions of investing in the UK are not just based on the UK's position as a gateway to Europe. What matters more are these facts:

- Britain is the world's fifth largest economy.
- Britain has a large and open market.
- Britain boasts world-class services.
- And, Britain is a global leader in many other business sectors.

To create a bright future of China-UK business relations, I think our two countries should continue to focus on the following aspects:

First, we need to expand investment and trade.

- We hope that Chinese investment will remain welcome in the UK.
- We need to advance the agreed cooperation projects, such as Hinckley Point.
- And, we can also discuss a higher-standard arrangement for bilateral trade and investment.

Second, we need to enhance our financial cooperation.

- We value London's position as a global financial centre.
- We will continue to support the building of the offshore RMB market in London.
- We will carry out more green financial cooperation between our two countries.
- We will encourage more Chinese banks to come to Britain.
- And, we also hope that the UK will reach with the EU a mutually beneficial financial service arrangement.

Third, we need to dovetail our respective development strategies.

- Both Chinese and British business communities should get deeply involved in our respective development strategies and plans. This includes the Chinese Belt and Road Initiative, the Yangtze River Economic Belt, and Britain's National Infrastructure Plan and the Northern Power house.
- We hope that we can leverage our respective strengths in technology, innovation and financing.
- We looks to more cooperation on infrastructure building, acquisition, financing, as well as international capacity cooperation.

Fourth, we need to work together for global growth and prosperity.

- China and the UK need to jointly advance the reform of world economic and financial governance.
- China and the UK need to facilitate the building of a multilateral trade system.

- China and the UK must stand against protectionism.
- And, China looks forward to working with the UK at the G20 Summit in Hangzhou, China. We should join hands to produce fruitful results.

Ladies and Gentlemen,

As I said just now, many uncertainties have arisen from the Brexit. These are added to many other rising uncertainties in the world economy. But the Chinese commitment remains unchanged:

- China will work with all countries to build up confidence and stand against challenges.
- China will join forces with the rest of world to restore stability and to seek a solution to the root cause of existing problems.
- And, at the same time, China will pursue steady economic growth at home. Steady growth in China is itself a contribution to global prosperity and stability.

Since early this year, the Chinese government has been making strenuous efforts to advance structural reform and create new economic drivers. The Chinese overall economic performance has been stable. There has been steady progress along the way:

- In the first quarter, the Chinese economy grew by 6.7%.
- And, the second quarter witnessed this steady trend of growth continued.

There is more good news:

- Business profits was picking up steadily.
- The service sector is developing rapidly.
- Sales grew steadily.
- CPI was kept stable and decline of producer prices slowed.
- And, the employment market was stable.

Meanwhile we are aware of the difficulties:

- The Chinese economy is still in transition.
- The foundation of steady growth are not solid enough.
- And there is still downward pressure and likely short-term fluctuations.

However, in China we are still confident in attaining the goals of economic and social development. This confidence is based on the facts that China has sufficient policy tools to keep the economy growing at a reasonable speed. In addition, China is capable of guarding against systemic and regional risks. To this end, China needs to make further efforts in the following aspects:

First, China will keep its macropolicy consistent and stable:

- China will continue to innovate ways of macro economic management.
- China will implement its proactive fiscal policy with greater intensity and efficiency.
- China will carry out a prudent monetary policy in a flexible and appropriate way.
- And, China will channel more resources into the new economy which facilitates transition and upgrading.

Second, China will continue to implement the five key development concepts, namely, innovation, coordinated development, green economy, opening-up and inclusiveness.

- China will expand overall demand appropriately.
- At the same time China will advance supply side reform steadfastly.
- China will cut overcapacity, reduce excessive inventory, deleverage, slash business costs, and shore up the weak links.
- And, this will enable China to maintain a medium-to-high growth rate and move to a higher development level.

Third, China will continue to strive for economic transformation and upgrading led by innovation:

- China will follow through the innovation-driven development strategy.
- China will grow a new economy, create new growth engines and encourage innovation and entrepreneurship.
- China will develop a sharing and start-ups friendly economy.
- And, China will create new growth points—such as with digital developments.

Fourth, the Chinese government will advance economic transformation and upgrading through comprehensive deepening of reform:

- China will streamline administration and delegate more central power to lower authorities.
- China will strive to eliminate overcapacity.
- China will advance reforms in a coordinated way. This will happen in key areas such as fiscal and taxation, the financial sector, state-run enterprises and market access.
- And, China will work to unleash the vitality of our economy.

Fifth, the Chinese government will transform and upgrade the economy through opening-up:

- China will make its economy more open.
- This means greater access to the service sector and general manufacturing sector.
- We will create a level playing field that is more transparent and predictable to investors.

Last week, President Xi spoke on the Chinese economy at an economic symposium in Beijing. Here are some key points:

- The fundamentals of the Chinese economy remain positive in the long run.
- The Chinese economy still has much resilience and huge potential and there is ample space for further growth.
- The foundations and conditions for growth remain positive.

- Structural adjustment and improvement continues to advance.

A recent KPMG survey of over 1,200 chief executives worldwide, shows most company bosses still consider China the most promising growth market. These top business leaders are confident about the Chinese future.

Ladies and Gentlemen,

Let me quote a famous line from a Chinese poem:

"Thousands of boats sail past the sunken ship by the shore, and millions of saplings spring forth from the dying tree."

Hard times will not stop the wheel of history. Challenges always come with opportunities.

This is why—despite the current uncertainties—I call on you to have confidence in a promising future.

Also, I call on you to seize the opportunities and stand up to the challenges.

Working together, we can navigate the uncharted water and ride through the waves.

Together, we can create a brighter and better future of China-UK business cooperation.

Thank you!

共建良好环境，共创中英经贸合作新局面 *

尊敬的英国保守党议会中国小组主席克利夫顿－布朗先生，
尊敬的英国国际发展部国务大臣贝茨勋爵，
各位议员，
女士们、先生们：
大家早上好！
很高兴第四次参加保守党议会中国小组早餐会。

克利夫顿－布朗主席希望我今天谈谈英国"脱欧"背景下中英经贸投资合作的机遇。

从我第一次参加保守党议会中国小组早餐会，整整七年过去了。在这七年时间里，我遍访英伦各地，从英格兰到苏格兰，从威尔士到北爱尔兰，从皇家属地马恩岛到海外领地百慕大，所到之处，我都能感受到英国各界人士发展对华合作的意愿和诚意，感受到中英关系的蓬勃生机和强劲动力。经贸合作一直是中英关系的"稳定器"和"助推器"，我认为可以用三个字来概括。

第一个字是"实"。中英互为重要贸易伙伴。2016 年，中国是英国第三大贸易伙伴、第二大进口来源国和第七大出口目的地国。2016 年，中英双边货物贸易额达 743.4 亿美元，在中国同欧盟国家双边贸易中位居第二。2017 年 1—7 月，中英双边货物贸易额为 443.4 亿美元，同比增长 7.1%。其中中

---

* 在英国保守党议会中国小组早餐会上的主旨演讲。2017 年 9 月 12 日，英国议会。

国对英出口316.6亿美元，同比增长3.5%；中国自英进口126.8亿美元，同比增长17.1%。在投资方面，近年来相互投资迅猛发展。英国是中国在欧盟内的第二大外资来源地，目前中国在英非金融类直接投资达180亿美元，居欧洲之首。有500多家中资企业落户英国，投资项目从贸易、金融、电信等传统部门向新能源、高端制造、基础设施、研发中心等新兴领域延伸。开曼群岛和英属维尔京群岛已成为除中国香港外，中国内地对外投资的第一和第二大目的地。在世界经济复苏乏力、贸易保护主义抬头的背景下，中英经贸和投资合作取得了亮丽的成绩。

第二个字是"先"。两国经贸合作敢为人先，不断探索合作新渠道，拓展合作新领域，打造合作新亮点，开创了多个第一：英国在西方大国中率先加入亚洲基础设施投资银行，也是继中国之后第二个向亚投行专门基金注资的国家；英国第一个发行人民币主权债券，伦敦已成为中国境外最大的人民币离岸市场。中国则在伦敦发行境外第一只主权债券；中国银行在伦敦发行30亿等值美元绿色债券，开辟双方绿色金融合作新领域；中广核成功参与欣克利角C核电站建设，打造旗舰项目；南汽集团、吉利公司整合英国企业，实现了英国设计和中国制造的完美结合。2017年初，中欧班列首次往返于义乌和伦敦，标志着丝绸之路延伸到欧洲的最西端。上述都生动体现了中英务实合作的创新性和前瞻性。

第三个字是"广"。中英两国在推动经济全球化、贸易自由化、投资便利化方面理念一致、利益融合。两国在推进自由贸易、完善全球经济治理、改革国际金融体系等方面进行有效沟通和合作。2016年中国成功主办二十国集团领导人杭州峰会，中英两国以二十国集团反腐败工作组共同主席身份，为打击跨国腐败行为制订行动计划；两国央行还领衔二十国集团绿色金融研究小组共同主席，推动各方就发展绿色金融达成全球共识，为推动世界经济走上强劲、可持续、平衡、包容增长之路发挥了积极作用。中英经贸合作已远远超出双边范畴，越来越具有全球影响。

女士们、先生们，

当前，英国"脱欧"是国际上的一件大事，英欧谈判仍是"进行时"。

尽管有人担心英国"脱欧"进程可能给中英经贸合作带来一些不确定性，但中英经贸投资合作的雄厚基础、内生动力和广阔前景都没有改变。我认为新形势下，两国经贸合作面临"三大机遇"。

一是伙伴关系的战略机遇。2015年习近平主席成功对英进行"超级国事访问"，双方同意构建面向21世纪全球全面战略伙伴关系。2016年二十国集团领导人杭州峰会和2017年二十国集团领导人汉堡峰会期间，习近平主席和梅首相两次会晤，再次确认中英关系的大方向。两国高层互动频繁，政治互信不断增强，为两国关系发展提供了强有力的政治引领，推动中英务实合作进入新时期。

二是优势互补的对接机遇。中英在经济发展模式、产业结构和国际分工、研发创新等方面各有千秋，两国正处于产业调整和转型的不同阶段，互补性突出，利益交汇点多，合作潜力巨大。两国应充分利用中方在装备制造和资金方面的优势，以及英方在创新研发、高端制造和金融服务方面的强项，通力合作，实现共赢发展。英国崇尚自由贸易，市场规范，法律健全，对中国投资持开放态度，中资企业可在基础设施、品牌创意、节能环保等领域加大对英国投资力度。

三是"一带一路"的合作机遇。"一带一路"已成为中英合作的新亮点，蕴含着巨大的商机与潜力。英国政府、工商、金融、智库等各界人士对中英"一带一路"合作热情高涨，积极建言献策。2017年5月，哈蒙德财政大臣作为梅首相特使出席"一带一路"国际合作高峰论坛，为两国"一带一路"合作注入新动力。英中贸易协会、汇丰银行等发布了多份"一带一路"调研报告，为英国企业参与"一带一路"建设提供了指南。英国作为"一带一路"的重要参与方，在金融服务、法律专业服务、项目运营、风险管控等领域经验丰富，中英可在"一带一路"框架下加强战略对接和政策协调，携手开发第三方市场，打造"一带一路"合作亮点。

女士们、先生们，

多年来，在中英双方共同努力下，两国经贸投资合作成果丰硕，前景广阔。在当前逆全球化和贸易保护主义抬头等背景下，我们要坚定信心，排除干扰,一心一意求合作,聚精会神谋发展,重点营造好"四个环境"。

一是政治环境。良好的政治环境是国家关系发展的前提,更是推动经贸投资合作的基础。中国崇尚"和为贵""和而不同",主张超越社会制度与意识形态的差异,谋求共同利益,致力于在交流互鉴中取长补短,在求同存异中共同进步,在互利合作中共赢发展。正如习近平主席指出的,"志同道合是伙伴,求同存异也是伙伴"。中英双方应以平等的视角相互尊重,以包容的心态相互理解,以开阔的胸襟相互信任,以友好的情谊相互交往,始终以长远和战略眼光看待两国关系;我们要尊重彼此核心利益和重大关切,以建设性方式处理分歧和敏感问题,确保中英关系行稳致远。

二是政策环境。梅首相多次表示,英国致力于建设"全球化英国",将继续坚持自由贸易,反对保护主义,积极发展和加强与全球伙伴的经贸关系。我们希望英方信守开放承诺,展现开放姿态,释放开放信号,增强外界对英发展前景的信心。我们也希望英国在制定投资政策时,坚持非歧视和透明化原则,充分考虑和维护包括中国企业在内各国投资者的合法权益,继续营造开放、公平、可预见的政策环境。

三是舆论环境。我注意到英国媒体十分关注中国,但对中国的报道仍有误解和偏见。比如近期炒作的所谓"中国投资威胁论",它们担心"中国买断英国",渲染中国投资威胁英国安全。这种论调把中国投资"妖魔化",不仅站不住脚,也是有害的。为此,我不久前在《旗帜晚报》就中国在英投资问题撰文。希望这有助于大家更深刻理解中英投资合作不是单向获利,更不是损人利己,而是互利共赢的。我想强调的是,中国企业到英国来,为的是寻求合作、寻求共赢。它们希望看到一个友善的、欢迎外资的环境。这既包括政策和法律环境,也包括舆论和社会环境。我希望它们的愿望能够实现。事实能够表明它们来英国投资的决定是正确的。

四是国际环境。当前,世界经济虽出现一些向好势头,但同时全球经济金融不稳定不确定因素也在增多,世界经济深层次问题远未解决。习近平主席在世界经济论坛 2017 年年会开幕式上指出,"要坚定不移发展全球自由贸易和投资,在开放中推动贸易和投资自由化便利化,旗帜鲜明反对保护主义"。我们愿与英方加强在国际治理领域协调合作，高举支持经济全球化、贸易自由化、投资便利化的旗帜，引领国际社会共同应对挑战，共同为建设创新、活力、联动、包容的世界经济做出贡献。

女士们、先生们，

中国有句古话："单则易折，众则难摧。"在当前国际形势深刻复杂变化、全球性挑战依然突出的背景下，中英两国更需要加强协调，携手合作，共迎挑战。英国保守党议会中国小组长期致力于加强中英交流与合作，为推动两国议会交往、促进双边经贸合作做出积极努力。2017年是中英建立大使级外交关系45周年，也是中英关系深入发展之年。我希望，在新形势下，保守党议会中国小组继续发挥建设性作用。我相信，只要中英双方秉持开放包容、合作共赢理念，牢牢把握中英合作"三大机遇"，积极营造"四个环境"，集思广益，通力合作，就一定能推动中英经贸投资合作结出更多成果，更好地造福两国和世界人民。

谢谢！

Create a Sound Environment for New Success in China-UK Business Cooperation[*]

Chairman Clifton-Brown,

Lord Bates,

My Lords and MPs,

Ladies and Gentlemen,

Good morning.

It gives me real delight to join you for the Conservative Parliamentary China Group's Breakfast Meeting for the fourth time.

Chairman Clifton-Brown asked me to talk about the opportunities for China-UK cooperation on trade and investment against the background of Brexit.

It's been seven years since I attended the first breakfast meeting of the Conservative Parliamentary China Group. In the past seven years, I visited many places around Britain, from England to Scotland, from Wales to Northern Ireland, and from the Crown Dependency the Isle of Man to the Overseas Territory of Bermuda.

Wherever I went, I always met with people from different sectors. Almost all of them have high hopes for cooperation with China and strong desire to see it grow. I believe that is the fundamental vitality that keeps China-UK relations moving forward.

Through my visits I also came to see that business cooperation between China and

---

[*] Keynote Speech at the Breakfast Meeting of the Conservative Parliamentary China Group. House of Commons, 12 September 2017.

Britain plays such a crucial role. It is the "stabilizer" and "propeller" of our bilateral ties. This is because our business cooperation brings tangible benefits, demonstrates a pioneering spirit and reaches to broad social sectors.

First, China-UK business cooperation brings tangible benefits to both our countries. China and Britain are important trade partners for each other.

- In 2016, China was Britain's third biggest trading partner, third largest source of import and seventh largest market for British goods.
- In 2016, bilateral trade in goods totalled 74.34 billion US dollars, making Britain China's second largest trading partner in the EU.
- From January to July in 2017, trade in goods reached 44.34 billion US dollars, up by 7.1%.
- China's export to Britain was 31.66 billion US dollars, up by 3.5% while China's import from Britain was 12.68 billion US dollars, up by 17.1%.

Mutual investment is also growing fast over the years.

- Britain is China's second biggest investor in the EU.
- China has 18 billion US dollar non-financial investment in Britain, more than in any other EU countries.
- More than 500 Chinese companies have settled down in Britain. Their investments are going to areas beyond conventional sectors such as trade, finance and telecommunication. They are reaching out to emerging industries such as new energy, high-end manufacturing, infrastructure, R&D centre, etc.
- Cayman Islands and British Virgin Islands are now the largest and second largest destinations only after Hong Kong for direct investment from the Chinese Mainland.

Undoubtedly, in the context of sluggish global economic recovery and rising protectionism, what China and Britain have achieved in our business and investment cooperation is extraordinary.

Second, China-UK business cooperation has always demonstrated a pioneering spirit.

Our two countries have always been daring to take the lead in establishing new models of business cooperation, in expanding it to new fields, and in creating new highlights.

Together we have set a series of records in being the "first":

- Britain was the first major Western power to apply to join the Asian Infrastructure Investment Bank, and the second only after China to contribute capital to the AIIB's special fund.
- Britain was the first in the world to issue RMB sovereign bonds and London is now the largest RMB offshore market outside China.
- On our side, China issued its first overseas RMB sovereign bonds in London.
- The Bank of China issued in London a three billion dollar green bond, breaking new ground for China-UK cooperation on green finance.
- The CGN is the first Chinese nuclear company participating in Britain's nuclear project. The Hinkley Point C nuclear plant has become a flagship project in China-UK relations.
- China's Nanjing Automotive Corporation and the Geely Group bought British automakers. Their acquisitions have resulted in a perfect match between British design and Chinese manufacturing capabilities.
- Early in 2017, a freight train of China Railway Express arrived in London before making a round trip back to the Chinese Yiwu. It marks the extension of the new Silk Road to the very western end of Europe.

The list can go on and on. These examples are all vivid reflections of the pioneering spirit in our creative cooperation.

Third, China-UK business cooperation reaches broad social sectors.

China and Britain have shared commitment to economic globalization, trade liberalization and investment facilitation. Our interests converge and our communication and cooperation have been effective in facilitating free trade, improving global economic governance and reforming the international financial system.

In 2016, China successfully hosted the G20 Summit in Hangzhou. China and Britain co-chaired the G20 Anti-Corruption Working Group and made the action plan for combating cross-border corruption. The G20 Green Finance Study Group, co-chaired by the central banks of our two countries, led to the global consensus on green finance. Our role in building a robust, sustainable, balanced and inclusive world economic growth has been strong and active. In this sense, China-UK business cooperation has an impact that reaches far beyond the bilateral scope.

Ladies and Gentlemen,

Brexit is a consequential event for the world. Although the Brexit negotiation is still on-going, some fear that Brexit will create uncertainties for China-UK business cooperation. However, I want to underscore this:

- The solid basis for China-UK business cooperation remains unchanged.
- The momentum of China-UK business cooperation remains unchanged.
- And the promising prospects for China-UK business cooperation remain unchanged.

As the situation unfolds, China-UK business cooperation faces three new opportunities.

The first is the strategic opportunity of China-UK partnership.

President Xi Jinping's successful state visit to the UK heralded our global comprehensive strategic partnership for the 21st century. During the G20 Hangzhou Summit in 2016 and the Hamburg Summit not long ago, President Xi and Prime Minister May reaffirmed the shared commitment to China-UK relations in their bilateral meetings.The frequent high level interactions and strengthening political mutual trust means there is strong political guidance for our relationship. And this will open a window of new opportunity for the business cooperation between our two countries.

Second, China and Britain can create the opportunity for common success if we match up our respective strengths.

China and Britain have respective advantages in development model, industrial structure and international division of labour, R&D and innovation, etc. We are at different stages of industrial adjustment and transition. Therefore there is much we can offer each other. In many areas the interests of our two countries converge and in more fields there is huge untapped potential for further cooperation. China is good at equipment building and has abundant financial resources. Britain is strong in innovation, R&D, high-end manufacturing and financial services. If we can work together and pool these strengths, we will achieve common success.

Moreover, Chinese businesses are enthusiastic about investing in Britain's infrastructure, branding, energy conservation and many other fields. Britain's commitment to free trade, your rule-based market, your sound legal system and your openness to Chinese investment, will all work in Britain's favour.

The third opportunity comes from China-UK cooperation on the Belt and Road.

As a new area of China-UK cooperation, the Belt and Road has huge business opportunities. Greater potentials remain to be tapped.

From the government to business community, from financial sector to academia, the rising enthusiasm for Belt and Road cooperation can be felt in this country. People from different industries are coming forward with their advice and suggestions.

In May, Chancellor Hammond attended the Belt and Road Forum for International Cooperation in Beijing as Prime Minister May's personal envoy. His participation brought new dynamics to China-UK Belt and Road cooperation.

CBBC and HSBC issued their Belt and Road reports, providing guidelines for British companies who are interested in the Belt and Road Initiative.

China regards Britain as a key partner in building the Belt and Road. Britain has rich experience in financial and legal services, project management and risk control. Our two countries can work to dovetail our development strategies and strengthen policy coordination within the framework of the Belt and Road. We could also engage in tripartite cooperation with countries along the Belt and Road. Such cooperation could become a new highlight.

Ladies and Gentlemen,

Thanks to our concerted efforts, China-UK business cooperation has produced fruitful results over the years. We can all look to an even brighter future.

However, given the rising anti-globalization and protectionism, we must stay true to our commitment, work together to remove obstacles and focus on the way ahead.

We should devote our efforts to making sure that our cooperation enjoys healthy and sound environments, which I have summarized as "four environments", namely, the political environment, the policy environment, the public opinion environment and the international environment.

First, the political environment.

Sound political environment is the precondition for growing state-to-state ties. It is fundamentally important to advance trade and investment cooperation.

In state-to-state relations, China has always valued the ideas of "peace being of paramount importance" and "harmony without uniformity".

Countries may differ in social system and ideology. But in dealing with each other, we should focus on what we have in common and seek shared interests.

China believes countries should learn from each other through exchanges and communication, build common grounds and engage in win-win cooperation.

As President Xi rightly put it, "Those who share the same ideal and follow the same path can be partners. Those who seek common ground while shelving differences can also be partners."

China and Britain should always view each other as equal partners and treat each other with respect. We should enhance mutual understanding on the basis of tolerance. We should build up mutual trust with an open mind. We should forge friendship as we deal with each other.

We should, at any time, approach our bilateral ties from a long-term strategic perspective. This requires us to always respect each other's core interests and major concerns. This also calls on both sides to deal with differences and sensitive issues in a constructive way.

Above all, China and Britain should build a sound political environment which will enable China-UK relations to endure.

Second, the policy environment.

Prime Minister May reiterated the UK's commitment to building a truly "global Britain". This means the UK will continue to support free trade, oppose protectionism, and actively develop and reinforce business ties with global partners.

We look forward to a Britain that continues to be open. The UK's commitment to staying open will send out a positive signal and help build up world confidence in Britain's future.

It is our hope that Britain will continue to be non-discriminative and transparent in its policy-making with regard to foreign investment. Policy-makers should take into account the legitimate rights and interests of all investors including the Chinese businesses. I hope that the policy environment in Britain will continue to be open, fair and predictable.

Third, the public opinion environment.

I noted that the British media focuses considerable attention on the Chinese development. But some of their reports on China are based on misunderstanding and prejudice.

Take for example the alleged "threat of Chinese investment." The so-called China's appetite to buy out Britain is pure fabrication. As for the claim that Chinese investment poses danger to the UK's national security, such demonization is groundless and harmful not only to Chinese companies but also to the UK.

Last month I wrote an article on this topic for the *Evening Standards*. I hope my article will help you see that Chinese investment in Britain is not China's gain at the cost of Britain's loss. It is not a China-win-Britain-lose scenario. Rather, Chinese investment in the UK is mutually beneficial.

I would like to highlight that, Chinese companies are here for cooperation and win-win results. They expect a friendly and welcoming environment for foreign businesses not only in policies and rules, but also in public opinions. I hope they will find what they are looking for here in Britain. I hope their decision to put their money here will prove to be a right one.

Fourth, the international environment.

At present, the world economy is showing some positive momentum. But on the whole, global economic and financial uncertainties and instabilities are still on the rise. Some deep-rooted problems remain unresolved.

President Xi said this at this year's World Economic Forum:

"We must remain committed to developing global free trade and investment, promote trade and investment liberalization and facilitation through opening-up and say no to protectionism."

China always stands ready to strengthen collaboration with the UK in the field of international governance. Our two countries must work together to uphold economic globalization, trade liberalization and investment facilitation. We must join hands to lead the international community in a joint response to challenges. This is what our two countries can do to contribute our part to building a global economy that is innovative, invigorated, interconnected and inclusive.

Ladies and Gentlemen,

In China people often say:

"A single twig is easy to snap but a bunch of twigs is too strong to break."

In face of the complicated, profound adjustment of international landscape and the daunting global challenges, China and Britain have every reason to enhance coordination and address challenges hand in hand.

The Conservative Parliamentary China Group has long been engaged in strengthening China-UK exchanges and cooperation. You have made active efforts in facilitating parliamentary communications and business cooperation between our two countries.

This year marks the 45th anniversary of China-UK ambassadorial diplomatic relations. It is also a year for consolidating China-UK relations.

- I hope the Conservative Parliamentary China Group will continue to play a constructive role.
- I hope China and Britain will continue to stay open and embrace the principles of openness, inclusiveness and win-win cooperation.
- I hope we will work together to seize the three opportunities and ensure four sound environments as I elaborated a moment ago.
- And I am confident that our shared commitment and joint efforts will enable China-UK business cooperation to bear more fruits and deliver more benefits to the people of our two countries and beyond.

Thank you!

把握新时代，开创新局面，迈上新台阶 *

尊敬的伦敦金融城市长鲍满诚先生，

各位来宾，

女士们、先生们：

今天是 2018 年 1 月 18 日，在中国文化里，"18"预示着吉祥如意、发家致富、大展宏图，两个"18"更是非常吉利的象征。

在这样一个吉祥的日子，出席由英国、中国商会举办的中英经济贸易论坛很有意义。我期待与中英工商界人士一道，共商中英关系的大发展，共谋两国经贸合作的大繁荣。

前不久，我回国出席 2017 年度驻外使节工作会议。习近平主席在接见使节们时指出，放眼世界，我们面对的是百年未有之大变局；世界多极化加速发展，国际格局日趋均衡，国际潮流大势不可逆转。正是在这样一个大发展大变革大调整的时代，中英伙伴关系步入加速发展的"快车道"。

回首 2017 年，我们充满获得感。中英以庆祝两国建立大使级外交关系 45 周年为主线，推动中英关系克服诸多不确定、不稳定因素，实现平稳健康发展。两国领导人在二十国集团领导人汉堡峰会期间举行会晤，并多次通话和互致信函。中英高级别人文交流机制会议、经济财金对话相继成功举行，取得丰硕成果。中英关系的战略定位更加清晰，双方政治互信进一步加强，合作内涵更加充实。

---

* 在中英经济贸易论坛上的主旨演讲。2018 年 1 月 18 日，伦敦金融城。

一年来，中英双方在贸易、核电、运输、金融、人文等领域合作均取得重要成果。2017年1—10月中英双边贸易额达651亿美元，英国对华出口同比上升11.3%，中国继续是英国增长最快的出口市场之一。欣克利角项目主体工程开工建设，"华龙一号"技术通用设计审查进入第二阶段。首趟义乌往返伦敦中欧班列开通，实现了中英贸易物流全陆地运输，使"一带一路"延伸到欧洲最西端。中国农业银行、浦发银行申请伦敦分行牌照获得英国监管机构批准，中国银行私人银行服务中心正式开业。

展望2018年，我们充满期待。2018年是中国全面贯彻中共十九大精神的开局之年，是中国改革开放40周年，也是"一带一路"倡议提出5周年。对中英关系而言，2018年也是十分重要的一年。特雷莎·梅首相即将对华访问，这是当前中英关系的重头戏。中英双方对此访都十分重视，期待以此为契机在更大范围、更高水平、更深层次推动中英互利合作。为此，我们应抓住"三大机遇"。

第一，抓住中国特色社会主义新时代机遇，推动中英关系行稳致远。

中共十九大报告指出，中国特色社会主义进入了新时代。这是中国发展新的历史方位，也标志着中国踏上全面建设社会主义现代化国家新征程。中国经济发展进入新时代的一个基本特征是，中国经济已由高速增长阶段转向高质量发展阶段。未来中国将贯彻新发展理念，加快建设创新型国家，建设现代化经济体系。同时，新时代意味着中国将日益走近世界舞台中央，日益为人类做出新的更大贡献。中国将深化全方位外交布局，拓展全球伙伴关系网，推动构建新型国际关系，推动构建人类命运共同体。

中英关系始终走在中国与西方国家关系前列。中国一贯坚持从战略高度和长远角度看待和发展中英关系，期待与英国加强战略对接，深化在政治、经济、人文以及全球治理等各领域务实合作，实现共同发展。正如梅首相2017年11月在金融城演讲中所说，英中携手可塑造世界格局。我相信，随着中国发展进入新时代，中英关系将面临新的历史性机遇和更加广阔的发展空间。

第二，抓住中国改革开放新阶段的机遇，为中英经贸合作提质升级注入新动力。

改革开放是当代中国发展进步的必由之路。2018 年是中国改革开放 40 周年。40 年来，改革开放使中国跃升为世界第二大经济体、第二大货物贸易国、第三大吸引外资国和第二大对外投资国，中国取得举世瞩目的发展成就。中国现在是世界上 124 个国家的最大贸易伙伴国，近年来每年为世界经济增长贡献率超过 30%。新的一年，中国将以庆祝改革开放 40 周年为契机，逢山开路，遇水架桥，将改革进行到底，将开放进一步扩大。一方面，我们将深化供给侧结构性改革，激发各类市场主体活力，积极推动政府职能转变，构建系统完备、科学规范、运行有效的制度体系；另一方面，我们将坚持"引进来"与"走出去"并重，实行高水平的贸易和投资自由化便利化政策，发展更高层次的开放型经济，推动形成全面开放新格局，促进贸易平衡，有效引导支持对外投资。

中英经贸合作基础良好，具有很强的互补性。中国的改革开放进程将继续为两国深化在经贸、基础设施、装备制造、高科技、新能源、金融服务等领域合作提供源源不断的动力。2017 年以来，中国推出一系列对外开放新举措，大幅度放宽市场准入，特别是服务业扩大开放进展明显。中方决定放宽外国投资者投资证券、基金、期货公司的投资比例限制，实施内外一致的银行业股权投资比例规则，还将在未来取消外资投资人身保险业务的投资比例限制。英国企业在相关领域优势突出，可抢抓合作机遇，积极赴华投资兴业，实现互利共赢。中国将于 2018 年 11 月在上海举办首届国际进口博览会，欢迎英国企业赴华参展参会，开拓双边贸易增长点。

第三，抓住"一带一路"合作机遇，打造中英引领全球开放型经济建设新平台。

"一带一路"倡议是中国实行全方位对外开放的重大举措，也是共同促进地区及全球发展振兴的重要公共产品。倡议提出五年来，以和平合作、开放包容、互学互鉴、互利共赢为核心的丝路精神在国际社会产生广泛共鸣，吸引了各国共同参与"一带一路"建设，成果丰硕，前景广阔。中国将继续积极促进"一带一路"国际合作，努力实现政策沟通、设施联通、贸易畅通、资金融通、民心相通，推动生产要素更加有序流动，资源配置效率不断提高，市场资源持续融合。

作为全球对贸易和投资最开放、最自由的大国之一，英国是"一带一路"建设的"天然合作伙伴"。英国不仅是第一个申请加入亚洲基础设施投资银行的西方大国，还是继中国之后第二个向亚投行专门基金注资的国家。2017年12月第九次中英经济财金对话期间，两国达成一系列重要合作共识，包括中英将成立首期10亿美元中英双边投资基金，以商业化和市场化为基础建立和运作，支持中英两国及第三方市场的投资机会。相信在双方共同努力下，中英"一带一路"不仅能为两国企业开拓地区及国际市场创造更多机会和平台，还能为促进全球贸易和投资自由化便利化，推动经济全球化朝着更加开放、包容、普惠、平衡、共赢的方向发展做出积极贡献。

女士们、先生们，

习近平主席在2018年的新年贺词中说，不驰于空想、不骛于虚声。无论机遇有多大、动力有多强、平台有多宽广，都需要我们一步一个脚印，踏踏实实地去落实。在此，我想提三点建议。

一是进一步推动两国发展战略对接。中方"一带一路"倡议与英"全球化英国"、现代产业战略等政策高度契合，将给两国企业深化合作带来更多机遇。希望双方继续积极推动战略对接，加强政策协调，为两国企业开展经贸合作创造更加优质的制度环境和政策保障。

二是进一步提升两国合作水平。英国在金融、法律、高端制造、清洁能源、创意产业、生命科学及医药等领域经验丰富，优势明显。中国市场巨大，经济结构不断优化，数字经济等新兴产业蓬勃发展，创新驱动发展战略有效实施，成果丰硕。希望中英两国企业家继续深挖合作潜力，拓展贸易投资合作，扩大产业和创新合作，真正实现优势互补和共同发展。

三是进一步丰富两国开展三方合作的内涵。中英共建"一带一路"潜力巨大、前景广阔。希望两国企业家加强"一带一路"框架下务实合作、探索第三方市场合作，将自身优势与"一带一路"建设需求相结合，与"一带一路"共建国家密切沟通协作，打造更多合作品牌和亮点，推动三方乃至多方互利共赢。

女士们、先生们，

九层之台，起于累土。我衷心期待，中英企业界能抓住新时代赋予我们的宝贵机遇，脚踏实地，开拓创新，齐心协力，为推动中英经贸合作不断迈上新台阶做出新贡献！

最后，预祝本次中英经济贸易论坛取得圆满成功！

谢谢大家！

Embrace New Era, Open up New Prospects and Scale New Heights*

Lord Mayer Alderman Charles Bowman,

Distinguished Guests,

Ladies and Gentlemen,

Good afternoon.

Today is a special day.

In the Chinese culture, 18 is a lucky number. It is believed to promise good fortune, thriving business and bright prospects. Today is January 18, 2018. With these two 18's I am sure our good luck will double.

So, on this auspicious day, I wish to say how delighted I am to join you for the China-UK Economic and Trade Forum organized by the China Chamber of Commerce in the UK. I look forward to lively discussions with you. And I hope this gathering of Chinese and British entrepreneurs will generate some productive ideas—ideas that will boost trade and economic cooperation between our two countries and advance China-UK relations as a whole.

Less than three weeks ago, I was called back to Beijing, as did all the Chinese diplomatic envoys from every corner of the world, for an annual conference. We had an important meeting with President Xi Jinping, where he shared with us his thoughts on the world today.

President Xi said, we are now in a world of unprecedented change. Accelerated

---

* Keynote Speech at the China-UK Economic and Trade Forum. City of London, 18 January 2018.

multi-polarization and increasing equilibrium in the international landscape have become an irreversible trend.

This is a time of great progress, tremendous transformation and profound adjustments. This is the big picture against which China and the UK have embarked on a fast track in building China-UK partnership.

As we look back at 2017, we have every reason to be proud.

We commemorated the 45th anniversary of the ambassadorial diplomatic ties.

We withstood uncertainties and maintained a sound and steady momentum in China-UK relations.

President Xi and Prime Minister May held a successful meeting during the G20 Summit in Hamburg. They also stayed in touch through letters and telephone calls.

The annual meetings of China-UK High-Level People-to-People Dialogue and the Economic and Financial Dialogue produced fruitful results.

China and the UK reconfirmed the strategic definition of the relationship, enhanced political trust, and enriched bilateral cooperation.

The year 2017 has seen fruitful results across the board, from trade to transport, from nuclear power to financial services and from cultural collaboration to people-to-people exchanges.

By October 2017, China-UK trade reached 65.1 billion US dollars, with British export to China increasing by 11.3% year on year. China remains one of the fastest growing export markets for the UK.

The construction of Hinkley Point C nuclear power station has begun. At the centre of this project, the generic design assessment of Hualong One technology has entered the second stage.

China Railway Express ran its first freight train between the Chinese Yiwu and London. This offered a new, on-land option for the movement of goods between China and Britain, and extended the Belt and Road to the very western end of Europe.

Here in the City, the Bank of China opened its Private Banking Service Centre. Applications from Agricultural Bank of China and Shanghai Pudong Development Bank to set up branches got the go-ahead from British financial regulators.

In 2018, we have a great deal to look forward to.

In China, this year will be the opening year for the implementation of the blueprint of the 19th National Congress of the Communist Party of China. It also marks the 40th anniversary of the Chinese reform and opening-up policy and the fifth anniversary of the Belt and Road Initiative.

For China-UK relations, 2018 is also an important year. Prime Minister May will pay an official visit to China. This is now high on the agenda of our bilateral relations.

Both China and the UK attach great importance to this visit. Both want to take this opportunity to expand, elevate and deepen our mutually-beneficial cooperation.

To achieve this goal, we need to seize three important opportunities.

The socialism with Chinese characteristics in a new era creates our first opportunity. This will ensure that China-UK relations is steady and will endure.

The 19th National Congress of the Communist Party of China points out that socialism with Chinese characteristics has entered a new era. This is a new historic juncture in the Chinese development. It marks the beginning of a new journey to build a modern socialist country in all respects.

The Chinese economic development has also entered a new era. This is marked by the transition from high-speed growth to high-quality growth.

China will follow a new development concept;

Growth will be driven by innovation;

And our economic system will be modernized.

This will also be a new era for the Chinese global role. China will increasingly take centre stage and make greater contribution to mankind.

China will deepen all-round diplomacy;

China will expand its global partnership network;

And China will promote the building of a new-type of international relations and a community with a shared future for mankind.

China-UK relations have always been a leader in the Chinese relations with other Western countries.

China has sought to develop its relations with the UK from a strategic and long-term perspective.

We hope to make our development strategies match with that of the UK.

We aim to deepen China-UK cooperation in political and economic areas, cultural and people-to-people exchanges, and global governance.

Working together, our two countries can achieve common development.

We are delighted by the message from the British side. Prime Minister May said this at the Lord Mayor's banquet last November:

"I am committed to maintaining the partnership with China... whose decisions together with ours will shape the world around us."

I believe as the Chinese development enters a new era, China-UK partnership will embrace new historic opportunities and more promising prospects.

Now, let me turn to the second opportunity. The Chinese reform and opening-up has come to a new stage. This will create a new driving force for upgrading trade and economic cooperation between China and the UK. This is the second opportunity that we must seize.

For China today, reform and opening-up is the only road leading towards growth and progress. Our forty years of experience has proven that this is the right way. We owe our breathtaking development to reform and opening-up.

Thanks to reform and opening-up, China is now the world's second largest economy, the second largest trader in goods, the third largest destination for foreign investment, and the second largest outbound investor in the world.

Also thanks to reform and opening-up, China is now the largest trading partner for 124 countries. It has contributed over 30% to world economic growth every year in recent years.

As we celebrate the 40th anniversary of reform and opening-up this year, China will be further resolved to "cut through mountains and bridge over waters" in order to deepen the reform and open wider to the world.

On reform, we will deepen supply-side structural reform and bring out the vim and vigour of various market entities. At the same time, we will transform the functions of governments, and put in place a system of rules and regulations that are well conceived, fully developed and effective.

On opening-up, we will continue to open our doors and encourage two-way traffic.

We will take measures to increase trade and investment liberalization and facilitation.

Our aim is to open up our economy at a higher level and in all aspects, promote balanced trade, and effectively guide and support out-bound investment.

I am glad to say that China and the UK have highly complementary economies.

Our economic cooperation and trade are solidly based and will be further powered by continued and deepening of reform and opening-up in China. Sectors that stand to benefit range from trade, infrastructure, equipment manufacturing to high-tech, new energy and financial services.

Let me give you an example. Last year, China adopted a series of new opening-up measures. These measures have greatly increased market access, especially in the service sector. They include:

- Raising the limit on foreign ownership in joint-venture firms involved in the securities, fund and futures market.
- Treating domestic and foreign investors as equals in terms of ownership in joint ventures in the banking sector.
- And gradually in the near future, removing caps on foreign ownership in life insurance business.

In all these areas, British companies have a competitive edge. Therefore, I encourage you to grab this opportunity and build up your business in China. I am sure both China and Britain will benefit from it.

Later this year, in November, the Chinese first International Import Expo will open in Shanghai. British companies are most welcome there to explore new area to grow our bilateral trade.

The third opportunity comes from the Belt and Road Initiative. Seizing this Initiative will give China and the UK a new platform and from this platform, we can go on to take the lead in an open global economy.

The Belt and Road Initiative represents a major effort of China to open up on all fronts. It is also an important public good that China provides to the region and the whole world. It is a public good for common development and global economic recovery.

This Initiative embodies the spirit of peace and cooperation. It calls for openness and inclusiveness. It advocates mutual learning and mutual benefit.

In the past five years since its inception, the Belt and Road Initiative showed enormous appeal all over the world. It has by far attracted wide participation and delivered fruitful results.

There is certainly a lot more to be expected going forward. China will continue to work vigorously to advance international cooperation along the Belt and Road. Through such cooperation, we will strive for connectivity in policy, infrastructure, trade, finance and people-to-people exchanges. This will in turn allow production factors to flow in a more orderly manner, enable more efficient allocation of resources and deliver the benefit of a better integrated market.

The UK is known for being open and free in trade and investment. It is, in the words of Chancellor Hammond, "a natural partner" in the Belt and Road Initiative. In fact, we have seen a few pioneering efforts in this respect.

The UK is the first major Western country to apply to join the Asian Infrastructure Investment Bank and the second country after China to contribute to an AIIB special fund.

During the ninth meeting of China-UK Economic and Financial Dialogue held in December 2017, our two countries reached important agreements. This includes agreement on the establishment of a bilateral investment fund, with an initial input of 1 billion US dollars. This commercially-based and market-oriented fund aims to support investment in the two countries as well as in potential third market.

I am confident that with our concerted efforts, China-UK cooperation on the Belt and Road Initiative will deliver more benefits.

It will create more opportunities and platforms for our companies to explore regional and international market.

It will advance trade and investment liberalization and facilitation around the world.

And it will contribute to making economic globalization more open, inclusive, balanced and universally beneficial.

Ladies and Gentlemen,

I believe I have painted a grand picture of huge opportunities, strong driving forces and broad platforms. However, as President Xi said in his New Year message, we must not indulge in mere dreams or rhetoric.

The more important thing we need to do is to adopt a down-to-earth attitude and deliver solid outcomes to translate this dream into reality. In this regard, may I share with you my three suggestions.

First, we need to match our development strategies.

There is a strong match between the Chinese Belt and Road Initiative, and the "global Britain" and Modern Industrial Strategy of the UK in terms of the goals they set out to achieve. This creates opportunities for companies from the two countries to deepen cooperation.

To help them seize these opportunities, I hope our two sides will continue to make our development strategies match and enhance policy coordination. This will provide a high-quality institutional environment and policy guarantee for companies to engage in economic and trade cooperation.

Second, we need to upgrade our cooperation to a higher level.

The UK is highly experienced and competitive in financial and legal services, high-end manufacturing, clean energy, creative industry, bio-science and medicine.

While in China, on top of a huge market, our economic structure is being improved, new sectors such as digital economy are thriving, and the innovation-driven development strategy has been effective and delivered fruitful results.

I look forward to continued efforts from you, both Chinese and British entrepreneurs, to put your strengths together. There is huge potential to be tapped in expanding trade and investment and enhancing industrial and innovation cooperation. Together, we could achieve common development.

My third suggestion is to enrich tripartite cooperation.

China and the UK have a huge potential and promising future in Belt and Road cooperation.

It is my hope that both Chinese and British businesses will step up practical cooperation under this framework and work together to explore a third market along the Belt and Road.

I encourage you to put your respective strengths to use as you work to meet the need of Belt and Road development.

I encourage you to go out there to connect with the countries along the Belt and Road.

I hope that in the process of cooperation, you could build your brand name and create the highlights of your business.

This will deliver win-win results to more than just China and Britain. This will benefit three or even more parties involved.

Ladies and Gentlemen,

As a Chinese saying goes, a nine-storey tower rises up from a pile of soil.

Building China-UK cooperation requires the same down-to-earth approach.

I sincerely hope that the business communities of our two countries will act in this spirit, seize the valuable opportunities of this new era, embrace new ideas and break new ground.

I am sure, by working together, we will make new contribution to and scale new heights in China-UK economic and trade cooperation.

To conclude, I wish the China-UK Economic and Trade Forum a complete success!

Thank you!

继往开来，携手奋进，筑牢中英合作共赢之路 *

尊敬的英国国际贸易部国务大臣斯图尔特先生，
尊敬的英国四十八家集团俱乐部主席佩里先生，
尊敬的英国政府"一带一路"特使范智廉爵士，
各位来宾，女士们、先生们：

大家下午好！

很高兴出席由英国中国商会主办的"庆祝中华人民共和国成立 70 周年暨第二届中英经贸论坛"。中英经贸论坛是两国工商界人士交流思想、对接需求、畅谈合作、共促发展的重要平台。今天的论坛，也是庆祝新中国成立 70 周年系列活动的一场重头戏。

2019 年是新中国成立 70 周年，也是中英建立代办级外交关系 65 周年，可谓是一个承前启后、继往开来的重要年份，具有特殊意义。今天，我想利用这个论坛谈谈如何承前启后，继往开来。

首先，我们从中英经贸合作的历史中得到许多启示，主要有四条。

一是相互尊重，维护大局。65 年来，在双方共同努力下，中英关系历经风雨、砥砺前行，战略性、务实性、全球性和包容性日益凸显。中英社会制度、文化传统不同，双方在一些问题上存在不同看法很正常。关键是双方要着眼大局，超越差异，切实照顾彼此核心利益和重大关切，正确看待和妥善处理分歧。中英关系的发展历程表明，只要双方尊重彼此核心利益和重大关

---

* 在"第二届中英经贸论坛"上的主旨演讲。2019 年 6 月 26 日，伦敦金融城市政厅。

切，平等相待，求同存异，中英关系就能保持正确方向，两国经贸合作之路就能越走越稳，越走越宽。

二是优势互补，战略对接。英国拥有世界领先的金融业，在设计、工程、金融和法律服务等领域经验丰富、优势突出。中国经过几十年的发展，不仅成为世界第一制造大国，而且成为世界第一贸易大国。中国不断开放的市场和日益完善的营商环境将为包括英国在内的全球伙伴提供互利共赢的机遇。近年来，中英两国加强战略沟通和政策协调，中方"一带一路"倡议、"十三五"规划与英国现代产业战略和"全球化英国"等政策进行有效对接，为两国企业深化经贸合作创造更良好的制度环境和政策保障。相信双方深挖合作潜力，发挥各自技术、产业和制度优势，必将更好地推动两国共同发展。

三是开放包容，互利共赢。新中国成立70年来，特别是改革开放40多年来，中国得出的一条重要经验就是，开放才能进步，封闭必然落后；发展中遇到的问题，只有通过开放合作才能解决；搞"本国优先""关起门来过日子"，不仅违背历史潮流，也终将错失发展机遇。英国素来秉持开放包容理念，倡导自由贸易，主张开放合作。我希望并相信，英国能顶住外来压力，继续为中国企业提供公正、公平、透明的营商环境。中英都是具有全球影响的大国，都致力于推进自由贸易和开放合作，都致力于推动世界经济强劲、可持续、平衡、包容增长。在当前保护主义盛行、单边主义抬头的背景下，中英应携手努力，对外发出反对保护主义、支持开放合作的强烈信号，为建设开放型世界经济贡献力量。

四是民亲心通，厚植民意。65年来，无论世事如何变迁，两国人民之间的友谊始终坚如磐石。目前，中英人文交流亮点纷呈，两国航线增多，友城覆盖面广，教育合作密切，给两国人民带来了实实在在的福祉。促进民心相通、夯实民意基础，不仅是中英两国政府的职责，也是两国企业家的责任。我希望两国工商界人士携手共担，为增进中英了解与互信，为促进两国民心相通与相亲做出应有贡献。

其次，我想谈谈中英经贸合作的未来，重要的是要抓住三大机遇。

一是牢牢抓住第四次工业革命浪潮的时代机遇。以 5G+ 物联网技术、人工智能、量子计算、大数据、新材料为代表的第四次工业革命正在引领新一轮经济全球化浪潮，移动互联网日益普及，国际空间距离不断拉近，高科技研发日新月异。在此背景下，中国正大力推行创新驱动发展战略，深化供给侧结构性改革，推动互联网、大数据、人工智能和实体经济深度融合，加快建设创新型国家。英国是科技强国，高度重视科学和创新，将其置于长期经济发展规划的核心。我希望中英加强合作，携手走在数字化、网络化、智能化潮流的前沿，推动两国经贸合作转型升级，从资金、产品上的相互"输血"走向技术上的相互"造血"，为双方合作共赢之路注入更多动力。

二是牢牢抓住中国新一轮高水平对外开放的政策机遇。习近平主席在第二届"一带一路"国际合作高峰论坛上宣布，中国将采取一系列重大改革开放举措，加强制度性、结构性安排，促进更高水平对外开放。这意味着中国将在更广领域扩大外资市场准入。中国已经实施准入前国民待遇加负面清单管理模式，未来将继续大幅缩减负面清单，推动现代服务业、制造业、农业全方位对外开放，并在更多领域允许外资控股或独资经营；将加快制定配套法规，确保严格实施《中华人民共和国外商投资法》。这意味着中国要更大力度加强知识产权保护国际合作，全面完善知识产权保护法律体系，加强对外国知识产权人合法权益的保护，杜绝强制技术转让，完善商业秘密保护，依法严厉打击知识产权侵权行为。这意味着中国将更大规模增加商品和服务进口。中国既是"世界工厂"，也是"世界市场"，拥有世界上规模最大、成长最快的中等收入群体，消费增长潜力巨大。中国将进一步降低关税水平，消除各种非关税壁垒，进一步打开中国市场大门，欢迎来自世界各国的高质量产品与服务。这必将为包括英国在内的世界各国企业提供更多机遇。第二届中国国际进口博览会将于 2019 年 11 月在上海举办，欢迎英国企业积极参与。

三是牢牢抓住"一带一路"建设的平台机遇。6 年来，在各方共同努力下，"一带一路"建设进展顺畅，"六廊六路多国多港"的互联互通架构基本形成，一大批合作项目落地生根，160 多个国家和国际组织同中国签署"一带一路"合作协议。从亚欧大陆到非洲、美洲、大洋洲，共建"一带一路"

为世界经济增长开辟了新空间，为国际贸易和投资搭建了新平台，为完善全球经济治理拓展了新实践，为增进各国民生福祉做出了新贡献，成为世界各国共同的机遇之路、繁荣之路。中英"一带一路"合作潜力巨大，前景广阔。2019年4月，哈蒙德财政大臣作为梅首相特别代表，出席了第二届"一带一路"国际合作高峰论坛。他指出，英方愿将英国在设计、法律、技术、金融等领域的优势与中国在制造、工程、建设等领域的优势强强联合。上周，双方签署了关于开展第三方市场合作谅解备忘录，并就探索吸引私人部门资金参与"一带一路"建设的融资机制达成共识。我坚信，未来"一带一路"高质量发展必将为中英关系在更大范围、更高水平、更深层次发展提供更多新机遇，为中英深化在国际标准、绿色金融、风险管理、第三方市场等领域合作创造更大空间。

女士们、先生们、朋友们，

"潮平两岸阔，风正一帆悬。"站在新中国70年奋斗史和中英关系65年发展史的新起点上，我希望中英两国企业家坚持从战略高度和长远角度看待中英经贸合作，抓住机遇，齐心协力，共筑中英经贸合作共赢之路！

谢谢！

Build on Past Achievements and Join Hands to Enhance China-UK Win-Win Cooperation*

Minister Graham Stuart,

Chairman Stephen Perry,

Sir Douglas Flint,

Distinguished Guests,

Ladies and Gentlemen,

Good afternoon!

It is a real delight to join you for the second China-UK Economic and Trade Forum hosted by China Chamber of Commerce in the UK.

This Forum has always been an important platform for business leaders from both countries to exchange ideas, assess needs, and discuss cooperation and development.

Today's Forum is more than that. It is part of this year's celebration of the 70th anniversary of the People's Republic of China. So allow me to say what a great pleasure it is to join you to mark this important anniversary.

This year also marks the 65th anniversary of the establishment of China-UK diplomatic relationship at the level of chargé d'affaires. So, it is a significant time for us to reflect on past achievements and look into the future.

First, what have we learned from China-UK business cooperation over the past

---

* Keynote Speech at the second China-UK Economic and Trade Forum. Guildhall, City of London, 26 June 2019.

years?

In my view, there are four main lessons. The first lesson is that we should always respect each other and keep the larger picture in mind.

In the past 65 years, thanks to the concerted efforts of both sides, the China-UK relationship has forged ahead despite winds and rains. Now this relationship has become increasingly strategic, pragmatic, global and inclusive.

China and the UK differ in social system and cultural tradition. It is natural that we do not always see eye to eye. What is important is that we keep the larger picture in mind and see beyond our differences. We should take concrete steps to accommodate each other's core interests and major concerns, and handle our differences properly.

China and the UK have come this far in developing our relationship because we are always able to respect each other's core interests and major concerns, treat each other as equals and seek common ground despite differences. That is why we have been able to keep our relationship on the right track. That is also why our business cooperation has been making steady progress and will have a broad prospect.

The second lesson is that we should leverage our comparative strengths and match our strategies.

The UK is a world leader in financial services. It also has rich experience and unique advantages in design, engineering and legal services.

After decades of development, China is now the world's largest manufacturer and largest trading country. Its increasingly open market and friendly business environment will create mutually-beneficial opportunities for global partners including the UK.

In recent years, China and the UK have increased dialogue on strategies and coordination on policies. There is an effective match between the Chinese Belt and Road Initiative, the 13th Five-Year Plan, and the UK's Modern Industrial Strategy and "global Britain" strategy. This has provided a sound institutional environment and strong policy guarantee for Chinese and British companies to deepen cooperation.

I am confident that our two countries will achieve common progress by further tapping the potential of cooperation and leveraging our technological, industrial and institutional strengths.

The third lesson is that we should stay open and inclusive, and engage in win-win cooperation.

The past 70 years since the founding of New China, especially the more than 4 decades of reform and opening-up, have taught us an important lesson, that is, openness is the only road to progress and isolation leads to backwardness.

Any problem that we encounter in development can only be solved through open cooperation. "Putting one's own country first" and "closing the door to the world" not only go against the trend of the times, but also result in missed opportunities.

The UK has always upheld openness, inclusiveness, free trade and cooperation. I hope and believe that the UK can resist external pressure and continue to provide a just, fair and transparent business environment for Chinese companies.

China and the UK are both major countries of global influence. We both uphold free trade and open cooperation. And we are both committed to robust, sustainable, balanced and inclusive growth of world economy.

Amid rising protectionism and unilateralism, it is all the more important that China and the UK join hands to send out a loud message about our opposition to protectionism and support for open cooperation. This will be our contribution to building an open world economy.

The fourth lesson is that we should strengthen the bond between our people and cement public support for China-UK relations.

The world has changed tremendously in the past 65 years, but the friendship between the Chinese and British people has remained strong as ever.

China-UK cultural and people-to-people exchanges have produced numerous highlights. There are more flights linking our two countries. There are more sister relations linking our cities. There is closer cooperation on education. And all these have delivered tangible benefits to our people.

The responsibility of building a closer bond between our people and cementing public support for our relations lies with not only the governments. The responsibility also lies with you, the business leaders of our two countries.

Therefore, it is my hope that members of Chinese and British business communities will join hands to enhance understanding and mutual trust between our two countries and make your contribution to building a closer bond between our people.

Now, let's look into the future of China-UK business cooperation. I think there are three major opportunities.

The first opportunity is the fourth industrial revolution.

The new technologies in this revolution, including 5G+the Internet of Things, artificial intelligence, quantum computing, big data and new materials, are leading a new round of economic globalization featuring wide application of mobile internet, shorter travel time and constant progress in high-tech.

Against this backdrop, China is pursuing innovation-driven development, deepening supply-side structural reform and promoting integration of the internet, big data and AI into the real economy. The goal is to build a country strong in innovation.

The UK is strong in technology. Science and innovation have always been given great importance and are placed at the centre of the UK's long-term development strategy.

It is my hope that our two countries could join hands to take the lead in digital, cyber and smart technology application so as to upgrade our business cooperation from trade in capital and product to mutual learning of advanced technology. This will provide more impetus for the win-win cooperation between our two countries.

The second opportunity lies in the Chinese new round of higher-quality opening-up.

President Xi Jinping announced at the second Belt and Road Forum for International Cooperation that China will take a series of important reform and opening-up measures and make stronger institutional and structural moves to boost higher-quality opening up.

Higher-quality opening-up means that China will increase market access for foreign capital in wider areas. On top of the existing management model known as pre-establishment national treatment plus a negative list, China will continue to shorten the list by a large margin to allow all dimensional access to modern services, manufacturing and agricultural sectors and approve foreign-controlled or wholly foreign-owned companies in more areas. China will also strictly enforce the Foreign Investment Law and speed up the making of supporting regulations.

Higher-quality opening-up also means that China will:

- enhance international cooperation on IPR protection,
- improve IPR-related legal system,
- safeguard the lawful rights and interests of foreign IP owners,

- prohibit forced technology transfer,
- step up protection of commercial secrets,
- and crack down on IPR infringement in accordance with law.

Higher-quality opening-up also means massive increase of import of goods and services.

China is not only the "factory of the world", but also a "market of the world". With the world's largest and fastest-growing middle-income population, China is a massive consumer market that promises enormous growth potential.

Going forward, China will cut tariffs further, remove non-tariff barriers and open its market wider to high-quality products and services from the world. This will create more opportunities for companies from all countries, including the UK.

This coming November, China will host the second China International Import Expo in Shanghai. We hope to see more British companies at the Expo.

The third opportunity is the Belt and Road Initiative.

In the past six years, thanks to the efforts of all the parties, BRI has made smooth progress.

- The basic framework of connectivity has been set up, consisting of six economic corridors, six routes, and ports in many countries.
- A large number of projects have been implemented.
- More than 160 countries and international organisations have signed agreements with China on BRI cooperation.

From the Eurasia Continent to Africa, from the Americas to Oceania, BRI is regarded as:

- A new space for world economic growth.
- A new platform for international trade and investment.
- A new endeavour to improve global economic governance.
- And a new contribution to better life for people of all countries.

It has become a road to opportunities and a road to prosperity for all countries in the world. China-UK cooperation on BRI promises enormous potential and broad prospects.

Last April, Chancellor Hammond attended the second Belt and Road Forum for International Cooperation as the special representative of Prime Minister May. He proposed to combine the best of British project design and legal, technical and financial services expertise with the best of Chinese manufacturing, engineering and construction.

Last week, at the 10th EFD, China and the UK signed an MOU on third market cooperation, and agreed to explore financing mechanisms to attract private investment to BRI.

I am confident that high-quality BRI development will create more opportunities for China-UK relations to develop in a wider scope, at a higher level and at greater depth. In specific, it will deepen China-UK cooperation in areas such as international standards-setting, green finance, risk management and third market development.

Ladies and Gentlemen,

Dear Friends,

I would like to quote an ancient Chinese poem to describe the promising prospects of China-UK cooperation:

"On the river wide at full tide; a sail with ease hangs in soft breeze."

After 70 years of strenuous efforts since the founding of the People's Republic of China, and after 65 years of China-UK diplomatic relations, we are standing at a new starting point.

I hope the business leaders from both our two countries will always take a strategic approach and long-term perspective in promoting China-UK business cooperation. I hope you will seize the opportunities and work hand in hand for win-win results.

Thank you!

胸怀大局，继往开来，深化合作 *

尊敬的英中贸易协会名誉主席沙逊勋爵，
尊敬的英中贸易协会主席古沛勤爵士，
女士们、先生们、朋友们：
大家上午好！

感谢英中贸易协会专门为我举办告别座谈会。在离任回国之际，很高兴有机会通过视频方式再次与英国工商界朋友畅叙友情，共话发展。

我从事外交工作47年，曾在非洲、美洲、亚洲、欧洲的6个国家常驻。出使英国11年，是我第三次担任中国驻外大使，也是我驻外时间最长的一次。我很荣幸地成为中英关系史上任期最长的中国驻英使节和中国历史上任期最长的驻外大使。

11年前，我刚刚来英履新不久，英中贸易协会在伦敦克拉里奇酒店为我举行了欢迎午宴。我在致辞中承诺，将以加强中英政治互信、深化两国各领域合作、扩大双方战略共识和利益为使命，推动中英关系不断向前发展。11年来，我夙夜在公，勤勉工作，忠实履行职责使命。

这11年，我们共同见证和推动中英互利合作引领新方向。2015年，习近平主席对英国进行"超级国事访问"，指明了中英关系和务实合作大方向。中英两国总理会晤、经济财金对话等高层对话机制，为中英合作注入了强劲动力。11年来，中英合作开风气之先，在中国与西方国家多个领域务实

---

* 在英中贸易协会告别座谈会上的演讲。2021年1月20日，中国驻英国大使馆。

合作中发挥了引领作用：英国在西方大国中第一个加入亚投行并向亚投行专门基金注资，第一个设立人民币结算中心，第一个发行人民币主权债券，第一个任命"一带一路"特使，第一个签署《"一带一路"融资指导原则》。

这11年，我们共同见证和推动中英贸易投资迈向新高度。一是双边贸易额快速增长。2010—2020年，中英双边货物贸易额从2010年的501亿美元增至924亿美元，特别是2020年在新冠疫情蔓延和国际贸易持续低迷的情况下，两国贸易额仍创历史新高。二是中英投资合作不断深入。截至2019年底，英国在华直接投资存量达253.9亿美元，中国对英直接投资存量达171.4亿美元，是2009年的约20倍，投资领域从传统行业向高端制造、信息科技、文化创意等新领域延伸，英国成为中国在欧洲第二大投资目的地国。三是大型项目取得重大进展。11年前，两国基本没有标志性的合作大项目；如今，在双方共同努力下，欣克利角C核电站、皇家阿尔伯特码头等多个中国在英投资旗舰项目正稳步推进。

这11年，我们共同见证和推动中英金融和"一带一路"合作取得新突破。中英积极推进绿色金融和金融科技等合作，在英设立分行的中资银行增加至8家；"沪伦通"正式开通，多家中资企业在伦交所上市，开中国与境外资本市场互联互通先河；伦敦成为世界第一大人民币离岸交易中心和第二大人民币离岸清算中心，人民币清算量超过50万亿元。英国将己作为"一带一路"的"天然合作伙伴"，两次派首相特别代表赴华出席"一带一路"国际合作高峰论坛；中英签署第三方市场合作协议，双方在第三方市场融资、提供专业技术与服务等方面积极开展合作。

女士们、先生们、朋友们，

中英互利合作的丰硕成果，给两国人民带来了实实在在的益处：中国投资的纯电动、低排放出租车驶上了伦敦街头；英国美食饮品通过"进博会"的平台走上了中国百姓餐桌；中国投资为英国当地创造了可观的税收和就业机会，也为英国企业转型升级和产业高质量发展提供了动力。展望未来，中英合作潜力巨大、前景广阔。我对此充满信心，也有三点期许。

一是要胸怀大局，互尊互信。历史告诉我们，只要相互尊重、平等相待、遵守国际法和国际关系基本准则，中英关系就会向前发展；反之则遭遇挫折，甚至倒退。一个健康稳定的中英关系，符合两国人民共同利益，也有利于世界的和平与发展。双方应着眼大局和长远，视彼此发展为机遇，而非挑战甚至威胁，始终尊重彼此核心利益和重大关切，推动中英关系持续健康发展，为深化两国务实合作创造良好条件。

二是要把握大势，坚定信心。当今世界正面临百年变局和世纪疫情的叠加冲击，单边主义、保护主义和逆全球化思潮抬头，不确定不稳定因素增多。中英合作机遇与挑战并存。我们要对经济全球化大趋势充满信心，对中国开放发展前景充满信心，对中英互利合作未来充满信心，共同高举自由贸易的旗帜，携手构建开放型世界经济，推动经济全球化朝着更加开放、包容、普惠、平衡、共赢方向发展。

三是要抓住机遇，深化合作。中英发展战略契合度高，经贸合作互补性强。当前，两国都处于新的重要发展时期：中国即将开启"十四五"规划新篇章，踏上全面建设社会主义现代化国家的新征程，加速构建国内国际双循环相互促进的新发展格局，推动高质量发展，实施更大范围、更宽领域、更深层次的全面开放。英国则完成"脱欧"，进入打造"全球化英国"和拓展全球合作伙伴的新阶段。中英应积极发挥各自优势，推进双方政策协调和战略对接，深化双方在贸易投资、基础设施、金融、高新科技等领域合作，打造更多合作成果，助力各自发展繁荣，更好地造福两国人民。

女士们、先生们、朋友们，

中英经贸合作今天取得的成就，离不开英中贸易协会和两国工商界人士的辛勤付出。多年来，英中贸易协会积极为中英两国工商界牵线搭桥，为双方深化务实合作献计献策。2020年疫情暴发以来，英中贸易协会协调两国企业和金融机构捐款捐物，两国工商界用实际行动演绎了中英携手抗疫、共克时艰的故事。借此机会，我谨对你们为推进中英合作所做贡献表示敬意！我还要特别感谢我的老朋友白乐威爵士、沙逊勋爵和古沛勤爵士，你们在过去11年先后担任英中贸易协会主席，为我在英履职提供了鼎力支持和帮助！

我衷心希望各位工商界朋友一如既往地关心中英关系发展，支持两国互利合作，支持中国驻英国大使馆和我的继任者新大使的工作，不断为中英关系稳定健康发展贡献智慧和力量。

再过 22 天，我们将迎来中国农历牛年春节。牛在中国文化中象征着忠诚勤劳、繁荣兴旺。借此机会，我给大家拜个早年，祝愿各位身体健康、事业兴旺，祝愿我们的友谊地久天长！

谢谢大家！

Keep Big Picture in Mind and Deepen Cooperation*

Lord Sassoon,
Sir Sherard,
Ladies and Gentlemen,
Dear Friends,
Good morning!

Let me begin with a big thank you to the China Britain Business Council (CBBC) for hosting this special roundtable for me to bid farewell.

It is a real delight to meet you again online to renew our friendship and talk about opportunities for development before I complete my tour of office and leave for China.

In my diplomatic career of 47 years, I have had 6 overseas postings on 4 continents: Africa, America, Asia and Europe. The 11 years spent in the UK constitute my third tour as Chinese Ambassador and the longest of my overseas postings. It is indeed an honour to be the longest-serving Chinese Ambassador both in the history of China-UK relations and of all Chinese ambassadors of all time.

When I first arrived in the UK 11 years ago, CBBC held a welcome lunch for me at Claridge's Hotel. In my remarks at the lunch, I promised to take it as my mission to deepen political mutual trust, enhance cooperation across the board, and expand strategic consensus and common interests of our two countries, so as to bring the China-UK relationship forward. Over the past 11 years, I have worked diligently to keep my words and fulfill my duty.

---

* Speech at the CBBC Farewell Roundtable. Chinese Embassy, 20 January 2021.

In these 11 years, we witnessed and worked together for the opening-up of new frontiers for China-UK mutually-beneficial cooperation.

In 2015, President Xi Jinping paid a "super state visit" to the UK. The visit charted the course for the overall China-UK relationship as well as practical cooperation. High-level dialogue mechanisms between China and the UK, including the Prime Ministers' Meeting and the Economic and Financial Dialogue, offered strong impetus for cooperation between our two countries. In the past 11 years, China-UK cooperation played a pioneering and leading role in many areas of productive cooperation between China and Western countries. Among major Western countries, the UK was:

- the first to join the AIIB and inject capital into the AIIB special fund;
- the first to set up an RMB clearing centre and issue RMB sovereign bond;
- and the first to appoint a special envoy to the Belt and Road Initiative and to sign the Guiding Principles on Financing the Development of the BRI.

In these 11 years, we witnessed and worked together for new records in China-UK trade and investment.

First, bilateral trade has surged.

From 2010 to 2020, China-UK trade in goods surged from 50.1 billion US dollars to 92.4 billion US dollars. Despite the pandemic and the contraction of international trade that follows, China-UK trade still hit a historical record.

Second, China-UK cooperation in investment has kept deepening.

By the end of 2019, FDI from the UK to China totaled 25.39 billion US dollars; in the other direction, FDI from China to the UK totaled 17.14 billion US dollars. This is about 20 times the level at the end of 2009, and has made the UK the second largest destination in Europe for Chinese investment.

Moreover, Chinese investment has expanded from traditional industries to new areas such as high-end manufacturing, information technology and cultural and creative industries.

Third, large-scale projects have made important progress.

11 years ago, there was basically no large-scale flagship project jointly built by our two sides. Now, with the efforts of both sides, several China-invested flagship projects

in the UK are making steady progress, including Hinkley Point C nuclear power plant and ABP Royal Albert Dock.

In these 11 years, we witnessed and worked together for new breakthroughs in China-UK cooperation on financial services and the BRI.

Both China and the UK have made vigorous efforts to advance cooperation in green finance and FinTech.

- Eight Chinese banks have opened branches in the UK.
- The Shanghai-London Stock Connect was officially launched, connecting for the first time the Chinese capital market with a foreign one, and enabling many Chinese companies to be listed here in London.
- London became the world's largest offshore RMB exchange centre and the second largest offshore RMB clearing centre. The total clearing volume has already exceeded 50 trillion RMB yuan.

The UK is a natural partner for China in BRI cooperation. The special representative of the Prime Minister of the UK has attended both sessions of the Belt and Road Forum for International Cooperation. China and the UK are also committed to working together in third markets. We have signed an agreement on such cooperation and worked together on financing, expertise and services.

Ladies and Gentlemen,

Dear Friends,

The productive China-UK business cooperation has delivered tangible benefits to the peoples of our two countries:

- China-invested electric, low-emission cabs are running in the streets of London.
- British food and drinks found their way to the dinner tables of Chinese families with the facilitation of, among others, the China International Import Expo.
- Chinese companies in the UK generated tax revenue and job opportunities for local communities and contributed to the transformation and upgrading of British businesses and the high-quality development of British industries.

Going forward, I am confident that our cooperation will enjoy enormous potential and promising prospects if China and the UK can follow three principles.

First, we should bear in mind the big picture, respect each other and strengthen mutual trust.

History tells us that when the principles of mutual respect and equality are followed, and international law and the basic norms governing state-to-state relations are observed, the China-UK relationship will move forward; otherwise, it will suffer setbacks or even retrogression.

A sound and stable China-UK relationship is not only in the common interests of our peoples but also conducive to world peace and development.

It is important that China and the UK always have in mind the big picture and long-term interests, view each other's development as opportunities, rather than challenges or threats, and respect each other's core interests and major concerns, so as to ensure the sustained and sound growth of China-UK relations and foster favourable conditions for deeper and productive cooperation between our two countries.

Second, we should follow the major trend of our times and shore up confidence.

Today, the world is experiencing the most profound changes in a century. These changes are happening not only amidst a pandemic unseen in a century. They have also come against surging unilateralism, protectionism and anti-globalisation sentiments, and growing uncertainties and instabilities in many places of the world.

For those of us who are committed to promoting China-UK cooperation, there are both opportunities and challenges.

It is important that we remain confident in the major trend of economic globalisation, in the prospects of the Chinese opening-up and development, and in the future of China-UK mutually-beneficial cooperation.

With such confidence, we should hold high the banner of free trade, work together to build an open world economy and ensure an open, inclusive, balanced and win-win economic globalisation.

Third, we should seek and seize opportunities to deepen cooperation.

China and the UK have highly-matching development strategies and complementary economies. At the moment, both our two countries are at a new, important development stage.

China is opening a new chapter. We will soon roll out the 14th Five-Year Plan and continue on the journey of building a modern socialist country in all aspects. The "dual circulation" development paradigm encourages a reinforcing interaction between the domestic and international markets. It means China will pursue high-quality growth and will open up wider and deeper.

The UK has just completed Brexit. It is now entering into a new stage of building a "global Britain" and expanding global partnership network.

China and the UK should leverage our respective strengths, coordinate our policies and dovetail our growth strategies. We should deepen cooperation in areas such as trade and investment, infrastructure, financial services and high and new technology, and make them more productive. This will boost development and prosperity in both our countries and deliver more benefits to our peoples.

Ladies and Gentlemen,

Dear Friends,

China-UK business cooperation has been productive and successful. This would not have been possible without the hard work of the business communities from both sides, especially CBBC.

Over the years, CBBC has made vigorous efforts to connect the Chinese and British business communities. You have also shared invaluable ideas and thoughts on deepening business cooperation between our two sides.

Since the outbreak of COVID-19, CBBC has brought Chinese and British business and financial institutions together to donate funds and supplies. It was a touching story of Chinese and British business communities taking concrete actions in time of difficulties and joining hands to fight the pandemic. I would like to take this opportunity to pay tribute to you for your contribution to China-UK cooperation!

My special thanks go to my old friends and the chairs of CBBC, Sir David, Lord Sassoon and Sir Sherard! Thank you for your all out support and assistance to me in the past 11 years!

I sincerely hope that my friends from the business sector will, as you always do, continue supporting China-UK relations and mutually beneficial cooperation. I also hope you will continue supporting the work of the Chinese Embassy and my successor the new ambassador. Your wisdom and efforts will continue to be the valuable source of strength for the steady and sound development of China-UK relations.

In 22 days, it will be the Chinese New Year, the Year of the Ox. In the Chinese culture, the Ox is a symbol of loyalty, hard work and prosperity.

I would like to take this opportunity to send you my very best and early wishes for a Happy Chinese New Year!

I wish you health and success! And I hope our friendship lasts forever!

Thank you!

第四章　金融合作

PART Ⅳ　Financial Cooperation

英国是世界金融大国，伦敦是世界金融中心之一，也是世界最大的外汇交易市场、保险市场、黄金现货交易市场和衍生品交易市场。中英金融合作起步早，创造了多个"第一"：伦敦是全球第一大人民币离岸外汇交易中心和第二大人民币离岸清算中心；2014年，英国首次发行30亿元人民币主权债券并将人民币纳入外汇储备，成为第一个发行人民币主权债券的西方国家；2015年，英国在西方大国中率先申请加入亚投行，成为创始成员；2016年，中国财政部在伦敦发行30亿元人民币国债，这是中国首次在境外发行人民币主权债券；2019年，中资银行首次在伦敦公开发行英镑债券。

本章从我的几十篇关于中英金融合作的演讲中收录了8篇，它们具有一定的代表性，包括中英两国政府发行人民币主权债券、人民币国际化、绿色金融、人民币清算行等。

The UK is a global financial powerhouse, with London being one of the world's financial centres and the largest market for foreign exchange trading, insurance, gold spot trading, and derivatives trading. China-UK financial cooperation started early and has created many "firsts". London is the world's largest offshore RMB trading centre and the second-largest offshore RMB clearing centre. In 2014, the UK issued RMB 3 billion of sovereign bonds for the first time and included RMB in its foreign exchange reserves, becoming the first Western country to issue RMB sovereign bonds. In 2015, the UK was the first among major Western countries to apply to join the Asian Infrastructure Investment Bank as a founding member. In 2016, the Chinese Ministry of Finance issued RMB 3 billion of government bonds in London, the first time China issued RMB sovereign bonds overseas. In 2019, a Chinese bank publicly issued GBP bonds in London for the first time.

This chapter includes 8 of my speeches, selected from dozens on China-UK financial cooperation, which are representative and cover topics such as the issuance of RMB sovereign bonds by the Chinese and British governments, RMB internationalization, green finance, and RMB clearing banks.

深化合作，互利共赢 *

尊敬的伦敦金融城市长先生，

尊敬的主席先生，

女士们、先生们：

我很高兴出席今天的伦敦"金融城之周"活动，并愿借此机会向大家介绍中国金融业发展状况，与大家共同探讨如何加强中英金融领域合作。

过去四年，提起"金融"这个词，人们首先想到的可能是：金融危机。如果提起"金融"和"伦敦"两个词，人们首先想到的可能是：伦敦超过纽约，成为世界第一大金融中心。如果提起"金融"和"中国"这两个词，那么人们首先该想到什么呢？我的答案是：长足发展。

尽管过去四年是国际金融危机发生、蔓延和深化的四年，世界经济形势极为复杂严峻，但中国经济保持了平稳较快发展，中国金融业取得了历史性进步。

第一，中国金融业实力大大增强。中国对金融机构实行了大刀阔斧式的改革，特别是对工农中建交五大国有控股商业银行完成了股份制改革。如今，这些大型商业银行公司治理逐步健全，盈利能力显著提高。过去，在全球十大银行中，清一色是欧美、日本的银行，现在中国工商银行等中资银行已成排行榜上的常客。截止到2011年11月末，中国金融业总资产达119万亿元人民币，比2006年末增长了149%。2011年9月末，商业银行资本充足

---

* 在伦敦"金融城之周"活动的主旨演讲。2012年2月6日，伦敦伊丽莎白二世会议中心。

率为 12.3%，比 5 年前提高 5 个百分点；不良贷款率为 0.9%，比 5 年前下降 6.2 个百分点。

第二，中国金融市场体系日益健全。中国已基本形成功能相互补充、交易场所多层次、交易产品多样化的金融市场体系。2011 年末，沪深两市上市公司 2342 家，总市值 21.5 万亿元人民币，位居世界第二。债券市场规模超过 20 万亿元人民币，位居世界第五。期货市场稳步发展，覆盖农产品、金属、能源、化工和金融等领域的期货品种体系初步形成。保险市场快速发展，2011 年中国保费收入 1.43 万亿元人民币，是 2006 年同期的近 3 倍。外汇市场交易主体增加，产品不断创新。

第三，中国金融抗风险能力大大增强。我们坚持正确把握金融宏观调控的方向、力度和节奏，综合运用利率、汇率、存款准备金率和公开市场操作等工具，促进货币信贷合理增长，调整优化信贷结构，较好地处理了金融支持经济发展、控制通货膨胀与防范金融风险的关系。我们立足基本国情，不断完善银行、证券、保险分业监管体制，加强金融监管协调。我们积极借鉴国际监管理念和标准，改进监管方式和手段，对系统性风险隐患早发现、早干预。我们不断强化市场基础性制度建设，推动完善企业公司治理。

我想强调的是，在发展金融产业的过程中，中国注意吸取从国际金融危机中得到的教训，始终坚持金融服务实体经济的本质要求，牢牢把握发展实体经济这一坚实基础，确保资金投向实体经济，防止虚拟经济过度自我循环和膨胀，防止出现产业空心化现象；中国始终坚持创新与监管相协调的发展理念，支持金融组织创新、产品和服务模式创新，提高金融市场发展的深度和广度，同时防止以规避监管为目的和脱离经济发展需要的"创新"。

第四，中国金融业日益对外开放。中国自 10 年前加入世贸组织以来，全面履行入世承诺，坚持"引进来"和"走出去"并重，大幅提高金融业市场开放度。在华外资金融机构规模扩大，截至 2011 年 9 月末，在中国注册的外商独资和中外合资法人银行业机构 14 家，73 家外国银行在中国设立 191 家分行和 61 家支行，183 家外国银行在中国设立 242 家代表处，在华外资银行资产总额高达 1051 亿美元。名列《财富》500 强中的 40 多家境外保险公司大多数已进入中国保险市场，其中包括英国的标准人寿、保诚集团和皇家太阳联合保险集团等。中国稳步推进股票市场、债券市场对外开放，实施合格境内机构投资者、境外机构投资者制度。截至2011年底，中国批准设立的合格境外投资者已经达到135家。中国稳步推动人民币汇率形成机制和利率市场化改革，中国与14个国家和地区签署了总额为1.3万多亿元人民币的双边本币互换协议，人民币结算额已上升至中国外贸总额的近10%，人民币国际地位明显提升。中国不断加强国际金融合作，积极参与国际经济金融治理机制建设，在国际货币基金组织和世界银行中的份额和投票权得到提高，在二十国集团中的作用日益突出。

现在，我想再问大家一个问题，如果同时提到"金融""英国""中国"这三个关键词，人们首先想到的会是什么？可能不同的人会有不同的联想。

中国中投公司董事长想到的可能是：加大在英国的金融投资。的确，就在上个月，中投公司投资入股了泰晤士水务公司，这是中英决定加强基础设施投资合作以来的首项重要成果。中国企业正加快对英投资步伐，领域从贸易、银行、电信、航运等部门延伸到高端制造业、创意产业、研发中心和基础设施。截至2011年底，中国对英非金融类直接投资超过了23亿美元，其中2011年一年就占近半，达11.3亿美元。我相信，随着中英双向投资的不断发展，两国金融业可以发挥更大的作用。

中国银监会主席想到的可能是：加强中英在金融监管领域的交流。不久前，英国改革了金融监管体制，设立了金融行为监管局。金融监管在中国发展历程相对较短，经验也不多。我认为，英国的改革思路、目标和效果及其对中国的参考借鉴，应当成为中英金融监管者今后密切沟通的主题。

英国财政大臣奥斯本想到的可能是：伦敦成为人民币离岸交易中心。2011年9月，在第四次中英经济财金对话时，中英双方就此已经进行了讨论。上月，奥斯本财政大臣访华时与香港金融管理局达成了合作协议，希望伦敦作为中国香港的一个补充，成为人民币离岸交易中心。我认为，中英双方可继续就此进行积极探索。

汇丰银行集团主席范智廉想到的可能是：尽快在上海证交所国际板上

市。尽管国际板目前尚无时间表，但推进上海证券市场国际板建设，支持符合条件的境外企业发行人民币股票，这是中国政府的既定方针。我知道，汇丰银行和渣打银行正争取乘上首趟列车。

中国农业银行行长想到的则可能是：如何在英国开展国际化经营。三天后，中国农业银行（英国）有限公司将在伦敦金融城正式开业，中国五大国有控股商业银行实现了齐聚伦敦，分别开设了五家子公司。我认为，中英双方金融机构应抓住机遇，加强交流，深化合作，两国政府、监管部门应积极为促进双方企业的合作创造良好条件。

这些就是中英未来金融合作的几个主要方向和领域，而我们的目标只有一个：互利共赢。

谢谢！

Seize the Opportunity to Deepen a Win-Win Partnership[*]

Lord Mayor,

Mr Chairman,

Ladies and Gentlemen,

It's a great pleasure to attend the City Week 2012 and this International Financial Services Forum.

This is a most valuable forum in which to share insights.

There is a great need for dialogue as we are in the fourth year of the global financial crisis. It is only through discussion that we can build the mutual understanding needed to secure stability in the financial markets of the world.

Over the past 4 years, whenever the word "Finance" is mentioned, it has always been associated with the financial crisis.

When "Finance" and "London" are put together, the first thing that comes to people's mind would probably be London replacing New York as the world's number one financial centre.

And when talking about "Finance" and "China", what do you have in mind?

My answer is: historic progress.

Today I will share with you my analysis of the historic progress of the Chinese financial industry.

Since the collapse of Lehman Brothers in September 2008, the crisis has rolled

---

[*] Keynote Speech at the City Week 2012 International Financial Services Forum. The Queen Elizabeth II Conference Centre, London, 6 February 2012.

around the world. As developed economies have stumbled, the Chinese economy showed strong resilience.

At the same time, the Chinese financial industry weathered the external shocks and achieved historic progress.

Now, let me explain what I mean by "historic progress".

First, the Chinese financial industry is more competitive.

China has introduced sweeping reforms to its financial institutions.

This ambitious plan transformed the "Big Five" stated-owned commercial banks, namely:

- Industrial and Commercial Bank of China.
- Agricultural Bank of China.
- Bank of China.
- China Construction Bank.
- And Bank of Communications.

Each of the "Big Five" has evolved into share holding financial groups.

Over the past few years, these banks have strengthened corporate governance and raised profitability.

The result has been dramatic.

The global ranking of the top 10 banks is no longer dominated by American, European and Japanese banks.

Today, Industrial and Commercial Bank of China and other Chinese banks have become heavy-weight players in the world.

In late November 2011 the Chinese financial industry was valued at 119 trillion RMB yuan, or 11.9 trillion pounds. That means a rise of 149% from the end of 2006.

By September 2011 Chinese commercial banks' capital adequacy ratio reached 12.3%. That is up by 5% compared with 5 years ago.

Also in this period, their non-performing loans ratio dropped to 0.9% from 7.1%.

My second point about "historic progress" is to highlight the growing maturity of the Chinese financial markets.

China now has strong and maturing financial markets. They have diverse products and trading facilities that reinforce each other. These are some of the key points:

- By late 2011, there were 2,342 listed companies at the Shanghai and Shenzhen Stock Exchanges. These have a total market capitalisation of 21.5 trillion RMB yuan, or 2.15 trillion pounds. The Chinese stock markets now rank as the world's second largest.
- With bonds, China has developed an over 20 trillion yuan, or 2 trillion pound market, which ranks fifth in the world.
- Futures trading in China continues to rise. Markets now span agricultural products, metals, energy, chemicals and financial products.
- As a measure of a flourishing insurance market, this industry posted a record premium of 1.43 trillion yuan, or 143 billion pounds, in 2011, which is about 3 times that of 2006.
- The forex market has also become more robust, attracting more traders and rolling out new investment products.

My third point about "historic progress" is how the Chinese financial system has grown resilient to risks.

There has been very different approaches to managing financial market risks in the world over the past 30 years.

Over the past 3 decades, the Chinese macro regulatory reform has kept the financial industry well regulated.

The Chinese government policy used a wide range of tools:

- Fine-tuning was flexible and timely.
- There was the fine-tuning of intensity and pace of regulation in the light of the wider economic environment and market conditions.
- China employed a full range of measures including interest rate, forex rate, bank reserve ratio for savings and open market operations.
- Care was taken with money and credit growth.
- The lending structure was improved. China highlighted the value of the financial sector macro management.

- This meant that China struck the right balance among supporting growth, managing inflation and preventing financial risks.
- Tailored to the Chinese economic conditions, we have developed a more effective and coordinated regulatory structure. This covers the banking sector, securities trading and insurance services.

China has adopted international concepts and standards to improve our regulatory approaches and vehicles.

At the heart of the Chinese risk management system is early warning of systemic risks and immediate intervention to prevent contagion.

At the same time, we have strengthened the institutional infrastructure and pushed for corporate governance to operate to higher standards.

What I hope to bring to your attention is that China is a serious student of the history of financial industry and global crises.

We are deeply aware of the centrality of the real economy in national prosperity. Chinese people know that the financial sector should have an important supporting role.

But at the same time, the financial sector should not expand excessively at the expense of the manufacturing base.

China provides crucial lessons for the world that finding the right balance of regulation of the financial sector is critical for winning stable and sustainable performance.

China will continue to keep financial innovation and financial regulation in balance.

On one side, we support the innovation of organisational structure, products and service models in the financial sector. China recognises that these are essential elements for the financial markets to reach greater depth and breadth.

On the other hand, we are determined to prevent the kind of innovation that sidesteps regulation or is divorced from the real economy.

My fourth point about "historic progress" in China is that our financial industry is increasingly open to the world.

China joined the WTO just over 10 years ago. Since then China has delivered its commitments. This means China has significantly opened its financial markets and encouraged its financial institutions to operate globally. These facts measure the progress:

- Foreign financial institutions have expanded their presence and secured a firm footing in the Chinese market. Foreign banking assets in China reached 105.1 billion US dollars.
- By September 2011, 14 wholly owned foreign banks and Sino-foreign joint-equity banks were registered in China. Now, 191 branches and 61 sub-branches of foreign banks are operating in China. There are another 242 offices of 183 foreign banks across the country.
- In the insurance sector, among some 40 global insurers on the *Fortune* 500 list, most have had operations in the Chinese insurance market. These include Standard Life, Prudential and RSA from Britain.
- The Chinese steady opening-up of its stock and bond markets is just as impressive and productive. A range of measures have been introduced, such as the QDII scheme and the QFII scheme. By the end of 2011, 135 qualified foreign institutional investors had been cleared to invest in the Chinese securities market.
- The reforms towards a managed floating RMB exchange rate and a market-driven interest rate scheme have made progress. China has signed 1.3 trillion RMB yuan, or 130 billion pounds, worth of bilateral currency swap agreements with 14 countries and regions. The fact that nearly 10% of the Chinese international trade annually is settled by RMB points to a significant rise of the currency's global status.
- China is keen to further deepen its global financial cooperation. We are an active participant in global economic and financial governance. Increasingly our voice is heard at key international forums. For example, China is now holding more quotas and voting shares in the IMF and the World Bank. the Chinese role in the G20 is growing.

Let me ask you another question. If the keywords "finance," "the UK" and "China" are put together, what will come to your mind?

Different people will give different answers.

Let me start with the Chairman of China Investment Corporation. He might say:

"Increase financial investment in Britain."

In January, CIC announced its equity investment deal with Thames Water. This was a major step following last November's China-UK infrastructure investment initiative.

This deal came as a wave of Chinese businesses show greater interest in investing in Britain. The areas of capital inflow include a broad spectrum of sectors, such as:

- Trade.
- Banking.
- Telecommunications.
- Shipping.
- Advanced manufacturing.
- Creative industries.
- Research and development.
- And infrastructure.

By the end of 2011, the Chinese direct investment in Britain totaled 2.3 billion US dollars. What's encouraging is that almost half that amount—or 1.13 billion US dollars—was invested in 2011 alone.

I have confidence as our two-way investment rises to a new level, the financial communities in China and Britain will have more opportunities to collaborate.

Now, how might the Chairman of China Banking Regulatory Commission answer the question? This may be: "Strengthen exchanges with British financial regulators."

We meet at a time of global economic and financial storm.

For the regulators worldwide, fixing institutional weaknesses and rebuilding the financial industry is the number one priority.

This is clearly an area where Britain can show its strength. As part of its financial regulatory reform, Britain has set up the Financial Conduct Authority.

Compared with the UK, financial regulation is relatively young in China. Our regulatory experience is not nearly as much as that of our British colleagues.

That's why Britain's reform agenda, fresh thinking and policy implications can be of great value for China. These topics should be front and centre between Chinese and British decision-makers in their financial regulatory dialogues.

What is on the mind of Chancellor George Osborne? He has made it very clear: "Build London into an offshore RMB centre."

This was an initiative on the agenda of the 4th China-UK Economic and Financial Dialogue last September.

On his China visit last month, Chancellor Osborne agreed with Hong Kong Monetary Authority on building collaborative ties on RMB trading.

The hope from the British side is London can over time become an RMB offshore trading centre as a supplement to Hong Kong. This is a good plan that should be worked on by the two countries.

Another obvious answer can come from HSBC Chairman Douglas Flint. HSBC has made it clear: "List the HSBC stock on the international board of the Shanghai Stock Exchange."

So far, there is no timetable of an "international board".

But the Chinese policy position is clear and consistent. We are determined to attract committed international players to list on Shanghai's capital market. And we support the issuing of RMB stock by qualified corporations outside China.

I know that the HSBC and the Standard Chartered are trying to catch the early tide.

What might be the answer from the President of the Agricultural Bank of China? This is likely to be: "Launch the bank's operations in Britain."

In just three days from today, Agricultural Bank of China (UK) Limited will officially open in the City. This marks the moment that all the "Big Five" state-owned commercial banks in China have established presence in London. By the end of this week each will have one subsidiary.

I encourage Chinese and British financial institutions to follow the example of those forerunners. They should seize opportunities to strengthen exchanges and deepen co-operation.

For this to happen, Chinese and British governments and regulatory authorities should also take up their responsibilities. This means they should work together to create a pro-business environment for our financial communities to chart a successful path forward.

As we "progress forward", the financial industries are an area where China and Britain have a huge potential to cooperate with each other.

All of us seek one objective.

This is stable and sustainable financial markets and a win-win future for all.

Thank you!

人民币国际化的"伦敦机遇" *

女士们、先生们：

非常高兴应邀出席由中国银行和《银行家》杂志联合主办的"崛起的人民币"论坛。

秋天是收获的季节，刚刚结束的第六次中英经济财金对话，双方就宏观经济、金融经贸、基础设施、城镇化、国际经济合作等议题进行深入沟通，取得丰硕成果，人民币国际化又迈出了坚实的步伐。

自 2009 年跨境人民币业务试点启动以来，在市场需求的推动下，跨境人民币业务和离岸人民币市场取得了显著进展，有效提升了中国与世界各地贸易投资的自由化和便利化程度。伦敦作为国际金融中心，敏锐地抓住了人民币国际化的机遇，自 2011 年中英经济财金对话启动伦敦离岸人民币市场以来，短短三年里，伦敦离岸人民币市场建设成绩斐然，创造了七项"第一"。

一是中英签署了 200 亿英镑的双边本币互换协议，这是中国与七国集团国家签署的首个此类协议。

二是英国成为亚洲以外首个获得人民币合格境外机构投资者初始额度的国家，意味着英国投资者可投资中国的股票、债券和货币市场。

三是伦敦人民币交易在亚洲之外名列第一。

四是亚洲以外首家人民币清算行落户伦敦，李克强总理 2014 年 6 月访英期间，中方宣布中国建设银行作为人民币清算银行在伦敦开展业务。

---

* 在"崛起的人民币"论坛上的主旨演讲。2014 年 9 月 23 日，伦敦股票交易所。

五是伦敦人民币计价金融产品屡开先河。2012年汇丰银行发行了20亿元人民币债券，成为首批在亚洲之外发行的人民币债券，2013年11月中国工商银行发行了20亿元离岸人民币高级债券，这是中国境内金融机构总部首次直接在伦敦市场发行离岸人民币债券，2014年1月中国银行伦敦分行首次以分行名义发行了25亿元债券，为英国及欧洲投资者提供了又一高品质的人民币投资产品。

六是中国国家开发银行2014年9月12日在伦敦成功发行20亿元人民币债券，这是首只登陆伦敦市场的中国准主权人民币债券。

七是2014年9月在第六次中英经济财金对话期间，英国政府宣布有意向发行以人民币计价的主权债券，因此成为第一个发行人民币主权债的外国政府。发债收入将作为外汇储备，使人民币成为英国的国家外汇储备货币之一，其意义和影响远超中英双边范畴。

作为中国驻英国大使，我见证了伦敦离岸人民币市场从无到有、从起步到驶入"快车道"的全过程。展望未来，我对伦敦成为全球最活跃的人民币市场之一充满信心。

第一，中国经济"稳中有进"是人民币国际化的动力源泉。一个国家货币的国际化，是综合实力发展的结果。中国改革开放30多年来，经济总量跃居世界第二，外贸总量跃居世界第一，对外直接投资跃居世界第三，人民币已成为全球第七大支付货币。但与中国的经济规模相比，人民币国际化仍存在巨大的发展潜力和空间。2014年上半年，中国GDP增速达7.4%，标志着中国经济正步入从高速转向中高速增长、从结构不合理转向结构优化、从要素投入驱动转向创新驱动的新常态。新常态下的中国经济发展仍处于重要战略机遇期，改革开放进入新的历史阶段，中国在国际贸易和投资领域的实力与日俱增，助推人民币国际化进程，有力支撑伦敦离岸人民币市场的建设。

第二，中英各领域合作不断深入是伦敦建设离岸人民币市场的基石。2013年，中英双边贸易额已达700多亿美元，现在两国3天的贸易量相当于30多年前1年的总量。中国对英投资增长迅猛，近3年合计180多亿美元，超过此前30年总和，英国已成为中国在欧洲最大投资目的地国。特别是2014年6月李克强总理访英时，两国签署了30多项合作协议，金额高达300多亿美元，内容涵盖能源、高铁、金融、投资等广泛领域。伦敦建设离岸人民币市场，将与中英贸易和投资"换挡提速"相互促进，为两国深化合作带来双赢局面。

第三，中英合作"顶层设计"和"基层参与"是保障。伦敦离岸人民币市场建设是一项长期的系统工程，中英两国间的总理年度会晤机制和经济财金对话机制为不同阶段的发展指明了方向，刚刚结束的第六次中英经济财金对话，再次将金融合作列为中英经贸关系的重中之重。同时，伦敦离岸人民币市场建设离不开积极协作的市场参与者。伦敦金融城最新研究表明，金融城启动人民币项目三年来，英国银行及其客户对于人民币的兴趣有增无减。随着中国各大银行在伦敦设立分行，发行人民币债券，这些中资金融机构将为伦敦离岸人民币市场建设注入新的动力。

同时，我们也应看到，人民币国际化不可能一蹴而就，必须循序渐进。中国将深化金融改革开放，遵循市场原则，顺应发展需要，为国内外金融和经济合作发展创造良好的条件。

我希望并相信，中英两国金融界将抓住机遇，携手合作，不断推进伦敦人民币离岸市场建设，带动两国金融合作迈上新台阶，为中英全面战略伙伴关系注入强劲动力。

谢谢大家！

The London Opportunity for the Internationalization of RMB[*]

Ladies and Gentlemen,

It is a real pleasure for me to speak at the Rise of RMB Forum co-sponsored by Bank of China and *The Banker* magazine.

Autumn is a season of harvest. The recent Sixth China-UK Economic and Financial Dialogue (EFD), just reaped a bumper harvest. The two sides had in-depth discussions on many topics:

- Macro-economy.
- Finance.
- Trade.
- Infrastructure.
- Urbanisation.
- And international economic cooperation.

On top of these, RMB internationalisation has taken a solid step forward.

Since the pilot programme in 2009, with buoyant market demand, cross-border and offshore RMB business has made marked progress. This has played a huge role in facilitating investment and liberalising trade between China and the rest of the world.

As a leading global financial centre, London has seized the opportunity. Following the EFD in 2011, London became an offshore RMB market. In just 3 years, London

---

[*] Speech at the Rise of RMB Forum. London Stock Exchange, 23 September 2014.

has come a long way and become pacemaker for offshore RMB business in 7 areas:

- First, China and the UK signed a currency swap agreement worth 20 billion pounds. This was the first of its kind between China and any other G7 members.
- Second, Britain was awarded the first RMB RQFII quota outside Asia. This quota allows the UK based asset managers to invest directly into onshore stock, bonds and equities.
- Third, London has the largest volume of RMB business outside Asia.
- Fourth, the first RMB clearing bank outside Asia found its place in London. During Premier Li Keqiang's visit in June, China announced China Construction Bank to be the first UK clearing bank for RMB.
- Fifth, London is a leader in RMB denominated financial products. In 2012, HSBC issued a two-billion RMB bond. This was the first issuance of RMB bonds outside Asia. In November 2013, Industrial and Commercial Bank of China issued 2 billion offshore RMB bonds. This was the first issuance of offshore RMB bonds in London by the headquarters of a Chinese domestic financial institution. In January 2014, Bank of China London branch for the first time issued 2.5 billion RMB bonds as a branch. This offered another quality RMB investment product for British and European investors.
- Sixth, on September 12, China Development Bank issued in London a 2 billion RMB bond. This was the first quasi-sovereign bond in London.
- Seventh, during the sixth EFD, the UK government announced its intention to issue RMB-denominated sovereign debt in London. This makes Britain the first foreign country to issue RMB sovereign debt. Income from it will become part of the UK's foreign exchange reserve. This makes RMB one of the UK's foreign exchange reserve currencies. Its significance and implication is well beyond the bilateral scope.

As Chinese Ambassador to the UK, I witnessed how London's offshore RMB business started from scratch and then grew from strength to strength. Looking ahead to the future, I am fully confident about London becoming one of the world's most active RMB markets. There are compelling reasons for my confidence.

First, the Chinese economy is making steady progress. This is the engine of RMB internationalization. Internationalization of a currency depends on the country's comprehensive strength. After more than three decades of reform and opening-up, China is now the second largest economy in the world. China has the largest foreign trade and third largest outbound investment in the world. RMB is the seventh largest currency of payment. Yet, given the size of the Chinese economy, RMB internationalisation still has great potential.

In the first half of 2014, the Chinese GDP grew by 7.4%. This means the Chinese fast growth has moderated to a more sustainable rate. Economic structure has improved. The growth model has shifted from being led by production factors to innovation driven. Under this new model, the Chinese economy still has strategic opportunities. Reform and opening-up has entered a new historic period. This will boost RMB internationalisation and support London's efforts to become an offshore RMB centre.

Second, deepening cooperation between China and the UK in a wide range of areas is the corner stone of London's offshore RMB business. In 2013, China-UK trade volume exceeded 70 billion US dollars. Now our trade in 3 days equals the trade in one year more than 30 years ago. Chinese investments in the UK are surging. Combined Chinese investments in Britain in recent 3 years totaled more than 18 billion US dollars. This was more than the total of previous 30 years.

Britain has become the largest destination of Chinese investment in Europe. In particular, when Chinese Premier Li Keqiang visited Britain in June, our two countries signed more than 30 cooperation agreements worth more than 30 billion US dollars. These agreements cover a great variety of areas, such as energy, high-speed railway, finance and investment. London's drive to become an offshore RMB center and the gearing-up of China-UK trade and investment will enhance each other. This will deepen our cooperation and create win-win for our two countries.

Third, the top-down design and mass participation is the guarantee of London's RMB business.

Nurturing the offshore RMB market in London is a long-term and systematic project. China-UK annual summit and EFD point out the direction for this project at different stages. The recent EFD once again identified financial cooperation as the top priority of China-UK economic links. At the same time we need the participation of market players. Records show that since the launch of RMB pilot program three years ago, British banks and their customers have shown a growing interest in RMB business. Now several major Chinese banks have set up branches in London and issued RMB bonds. These Chinese financial institutions will add new impetus to London's RMB business.

Having said the above, we should be aware that RMB internationalization can not be accomplished overnight. It must go ahead in a step-by-step manner. China will deepen reform and opening-up further in the financial sector. It is important to follow market rules and adapt to the changes so as to create conditions for the Chinese financial and economic cooperation with the world.

I hope Chinese and British financial sectors will seize the opportunities.

They must work together to push forward London's RMB business and raise China-UK financial cooperation to a higher level.

All these, I believe, will lend a powerful driving force to the China-UK comprehensive strategic partnership.

Thank you!

人民币国际化在英国迈出坚实步伐 *

尊敬的财政部经济大臣利德索姆女士，
尊敬的伦敦证券交易所首席执行官贾思涵先生，
各位来宾，
女士们、先生们：

非常高兴出席伦敦证券交易所开市仪式。首先，我热烈祝贺英国政府10月14日成功发行30亿元、3年期的人民币主权债券。至此，英国成为首个发行人民币主权债的外国政府，人民币也将成为英国的国家外汇储备货币之一，其意义和影响十分深远。

一是体现了英国政府对建设伦敦离岸人民币市场的"新承诺"。自2011年伦敦启动建设离岸人民币市场以来，短短3年里，英国在签署双边本币互换协议、获得人民币合格境外机构投资者初始额度、发行人民币计价金融产品等多个领域屡开先河。特别是此次英国政府发行人民币主权债券，凸显了英国政府将伦敦建成全球最活跃的人民币离岸市场的坚定承诺。

二是创造了人民币国际化的"新里程碑"。经过改革开放30多年的快速发展，中国经济规模跃居世界第二，外贸总量跃居世界第一，对外直接投资跃居世界第三，人民币已成为全球第七大支付货币。此次市场对英国政府发售的人民币主权债券需求十分旺盛，认购额高达58亿元人民币，充分体现

---

* 在英国政府发行30亿元人民币主权债券上市交易仪式上的讲话。2014年10月21日，伦敦证券交易所。

了各界对人民币国际地位的信心、对中国经济前景的信心。我相信，英国作为首个发行人民币国债并将人民币纳入储备货币的西方经济大国，将在国际上起到重要的示范作用。

三是为中英经贸合作注入"新动力"。英国政府发行人民币主权债券体现了中英经贸关系快速发展的需求。自 2013 年中英贸易额创新高之后，2014 年前三季度中英贸易又增长 20%，远远超过中国与欧盟的贸易增幅，全年两国贸易额有望超过 800 亿美元。中国对英投资增长迅猛，近 3 年合计 180 多亿美元，超过此前 30 年总和，英国已成为中国在欧洲最大投资目的地国。伦敦加快建设人民币离岸市场，将有力促进中英企业界的业务往来和经济联系，为两国深化贸易和投资合作带来双赢局面。

最后，我祝伦敦人民币离岸市场建设步伐越走越实，越走越大，越走越好！

谢谢大家！

Advancements of RMB Internationalization in the UK*

Economic Secretary Andrea Leadsom,

Chief Executive Office Alexander Justham,

Distinguished guests,

Ladies and Gentlemen,

It is a real pleasure for me to attend the opening ceremony of London Stock Exchange. I warmly congratulate the UK government on the successful issuance of a 3 billion sovereign bond in the Chinese currency, the RMB. The bond, issued on October 14 with a maturity of three years, has made the UK government the first non-Chinese issuer of RMB sovereign debt. RMB will also become one of Britain's foreign exchange reserve currencies. It has great significance in the following three aspects.

First, it renewed British government's commitment to making London a centre for offshore RMB business. Since the initiative was launched in 2011, Britain has created a number of records within a short span of three years. Here are some examples:

Britain and China signed the first currency swap agreement.

Britain was awarded the first RMB RQFII quota outside Asia.

Britain issued the first RMB denominated financial products.

The issuance of sovereign debt in RMB has accentuated British government's firm commitment to building London into one of the most dynamic offshore RMB markets.

Second, it created a new milestone of RMB internationalization. After more than

---

* Speech at the Launch of the UK Government RMB Bond. London Stock Exchange, 21 October 2014.

three decades of fast growth since reform and opening-up, China has surged to be the world's largest trading nation, the second largest economy, and the third largest outbound direct investor. RMB has become the world's seventh largest payment currency.

On the day of issuance, the order book closed with orders totaling 5.8 billion RMB. This fully demonstrates international market's confidence in RMB and in the Chinese economic prospect. I believe that as the first major Western country to issue RMB sovereign bond and by taking RMB as one of its reserve currencies, Britain will play an exemplary role in the world.

Third, it provided a new driving force for China-UK economic cooperation. This issuance reflected the demand of fast growing economic ties between China and the UK. Our bilateral trade hit a record high in 2013. The first three quarters of this year saw another increase of 20%. This was much higher than the increase of trade between China and the EU. The total trade volume this year is expected to top 80 billion US dollars.

In the meantime, Chinese investment in Britain is soaring, with 18 billion US dollars in the recent three years. This is more than the total investment in previous three decades.Britain is now the largest recipient of Chinese investment in Europe. The fast advance of London as an offshore RMB market will create win-win results, as it will greatly boost China-UK business links and economic ties. It will also deepen our bilateral trade and investment.

In conclusion, I wish every success for building offshore RMB centre in London.

Thank you!

硕果累累，精彩无限 *

尊敬的中国财政部副部长史耀斌先生，
尊敬的英国财政部经济大臣哈里特·鲍德温女士，
尊敬的伦敦证券交易集团主席唐纳德·布瑞敦先生，
女士们、先生们：

非常高兴再次出席伦敦证券交易所开市仪式。记得上次是 2014 年 10 月出席英国财政部发行的人民币主权债券上市仪式，那是一次里程碑式的事件。

今天，我们又迎来了中国财政部成功发行 30 亿元、3 年期的人民币债券并上市，这同样是一次里程碑式的事件。

第一，这是中英关系中的一件大事。2015 年习近平主席对英国进行了"超级国事访问"，访问取得丰硕成果。习近平主席在记者会上亲自宣布，中方将在伦敦发行中国之外首只人民币主权债券。这次中方兑现承诺，既是积极落实习近平主席访英成果，也为中英关系增添了极富"含金量"的亮点。我相信，它将有力助推两国在经贸、金融等各领域的合作提质升级。

第二，这是伦敦国际金融中心的一件大事。伦敦一直积极致力于发展人民币离岸业务，现已成为全球第二大人民币离岸结算中心。此次中国成功在伦敦发行人民币国债，全球投资者认购踊跃，既彰显了中国对伦敦成为全球领先的人民币离岸市场的积极支持，也反映出国际投资者对伦敦市场的一致看好。

---

* 在中国政府发行人民币主权债券上市仪式上的讲话。2016 年 6 月 8 日，伦敦证券交易所。

第三，这是人民币国际化进程中的一件大事。从全球贸易货币到投资货币，再到储备货币，这是人民币国际化进程中不可或缺的步骤。近两年来，人民币国际化进程加速发展，从英国政府在伦敦发行首只人民币主权债券，到国际货币基金组织将人民币纳入特别提款权货币篮子，再到今天中国政府在伦敦发行首只海外人民币债券，人民币经历了一个又一个历史性时刻，实现了一个又一个历史性突破。这充分体现出全球投资者对人民币的坚定信心，更体现了国际社会对中国经济的坚定信心。

最后，我祝今天的人民币主权债券上市圆满成功！

谢谢！

Let China-UK Cooperation Bear More Fruits*

Vice Minister Shi Yaobin,

Secretary Harriet Baldwin,

Chairman Donald Brydon,

Ladies and Gentlemen,

It is such a great pleasure to be back at the London Stock Exchange for this listing ceremony.

Last time I was here, in October 2014, I witnessed the listing of the RMB sovereign bond issued by HM Treasury. That was truly a milestone event.

Today, we are here for the listing of a three billion, three-year RMB bond issued by the Chinese Ministry of Finance. We are marking yet another milestone.

It is a milestone of three significances.

First of all, this is a significant moment in China-UK relations. In 2015, President Xi Jinping's "super state visit" to the UK was immensely fruitful. President Xi announced in person at a press conference that China would issue its first overseas RMB sovereign bond here in London. With today's listing, China means what it says.

We are here to deliver the results of President Xi's state visit. This will add a "golden shine" onto China-UK relations. I am confident what we are doing today will help strengthen and upgrade China-UK cooperation in business, in finance and in many other areas.

---

* Remarks at the Listing Ceremony of RMB Sovereign Bond in London. London Stock Exchange, 8 June 2016.

The second significance is that this bond listing is a momentous event for London as a global financial centre. London has always taken an active part in RMB offshore business. The result is that London is now the world's second largest clearing centre for RMB.

The enthusiastic subscription from international investors says it all about the tremendous success of the Chinese issuance of this RMB bond in London. This encouraging success demonstrates the Chinese strong support for London to become the world's leading RMB offshore market.

The third significance I want to leave with you is that today we are witnessing another major milestone for RMB internationalization.

To become a truly international currency, the RMB has to go through these stages:

- The RMB must become a currency for global trade.
- The RMB needs to be an investment currency.
- And finally the RMB has to be a reserve currency.

This process has taken on a faster pace.In a matter of less than two years,we have witnessed a number of crucial steps:

From the issuance of the first RMB sovereign bond in London by the British government, to the inclusion of RMB into the SDR basket of IMF, and to the first overseas RMB bond issued by the Chinese government here today.

These are historical moments and breakthroughs for the RMB. They reflect international investor's firm confidence in the RMB. And they also show the world's confidence in the Chinese economy.

In conclusion, I wish today's listing a complete success!

Thank you!

共同塑造中英金融合作的美好未来 *

尊敬的汇丰集团总裁欧智华先生，

女士们、先生们：

很高兴出席汇丰集团举办的汇丰中国与人民币论坛。本次论坛的举办可谓恰逢其时，其主题是"迎接挑战，塑造不同的未来"。正如一枚硬币的两面，机遇和挑战往往相伴相生。中英金融合作也是如此，而且机遇远远大于挑战。我的信心主要来自三个方面。

第一，人民币国际化进程正在加速推进。近年来，中国一方面有序开展人民币汇率市场化改革，逐步开放国内资本市场；另一方面稳步推动人民币"走出去"，提高金融业国际化水平。随着中国经济保持长期稳定发展，人民币在跨境投资和贸易中的使用率不断提升。2015年，人民币跨境直接投资结算业务额达2.32万亿元，离岸人民币债券发行规模达3930亿元。

就在本月第一天，也就是中国的国庆日，根据国际货币基金组织决定，人民币正式进入特别提款权货币篮子。这一标志性事件，不仅有利于进一步推动人民币国际化进程，而且有助于促进国际货币体系改革，也将为中英金融合作注入新的活力和动力。

伦敦作为全球最大金融中心，在人民币国际化进程中发挥着日益重要的作用。从2014年英国政府在全球率先发行人民币主权债券，到2015年中国人民银行在伦敦首次发行以人民币计价的央行票据，再到2016年5月中国

---

* 在汇丰中国与人民币论坛上的主旨演讲。2016年10月11日，伦敦洲际酒店。

财政部在伦敦首次发行人民币国债,伦敦在人民币债券方面已经创造了多项"第一"。同时,中资金融机构已纷纷在伦敦开设分支机构。2016年3月,伦敦超越新加坡成为全球仅次于中国香港的人民币清算中心。可以说,这些重要成果为中英金融合作不断提质升级打下坚实基础。

第二,中国全方位对外开放保持坚定步伐。坚定不移扩大对外开放,是中国的战略选择。正如习近平主席在二十国集团工商峰会开幕式上所说,中国对外开放不会停滞,更不会走回头路。下一步,我们将加大放宽外商投资准入力度,提高便利化程度,促进公平开放竞争,全力营造优良营商环境。目前,上海等4个自贸试验区初步建立起开放型经济新体制,中国决定增设7个自贸试验区。展望未来,中国对外开放的大门只会越开越大,各位工商界朋友到中国投资兴业的环境只会越来越规范、友好、透明。

"一带一路"倡议是中国在新的历史条件下实行全方位对外开放的重大举措。倡议实施以来,已经有包括英国在内的70多个国家和国际、地区组织表达了支持和参与的积极意愿,一系列重点项目和经济走廊建设稳步推进。中欧班列迄今成功开行1500多列,形成常态化运输机制。区域贸易和投资年均增速高于全球平均水平近一倍,2015年中国同"一带一路"共建国双边贸易额已突破1万亿美元。亚投行开业运营,丝路基金首批投资项目顺利启动,共建国家积极探讨建立或扩充各类双多边金融合作基金,为重点项目建设提供了强有力的金融支撑。

"一带一路"倡议是中国提出的,但机遇是世界的。"一带一路"不仅有利于地区乃至全球经济的发展振兴,也必将为中英在金融、贸易、投资等领域加强合作带来更多机遇。

第三,中英共同打造两国伙伴关系的动能有增无减。2015年10月习主席对英国进行"超级国事访问",两国宣布共同构建面向21世纪全球全面战略伙伴关系。

尽管英国公投"脱欧"后发生了很多变化,但中英关系的基本面没有变,中英关系的基础依然牢固。不久前,英国首相梅赴华出席二十国集团领导人杭州峰会并与习主席成功举行双边会见,两国领导人再次确认,双方致力于推动两国全面战略伙伴关系迈上更高水平。年底前，双方还将共同举行中英经济财金对话、中英战略对话、中英高级别人文交流机制会议等一系列高层互访和对话，进一步推动经贸、金融、国际、人文等领域务实合作。

女士们、先生们，

我常说，塑造一个美好的未来，不仅需要充满信心，更需要抓住机遇，脚踏实地，积极进取，不断取得更多更好的合作成果。为此，我们应当：

第一，抓住人民币国际化带来的难得机遇。人民币国际化是一个循序渐进、水到渠成的过程，既符合中国经济深度融入全球经济的发展趋势，也有助于改善世界发展的货币金融环境。作为中英金融合作的重要内容，人民币国际化日益成为中英在双边合作中实现优势互补、互惠互利的一大品牌。

下一步，随着人民币汇率制度市场化改革的稳步推进，人民币将逐渐从贸易融资货币向计价货币、储备货币演进，伦敦的全球金融中心优势将进一步得到发挥，人民币离岸业务在伦敦将取得飞速发展。双方可以加快伦敦人民币离岸中心建设，在丰富金融产品、扩大交易规模等方面多下功夫，积极推进两国金融市场互联互通准备工作，不断拓展人民币国际化合作的广度和深度，做大共同利益"蛋糕"。

第二，用好"一带一路"建设的广阔平台。中国的对外开放不是一家唱独角戏，而是欢迎各方搭乘发展快车，欢迎各方共同参与。"一带一路"以贸易和投资便利化为纽带，以金融互利合作为重要保障，将致力于打造多主体、全方位、跨领域的合作平台。英国在"一带一路"建设中具有独特优势，可以为共建国家提供高质量的金融服务、法律保障、人才培养等。

在金融服务方面，英国具备丰富的国际金融经验和成熟的管理制度，与众多共建国家金融往来密切。随着共建国家金融创新合作步伐的加快，中英与共建国家开展金融合作的潜力巨大。

在法律保障方面，英国是普通法系发源地和法律大国，国际商事仲裁和争端解决水平处于全球领军地位，"一带一路"法律合作有望成为中英司法交流合作的新亮点。

在人才培养方面，英国同样拥有许多知名智库和世界一流的教育资源，中英可以就合作内容和形式进行深入探讨，共同为"一带一路"建设提供强有力的智力支撑。总之，中英以"一带一路"建设为平台开展多种形式合作的前景十分广阔。

第三，发挥重大合作项目的引领作用。英国是中国在欧洲的主要贸易伙伴和投资目的地国。英国公投"脱欧"并没有改变中国企业来英投资的热情，反而为双方探讨建立更高水平的双边贸易和投资安排创造了积极条件。9月底，中、英、法三国代表签署了欣克利角C核电项目一揽子投资协议。这一旗舰项目是中国在英最大的单笔投资，也是在欧洲最大的投资项目，标志着中英两国互惠合作进入新的阶段。我们期待一揽子合作协议能顺利执行，为中英两国人民增添福祉，为各领域务实合作发挥引领和示范作用。

从现代经济发展的普遍规律看，重大项目合作往往更需要金融业的有力支持和优质服务，同时也会进一步带动金融业蓬勃发展。中方在参与对英重大项目合作时，非常看重英国金融服务业的优势和支撑作用，希望两国能进一步深化发展战略对接，积极推动核能、高铁、基础设施等重大项目合作，扩大双边投资和经贸合作规模，这也将为中英金融合作提供更大空间。

第四，促进全球经济金融治理机制改革。中英都是具有全球影响的大国，两国关系早已超越双边范畴，正不断彰显战略意义和全球影响。前不久，正是在中英及与会其他各方的共同努力下，二十国集团领导人杭州峰会取得圆满成功。峰会成果凝聚了国际社会关于全球经济治理的共识，为深化国际经济合作指明了方向。各方一致同意加强落实各项金融改革举措，密切监测和应对金融体系潜在风险和脆弱性，深化普惠金融、绿色金融领域合作，共同维护国际金融市场稳定。近年来，中英在绿色金融领域合作取得很大进展，共同为经济资源向绿色产业转移做出突出贡献。未来，中英双方可以与二十国集团其他成员一道努力，大力推动落实杭州峰会成果与共识，加强在国际货币基金组织、世界银行、亚投行等多边金融机构合作，共同构建公正高效的全球金融治理格局。

女士们、先生们，

汇丰集团一直是人民币国际化的积极支持者，也是中英金融合作的领军者。在座各位是英国政、商、学术等各界杰出代表，我希望大家能充分利用本次论坛平台，集思广益，坚定信心，携手迎接挑战，抓住机遇，共同塑造中英合作的美好未来。

最后，预祝本次论坛取得圆满成功！

谢谢！

Work Together for a Promising Future of China-UK Financial Cooperation[*]

Mr Stuart Gulliver,

Ladies and Gentlemen,

It gives me great pleasure to join you today at this HSBC China and RMB Forum on the theme of "Rising to the Challenges, Shaping a Different Future".

The topic is most timely and offers immense opportunity.

Just as every coin has two sides, every challenge comes with opportunities. And in the financial cooperation between China and the UK, there are far more opportunities than challenges. Here are the three reasons why I am confident of this.

First, the internationalization of RMB is accelerating.

- At home, China has in recent years taken measured steps to make the RMB exchange rate more market-oriented.
- And the Chinese capital market has been gradually opened up.
- In the global market, the RMB is steadily becoming an international currency.
- And the Chinese financial sector is operating to a higher international standard.

With the long-term steady growth of the Chinese economy, the RMB is now used more frequently than ever in cross-border investment and trade:

---

[*] Speech at the HSBC China and RMB Forum. InterContinental London Park Lane, 11 October 2016.

- In 2015, more than two trillion RMB yuan was used in the settlement of cross-border direct investment, and the offshore RMB bond totalled 393 billion yuan.

Recently there was a highly significant advance of the internationalization of the RMB. On the first day of this month, which was the Chinese National Day, the IMF announced the official inclusion of the RMB in the SDR basket:

- This is a milestone.
- It will boost the RMB's internationalization.
- It is a fresh push on the reform of the international monetary system.
- And it will also generate new vigour and vitality for China-UK financial cooperation.

London as the largest global financial centre has been playing an increasingly important role in RMB internationalization:

- In 2014, the British government issued the world's first RMB sovereign bond here in London.
- A year later, the People's Bank of China issued the first RMB-denominated central bank bills also here in London.
- In May this year, the Chinese Ministry of Finance issued the first RMB treasury bonds once again here in London.
- In a few years time, this city has witnessed a number of "firsts" in RMB bond issuance.
- At the same time, Chinese financial institutions have come to London one after another to set up branches.
- In March this year, London overtook Singapore to become the world's major RMB settlement centre, second only to Hong Kong.
- Such progress has helped cement the foundation of China-UK financial cooperation.
- And it has made further improvement and upgrading of our financial cooperation possible.

The second reason for my confidence is the Chinese continued commitment to overall opening-up:

- For China, opening-up is a core strategic choice.
- As President Xi Jinping said at the Opening Ceremony of the B20 Summit, the Chinese opening-up will not stall, still less will it reverse course.
- Going forward, China will continue to lower the threshold for foreign investment, improve facilitation, promote fair and transparent competition, and create a more business-friendly environment.
- Now a new system for developing an open economy is taking shape, with the establishment of four pilot free-trade zones, including the one in Shanghai.
- And seven more are to be designated.

In the years ahead, China will open its door wider than ever to foreign investment. Please be sure, my friends from the UK business sector, of this certain advancing trend. Going forward you will find a more rule-based, business-friendly and transparent commercial environment in China.

One commitment to openness is the Belt and Road Initiative. This is a major plan of China to deliver an all-round opening-up. Britain and some 70 other countries, international and regional organizations have expressed their readiness to support and participate in this initiative.

Now a number of projects are making steady progress and the building of the economic corridors are underway:

- The China Railway Express has to date made over 1,500 routine journeys over land between China and Europe.
- Trade and investment in regions along the Belt and Road routes are growing at a speed almost twice the global average.
- In 2015, the Chinese trade with Belt and Road partner countries exceeded one trillion US dollars.
- Notably, the Belt and Road projects have strong financial support.
- The support comes from the Asian Infrastructure Investment Bank.

- It comes from the investment of the Silk Road Fund.
- And it comes from the bilateral and multilateral financial cooperation funds that the BRI partner countries are actively involved to establish or expand.

The Belt and Road is an initiative by China but an opportunity for the world:

- It will benefit regional development.
- It will boost global growth.
- And it will definitely bring more opportunities to facilitate closer cooperation between China and Britain in finance, trade, investment, and in many other areas.

My third reason for confidence is the increasing dynamics for China-UK partnership that our two countries are committed to:

- Last October, President Xi Jinping paid a very successful "super state visit" to the UK.
- Our two countries announced our commitment to jointly building a global comprehensive strategic partnership for the 21st century.

Despite many unexpected changes following the Brexit referendum, the fundamentals of China-UK relations have remained unchanged. The vital interests that bond our two countries together have remained secure:

- Last month, Prime Minister May was in Hangzhou for the G20 Summit. She had a successful bilateral meeting with President Xi.
- The two leaders reiterated their shared commitment to bringing our global comprehensive strategic partnership to a higher level.
- In the coming months, China and the UK will co-host the Economic and Financial Dialogue, Strategic Dialogue and the High-Level People-to-People Dialogue.
- And these high-level mutual visits and dialogues will further promote our practical cooperation in the field of business, finance, cultural, international and

people to people exchanges.

Ladies and Gentlemen,

I often say that we should be confident in a promising future for China-UK relations. What is more, we should seize the opportunities when they come along. We must work hard and take real actions to deliver more fruits. I believe more efforts are needed in the following aspects.

First, we must seize the valuable opportunities of the internationalization of RMB:

- The internationalization of RMB is a step-by-step process. It is a process that will not stop and cannot be stopped, as it is in line with the trend of the Chinese deeper integration into the global economy.
- And it will also help improve the global monetary and financial environment for growth.

For China and the UK, RMB internationalization is an important part of our bilateral financial cooperation:

- This is an area where we can dovetail respective strengths and produce mutual benefit.
- And this is an area where we can create a brand name for China-UK cooperation.

As the Chinese market-based reforms of the exchange rate regime continues, RMB will gradually grow from a trade currency to a quote currency and finally to a reserve currency. That will give London a further advantage and allow the offshore RMB business in London to grow at an even faster speed.

Therefore, China and the UK can work together to speed up the building of RMB offshore centre in London:

- We can work together on the variety of financial products and the scale of transactions.
- We can work together on the preparations for the interconnectivity between our

financial markets.
- We can work together to expand and deepen cooperation on RMB internationalization.
- And together, we can make the pie of common interests bigger.

Secondly, we need to make good use of the platform of the Belt and Road:

- The Belt and Road Initiative is not the Chinese one-man-show. Anyone is welcome to join in and catch this express train bound for a future of development.
- The Belt and Road links countries together through trade and investment facilitation and offers opportunities for win-win financial cooperation.
- And our vision for the Belt and Road is to build a platform for all-dimensional, cross-field cooperation among multi-entities.

Here, the UK has unique advantages. These include the financial and legal services as well as talent resource it can offer to the BRI partner countries.

In financial services, Britain has rich experience in international financing and mature management expertise. You have close financial interactions with the partner countries, who will soon be in need of innovative financial cooperation to bring in capital, expertise and experience. China and the UK will find huge potential for financial cooperation with these countries.

In legal services, Britain is a world leader and the origin of the common law. British leadership in international commercial arbitration and dispute resolution is widely acknowledged. Legal services in Belt and Road projects can be a new area for China-UK legal exchanges and cooperation.

With respect to human resource training, the UK is also well placed, given its world-renowned think tanks and prestigious universities. China and the UK can join hands to explore ways and means of cooperation in this regard so as to offer strong intellectual support to the building of the Belt and Road.

In short, the Belt and Road is setting the stage for China and Britain to engage in multiple forms of cooperation. The opportunities are limitless.

Turning to a third area for leveraging the exemplary role of major cooperation projects so as to spur more cooperation:

- Britain is the Chinese major trading partner and investment destination in Europe.
- The Brexit referendum has certainly not dampened the enthusiasm of Chinese companies about investing in the UK.
- And, on the contrary, it opens a door to the possibility of exploring a higher level of bilateral trade and investment arrangement.

Two weeks ago, China, Britain and France signed a package deal on Hinkley Point C nuclear project:

- This flagship project is so far the single largest Chinese investment in the UK.
- It is in fact larger than any other Chinese investment in Europe.
- And it is a symbol of China-UK win-win cooperation moving up to the next level.
- We look to the smooth execution of the package deals related to the Hinkley project.
- We hope that their implementation will benefit the people of both countries and serve as a fine example for cooperation in other fields.

The development of modern economy shows that sufficient funding and quality financial services are key to the success of big projects. Big projects will in turn enable the financial sector to thrive. That's why when China participates in major British projects, we highly value the UK's strength in the financial sector:

- Our two countries can probe deeper to find out where our development strategies can dovetail.
- We can encourage greater cooperation on nuclear, high-speed rail, infrastructure building and other major projects.
- We can continue to expand the scale of mutual investment and trade.
- And these endeavours will open up more space for China-UK financial cooperation.

Fourth, we can collaborate to advance reforms of the global economic and financial governance:

- Both China and the UK are countries with global influence.
- And our relationship has been growing in strategic importance and global significance. It goes far beyond the bilateral scope.

The G20 Hangzhou Summit is a recent example.

Thanks to the concerted efforts of China, Britain and all other member states, the summit was a complete success. The outcome of this summit reflects the international consensus on global economic governance and charts the course for deeper international economic cooperation.

The parties agreed on the following:

- They will implement the financial reform measures.
- Closely monitor and address the underlying risks and vulnerability of the financial system.
- Deepen cooperation on financial inclusion and green financing.
- And jointly maintain stability in international financial markets.

In the recent years, China and the UK have achieved much progress in our cooperation on green financing. We have jointly contributed to transferring more economic resources to green industries.

Going forward, China and the UK need to continue working with other G20 members towards a more just and efficient global financial governance. To achieve that, we must work hard to implement the outcomes and consensus of the G20 Hangzhou Summit.

In addition, we need to reinforce the cooperation within multilateral financial institutions such as the IMF, World Bank and AIIB.

Ladies and Gentlemen,

HSBC has always been an active supporter of the RMB internationalization and a leader in China-UK financial cooperation. I thank HSBC for hosting this forum and for bringing together a wealth of British political, business and academic leaders:

- I hope you will make good use of this forum.
- I hope you will share your thoughts and draw on each other's ideas.
- And I also hope you will maintain and boost your confidence in a better future of China-UK financial cooperation.

I am ready to join hands with you to rise to the challenges and seize the opportunities to shape a bright future for both our countries.

In conclusion, I wish today's Forum a complete success.

Thank you!

坚定信心，共创未来[*]

尊敬的伦敦金融城市长埃斯特林先生，

尊敬的各位大臣、各位议员、各位嘉宾，

女士们、先生们、朋友们：

大家下午好！

感谢伦敦金融城授予我"荣誉市民"称号，感谢各位嘉宾的莅临。金融城"荣誉市民"称号是一个很高的荣誉。英国朋友告诉我，如果我在200年前获得这一殊荣，就可以在金融城"持剑行走"，还能"赶着羊群通过伦敦桥"。

今天这个称号仍具有很高的"含金量"，金融城用数字来概括就是"1、2、3、4"：在1平方英里[①]的土地上，云集了2000多家金融机构，创造了英国3%的国内生产总值，汇聚了全球4万多亿美元的庞大资产。

因此，我十分珍惜这一称号。我认为，这个称号不仅是给予我个人的荣誉，也是对中国驻英国大使馆工作的认可，更体现了伦敦金融城对中英金融合作的高度重视和对中国人民的美好情谊。

我担任中国驻英国大使近9年来，造访过无数次伦敦金融城，每次都能感受到它深厚的底蕴和勃勃的生机，体会到中英两国金融合作的巨大潜力和广阔前景。我初步统计了一下，中英金融合作至少为两国关系贡献了"三个最"。

---

[*] 在伦敦金融城"荣誉市民"授勋仪式上的讲话。2018年12月3日，伦敦金融城市政厅。

[①] 1英里约等于1.609千米。——编者注

第一，创造的"第一"最多。英国是第一个加入亚投行、第一个向亚投行专门基金注资、第一个签署《"一带一路"融资指导原则》的西方大国。伦敦目前是全球最大的人民币离岸交易中心和第二大人民币离岸清算中心，英国还是首个发行人民币主权债券的西方国家。2016年，中国银行在伦敦发行首只中国绿色资产担保债券；中国财政部发行的30亿元人民币国债在伦敦证券交易所上市交易，这是中国首次在境外发行人民币主权债券。所有这些"第一"不仅彰显了两国金融合作的活力，而且体现了金融合作在两国务实合作中的引领作用。

第二，合作的成果最丰硕。2018年是中英经济财金对话机制成立10周年。10年来，这一机制日益成为两国金融政策协调和发展对接的重要平台。在2017年第9次对话达成的72项成果中，一多半都属于金融领域。截至目前，包括中国五大国有银行在内的7家中资银行在伦敦设立了分行，其中6家是在我任期内开设的。唯一例外的是中国银行分行，它早在1929年就于伦敦设立了。中国再保险公司、中国人保、太平保险等其他金融机构也在伦敦开设了分支机构。中国银行还在伦敦设立了私人银行服务中心，这是在亚洲以外设立的第一家。在当前英国"脱欧"的大背景下，这些中资银行开设的分支机构，无疑是对伦敦金融城投下的支持票和信任票。

第三，产生的影响最广泛。中英金融合作已远超双边范畴。中英共同发起成立的二十国集团绿色金融研究小组，共同发布的《中英金融服务战略规划》，支持建立的由私营部门牵头的中英金融服务峰会，不仅为提升两国金融合作的全局性、战略性奠定了坚实基础，也引领了相关领域的国际合作，产生了广泛而深远的影响。

女士们、先生们，

荣誉源自信赖，荣誉传递信心。今天，我与各位分享荣誉之时，也愿与大家共享我对中英合作的信心，这份信心来自三个方面。

一是对中国进一步深化改革开放的信心。2018年是中国改革开放40周年。习近平主席已多次宣布，新时代中国的大门不会关闭，只会越开越大。金融将是中国下一阶段对外开放的重要领域，中国金融市场准入还将大幅放宽，中英双方将加快推进"沪伦通"。中国进一步深化改革、扩大开放，必将为中英在更高层次、更广领域拓展金融合作带来更多商机。

二是对中英共建"一带一路"的信心。2018年是"一带一路"倡议提出5周年。"一带一路"坚持对话协商、共建共享、合作共赢、交流互鉴，为世界可持续发展开辟了新方向。目前，已有140多个国家和国际组织与中国签署了"一带一路"合作协议。中国正积极推进在"一带一路"共建国家设立金融服务平台，金融成为"一带一路"建设的重要内容。英国在国际金融领域经验丰富、制度成熟，与众多共建国家保持密切沟通和良好合作，在融资、PPP（政府和社会资本合作模式）、保险、绿色金融等领域优势突出，是中国"一带一路"合作的"天然伙伴"。2019年，中国将举办第二届"一带一路"国际合作高峰论坛，努力将"一带一路"国际合作提升到新高度，这将为中英合作特别是金融服务合作带来新机遇。

三是对中英关系的信心。在21世纪第二个10年，中英建立起面向21世纪的全球全面战略伙伴关系，两国贸易、投资、金融、科创、人文等各领域合作成果丰硕。这一局面来之不易，凝结着两国各界人士几十年的心血和不懈努力，值得我们倍加珍惜、精心呵护。我希望并相信，中英双方能从全球视角和战略高度审视两国关系，尊重彼此核心利益和重大关切。

女士们、先生们，

古罗马哲学家西塞罗说过，"信心就是抱着足可确信的希望与信赖，奔赴伟大荣誉之路的感情"。我相信，只要我们坚定信心，携手努力，攻坚克难，开拓进取，就能共同开创中英关系更加美好的明天！

谢谢大家！

Firm Confidence in a Brighter and Shared Future[*]

Lord Mayor Peter Estlin,

Ministers,

Councillors,

Distinguished Guests,

Ladies and Gentlemen,

Dear Friends,

Good afternoon!

I would like to begin by expressing my appreciation to the City of London Corporation for bestowing upon me the honour of the Freedom of the City.

I also wish to thank all of you who are present today for joining me on this significant occasion.

Being a "Freeman" is an extremely high honour. My British friends told me that two hundred years ago, being a Freeman would have given me the privilege to "carry a naked sword in public" or "drive sheep over London Bridge".

Today, it is still a great privilege to be a City Freeman. The City of London is such an extraordinary institution. My summary of the City's status is as simple as one, two, three, four: In a space of one square mile, the City hosts two thousand financial institutions, contributes to three percent of the UK's GDP and manages four trillion US dollars of assets.

---

[*] Speech at the Freedom Ceremony of the City of London. Guildhall, City of London, 3 December 2018.

I cherish this honour of the Freeman.

- I believe it is a recognition of the work of not just myself but the Chinese Embassy.
- It demonstrates the importance that the City of London attaches to China-UK financial cooperation.
- And it embodies the friendship between the people of our two countries.

In nearly 9 years as the Chinese Ambassador to the UK, I have visited the City of London numerous times. Each time, I was impressed by its profound strength and exhilarating dynamism. Each time, I could sense the enormous potential and broad prospects of China-UK financial cooperation.

Such cooperation has contributed to at least three important records in our bilateral relations.

First, it has achieved the greatest number of "firsts".

- The UK was the first major Western country to apply to join the Asian Infrastructure Investment Bank, the first to contribute to the AIIB special fund, and the first to sign the Guiding Principles on Financing the Development of the Belt and Road with China.
- The UK is also the first Western country to issue RMB sovereign bond. It is only natural that London becomes the world's largest RMB offshore trading centre and the second largest RMB offshore clearing centre.
- It was in London that the Bank of China issued the first Green Covered Bond in 2016.
- It was at the London Stock Exchange that the Ministry of Finance of China made its first overseas issuance of RMB sovereign bond of three billion yuan.

These "firsts" demonstrate the vitality of China-UK financial cooperation. They also emphasise the leading role of the financial sector in the business cooperation between our two countries.

Second, of all sectors, China-UK cooperation in financial service has been most productive.

This year marks the tenth anniversary of the launch of the China-UK Economic and Financial Dialogue. After ten years of strenuous efforts on both sides, EFD has become an important platform for our two countries to enhance macro policy coordination and match development strategies in the financial sector. Of the 72 outcomes of last year's EFD, more than half are related to financial services.

As of today, seven Chinese banks, including the top five state-owned commercial banks, have set up branches in London. Six of the branches were opened during my tenure as the Chinese Ambassador to the UK. The only exception, the Bank of China London Branch, was established in 1929, well before I was born.

Other Chinese financial institutions, including China Re, PICC and China Taiping Insurance Group, have also set up branches in London. Moreover, the Bank of China has opened the Private Banking Service Centre in London, which is the first of its kind outside Asia.

By opening these branches, the Chinese financial institutions have cast their vote of support and confidence for the City of London as Britain leaves the EU.

Third, China-UK financial cooperation has the most extensive and far-reaching significance.

Such significance has gone far beyond the bilateral scope.

- China and the UK have established the G20 Green Finance Study Group.
- We have issued the China-UK Strategic Plan for Financial Services.
- And we helped launch the China-UK Financial Services Summit led by the private sector.

Through these efforts, our two countries are not only engaged in more comprehensive and strategic bilateral cooperation. We are also taking the lead in international cooperation in the financial sector.

Ladies and Gentlemen,

The Freedom award is an honour. This honour is based on trust. This honour imparts confidence.

Today, I want to share this honour with you. I also want to share with you my confidence in China-UK cooperation. My confidence comes from the following three aspects:

First, I have confidence in deeper reform and further opening-up in China.

This year marks the 40th anniversary of the Chinese reform and opening-up. President Xi Jinping has reiterated on many occasions that China will not close its door; instead, it will open its door even wider to the world.

The financial sector will be a key area for opening-up in the next stage. China will significantly increase access to its financial market. We will work with the UK to accelerate the preparations for the Shanghai-London Stock Connect.

Deeper reform and further opening-up will create more business opportunities for China-UK financial cooperation at a higher level and in a wider scope.

Second, I have confidence in China-UK cooperation on the Belt and Road Initiative.

This year marks the fifth anniversary of the BRI. In the past five years, the BRI has:

- adhered to dialogue and consultation,
- invited all partners to pitch in,
- shared the benefits of win-win cooperation,
- pursued cultural exchanges and mutual learning,
- and showed a new direction for sustainable development in the world.

As of today, more than 140 countries and international organisations have signed cooperation agreements with China on the BRI.

Financial cooperation is an important part of BRI cooperation. China is encouraging the establishment of financial services platforms in the partner countries.

The UK has extensive knowledge and expertise in international financial services, and close ties with many BRI partners. These have given the UK a unique strength in BRI project financing, Public Private Partnership, insurance and green finance. There is no doubt that the UK is a natural partner of China in advancing the BRI.

Next year, China will host the second Belt and Road Forum for International Cooperation to lift international cooperation on the BRI to a new level. This will create new opportunities for China-UK cooperation, in particular, on financial services.

Third, I have confidence in a sound China-UK relationship.

As China and the UK stepped into the second decade of the 21st century, we established the global comprehensive strategic partnership for the 21st century, and have since achieved fruitful results in our cooperation on trade, investment, financial services, science, innovation, and cultural and people-to-people exchanges.

The progress has not come easy. It is a result of decades of relentless efforts of people from all walks of life of both our countries. It is important that we treasure and take good care of the sound momentum of our relationship.

I hope, and I believe, that our two countries will view our relationship from a global and strategic perspective, and respect each other's core interests and major concerns.

Ladies and Gentlemen,

The ancient philosopher Cicero said, "Confidence is that feeling by which the mind embarks in great and honourable courses with a sure hope and trust in itself."

I believe, with firm confidence, we will overcome difficulties and strive ahead together to create an even brighter future for China-UK relations!

Thank you!

走绿色发展之路，谱金融合作新篇 *

尊敬的伦敦金融城政策与资源委员会主席孟珂琳女士，

女士们、先生们：

大家早上好！

很高兴出席亚洲金融合作协会（以下简称亚金协）2019 年绿色金融国际论坛（伦敦）暨《亚金协绿色金融实践报告（2019）》发布会。

2019 年是中华人民共和国成立 70 周年，也是中英建立代办级外交关系 65 周年。70 年来，中国发展日新月异，经济实力和综合国力名列世界前茅，走完了西方发达国家几百年走过的发展之路。65 年来，中英关系历经风雨，实现跨越式发展，建立起面向 21 世纪全球全面战略伙伴关系。中国的快速发展，为中英合作特别是金融合作带来巨大机遇。

我出任中国驻英国大使 9 年多来，无数次到访金融城，每次都感到既熟悉又新鲜。

说到"熟悉"，是因为中英金融合作成果丰硕、前景广阔，我每次来访都倍感亲切。我在这里多次出席中资银行分行开业、两国合作项目启动、合作成果庆典，2018 年还荣获伦敦金融城"荣誉市民"称号。就在 小时前，我出席了在伦敦证券交易所举办的第十五届世界华商大会推介会。

说到"新鲜"，是因为国际金融业蓬勃发展，我每次来访都能收获新知

---

* 在亚洲金融合作协会 2019 年绿色金融国际论坛（伦敦）暨《亚金协绿色金融实践报告（2019）》发布会上的主旨演讲。2019 年 9 月 3 日，伦敦金融城市政厅。

识，结识新朋友，开阔新视野。绿色金融就是在当今逆全球化暗流涌动、环境治理等全球性挑战日益突出的背景下，世界各国所面临的一个新课题。

今天，中英两国金融界人士在此共同探讨绿色金融合作、推动绿色金融发展，可谓恰逢其时。我认为有三个重要意义。

第一，为中英深化金融合作注入"新动力"。中英两国都是绿色发展的"领军者"。中国农业银行早在 2015 年就在伦敦证券交易所发行了等值 10 亿美元的绿色债券；吉利集团于 2016 年发行总额达 4 亿美元的绿色债券，支持其英国子公司伦敦出租车公司开发具有零排放能力的经典伦敦黑色出租车；中国工商银行于 2018 年在伦敦正式发行 15.8 亿美元等值双币种多段绿色债券，并于 2019 年 6 月与汇丰银行、法国巴黎银行签署绿色融资合作意向书。2019 年 6 月举行的第十次中英经济财金对话期间，两国就绿色金融达成了多项重要共识，双方重申彼此在绿色金融领域互为主要合作伙伴，将加强绿色标准协调，开发创新产品等合作。展望未来，绿色金融将成为中英务实合作的重要"增长点"，潜力巨大、前景广阔。

第二，为中英共建"一带一路"提供"新机遇"。"一带一路"是一条绿色之路。2018 年 11 月，中英绿色金融工作组共同发布《"一带一路"绿色投资原则》，将低碳和可持续发展议题纳入"一带一路"倡议，以提升投资环境和社会风险管理水平，推动"一带一路"投资的绿色化。2019 年 4 月举行的第二届"一带一路"国际合作高峰论坛开启了高质量共建"一带一路"新征程，此次论坛一个重要成果就是正式成立了绿色发展国际联盟。伦敦是首屈一指的国际金融中心，英国是绿色"一带一路"建设的天然伙伴。中英双方可积极利用绿色金融专业知识和领导能力，加强优势互补，研发绿色产品，推动"一带一路"合作高质量发展。

第三，为完善全球金融治理贡献"新思路"。中英绿色金融合作不仅限于双边范畴，也具有重要全球影响。2016 年，中英两国率先在二十国集团框架下成立绿色金融研究小组，向二十国集团领导人杭州峰会提交了《G20 绿色金融综合报告》，共同作为"引领者"在全球范围内推动绿色金融发展。中英两国应进一步加深绿色金融理论研究，构建绿色金融标准体系，深化绿色金融产品服务创新，共同推动全球金融治理框架不断完善，促进全球金融合作更加健康、可持续发展。

女士们、先生们，

2015年，习近平主席在博鳌亚洲论坛讲话中提出，探讨搭建亚洲金融机构交流合作平台。亚金协就此应运而生。亚金协成立以来，本着"联通合作、共治共享"的宗旨，努力搭建金融务实合作平台，深入研究金融发展理论，大力整合区域金融资源，积极参与国际金融治理，受到域内外金融界的高度关注和支持。伦敦金融城成为亚金协绿色金融合作委员会常务副主任单位，这为两国绿色金融合作增添了新的着力点。

女士们、先生们，

中国有句古语，"万物得其本者生，百事得其道者成"。当今世界正处于百年未有之大变局，和平、发展、合作、共赢的时代潮流不可阻挡。中英关系正处于承前启后的重要时刻，站在新的历史起点上。在当前保护主义、单边主义不断抬头的背景下，中英金融合作不仅惠及两国，也具有世界意义。我衷心希望，中英两国金融界抓住机遇，携手努力，拓展合作，促进中英绿色金融合作走深走实，推动全球绿色金融合作行稳致远！

最后，预祝今天的论坛暨《亚金协绿色金融实践报告（2019）》发布会取得圆满成功！

谢谢大家！

Pursue Green Development and Write a New Chapter of Financial Cooperation*

Ms Catherine McGuinness,

Ladies and Gentlemen,

Good morning!

It is a real delight to join you at the AFCA International Forum for Green Finance (London) and *AFCA Green Finance Practice Report 2019* Launching Event.

This year marks the 70th anniversary of the founding of the People's Republic of China and the 65th anniversary of the establishment of China-UK diplomatic relationship at the level of chargé d'affaires.

In the past 70 years, China experienced rapid growth. It is now leading the world in economic power and comprehensive national strength. China has accomplished in 70 years what had taken Western industrialised countries hundreds of years to achieve.

In the past 65 years, the China-UK relationship has made leaps and bounds despite wind and rain. Now China and the UK have established a global comprehensive strategic partnership for the 21st century. In this process, the Chinese rapid development has created enormous opportunities for China-UK cooperation especially in the financial sector.

In my more than 9 years as Chinese Ambassador, I have visited the City of London many times. Yet I find it both familiar and fresh.

---

* Keynote Speech at the AFCA International Forum for Green Finance (London) and *AFCA Green Finance Practice Report 2019* Launching Event. Guildhall, City of London, 3 September 2019.

I find it familiar because the fruitful and promising financial cooperation between China and the UK has resulted in my frequent visits and emotional attachment to the City of London. I have attended many openings of Chinese bank branches, launches of China-UK joint projects and celebrations of cooperation outcomes. In 2018, I had the honour of becoming a Freeman of the City. Just one hour ago, I was at London Stock Exchange for the Market Open in honour of the 15th World Chinese Entrepreneurs Convention coming to London.

I also find it fresh when I visit the City each time. There are always new things to learn, new faces to meet and new frontiers to explore. I think this is attributable to the City's thriving international financial sector. In curbing anti-globalisation and tackling global challenges in environmental governance, green finance is one of the new frontiers.

Therefore, it is timely that representatives from the financial sectors of our two countries have come together today to discuss how we could work together for new progress in green finance. In my view, green finance has the following three-fold significance for China and the UK.

First, it is a "new driving force" for deeper financial cooperation.

Both China and the UK champion green development.

- As early as 2015, the Agricultural Bank of China listed green bond equivalent to 1 billion US dollars at the London Stock Exchange.
- In 2016, Geely issued 400 million US dollars of green bond to support the development of the classic London black cabs with zero emission.
- In 2018, the Industrial and Commercial Bank of China issued dual-currency green bond segment in London equivalent to 1.58 billion US dollars.
- In June, ICBC signed the Mandate Letter on Green Loan with HSBC and BNP Paribas.

At the tenth China-UK Economic and Financial Dialogue concluded in June, our two countries reached a number of important agreements on green finance. According to these agreements, China and the UK restate their recognition of each other as their primary partner in green finance. We have also pledged to work on harmonisation of green standards and develop innovative product.

Looking ahead, green finance, as an important new "growth point" for China-UK business cooperation, will achieve its huge potential and embrace a promising future.

Second, green finance creates "new opportunities" for China-UK cooperation on the Belt and Road Initiative.

The BRI is a green initiative.

Last November, the China-UK Green Finance Taskforce issued the Green Investment Principles for Belt and Road Development. Low-carbon and sustainable development became a BRI objective. There will be increased emphasis on the capability to manage environmental and social implications so as to make BRI investment greener.

The second Belt and Road Forum for International Cooperation held in April marked the beginning of high-quality BRI. One important outcome of the Forum is the establishment of the BRI International Green Development Coalition. This is another indication that BRI is becoming greener.

London is a top international financial centre. Britain is a natural partner for China in building a green BRI. China and the UK could leverage our expertise and leadership in green finance. We could match our strengths and develop more green products so as to build a high-quality and greener BRI.

Third, green finance offers a "new solution" to global financial governance.

China-UK cooperation on green finance is more than bilateral. It has global significance.

In 2016, China and the UK took the initiative to set up the G20 Green Finance Study Group. This led to the *G20 Green Finance Synthesis Report*, which was submitted to the G20 Hangzhou Summit.

China and the UK should focus on further research, standardization, and product and services innovation on green finance. This will enable us to make concerted efforts to improve global financial governance framework and facilitate healthier and more sustainable financial cooperation in the world.

Ladies and Gentlemen,

At the Annual Conference 2015 of the Boao Forum for Asia, President Xi Jinping proposed to establish a platform for exchanges and cooperation between the financial institutions in Asia. In response to this proposal, the Asian Financial Cooperation Association was set up.

AFCA follows the principles of "Connectivity, Cooperation, Joint Governance and Shared Benefits". Since its establishment, AFCA has served as:

- A platform for financial cooperation.
- A centre for in-depth research on financial theories.
- A hub for integrating regional financial resources.
- And an active participant in global financial governance.

These efforts have been highly recognised and greatly endorsed by the financial sector in Asia and beyond. The City of London is the Executive Deputy Director of AFCA's green finance committee. This is providing yet another effective platform for China-UK cooperation on green finance.

Ladies and Gentlemen,

A Chinese adage goes,

"With strong roots, plants will grow; With good deeds, people will succeed."

The world is undergoing profound changes unseen in a century. Peace, development and win-win cooperation are the irreversible trend of our times.

Now is a critical moment for the China-UK relationship. Both our countries are standing at a new historical starting point. We should build on our past achievements and move on to embrace the future. Against the backdrop of surging protectionism and unilateralism, China-UK financial cooperation will not only benefit our two countries but also carry global significance.

I sincerely hope that the financial community of our two countries will seize the opportunities to expand cooperation. We should join hands to deepen and substantiate China-UK cooperation on green finance and promote the steady and sustained global cooperation on green finance!

In conclusion, I wish today's Forum and the *AFCA Green Finance Practice Report 2019* Launching Event great success!

Thank you!

推进高水平金融合作，打造开放共赢成果 *

女士们、先生们：

大家下午好！

很高兴出席中国建设银行举办的"双庆"活动。2014年，作为李克强总理访问英国的成果之一，中国建设银行在伦敦成立人民币业务清算银行。5年来，中国建设银行伦敦分行业务蓬勃发展，人民币累计清算量突破40万亿元，成为亚洲地区以外规模最大的清算银行，书写了建行历史上具有里程碑意义的新篇章！我谨对这一成就表示热烈祝贺！

2019年是中华人民共和国成立70周年，也是中英建立代办级外交关系65周年。在这样一个回顾历史、展望未来的重要年份，我们庆贺中国建设银行伦敦人民币清算银行取得的成就具有重要意义，体现了"三个标志"。

第一，这标志着中英金融合作正不断走深走实。金融合作是中英合作最具活力、最具潜力的领域之一。中国建设银行人民币清算银行地处伦敦这一全球金融中心，借助独特时区优势，协同北京和纽约两大资源，不仅实现了人民币清算业务对亚洲、欧洲和北美洲主要工作时段的覆盖，更使伦敦成为中国与世界各国开展离岸人民币业务的重要平台。目前，伦敦已成为世界第一大人民币离岸外汇交易中心和全球第二大人民币离岸清算中心。

第二，这标志着中国金融业正坚定走向世界。改革开放40多年来，中

---

* 在中国建设银行人民币清算银行成立5周年暨清算量突破40万亿元庆祝会上的讲话。2019年11月7日，伦敦城俱乐部。

国坚定不移扩大对外开放，奉行互利共赢的开放战略，有力提升了中国对外开放与国际合作水平。中国建设银行人民币清算银行在伦敦的设立和发展，是中国金融业深度融入世界、惠及世界的一个缩影。下一步，中国将扩大服务业特别是金融业对外开放，与包括英国在内的各国扩大双向投资，促进贸易和金融往来，在开放中增进共同利益，在合作中实现互利共赢。

第三，这标志着人民币国际化正日益展现广阔前景。随着中国推进人民币汇率市场化改革，人民币国际化水平不断提高。目前，人民币市场已得到更多跨国企业认可，汇丰、渣打、巴克莱、摩根大通、花旗、芝加哥商业交易所、巴西中央银行等世界74家金融机构均在建行人民币清算银行开通账户，客户来源遍布五大洲。人民币已成为全球第七大支付结算货币、第九大外汇交易货币，在全球货币体系中的重要性稳步提升。

展望未来，我认为，中英金融合作把握以下三点至关重要。

一是坚定开放合作。经济全球化是不可逆转的时代大势，单边主义、保护主义行径损人害己，零和博弈、以邻为壑只能画地为牢。中英双方要坚定地站在历史前进的正确一边，做经济全球化的积极参与者和坚定支持者，通过更高水平的开放合作，推动建设开放型世界经济。

二是引领创新潮流。近年来，新技术的兴起深刻改变了金融业态。中英金融科技创新创业活跃，市场需求广阔，发展势头强劲。英国在消费金融、数字化银行、大数据分析等方面经验丰富，中国在市场规模、移动支付、普惠金融等方面优势明显。双方可在金融科技等领域加大创新合作力度，提升金融服务的广度、深度和效率，为中英金融合作注入更强劲的动力。

三是打造共赢成果。中英是共建"一带一路"的天然合作伙伴。"一带一路"建设不仅需要投融资合作，而且涉及大量配套金融服务。英国具有丰富的金融运作经验和成熟的管理制度，中国在基础设施、互联互通、融资等方面具有优势。双方可依托"一带一路"平台，在投融资、保险、绿色金融、第三方市场等领域加强合作，实现优势互补、互利共赢，更好地造福两国和世界人民。

女士们、先生们，

历史照亮未来，征程未有穷期。中共十九届四中全会的召开，标志着中国将继续毫不动摇走中国特色社会主义道路，继续为世界和平、发展、繁荣、进步做出贡献。此时此刻，第二届中国国际进口博览会正在上海举行，习近平主席在开幕式上发表了重要讲话，提出共建开放合作、开放创新、开放共享的世界经济，宣布五项推进更高水平的对外开放措施，进一步彰显了中国以开放合作促进世界共同发展的大国担当。所有这些都将给世界各国带来更多发展机遇，提供更广阔的合作空间。

我衷心期待，中英两国金融界朋友们抓住机遇，加强合作，不断开拓两国经济金融合作新前景，为中英关系贡献更多合作成果！

最后，祝中国建设银行事业蒸蒸日上！祝建行伦敦分行及人民币清算银行不断开创新业绩！

谢谢！

Enhance Financial Cooperation and Deliver More Fruits*

Ladies and Gentlemen,

Good afternoon!

It is a real delight to join you at the event of double celebration for China Construction Bank. Back in 2014, CCB launched the RMB clearing services here in London. It was one of the outcomes of Premier Li Keqiang's visit to the UK. And it marked the beginning of a new chapter in the history of CCB.

Over the past 5 years since then, CCB London has achieved remarkable progress, with a total clearing volume of 40 trillion RMB yuan. It is now the largest RMB clearing bank outside Asia. I would like to extend my warmest congratulations to CCB on this major milestone!

This year marks the 70th anniversary of the founding of the People's Republic of China and the 65th anniversary of China-UK diplomatic relationship at the chargé d'affaires level. This is an important year! As we review our progress and look into the future, today's event bears three-fold significance.

First, CCB's achievement bears witness to the ever-deeper and more substantial financial cooperation between China and the UK.

Financial sector is one of the most vigorous and promising in China-UK cooperation. London is a global financial centre. CCB London joins clearing banks in Beijing and New York to make sure that RMB clearing services can be offered during the majority of

---

* Speech at the Celebration of the Fifth Anniversary of CCB London's Launch of the UK RMB Clearing Services. City of London Club, 7 November 2019.

the working hours in Asia, Europe and North America.

CCB's RMB clearing services has also made London an important platform for RMB offshore transaction between China and other countries. London is now the world's largest RMB offshore trading hub and second largest RMB offshore clearing centre.

Second, CCB's achievement represents a firm step to integrate the Chinese financial sector with the world.

In the past 40 plus years since the beginning of reform and opening-up, China has been committed to opening its market and pursuing win-win cooperation at a higher level. The launch and growth of the RMB clearing services in London is an epitome of the Chinese financial sector integrating with and delivering benefits to the world.

Going forward, China will open its services market wider, especially in the financial sector. China is ready to work with all countries, including the UK, to expand investment both ways, and enhance trade and financial exchanges. Through open cooperation, China hopes to expand common interests with other countries and achieve win-win results.

Third, CCB's achievement heralds a promising prospect of RMB internationalization.

As the market-based reform in RMB exchange rate regime deepens, RMB is increasingly becoming a global currency and has been accepted by more and more trans-national enterprises.

Seventy-four financial institutions, including HSBC, Standard Chartered, Barclays, J.P. Morgan, Citibank, Chicago Mercantile Exchange and Banco Central do Brasil, have all opened accounts with CCB London, who has customers in every corner of the world.

Today, RMB is the world's seventh most traded currency and the ninth largest foreign exchange trading currency. It is playing an increasingly important role in the global currency system.

Looking forward, I think China and the UK should make the following three efforts in our financial cooperation:

First, our two countries should remain committed to open cooperation.

Economic globalisation is irreversible. Unilateralism and protectionism are double-edged swords that will hurt both ways. Zero-sum games and "beggar-thy-neighbour" approach will only backfire.

China and the UK should stand on the right side of history. We should be active participants and firm supporters of globalisation. We should engage in open cooperation at a higher level and work to build an open world economy.

Second, China and the UK should take the lead in innovation.

The development of new technologies in recent years has changed the business models in the financial sector.

China and the UK are known for active FinTech innovation and entrepreneurship. We both have a large market and strong growth momentum in this aspect.

In particular, the UK has rich experience in consumer finance, digital banking and big data analysis. China has a huge market, advanced mobile payment and inclusive finance. Cooperation between our two countries on FinTech innovation will enable us to provide broader, more in-depth and more efficient financial services. It will also give a strong boost to the overall China-UK financial cooperation.

Third, China and the UK should deliver more mutually-beneficial outcomes.

Our two countries are natural partners in building the Belt and Road Initiative. BRI development needs not only cooperation on investment and financing. It also needs a wide range of supportive financial services.

The UK has rich experience in financial operation and mature management mechanisms. China is strong in infrastructure, connectivity and financing. China and the UK could enhance cooperation on BRI in the areas of investment, financing, insurance and green finance and in third markets. Complementing our strengths and engaging in win-win cooperation will enable our two countries to deliver more benefits to our peoples and the people of the world.

Ladies and Gentlemen,

History sheds light on our way ahead, and we must forever march on.

The fourth plenary session of the 19th Central Committee of the Communist Party of China was concluded a few days ago. This important meeting once again sends the message that China will remain committed to the path of socialism with Chinese characteristics, and will continue to contribute to world peace, development, prosperity and progress.

As we speak, the second China International Import Expo is being held in Shanghai. President Xi Jinping delivered an important speech at the opening ceremony. He proposed to work together to build an open world economy through cooperation, with innovation and for mutual benefits. He also announced five measures to bring about opening-up at an even higher level. He further emphasized the Chinese determination to shoulder its responsibility as a big country and promote common development in the world through open cooperation.

All these will create more opportunities for development and provide broader space for cooperation between countries of the world.

I sincerely hope that the financial communities of China and the UK will seize these opportunities and enhance cooperation. I hope you will open up new prospects for China-UK economic and financial collaboration, and deliver more fruits for China-UK relations!

In conclusion, I wish CCB great success! And I wish CCB London and its RMB clearing services new progress!

Thank you!

2017年9月19日
在苏格兰商会晚宴上发表主旨演讲：《深挖潜力，开拓中苏（格兰）合作美好未来》

2018年1月18日
在中英经济贸易论坛上发表主旨演讲：《把握新时代，开创新局面，迈上新台阶》

2018年4月25日

在"贵州全球推介活动——走进英国"活动上发表讲话:《抓住"宝贵机遇",推进贵州对英合作》

2018年6月11日

在"深圳-伦敦经贸交流会"上发表讲话:《永立改革开放时代潮头,推进中英全面战略伙伴关系》

2018年7月13日
在海南自贸区伦敦综合推介会上发表主旨演讲：《打造改革开放新高地，助力中英关系新发展》

2018年12月3日
出席伦敦金融城"荣誉市民"授勋仪式并发表讲话：《坚定信心，共创未来》

● 2018年12月18日

在曼彻斯特工商界晚宴上发表主旨演讲：《高举开放旗帜，携手开创未来》

● 2018年12月18日

在英国曼彻斯特大学发表主旨演讲：《以创新推动发展，以创新促进合作》

2019年1月28日

在英国议会跨党派中国小组新春招待会上发表讲话：《聚同化异，淬炼真金》

2019年2月13日

在英国保守党议会中国小组早餐会上发表主旨演讲：《中英关系的"三要三不要"》

● **2019年3月28日**
在"湖南-英国未来创新峰会"上发表讲话：《创新引领未来，合作共谱华章》

● **2019年6月26日**
在"第二届中英经贸论坛"上发表主旨演讲：《继往开来，携手奋进，筑牢中英合作共赢之路》

2019 年 9 月 3 日
在伦敦金融城市政厅发表演讲：《走绿色发展之路，谱金融合作新篇》

2019 年 10 月 11 日
在第十七届 "21 世纪中国" 论坛上致辞：《引领开放创新潮流，打造合作共赢成果》

2019年11月7日

出席中国建设银行人民币清算银行成立5周年暨清算量突破40万亿元庆祝会并发表讲话：《推进高水平金融合作，打造开放共赢成果》

2021年1月25日

在离任招待会上发表讲话：《精诚如一，善始令终》

第五章　科技合作
PART V　Cooperation on Science and Technology

英国是世界科技大国，以不到世界 1% 的人口，从事世界 5% 的科学研究工作，研究范围几乎涉及所有科学领域，尤其在生物技术、航空、国防方面具有较强的实力。英国科学家发表学术论文数量占全球总量的 9%，引用量占 15.2%，获国际重要奖项人数占总数的 10%。迄今共有 130 多人获得诺贝尔科学奖项，居世界第二。

英国对科技敏感、行动超前，宣布投资 6 亿英镑，支持大数据、空间技术、机器人和自动系统、合成生物学、再生医药、农业科技、先进材料、能源储蓄八大未来技术领域。根据世界知识产权组织《2021 年全球创新指数报告》，英国排名第四，仅次于瑞士、瑞典、美国。

中英科技交流广泛而深入，2019 年中英合作发表论文 1.6 万多篇，占英国论文总量的 11%，仅低于英美合作占比 19%。中国已超过德国，成为英国第二大科研合作伙伴。中英在人工智能、计算机、科学等 20 多个重要学科领域合作发表论文数量占英国论文产出总量的 20%，而且质量不断提升。中英科研合作的特点是以双边为主，占比 52%。而英美、英澳、英欧盟科研合作以多边为主。中国许多大学与英国的高校建立了国际联合实验室，在空间科技与技术、新能源材料、化学等多个领域开展合作研究。英国一些名校也分别在中国建立研究院和创新中心。2013 年中英签署了中英研究创新合作谅解备忘录，决定设立总额 2 亿英镑的联合科学创新基金。2015 年中英建立创新合作伙伴关系。2017 年双方共同发布《中英科技创新合作战略》。

本章收录了我的 5 篇演讲，内容涵盖医药卫生、生命科学、科技创新、产业合作、区域发展等。

The UK is a global science and technology powerhouse, with less than 1% of the world's population conducting 5% of the world's scientific research, covering almost all scientific fields, particularly in biotechnology, aviation, and national defense. British scientists publish 9% of the world's academic papers, account for 15.2% of citations, and make up 10% of the recipients of major international awards. To date, Britain boasts more than 130 Nobel Prize winners, ranking second in the world.

The UK is sensitive to and proactive in technology, announcing an investment of 600 million pounds to support eight fields of future technology: Big data, space technology, robotics and autonomous systems, synthetic biology, regenerative medicine, agricultural technology, advanced materials, and energy storage. According to the *Global Innovation Index 2021*, a report issued by the World Intellectual Property Organization, the UK ranks fourth, behind Switzerland, Sweden and the United States.

China-UK exchanges in science and technology are extensive and deep. In 2019, China and the UK co-authored over 16,000 papers, accounting for 11% of the UK's total, second only to the UK-US collaboration at 19%. China has surpassed Germany to become the UK's second-largest scientific research partner. China-UK cooperation in more than 20 key academic fields, including artificial intelligence and computer science, accounts for 20% of the UK's paper output, with continuous improvement in quality. China-UK scientific research cooperation is mainly bilateral, accounting for 52%, whereas UK-US, UK-Australia, and UK-EU scientific research cooperation is mainly multilateral. Many Chinese universities have established international joint laboratories with British universities, conducting cooperative research in fields such as space technology, new energy materials, and chemistry. Some prestigious British universities have also established research institutes and innovation centres in China. In 2013, China and the UK signed a Memorandum of Understanding on Research and Innovation Cooperation, establishing a joint science and innovation fund totaling 200 million pounds. In 2015, China and the UK established an innovation cooperation partnership. In 2017, the two sides jointly released the China-UK Science and Innovation Cooperation Strategy.

This chapter includes 5 of my speeches, covering topics such as medical and health care, life sciences, scientific and technological innovation, industrial cooperation and regional development.

合作共赢，造福人类 *

女士们、先生们：

欢迎大家来到中国驻英国大使馆做客。

在我为英国心脏细胞基金会举行午餐会之前，我查阅了一下相关资料。令我吃惊的是，据世界经济论坛发布的报告，在影响世界经济的众多因素中，慢性病造成的疾病风险和经济负担高达1万亿美元，甚至大于金融危机的影响。而在各种慢性病中，根据世界卫生组织的研究，心血管疾病成为威胁人类生命的"头号杀手"。在中国，每十个成年人就有两人患有心血管疾病，可能与英国的发病率相差无几。因此，中国《国家中长期科学和技术发展规划纲要（2006—2020年）》将"心脑血管病、肿瘤等重大非传染疾病防治"列为人口与健康领域的优先主题。

人类应对心血管疾病，首先要从预防着手，培养良好的生活习惯，比如注意饮食均衡和经常锻炼身体，但一旦患病，积极治疗也是必不可少的。在此，我要赞赏英国心脏细胞基金会，你们大力筹募善款，支持利用干细胞治疗心脏系统疾病的临床研究，帮助患者重获新生。

你们所支持的研究，我想不仅对英国是一件大好事，而且有益于世界，因为"科学无国界"，健康是人类共同的福祉。

近年来，中英在健康和卫生领域开展了良好的合作与交流。昨天，中国

---

* 在为英国心脏细胞基金会举行的午餐会上的讲话。2011年6月28日，中国驻英国大使馆。

国务院总理温家宝刚刚成功结束对英国的正式访问。访问的目的就是推动中英各领域的合作，其中包括生命科学和卫生领域的合作。

在 6 月初举行的中英政府间科技合作第六次联委会会议上，中英双方决定共同将人口健康领域确定为两国在今后两年重点科技合作领域之一。

中国当前也在完善基本医疗卫生制度，特别是加强社区卫生服务体系，而英国是现代社区医疗服务的发源地，有不少成功经验。我听说，中国不少地方专门请英国的社区卫生服务专家赴华讲课指导和传授经验。我上周还看到报道，中国决定建立全科医生制度，而我们知道，早在整整 100 年前，也就是 1911 年，英国就在世界上首创了这一制度。

近年来，中国科学家在利用干细胞治疗心脏系统疾病方面做出了不懈努力，也取得了一定成果。但在一些前沿领域，例如成体干细胞应用技术方面，中国与世界先进水平还有差距，因此我们鼓励和支持中国科学家与包括英国在内的国际同行加强合作和交流。

我希望中英两国在包括干细胞治疗心脏病等生命科学、卫生健康领域的交流与合作不断加强，取得更多更新的成果。

最后，祝愿英国心脏细胞基金会越办越好，帮助更多需要帮助的人，救治更多需要救治的人。

谢谢！

Win-Win Cooperation for Mankind[*]

Ladies and Gentlemen,

A very warm welcome to the Chinese Embassy.

Before I host this lunch for the Heart Cells Foundation, I looked up some background information about the correlation between health and the economy. I had some surprise findings. Apparently, the annual report of the World Economic Forum on global risks puts chronic diseases as a leading factor affecting the health of the global economy. Treatment of these diseases costs the world 1 trillion US dollars every year. This means a greater burden on the global economy than even the financial crisis. Cardiovascular diseases cause particular damage. According to the WHO, they are the "number one killer" among deaths caused by diseases. In China, every two out of ten adults suffer from some form of cardiovascular illnesses, similar to the figure in the UK. That is why the Chinese Guideline for National Scientific and Technological Development for the Medium to Long Term (2006—2020) has taken the prevention and treatment of cardiovascular diseases as a priority area in the field of population and health.

Prevention is the best way to deal with cardiovascular diseases. We can protect ourselves through a healthy way of living. We should have a balanced diet and regular exercises. But active treatment is equally important if unfortunately the illness occurs. One potential treatment is through stem cell research. The Heart Cells Foundation has been raising funds to support clinical research on finding the latest cure of this

---

[*] Remarks at the Lunch in Honour of the Heart Cells Foundation. Chinese Embassy, 28 June 2011.

killer disease through stem cell. This research could lead to lives being saved. I highly admire and commend your efforts.

The research you are funding is not only beneficial to people in this country, but for the whole world. Science goes beyond national borders. Health and well-being is a common blessing for all mankind.

China and the UK have worked closely together in addressing health challenges in recent years. Chinese Premier Wen Jiabao has just concluded his two-day official visit to the UK. His visit produced important results in further promoting our cooperation in two-way trade and investment, and people-to-people exchanges. The two sides also explored potential cooperation in the areas of life sciences and health.

Earlier this month we convened the sixth session of the China-UK Joint Commission on Science and Technology. During this session, population and health was identified as a key area of scientific cooperation between our two countries in the coming two years.

China is engaged in an ongoing effort to build and improve its basic medical care system. Special emphasis will be given to community health services.

As the birthplace of modern primary health services, Britain has a lot of useful experience that may offer guidance to other countries. I am glad to learn that British health care experts were invited to several cities in China to give lectures and share good practices with Chinese hospitals and health care agencies. Another report last week also shows that China has decided to establish general practice clinics, another institution that has its origins in Britain a hundred years ago.

Chinese scientists have worked hard in recent years to explore stem cell treatment of cardiovascular diseases. Some progress has been made. But China still lags behind in some cutting-edge areas such as adult stem cell application. We would very much hope to see greater exchanges and collaboration among the scientific communities of our two countries across the whole range of science and health areas. Stem cell research on heart diseases should no doubt be part of our exchanges.

Greater collaboration benefits both of us, as it helps to strengthen our respective capacities to deliver better and more effective health care to our two peoples.

Before I conclude, I wish the Heart Cells Foundation every success in your future endeavours.

I hope and I am sure that the stronger you become, the more people you will be able to help.

Thank you!

凡事预则立，不预则废 *

尊敬的英国财政部商业国务大臣奥尼尔勋爵，
各位使节，
女士们、先生们：
很高兴出席英国关于抗生素耐药性问题研究报告的发布会。

关于抗生素耐药性问题的重要性和迫切性，刚才奥尼尔国务大臣及英国首席医学官戴维斯教授等已经讲得很透彻。这正应了中国一句古语："道高一尺，魔高一丈。"人类社会在发展进程中，尽管取得了无数的进步与成就，但仍然不断面临困难与阻力。愈进愈阻，愈阻愈进，永无止息，这大概就是整个人类文明史的真实写照。在医学领域，青霉素的发现就是一大突破，拯救了无数患者的生命，但随之而来的抗生素耐药性却给医学带来了新的挑战。

当前，由于全球人口移动频繁以及抗菌药物使用不当，病菌繁殖进化高速演变，抗生素耐药性问题日益加剧，正成为人类生命安全和社会可持续发展的巨大威胁。

孔子说："人无远虑，必有近忧。"面对抗生素耐药性的挑战，各国都加强研究对策，并积极寻求国际合作。今天英方发布的报告体现了多国合作的最新研究成果，对国际社会共同应对抗生素耐药性挑战具有重要意义。

中国政府高度重视抗生素耐药性问题，不仅组织力量开展相关研究，而

---

* 在英国关于抗生素耐药性问题研究报告发布会上的讲话。2016年5月19日，伦敦兰卡斯特宫。

且结合自身国情采取积极措施和行动，包括加强抗生素药物管理，建立处方点评评估制度，开展抗生素药物临床应用监测和抗生素耐药监测，并充分运用信息化手段，重点对抗生素药物使用量、使用强度及变化趋势等进行监测和评价。在国家层面，中国政府还积极构建抗生素耐药多部门联防联控机制，制订抗生素耐药国家行动计划，并积极参与抗生素耐药性的国际合作等。

中国与英国在抗生素耐药性问题上进行了密切交流与合作，这些合作涉及政策磋商、人员培训、公众教育、新药研发等各个方面。两国政府还通过联合设立的中英联合科学创新基金（牛顿基金），共同出资900万英镑支持两国科学家合作开展相关研究，首批项目正在由中国国家自然科学基金委员会和英国研究理事会进行评审。中国将于2016年9月主办二十国集团领导人峰会，中英双方正在二十国集团领导人框架内就抗生素耐药性问题加强协调，推动各方专家开展讨论。

"凡事预则立，不预则废。"我相信，只要国际社会一起行动起来，加强科学研究、政策协调、资金支持与行动配合，我们就能应对抗生素耐药性这一全球性的挑战，就能防止大规模传染性疾病的暴发，就能捍卫人类的生命健康和安全！

谢谢！

Forewarned Is Forearmed[*]

Lord O'Neill,

Fellow Ambassadors,

Ladies and Gentlemen,

It is a pleasure to join you for the briefing of the AMR review final report.

Just now, Lord O'Neill and Professor Davis gave us incisive analysis of how essential and urgent it is to tackle the problem of drug-resistant infections.

As the Chinese saying goes, "As virtue rises one foot, vice rises ten." Men have always been making progress and achievements. Yet we are also always faced with difficulties and challenges. Making progress is a process of overcoming one hurdle after another. This is a true reflection on the journey of human civilizations.

In the field of medical science, the discovery of penicillin was a significant breakthrough that has saved innumerable lives. But the problem of resistance that followed is now becoming a new challenge.

In today's world, greater global mobility of people and improper use of antimicrobials is giving rise to faster evolution and stronger resistance of bacteria. This is posing a real and huge threat to the safety and sustainability of mankind.

Confucius said: "He who does not plan for the future will find trouble at his doorstep." Countries around the world are now working hard to find a solution to AMR and vigorously engaging in international cooperation. The final report released today is the latest outcome of joint international efforts in this field. It will be of great value to closer international cooperation in responding to this global challenge.

---

[*] Remarks at the Briefing of the AMR Review Final Report. Lancaster House, 19 May 2016.

The Chinese government takes AMR very seriously. We have put in enormous efforts into AMR research. We have also taken a string of concrete actions in line with the Chinese national conditions. These actions include:

- Tighten control on the use of antimicrobials.
- Establish a prescription evaluation system.
- Monitor the clinical application of antimicrobials and the drug resistance cases.

These measures, supported by the information technology, are mainly designed to monitor and assess the antibiotic consumption, dose-intensity and the trend of changes.

The Chinese government is also putting in place a national-level cross-department AMR management mechanism. This mechanism will be responsible for making a national AMR action plan and participating in international cooperation.

At present, China and the UK are engaged in close exchanges and cooperation in tackling AMR. This includes policy consultations, training programs, public education, and R&D of new drugs. Through our co-established platform of Newton Fund, our two governments have jointly pledged a total of nine million pounds to support scientists from both countries to cooperate on relevant research. The first projects are now under evaluation by the National Natural Science Foundation of China and the Research Councils UK. China is going to host G20 Summit in September. Currently China and the UK are coordinating with other member countries on expert-level with regard to how G20 would respond to tackling this global challenge.

As we say, "Forewarned is forearmed."

I am confident that,

as long as countries of the world work together,

as long as we all enhance scientific research, align our policies and pledge adequate funding,

we can address this rising global challenge of AMR,

we can prevent the explosive spread of infectious diseases,

and we can safeguard the health and safety of mankind.

Thank you!

以创新推动发展，以创新促进合作 *

尊敬的曼彻斯特大学校长罗思韦尔爵士，

老师们、同学们，

女士们、先生们：

大家下午好！

很高兴第三次访问曼彻斯特大学（以下简称曼大）。3 年前，我曾两度到访曼大，第一次是为习近平主席访问打前站，第二次是陪同习近平主席进行国事访问。曼大开放创新、追求卓越的精神给我留下深刻印象。时隔 3 年，故地重游，我倍感亲切。

曼大是英国乃至全球知名高等学府，综合实力、学科建设均位居世界前列。曼大人才辈出，迄今已培育了 25 名诺贝尔奖得主，贡献了诸多改变人类命运的重大科技成果，例如原子分裂、石墨烯的发现及世界第一台可储存程序计算机等。这些成果充分彰显了曼大"知识、智慧和人文精神"的校训。

校方领导希望我谈谈创新以及中英在创新和城镇发展等领域的合作，今天我想结合曼大的校训谈谈上述话题。

知识就是力量，也是叩开创新之门的钥匙。没有知识，就没有人类的进步；没有创新，人类社会就没有未来。当前，新一轮科技革命和产业变革方兴未艾。只有勇立世界科技创新潮头，才能推动人类文明进步取得更大发展。中国正积极落实创新、协调、绿色、开放、共享的新发展理念，推动经

---

* 在英国曼彻斯特大学的主旨演讲。2018 年 12 月 18 日，英国曼彻斯特大学。

济从高速增长阶段转向高质量发展阶段，加快建设创新型国家。对中国而言，抓创新就是抓发展，谋创新就是谋未来。中国的创新驱动发展有三个主要特点。

一是坚持高质量发展。创新是引领发展的第一动力。中国经济正处于新旧动能转换期，重在打造发展新引擎，培育发展新动力，推动发展从依靠自然资源和资本等要素驱动转变为依靠科技、管理、业态和文化等创新驱动，持续提升经济发展的质量和效益。与此同时，中国的创新驱动发展与区域协调发展协同推进，跨区域整合创新资源，构建各具特色的区域创新发展布局，促进区域产业合理分工和竞争力提升。例如，推动北京、上海打造具有全球影响力的科技创新中心，在中西部地区着力培育壮大区域特色经济与新兴产业，在东北地区以技术与管理创新带动老工业基地振兴。中国坚持以创新方式推动城市改造，优化城市功能，带动产业升级。例如，以疏解北京非首都功能为"牛鼻子"，推动京津冀协同发展，建设河北雄安新区，就是紧扣高质量发展，以创新引领区域协调、平衡与可持续发展的最新例证。

二是坚持人才优先。人才是创新的根基和第一资源，创新驱动的实质就是人才驱动。中国坚持以人为本，调动各类人才的积极性和创造性，尊重创新创造的价值，着力培育一批世界一流的科研机构、大学和创新型企业，培养高水平人才特别是高端技术创新人才，推动教育和就业培训的创新实践。2017 年，中国研发人员总量达 621.4 万人，连续 5 年稳居世界首位；研发经费投入达 2589 亿美元，居世界第二位，每年对全球研发经费投入贡献超过 1/6。中国大力鼓励创新创业，激发全社会创造活力，形成大众创业万众创新的生动局面。去过中国的英国朋友一定感受过中国"新四大发明"——高铁网络、电子商务、移动支付、共享经济——的便捷、高效，这正是人才培养与创新文化相互促进的结果。

三是坚持开放包容。2018 年是中国改革开放 40 周年。40 年来我们得出的一条重要经验就是：以开放引领创新，以创新推动开放。在经济全球化深入发展的今天，封闭狭隘的保护主义只会是一条越走越窄的死胡同，开放包容、互利共赢才是通向共同发展的阳光大道。各国既要立足自身发展，充分挖掘创新潜力，也要敞开大门，鼓励新技术、新知识传播，让创新成果造福更多国家和人民。中国始终以开放的全球视野谋划和推动创新，积极推进国际创新合作。

以知识产权保护为例。知识产权保护是创新的重要基础和保障。近年来，中国知识产权的"量"与"质"同步提升，知识产权保护水平日益提高。2018年4月和11月，习近平主席分别在博鳌亚洲论坛年会、首届中国国际进口博览会开幕式上宣布了一系列中国扩大开放新举措，其中特别提出加大知识产权保护力度。目前，中国已建立了符合国际通行规则和中国国情的知识产权法律体系，在北京、上海、广州设立了知识产权法院，在15个城市建立了知识产权专门审批机构。2001年加入世贸组织时，中国对外支付的知识产权使用费仅有19亿美元，2017年已达286亿美元，增长了14倍多。中国也高度重视保护英国企业的知识产权，这从英国在华活跃的专利申请可见一斑，英国在华专利申请累计已超过2万件。中国还积极推动在"一带一路"、金砖国家等框架下开展知识产权合作，与英国、欧盟、美国等建立了知识产权对话交流机制，与超过20个国家和地区签订了"专利审查高速路"合作协议，为推动全球知识产权体系向平衡、普惠、包容方向发展做出了积极贡献。

女士们、先生们，

中英都是崇尚创新、勇于创造的国家，都为人类文明进步做出了重要贡献。当今世界，各国利益交融、休戚与共，共享创新成果是国际社会的一致呼声。我认为，中英加强创新合作面临三大机遇。

一是中英关系的发展机遇。当前，中英关系保持稳定发展，两国领导人多次重申坚持中英关系的大方向，为双方加强创新合作提供了坚实的政治保障。近年来，中英"一带一路"合作逐渐走深走实，成为两国务实合作的新亮点，也为两国创新合作开拓了新空间。11月，英国约克公爵安德鲁王子、福克斯国际贸易大臣率团出席在上海举办的首届中国国际进口博览会，其间双方签署了一系列创新创意领域合作协议。

二是优势互补的独特机遇。英国是世界创新强国，处于全球科学研究的前沿，拥有强大的基础科学研究和创新实力。英国正大力推进"全球化英国"，实施产业发展战略，积极推进在人工智能、健康和老龄化、绿色增长、文化创意等领域的创新发展与国际合作。中国正在加速推进创新驱动发展，不断提升科技、工程、产业自主创新能力，在信息通信、航空航天、高铁、核能等方面处于世界先进水平。在进一步扩大开放的进程中，中国庞大的市场规模、完备的产业体系、多样化的消费需求、互联网时代的创新效率，孕育着巨大的国际合作空间。中英在创新领域目标一致、优势互补，以创新合作促进两国共同发展，符合中英双方共同利益。

三是基础扎实的合作机遇。经过双方的不懈努力，中英已经形成机制完善、主体多元、形式多样的科技及创新合作局面。中英建有科技创新合作联委会机制，设立了研究与创新合作伙伴基金，并在基金框架下支持240个中英机构开展了460多个合作项目。2017年底双方共同发布《中英科技创新合作战略》，为两国深化创新合作规划了新蓝图。近日，中英科技创新合作联委会第9次会议在伦敦举行，双方就中英联合科学创新基金、中英旗舰挑战计划、中英创新创业与人员交流合作等达成重要共识。此外，安德鲁王子发起的创新创业项目"龙门创将"在中国受到热烈响应，青岛中英创意产业园等新项目正在稳步推进。

著名创新作家吉斯·范·伍尔芬说过，"可以凭一己之力创造，但无法凭一己之力创新"。中英双方应如何抓住机遇，做大创新合作"蛋糕"，携手引领国际创新发展与合作？要回答这个问题，我们需要运用曼大校训的第二个关键词——"智慧"，积极开动脑筋，创新思路，重点在以下三个方面共同努力。

第一，进一步加强创新发展战略对接。中英双方应加强中国创新驱动发展战略和英国促进增长的创新与研究战略、产业发展战略等对接，以《中英科技创新合作战略》为牵引，加强中英创新合作的顶层设计与战略规划；加强就知识产权保护、绿色制造业创新等政策进行交流与对话；共同参与全球科技创新治理，积极参与和引领全球创新规则和标准制定，共同应对粮食安全、能源安全、气候变化及公共卫生等全球性挑战。

第二，进一步深化科技和产业创新合作。中英应利用好两国科技创新合作联委会、中英研究和创新伙伴基金、年度旗舰挑战计划、产业创新基金、中英创意产业园等平台和资源，推动从基础研究到成果转化的全链条创新合作。针对双方发展需求，明确优先合作领域与重点项目，在智能技术和机器人、低碳和绿色制造、遥感和卫星技术、新能源、新种业、先进治疗、抗生素耐药性、人口老龄化、创意经济、金融风险管理等领域开展产学研用合作。积极探讨在"一带一路"共建国家开展科技、知识产权保护、金融创新等第三方合作，扩大中英创新合作的辐射影响。

第三，进一步推进区域创新发展合作。曼大所在的英格兰北部地区是工业革命的发源地。200多年后的今天，该地区正以"英格兰北方经济中心"计划为引擎，实现转型升级与创新发展。中英双方应以友好省市为平台，发挥"一带一路"倡议、中国区域协调发展战略及"英格兰北方经济中心"、"中部引擎"等战略协同效应，不断深化地方创新发展合作。双方可分享城市发展经验，探讨城市升级改造合作试点和老工业区改造等合作，推动可持续城镇化合作，共建绿色、智慧、包容性未来城市；办好大连制造业产业示范园、青岛创意产业园等项目，带动中国城市转型；鼓励和支持中国企业参与"英格兰北方经济中心"战略有关基础设施建设，促进该地区互联互通与联动发展；共同推进中英雄安金融科技城合作项目，助力京津冀协同发展。

曼大校训中的第三个关键词是"人文"。在这个领域，中英合作始终走在中西方交流的前列。目前，在英中国留学生超过17万人，华人教授学者6000多人，每年在华工作的英方专家超过4万人次，这些数字都高居欧洲国家榜首。他们都是中英创新合作的重要人才基础和推动力量。近年来，我曾多次为全英高层次人才创业大赛获奖人员颁奖。就在上周，我作为评委参加约克公爵安德鲁王子举行的第三届"龙门创将"全球总决赛，见证了中国企业家的出色表现。每次参加这类活动，我都深深被中英创新创业人才的热情与创造力感染。中英应着力推动科学设施相互开放，重点加强在生命科学与数学、物理等基础学科的科研交流以及重大科学项目的联合研究，不断拓展在技术商业化领域的合作。充分调动创新人才积极性，加强创新创业者培训和职业教育等能力建设，继续开展好"龙门创将"等创新创业活动，为中英创新合作不断输送有生力量。我们欢迎英国作为唯一主宾国出席 2019 年 4 月在中国深圳举办的中国国际人才交流大会，这必将推动中英人才交流和人文合作再上新台阶。

曼大与中国企业在石墨烯科研和产品研发领域，与北京大学、清华大学等中国高校在先进材料、生命科学等领域开展了富有成效的合作，可以说曼大是中英创新合作的"先驱者"。我衷心希望曼大继续发挥优势，秉持"知识、智慧和人文精神"，与中方深化创新领域合作，加强人才培养与技术交流，打造曼大在中英创新合作中的"金字招牌"。同时，我也希望更多的曼大学子积极投身中英创新合作，为中英友好合作贡献更多智慧和力量。

女士们、先生们，

中国有句古语："苟日新，日日新，又日新。"创新永无止境，合作永无终点。我们愿与英国各界人士携手努力，以创新精神推动中英合作，以创新成果丰富中英伙伴关系，共同为中英关系发展增光添彩！

谢谢大家！

Promote Development through Cooperation on Innovation[*]

Vice-Chancellor Dame Nancy Rothwell,
Faculty Members and Students,
Ladies and Gentlemen,
Good afternoon!

It is a real delight to visit the University of Manchester for the third time. The previous two visits were both three years ago. The first was a "reconnaissance trip" for President Xi Jinping's visit, and the second was to accompany President Xi during his state visit.

On both trips, the University of Manchester impressed me deeply as an open and innovative institution forever reaching for the best. Now after three years, I am pleased to be back and it feels really good to reconnect with you.

As a renowned institution of higher learning both in Britain and the world, the University of Manchester is the world's leading university in comprehensive strength and academic disciplines. You have an outstanding list of alumni, including 25 Nobel laureates. You are also the birthplace of many important scientific and technological findings, including "the splitting of the atom", the isolation of graphene and the creation of the world's first stored-program digital computer.

These achievements are a testament to the University's motto: "Knowledge, Wisdom, Humanity."

---

[*] Keynote Speech at the University of Manchester. University of Manchester, 18 December 2018.

I am asked to talk about China-UK innovation and urban development. So let me share with you my views on these topics in the order of your motto, starting with "knowledge".

Knowledge is power. It is the key to innovation. Without knowledge, there would be no human progress. Without innovation, there would be no future for humanity.

A new round of scientific and technological revolution and industrial transformation is unfolding. One must catch up with this round of innovation to achieve greater progress for mankind.

China is pursuing innovative, coordinated, green, open and shared development. The economy is shifting from high-speed growth to high-quality growth which relies on innovation as the driving force. That means the Chinese development hinges upon innovation. Innovation holds the key to the Chinese future.

Innovation-driven development in China has three main features.

The first feature is the emphasis on high-quality development.

Innovation is the primary force of development. China is now in the process of replacing traditional growth engines with new ones. We are shifting from a resource-and-capital-intensive growth model to one that is driven by innovation in science, technology, management, business format and culture. The goal is to improve the quality and efficiency of economic growth.

At the same time, innovation is also a key factor in achieving coordinated development of different regions. The innovative strengths of different regions in China complement one another and could be leveraged in a way that form a synergy between regions and facilitate coordinated development. Each region will have a reasonable place in the overall industrial distribution, and this strengthens their competitiveness. For example:

- In Beijing and Shanghai, we are building world-class scientific, technological and innovation centres.
- In central and western regions of China, we are fostering local and emerging industries.
- In the traditional industrial bases in the Chinese northeast, we focus on regeneration by promoting innovation in technology and management.

China has also been innovative in urban transformation. This is aimed at optimising urban functions and promoting industrial upgrading. Take for example the relocation of non-capital functions out of Beijing. This will stimulate coordination between the Capital and nearby Tianjin Municipality and Hebei Province in the development of the triangular region called the Xiong'an New Area. It is the latest example of coordinated, balanced and sustainable regional development driven by innovation and aiming at high-quality growth.

The second feature of innovation-driven development in China is the focus on fostering the best minds.

People are the basis and primary resources for innovation. Innovation-driven development is in essence people-driven development.

Therefore, in China, we put people first, value the initiative and creativity of the people and respect innovative and creative outcomes. We have been building world-class research institutions, universities and innovative companies. This is aimed at fostering the best minds in innovation, especially high-tech innovation, and encouraging innovation in education and job training.

China has the largest number of R&D professionals in the world for five consecutive years. The total number was 6.214 million in 2017. In terms of R&D spending, China accounts for more than one sixth of the world's total. In 2017, we spent an equivalent of 258.9 billion US dollars, ranking the second in the world.

China also encourages the general public to engage in innovation and entrepreneurship. If you have been to China, I am sure you have experienced the convenience and efficiency brought by the Chinese "new four great inventions," namely, high-speed rail network, e-commerce, mobile payments and sharing economy. These inventions are the results of effective talent training in a society that values creativity.

The third feature of innovation-driven development in China is the pursuit of openness and inclusiveness.

This year marks the 40th anniversary of the Chinese reform and opening-up. An important lesson we have learned from these 40 years is that openness stimulates innovation, and innovation in turn leads to greater openness.

In a globalised world, protectionism only leads to a dead end. Openness, inclusiveness and win-win cooperation are the right choice if we want development for all. When it comes to innovation, self-reliance and tapping domestic potential are important to a country's development. But innovation by nature requires an open environment. Therefore it is also important for countries to open the door to exchanges of new technologies and new knowledge. In this process, innovations could reinforce one another and their outcomes could benefit more countries and people. China has adopted an open, global vision. We have actively engaged in cooperation with other countries on innovation.

Take for example the protection of intellectual property rights, which is an important basis and guarantee for innovation.

At the Annual Conference 2018 of the Boao Forum for Asia in April and the opening ceremony of the first-ever China International Import Expo last month, President Xi Jinping announced a number of new measures for further opening up the Chinese market. He laid special emphasis on strengthening IPR protection.

In recent years, China has expanded and improved IPR protection. We have established a full-fledged system of domestic laws and regulations for IPR protection that conforms to both international practice and the Chinese national conditions. Intellectual property courts have been set up in Beijing, Shanghai and Guangzhou and specialized IP tribunals have been put in place in 15 cities.

In 2001, the first year as a WTO member, China paid 1.9 billion US dollars in intellectual property royalties to overseas rights owners. Fast forward to 2017, this figure increased by 14 times to 28.6 billion US dollars.

China has attached great importance to protecting the IPR of British companies. The number of patent applications by British companies in China, which tops 20,000 in total, says it all.

China has also engaged in various forms of international cooperation on IPR protection.

- We have actively promoted IPR protection under the framework of the Belt and Road Initiative and within the BRICS.
- We hold regular dialogues on IPR protection with the UK, the European Union and the United States.
- And we have signed agreements with over 20 countries and regions on Patent Prosecution Highway.

These are a few highlights of the Chinese active efforts in promoting a global intellectual property system that is more balanced, inclusive and beneficial for all.

Ladies and Gentlemen,

Both China and the UK value the spirit of innovation. In our courageous pursuit of innovation, we have both made important contribution to human progress.

In today's world, countries have interconnected interests and share weal and woe. There is a broad consensus that the outcomes of innovation could benefit as many people as possible. Therefore, it is important that China and the UK enhance cooperation on innovation. I think there are three opportunities for such cooperation.

First, the opportunity of the development of China-UK relations.

China-UK relations maintain stable development. The leaders of our two countries have on many occasions renewed their commitment to China-UK relations. This has provided firm political guarantee for our two countries to enhance cooperation on innovation.

In recent years, China-UK cooperation on the Belt and Road Initiative has gone deeper and become more substantial. This has become a new highlight of China-UK business cooperation. It has also opened up new prospects for building closer partnership in innovation between our two countries.

Last month, The Duke of York and the Secretary of State for International Trade Liam Fox led a delegation to the first-ever China International Import Expo in Shanghai. During the Expo, our two sides signed a number of cooperation agreements in the areas of innovation and creative industries.

Second, the unique opportunity arising from comparative strengths.

The UK is a world leader in innovation and scientific research, with great strength in basic science.

To build a "global Britain" and achieve the goals of its industrial development strategy, the UK is promoting innovation and international cooperation in areas such as artificial intelligence, health care, elderly care, green growth and cultural and creative industries.

Likewise, China is fostering innovation-driven development. In this process, China is improving its independent innovation capability in science, technology, engineering and industries. Right now, China is leading the world in telecommunication, aerospace, high-speed rail and nuclear energy.

China has a huge market, a complete industrial system and diverse consumer needs. It is also noted for its innovation and efficiency in the digital economy. As China opens its market wider, the world stands to benefit from the huge potential of its cooperation with China.

China and the UK have the same goals and comparative strengths in innovation. Closer cooperation on innovation between our two countries will promote common development and serve the interest of both sides.

Third, the cooperation opportunity based on a solid foundation.

Thanks to the tireless efforts of both sides, China-UK cooperation on science, technology and innovation has well-rounded mechanisms, attracts a rich variety of participating entities and takes diverse forms.

Our two countries have established the Joint Commission on Cooperation in Science, Technology and Innovation, which held the ninth meeting in London last month. During the meeting, our two sides reached important agreements on the Research and Innovation Partnership Fund. It has provided support to 240 institutions from both countries in more than 460 cooperation projects. The Joint Commission also agreed on the Flagship Challenge Programme and cooperation on innovation, entrepreneurship and personnel exchanges.

Towards the end of 2017, our two countries signed the Joint Strategy for Science, Technology and Innovation Cooperation. This is a new blueprint for building closer partnership between our two countries in innovation.

Examples of specific projects include: The Pitch@Palace, which was founded by The Duke of York to support innovation and entrepreneurship. This has attracted active participation in China. Another one, the China-UK Innovation Industrial Park in Qingdao, is also making good progress.

Gijs van Wulfen, a recognised author on innovation, once said, "You can invent alone, but you cannot innovate alone."

China and the UK should work together to seize the opportunities, make the pie of innovation bigger and take the lead in innovation-driven development and international cooperation. But how do we achieve all that?

The answer can be found in the second word of your motto "wisdom". We should use our wisdom, and embrace new ideas. In my opinion, we should make joint efforts in the following three aspects.

First, we should match our strategies in innovation-driven development.

These strategies include the Chinese innovation-driven development strategy as well as the UK's Industrial Strategy and its innovation and research strategy for growth. Synergy between these strategies, along with the guidance of the China-UK Joint Strategy for Science, Technology and Innovation Cooperation, will enable our two countries to enhance top-level design and strategic planning for our cooperation on innovation.

Our two countries should also enhance policy exchange and dialogue on IPR protection and innovation in green manufacturing.

Moreover, our two countries can join hands to engage in global governance in science, technology and innovation. We should play an active role and take the lead in setting global rules and norms on innovation. We should work together to address global challenges such as food security, energy security, climate change and public health.

Second, China and the UK should deepen cooperation on science, technology and industrial innovation.

Our two countries can fully leverage existing bilateral platforms and resources. These include:

- The Joint Commission on Cooperation in Science, Technology and Innovation.
- The Research and Innovation Partnership Fund.
- The Flagship Challenge Programme.
- The three competitions organised and funded by Innovate the UK and Jiangsu, Shanghai and Guangdong.
- And the Innovation Industrial Park.

Through these platforms and resources, our cooperation could cover the complete chain of innovation, from basic research to commercialisation.

We should also identify priority areas and key projects for cooperation according to the development needs of our two countries. These priority areas could include smart and robot technology, low-carbon and green manufacturing, remote sensing and satellite technology, new energy, agricultural seeds, advanced medical treatment, antibiotics resistance, population aging, creative economy and financial risks management.

Moreover, our two countries could explore trilateral cooperation involving BRI partners on science, technology, IPR protection and financial innovation. This could expand our cooperation on innovation beyond bilateral scope.

Third, China and the UK should enhance subnational cooperation on innovation.

Northern England, where the University of Manchester is located, was the cradle of the Industrial Revolution. Now, after more than 200 years, economic restructuring and upgrading and innovation-driven development become the key words for this region. The strategies of the "Northern Powerhouse" and "Midlands Engine for Growth" are guiding the rejuvenation of this traditional industrial basis of Britain.

These strategies could form a perfect synergy with the Chinese Belt and Road Initiative and strategy of balanced development between different domestic regions.

Northern England has many sister provinces and cities in China. The sister relationships could provide a platform for China and the UK to deepen regional cooperation on innovation.

Urban development is another area for potential cooperation. Our two sides could share experience and explore pilot projects on urban upgrading and the regeneration of the rusty-belt areas. We could also focus on sustainable urbanisation and building green, smart and inclusive cities for the future. A couple of such projects are already making good progress, such as the Sino-British Advanced Manufacturing Industry Demonstration Park in Dalian and the China-UK Innovation Industrial Park in Qingdao.

Here in the UK, we could encourage and facilitate Chinese companies in taking part in infrastructure building under the "Northern Powerhouse" strategy, in order to improve connectivity and interconnected development in the region.

In China, a finance and technology park is being developed in Xiong'an New Area, which is a key part of the coordinated regional development of Beijing, Tianjin and Hebei. This certainly offers a great opportunity for British companies to play a role.

The third word of your motto is "humanity". In this aspect, China-UK cooperation has been a leader of exchanges between China and other Western countries.

As we speak, there are more than 170,000 Chinese students and over 6,000 Chinese professors and scholars in Britain. Every year, more than 40,000 British experts work in China. All these numbers top all other countries in Europe. These people form the solid foundation for China-UK cooperation on innovation.

In recent years, I have presented the awards for several competitions of the CSSA-UK High-level Entrepreneurship Challenge. Last week, I was invited to sit on the judge panel of the Pitch@Palace Global 3.0 held by The Duke of York, and witnessed the outstanding performance of Chinese entrepreneurs. At such events, I was always deeply impressed by the enthusiasm, creativity and entrepreneurship of the talents from both China and the UK.

Going forward, our two countries should continue to encourage our respective scientific facilities to open to each other. We should give priority to exchanges in bio-science and basic disciplines such as mathematics and physics, and carry out joint research on major scientific programmes. We should also expand our cooperation on the commercialization of technology.

At the same time, we should encourage more people to engage in innovation, enhance capacity building in training and vocational education for those who wish to engage in innovation or start new businesses, and provide facilitation for events such as Pitch@Palace. We should be creative in boosting China-UK cooperation on innovation.

China welcomes the UK's participation as the only country of honour at the China International Talent Exchange Conference to be held in Shenzhen next April. I am sure this Conference will lift China-UK talent exchange and cooperation to a new stage.

The University of Manchester has worked with Chinese companies on graphene research and products development. It has also carried out productive cooperation with the Chinese Peking University and Tsinghua University in the areas of advanced materials and bio-science. I must say that the University of Manchester is indeed a pioneer in China-UK cooperation on innovation.

I sincerely hope that the University of Manchester will continue to leverage its strengths, deepen cooperation with China on innovation in the spirit of "knowledge, wisdom and humanity", and enhance exchanges in personnel training and technology. I am sure you will become a leading brand of China-UK cooperation on innovation.

Meanwhile, I hope that more and more students from this university will become active participants in building closer partnership between China and the UK in innovation. I encourage you to contribute your wisdom and strength to China-UK friendship and cooperation.

Ladies and Gentlemen,

I want to quote an old Chinese saying to conclude my speech.

"If you can improve yourself in a day, do so each day and forever build on the improvement."

There is no limit to innovation. There is no end to cooperation. China stands ready to work with people from all walks of life in Britain to advance China-UK cooperation in the spirit of innovation, enrich China-UK partnership with outcomes of innovation, and make more contribution to China-UK relations!

Thank you!

坚持正确方向，开创共赢未来[*]

尊敬的英国约克公爵安德鲁王子殿下，
尊敬的英国哈德斯菲尔德大学校长克莱恩先生，
女士们、先生们、朋友们：
大家上午好！

很高兴时隔一年再次访问哈德斯菲尔德大学。首先，我谨对华东理工大学与哈德斯菲尔德大学合作成立科技创新孔子学院表示热烈祝贺！我也要感谢安德鲁王子殿下、哈德斯菲尔德大学和华东理工大学长期以来对中英教育交流与合作的重视与支持。

哈德斯菲尔德大学科技创新孔子学院是在英国创办的第30所孔子学院。孔子说，"三十而立"，意思是人到这个年纪就明确了人生目标和方向。哈德斯菲尔德大学科技创新孔子学院也是首个以科技创新为主题的孔子学院，标志着中英孔子学院合作进入新阶段。这个新阶段有三大特点。

一是推动科技创新。中英都是科技创新大国，两国金融科技独角兽公司、人工智能企业数量和影响力全球领先。在世界知识产权组织2018年全球创新指数排行榜中，英国位列第四，中国是唯一进入前20名的发展中国家和中等收入经济体。科技创新也是中英合作最具潜力的领域之一。安德鲁王子创立的"龙门创将"项目，已成为两国科技创新合作的经典品牌。6月，第十

---

[*] 在英国哈德斯菲尔德大学科技创新孔子学院成立签约仪式上的致辞。2019年7月8日，英国哈德斯菲尔德大学。

次中英经济财金对话成功举行，双方同意进一步落实《中英科技创新合作战略》，在农业科技、健康老龄化、民用核能、金融科技等领域加强合作。

二是弘扬开放精神。教育的使命不仅是"授业"，还有"传道"。哈德斯菲尔德大学和华东理工大学都是开放精神的践行者和受益者。随着经济全球化深入发展，各国以不同资源禀赋和比较优势，通过市场竞争和选择，形成结构高度互补、利益深度交融的全球经贸网络。这是世界大势，不可逆转。只有坚持开放的全球视野，跟上历史潮流，才能赢得更加光明的未来。在当前全球经济遭遇保护主义、单边主义逆风的背景下，我们更要弘扬开放精神，做好"开放合作"与"封闭自守"之间的选择题。

三是深化情感纽带。2018年，全英约有19万人在孔子学院和孔子课堂学习，170多万人次参与孔子学院开展的各类文化活动。在这个值得庆贺的日子里，我宣布2019年中国政府将给予哈德斯菲尔德大学20个短期赴华留学奖学金名额。我们欢迎更多英国青年学生到中国留学，亲身感知中国，真正读懂中国，做增进中英两国人民理解与情感的使者。

中国古代著名词人辛弃疾曾写道："乘风好去，长空万里，直下看山河。"我衷心祝愿哈德斯菲尔德大学科技创新孔子学院以今日为起点，坚持正确方向，在中英友好合作的万里长空展翅翱翔，携手谱写中英理解互信、合作共赢的新篇章！

谢谢！

Keep to the Right Direction and Open up a Win-Win Future *

Your Royal Highness The Duke of York,

Vice-Chancellor Cryan,

Ladies and Gentlemen,

Dear Friends,

Good morning!

It is a real delight to be back at the University of Huddersfield after my last visit one year ago. Let me begin by extending my warmest congratulations to the East China University of Science and Technology and the University of Huddersfield on the opening of the Confucius Institute of Science and Technology Innovation!

I would also like to express my thanks to HRH The Duke of York and all those at the University of Huddersfield and East China University of Science and Technology for your care and support for China-UK education exchanges and cooperation.

The Confucius Institute of Science and Technology Innovation at the University of Huddersfield is the 30th Confucius Institute in the UK. Confucius said, "At 30, one has established himself." It means that at the age of 30, one should be clear about the goal and direction in life.

This Confucius Institute is also the first one focused on science and technology innovation. Its opening marks the beginning of a new stage in China-UK cooperation on Confucius Institutes. This new stage has three features.

---

* Remarks at the Signing Ceremony of the Confucius Institute of Science and Technology Innovation at the University of Huddersfield. University of Huddersfield, 8 July 2019.

The first feature is science and technology innovation.

Both China and the UK are strong in science and technology innovation. Our two countries lead the world in both the number and influence of FinTech unicorns and AI companies. According to the Global Innovation Index 2018 by the World Intellectual Property Organisation, the UK is the fourth most innovative nation, and China is the only developing country that has made to the top 20.

Science and technology innovation is also one of the most promising areas of China-UK cooperation. Take for example the Pitch@Palace initiated by HRH The Duke of York. It is a flagship programme of China-UK science and technology innovation.

At the tenth China-UK Economic and Financial Dialogue, which was successfully held last month, our two sides agreed to take further steps to implement the China-UK Joint Strategy for Science, Technology and Innovation Cooperation. We also decided to enhance cooperation on agri-tech, healthy aging, civil nuclear energy and FinTech.

The second feature is the spirit of openness.

Education is not only about imparting knowledge. It is also the mission of education to uphold important values, including the value of openness. The University of Huddersfield and the East China University of Science and Technology are both practitioners and beneficiaries of the spirit of openness.

Globalisation has led to a highly interdependent and deeply integrated economic and trade system where the endowments and strengths of different countries are fully leveraged through market competition and selection. This is an irreversible trend. Only those with a global vision and willing to open up could seize this trend and embrace a brighter future.

As the world economy battles the headwinds of protectionism and unilateralism, it is all the more important that we uphold the spirit of openness and choose between "open cooperation" and "isolation" wisely.

The third feature is a close bond between the people.

In 2018, about 190,000 students were enrolled at the Confucius Institutes and Confucius Classrooms in Britain, and more than 1.7 million people took part in a wide variety of cultural events hosted by the Confucius Institutes.

Today, I have another good news to announce: This year, the Chinese government will offer scholarships to 20 students from the University of Huddersfield for short-term study in China.

I hope more British young students will choose to study in China so as to see the country with their own eyes and get to know the real China. By doing so, they will find in their heart a mission to enhance understanding and to build a closer bond between the people of our two countries.

Xin Qiji, a 12th century Chinese poet, wrote,

On wings of wind 'neath the boundless sky I fly,

Overlook mountains and rivers from above high.

For the Confucius Institute of Science and Technology Innovation at the University of Huddersfield, the boundless sky of China-UK friendly cooperation sets no limit. I sincerely hope that you will spread your wings, keep to the right direction and write a new chapter of better understanding, deeper trust and win-win cooperation between China and the UK!

Thank you!

引领开放创新潮流，打造合作共赢成果 *

尊敬的中国全国人大常委会副委员长、欧美同学会会长陈竺先生，
尊敬的英国皇家学会副主席卡特洛教授，
尊敬的英国议会上院前副议长贝茨勋爵，
女士们、先生们：

上午好！

很高兴来到历史悠久、享誉世界的英国皇家学会，出席由欧美同学会举办的第十七届"21世纪中国"论坛。首先，我谨向远道而来的陈竺会长和代表团一行表示热烈欢迎！

当今世界正经历百年未有之大变局，新一轮科技革命方兴未艾，新一轮产业变革风起云涌。科技与金融相互交融，正对世界发展产生广泛而深远的影响。在这个大背景下，本届论坛聚焦"中英科技与金融合作"主题，可谓恰逢其时。

10天前，我们刚刚庆祝中华人民共和国成立70周年。70年来，中国创造了人类发展史上的奇迹，迎来了从站起来、富起来到强起来的伟大飞跃。中国科技创新成果不断涌现，在量子通信、超级计算、航空航天、人工智能、5G网络、移动支付、高速铁路等领域世界领先。70年来，中国金融业也取得长足发展，已建立比较完备的宏观调控体系、有力的金融监管体系、较为健全的金融组织体系以及有效的金融市场体系。

---

* 在第十七届"21世纪中国"论坛上的致辞。2019年10月11日，英国皇家学会。

中国的发展成就不仅属于中国，也属于世界。中国坚持扩大对外开放，深化与各国的互利合作，让科技创新成果更好地造福世界各国人民，在应对1997年亚洲金融危机、2008年国际金融危机中体现了大国担当。展望未来，中国的发展前景将更加美好。我们将坚定不移奉行互利共赢的开放战略，实现更大力度、更高水平的对外开放，与各国共同创造更多合作机遇，分享更多发展红利。

女士们、先生们，

2019年是中英建立代办级外交关系65周年。65年来，中英关系历经风雨，实现跨越式发展。2015年习近平主席对英国成功进行国事访问，为两国各领域合作指明了方向。2019年6月，双方成功举行第十次经济财金对话，在金融、创新等领域达成69项成果，为中英深化合作注入了强劲动力。我认为，两国科技、金融合作有三个突出特点，面临三个重要机遇。

第一，基础坚实。1978年中英签订政府间科技合作协定，41年来两国科技合作不断深化。2017年，中英两国共同制定《中英科技创新合作战略》，双方科创合作成果丰硕。英国已成为中国在全球的第二大科研合作伙伴国。金融合作则是中英合作最具活力、最具潜力的领域。英国在西方大国中首个发行人民币主权债券，率先申请加入亚洲基础设施投资银行。目前，伦敦已成为中国之外全球最大的人民币离岸交易中心和第二大人民币离岸清算中心。2019年6月，中英成功启动"沪伦通"，开了中国与境外资本市场互联互通的先河。

第二，优势互补。英国是科技强国，是工业革命的发源地，具有丰富的创新经验、独特的创新文化和强大的创新能力。中国工程技术创新能力强、人才储备丰富、创新创业活跃，具有广阔的市场需求。伦敦是首屈一指的国际金融中心，拥有悠久的历史、丰富的金融管理经验和充足的人才资源。中国金融业正在加快对外开放，2019年7月已宣布一系列对外开放新举措。中英在科技、创新、金融等方面互补优势显现，有望形成"一加一大于二"的效果。

第三，前景广阔。在"脱欧"背景下，英国提出建设"全球化英国"和以创新为核心的产业战略。进入新时代的中国，正在实施创新驱动发展战略，高水平的创新供给和高素质的人力资本成为中国经济社会发展的新动力。展望未来，中英在可持续发展、气候变化、清洁能源、"一带一路"等方面合作潜力巨大，双方进一步加强合作，必将为两国发展插上腾飞的翅膀，为世界发展做出更大贡献。

近年来，新技术的兴起深刻改变了传统金融业态，其中科技与金融的结合——金融科技——在提升金融服务效率、促进普惠金融等方面发挥了重要作用。金融科技正成为中英合作的新领域和新机遇。中国金融科技创新创业活跃、市场需求广阔，其中移动支付、网络信贷等领域发展势头强劲。英国在支付和消费金融、数字化银行、大数据分析等方面经验丰富，创立了行之有效的"监管沙盒"模式。双方可进一步加强优势互补，扩大对金融科技企业的支持和引导，引领建立有利于金融科技发展的国际新规则，为全球数字经济特别是发展中国家数字普惠金融提出创新解决方案，实现互利双赢、互利多赢。

女士们、先生们，

2013年10月，习近平主席在欧美同学会成立100周年庆祝大会上曾说："创新是一个民族进步的灵魂，是一个国家兴旺发达的不竭动力。"中英两国都高度重视创新，都是具有全球影响力的大国，双方应把握时代大势，坚持开放创新，深化合作共赢，共同引领国际创新合作，打造更多创新成果，造福中英两国人民和世界人民。

最后，预祝今天的论坛取得圆满成功！

谢谢大家！

Take the Lead in Open Cooperation on Innovation and Deliver Win-Win Results[*]

Vice Chairman and President Chen Zhu,

Professor Richard Catlow,

Lord Bates,

Ladies and Gentlemen,

Good morning!

It is a real delight to join you at the time-honoured and prestigious Royal Society for the 21st Century China Forum. This is the 17th such event hosted by the Western Returned Scholars Association. Let me begin by extending a warm welcome to Vice Chairman and President Chen Zhu and his delegation!

The world we are living in is undergoing profound changes unseen in a century. As the new round of scientific and technological revolution and industrial transformation unfold, the integration of technology and finance is having an extensive and far-reaching impact on the development of the world.

This is a particularly opportune moment for intellectuals and entrepreneurs from both China and the UK to come together and focus on the theme of cooperation in "Technology and Finance".

Ten days ago, we celebrated the 70th anniversary of the founding of the People's Republic of China. The past 70 years witnessed the Chinese miracle in the history of human development, from gaining independence to becoming prosperous and growing strong.

---

[*] Remarks at the 21st Century China Forum. Royal Society, 11 October 2019.

In this process, China has achieved fruitful results in science, technology and innovation. It now leads the world in quantum communication, super-computing, aerospace, artificial intelligence, 5G network, mobile payment and high-speed rail.

In the past 70 years, China also achieved remarkable success in the financial sector. We have established a well-rounded macro-regulatory system, an effective supervision framework, a complete institutional network, and an effective financial market.

The Chinese development is not only an achievement for China itself but also a contribution to the whole world. China has been committed to opening its market wider to the world and deepening mutually-beneficial cooperation with other countries. This means the Chinese progress in science, technology and innovation has delivered benefits to the people of the whole world. China has lived up to its responsibility as a big country, standing firm during the Asian financial crisis of 1997 and the international financial crisis of 2008.

The future is promising for the Chinese development. Going forward, we will continue to follow the strategy of open and win-win cooperation, and we will continue to open our markets in more areas and at a higher level. This will create more opportunities for cooperation between China and other countries to ensure that the benefits of development will be shared by all.

Ladies and Gentlemen,

This year marks the 65th anniversary of China-UK diplomatic relationship at the chargé d'affaires level. In the past 65 years, China-UK relationship has achieved great progress despite winds and rains.

In 2015, President Xi Jinping paid a successful state visit to the UK, which charted the course for China-UK cooperation across the board.

The tenth China-UK Economic and Financial Dialogue concluded in June saw 69 outcomes reached in financial services, innovation and other areas. This has given a fresh boost to deepening cooperation between our two countries.

In my opinion, China-UK cooperation on science, technology and financial services bears three salient features and faces three important opportunities.

First, our cooperation has a solid foundation.

Since the governments of our two countries signed the Science and Technology Cooperation Agreement in 1978, China-UK cooperation on science and technology has been deepening over the past 41 years. In 2017, our two countries issued the China-

UK Joint Strategy for Science, Technology and Innovation Cooperation. This has facilitated more fruitful cooperation. The UK is now the Chinese second largest partner in scientific research.

Financial services sector is the most vigorous and promising in China-UK cooperation. The UK is the first major Western country to issue RMB sovereign bond and the first to apply to join the Asian Infrastructure Investment Bank. London is now the world's largest RMB offshore trading centre and the second largest RMB offshore clearing centre outside China. In June, our two countries successfully launched the Shanghai-London Stock Connect, which for the first time connected the Chinese and a foreign capital market.

Second, our cooperation has the benefit of complementary strengths.

The UK, as the cradle of the Industrial Revolution, is strong in science and technology. It is also known for its rich experience, unique culture and capability in innovation. China is strong in engineering, and has a rich talent pool and a vibrant ecosystem for innovation and entrepreneurship. It also has a huge market.

In financial services, London is a world-leading financial centre, with a time-honoured history, rich management experience and adequate professionals. China is accelerating the opening-up of its financial sector. In July, it announced a number of new opening-up measures.

With these complementary strengths in science, technology, innovation and financial services, China and the UK working together will achieve multiplying effect.

Third, our cooperation enjoys a promising future.

Against the backdrop of Brexit, the UK chose to build a "global Britain" and followed an industrial strategy centred on innovation.

China is pursuing innovation-driven strategy as it enters a new era of development. High-level innovation and a high-calibre labour force will be the new drivers of the Chinese economic and social development.

Going forward, China and the UK have enormous potential in their cooperation on sustainable development, climate change, clean energy and the Belt and Road Initiative. Enhancing cooperation in these areas will give wings to the development of our two countries and make greater contribution to the development of the world.

As new technologies continue to make progress in recent years, traditional financial models are undergoing profound changes. FinTech, which combines technology and financial services, is playing an important role in improving the efficiency of financial services and promoting inclusive finance. It is becoming a new area for China-UK cooperation and it is creating new opportunities.

China has a vibrant ecosystem for FinTech innovation and entrepreneurship. The market is huge, and there is a particularly strong growth momentum in mobile payment and online loans. The UK has rich experience in consumer finance, digital banking and big data analysis. It is also the birth place of effective "regulatory sandbox".

With these complementary strengths, China and the UK could work together to give more support and guidance to FinTech companies and take the lead in international rule-making to facilitate the growth of FinTech. We could also explore innovative solutions for the global digital economy, especially to promote digital financial inclusion in developing countries. This will be win-win for our two countries and for the world.

Ladies and Gentlemen,

At the 100th anniversary of the Western Returned Scholars Association in October 2013, President Xi Jinping said, "Innovation is the soul of the progress of a nation and the inexhaustible driving force behind the prosperity of a country."

China and the UK both attach great importance to innovation. As major countries of global influence, our two countries should follow the trend of our times, stay committed to innovation and openness, deepen our win-win cooperation, and take the lead in international cooperation on innovation. Working together, we can deliver more benefits to the people of our two countries and to the people of the world.

In conclusion, I wish today's forum great success!

Thank you!

第六章 生态环保

PART VI Ecological and Environmental Protection

保护生物多样性、应对气候变化是中英合作的重要领域，也是中英两国作为具有全球影响的大国应肩负的使命。中英分别作为联合国《生物多样性公约》缔约方大会第十五次会议和《联合国气候变化框架公约》第二十六次缔约方大会主席国，双方相互协调，相互支持，确保会议取得成功。能源也是中英互利合作的重要组成部分。中英不仅就传统的石油、天然气等化石能源积极开展合作，还在清洁能源和可再生能源合作方面保持良好势头。中国企业积极参与英国核电、海上风电、太阳能发电、生物质发电等新能源项目。中英企业在电动大巴、低排放出租车等新一代绿色交通工具方面的合作也取得重要进展。

本章收录了我的 6 篇关于中英生态环保合作的演讲，内容涵盖气候变化、生态文明、野生动物保护、生物多样性、能源转型、环境治理等。

Protecting biodiversity and addressing climate change are important areas of China-UK cooperation and missions that both countries, as influential global players, should shoulder. China and the UK, as the host countries of the 15th meeting of the Conference of the Parties to the UN Convention on Biological Diversity and the 26th Conference of the Parties to the UN Framework Convention on Climate Change respectively, have coordinated and supported each other to ensure the success of these conferences. Energy cooperation is also an important part of China-UK mutually beneficial cooperation. In addition to traditional fossil energy such as oil and natural gas, China and the UK have maintained a good momentum in cooperation on clean energy and renewable energy. Chinese companies have actively participated in new energy projects in the UK, including nuclear power, offshore wind power, solar power, and biomass power generation. China-UK cooperation in new generation green transportation, such as electric buses and low-emission taxis, has also made significant progress.

This chapter includes 6 of my speeches on China-UK ecological and environmental cooperation, covering topics such as climate change, ecological civilization, wildlife protection, biodiversity, energy transition and environmental governance.

十年树木，百年树人[*]

尊敬的英国气候组织主席莱弗莫尔先生，

尊敬的英国气候组织总裁肯伯先生，

女士们、先生们：

首先，我谨祝贺英国气候组织成立十周年。十年来，英国气候组织在世界各国商界和政界人士的支持下，专注于气候变化解决方案，积极推动低碳技术的市场化应用，促进经济增长和繁荣，为应对气候变化这一全球性挑战做出了突出贡献。

今天的庆祝会同时也是一次面向未来国际气候变化谈判的研讨会，我听说大家已就联合国政府间气候变化专门委员会工作组新发表的报告进行了交流和讨论，大家的普遍共识是2015年巴黎气候变化大会应成为国际气变谈判的重要里程碑。

气候变化这个问题自20世纪末提上议事日程以来，中国始终积极致力于与国际社会合作，共商应对之法，共图解决之道。我们认为气候变化问题是人类面临的共同安全挑战，各国都应付出不懈努力。我们主张应对气候变化问题应考虑温室气体排放的历史责任，考虑各国的发展水平差异，坚持共同但有区别的责任原则、公平原则和各自能力原则。

中国致力于推动2015年气候变化谈判取得成功，以不断加强《联合国

---

[*] 在英国气候组织成立十周年庆祝活动上发表闭幕主旨演讲。2014年4月28日，伦敦国王会展中心。

气候变化框架公约》在2020年后的全面、有效和持续实施。2014年2月，中国与美国发表《中美气候变化联合声明》，重申两国将为2015年全球应对气候变化挑战的努力做出重要贡献。3月，中国国家主席习近平访欧期间签署的中欧、中法、中德等联合声明中均专门谈及气候变化合作，强调应推动巴黎气候变化大会通过《联合国气候变化框架公约》之下适用于所有缔约方的一项议定书、另一法律文书或具有法律效力的议定成果，并强调致力于通过可信、可核查的国内行动实施重大温室气体减排。

对于推动气候变化谈判，我们不能学习唐宁街10号的御猫拉里。拉里曾被寄予捕鼠厚望，但可惜它的工作永远只是处在"战术计划准备阶段"。

在应对气候变化问题上，中国绝不是纸上谈兵，而是积极采取行动，而且许多是单方面的自主减排行动。我们不仅将应对气候变化问题作为中国与全球共同承担的一份重要使命和责任，更视之为自身实现可持续发展、产业升级转型的内在需求。中国正在积极主动作为，建设绿色发展、循环发展、低碳发展的"美丽中国"，不懈应对全球性气变挑战。

大家知道，早在2009年中国就主动公布到2020年单位国内生产总值二氧化碳排放比2005年降低40%~45%、非化石能源占一次能源比重达到15%、森林蓄积量增加13亿立方米的行动目标。目前，经过短短5年，中国已实现碳强度下降28%，减少二氧化碳排放23亿吨，非化石能源占比达到9.6%。2014年3月李克强总理在《政府工作报告》中明确了2014年节能减排的"硬任务"，在保持经济增长7.5%左右的情况下，要实现单位GDP能耗下降3.9%的目标。

中国大规模发展清洁能源，投入高居世界各国之首。到2014年底，中国太阳能发电总装机规模将达3000万千瓦，是2011年的10倍。预计到2050年，中国清洁能源装机总容量将达24.8亿千瓦，占全国总装机容量的62%和总发电量的58%，届时中国电力结构将实现从以煤电为主向新一代清洁非化石能源发电为主的历史性转变。

中国大力发展节能环保产业，淘汰高排放、高能耗落后产能。节能环保产业吸收3000万人就业，预计到2015年，节能环保产业总产值将达4.5万亿元，成为拉动中国经济的新增长极。2014年中国将淘汰钢铁2700万吨、水泥4200万吨、平板玻璃3500万标准箱等落后产能。中国下决心走出一条能耗排放做"减法"、经济发展做"加法"的新路子。

中国加快推动碳排放交易。中国正在实行碳交易试点，实际建设步伐远快于设想。2013年，深圳市、北京市、上海市、天津市等碳市场相继开始交易。2014年中国还将出台全国碳排放交易新的管理办法。

如同中国为世界减贫做出最大贡献一样，中国也致力于为全球减排做出最大的"绿色贡献"。我们在国内大力减排的同时，还鼓励中国企业积极"走出去"为世界减排贡献力量。就在五天前，我出席了中英再生能源及节能峰会，见证了中国企业在英国投资、开发建设地面光伏电站项目的签约仪式。这进一步表明，中国愿与包括英国在内的世界各国一道，共同努力应对气候变化，呵护好我们赖以生存的美丽家园。

女士们、先生们，

2014年是英国气候组织成立十周年。中国有句成语："十年树木，百年树人。"意思是说培植树木需要十年，培育人才需要百年。同样，一个组织从小到大、从弱到强需要一个过程，但要成就一番伟业则需要更长的时间。我高度赞赏英国气候组织过去十年为应对全球气候变化做出的积极贡献，更期待你们在下一个十年谱写新的篇章，为保护和改善人类赖以生存与发展的百年大计做出新的更大贡献。

谢谢！

Hundred Years to Rear People*

Chairman Phil Levermore,

CEO Mark Kenber,

Ladies and Gentlemen,

I warmly congratulate the 10th anniversary of the Climate Group.

Over the past 10 years the Climate Group has won support from an array of business and political leaders all over the world—including China.

The Climate Group deserves great praise for its focus on finding solutions to climate challenges and its active role in promoting commercialization of low carbon technologies.

All these efforts by the Climate Group have advanced economic growth and prosperity. But most important of all, the Climate Group has made a considerable contribution to tackling the global scourge of climate change.

Today's celebration is also a seminar on future climate change negotiations. I understand you have had discussions about the newly released IPCC reports. A common view is that the Paris Conference in 2015 should be a milestone in international negotiations on climate change.

Climate change rose to prominence as a core issue of global concern late last century. Since then, China has been committed to addressing the challenge through cooperation with the international community.

China sees climate change as a common challenge facing the entire humanity. There

---

* Speech at the Climate Group's 10 Year Anniversary Special Event. Kings Place, London, 28 April 2014.

are compelling reasons for all countries to collaborate and make urgent efforts for a resolution of climate change issues.

China believes that historical responsibilities for greenhouse gas emissions and the development stages of countries should be taken into consideration.

China also believes that the principles of common but differentiated responsibilities, equity and respective capabilities should be followed.

Looking forward to possible solutions China is dedicated to the success of the 2015 climate change negotiations. Our goal is to strengthen full, effective and sustained implementation of the UNFCCC beyond 2020.

In February, China and the United States issued Joint Statement on Climate Change. This reiterated our shared commitment to making important contributions to the global fight against climate change in 2015. Last month Chinese President Xi Jinping visited Europe. During the visit China signed joint statements with the EU, France and Germany. All these documents have paragraphs on climate change cooperation. They stressed that efforts should be made to adopt at the Paris Conference a protocol, another legal instrument or an agreed outcome with legal force under the UNFCCC applicable to all parties. Also underlined was a joint commitment to making significant cuts in greenhouse gas emissions through credible and verifiable domestic action.

In advancing climate change negotiations, we must not follow in the steps of "Larry the Cat". I am sure you all heard about the story of "Larry the Cat" who is famous as the "Chief Mouser" of the British government Cabinet Office. Everyone expected "Larry" to bring down the rat population around Downing Street. Regrettably he has earned a reputation as always remaining in a "tactical planning stage".

Similarly, in fighting against climate change, China would rather like to "war-war" than to "jaw-jaw".

In China we have taken a lot of actions to cut emissions. Many of them are voluntary and unilateral.

China approaches mitigating climate change from two directions:

- First, preventing climate change is a shared responsibility with the world.
- Second, stopping climate change is also an imperative for the Chinese own sustainable development as well as industrial upgrading.

China is endeavoring to build a "beautiful China" through green development, a circular economy and low carbon development.

This Chinese commitment is not new. In 2009, China had already announced major targets for 2020. These include:

- Reduce CO_2 emission by between 40% and 45%.
- Raise the share of non-fossil fuels in primary energy to 15%.
- Increase forest stock volume by 1.3 billion cubic meters.
- And all these targets are on the basis of 2005 levels.

After just 5 years, China had achieved these goals:

- Reduced carbon intensity by 28%.
- Saved 2.3 billion tons of CO_2 emission.
- Now non-fossil fuels already make up 9.6% of our energy mix.

In his Report on the Work of the Government in March, Chinese Premier Li Keqiang set out the mandatory target for this year. This is to bring down energy intensity by 3.9% while securing a 7.5% growth of the economy.

The approach in China is a multi-pronged one.

The Chinese investment in clean energy is the largest in the world. By the end of 2014 the Chinese solar power capacity will reach 30 million kilowatts. This will be 10 times of 2011. It is estimated that in 2050 the Chinese clean energy power capacity will amount to 2.48 billion kilowatts. This will account for 62% of the Chinese total installed capacity and 58% of its total power generation. These goals will mark a historic shift in the Chinese power generation from the dominance of coal to clean non-fossil energy sources.

China is making an all-out effort to encourage the development of energy conservation and environmental protection sector, also known as the green industry. An important means is to phase out high-emission and energy-intensive capacity. Now the green industry in China has employed 30 million people. It is projected that by the next year the total output of green industry will reach 4.5 trillion RMB. This will be a new engine of the Chinese economic growth.

This year China will wind down major sources of pollution. For example:

- Iron and steel capacity will be reduced by 27 million tons.
- Cement capacity by 42 million tons.
- Plate glass by 35 million TEU.

The Chinese strategy is to reduce emissions and energy consumption while adding to economic development.

China is also carrying out carbon emissions trading. Pilot programs are operating and they are going faster than expected. In 2013 carbon emission trading was introduced in big cities of China, including Beijing, Shanghai, Tianjin, Guangzhou and Shenzhen. This year, China will formulate some new rules and regulations on carbon trading.

Just as being the biggest contributor to global poverty reduction, China is well on her way to become the biggest green contributor to global emission reduction. While making domestic emission cuts, we also encourage Chinese companies to go global and contribute their part to emissions cuts worldwide.

Only five days ago, I attended the UK-China Sustainable Energy Summit and witnessed the signing of several MOUs on Chinese investment and building of solar parks in Britain. This further shows that China is committed to working with the UK and the rest of the world to grapple with climate change and look after our Mother Earth.

Ladies and Gentlemen,

This year marks the 10th anniversary of the Climate Group. As a Chinese saying goes, "It takes ten years to grow trees, but one hundred years to rear people." Likewise, it takes time for any organization to grow. And it will only take longer for this organization to accomplish great tasks. I highly appreciate the Climate Group's positive contribution to the global fight against climate change over the past decade. I expect the Climate Group to compose a new chapter in the next decade and make even greater contribution to safeguarding and improving mankind's survival and development, which is a great task that will take one hundred years and even longer.

Thank you!

加强中英能源合作，为构建人类命运共同体贡献力量[*]

女士们、先生们：

很高兴出席英国能源投资峰会。

能源与我们的日常生活息息相关，也是事关世界经济走向和人类前途命运的一项重要议题。关于如何看待当今世界经济和全球治理，我想前不久中国国家主席习近平在世界经济论坛年会的主旨演讲，提供了非常精彩的答案。那就是，我们不能把困扰世界的许多问题归咎于经济全球化，而是要树立人类命运共同体意识，适应和引导好全球化，在创新中寻找出路，在开放中分享机会，使发展成果更好地惠及每个国家和民族。今天，我想从人类命运共同体视角出发，谈谈对能源问题的看法，并就中英能源合作提一些建议。

谈到能源问题，我们首先应当看到能源为人类成为"你中有我、我中有你"的命运共同体提供了强大动力。纵观漫长的人类文明史，无论是火的发现还是电的应用，无论是化石燃料的开发利用还是可再生能源的迅猛发展，能源的每一次发现和更新都在人类社会进步中发挥了关键作用。能源的大规模开发利用不仅极大地提高了社会生产率，还促进了经济全球化与科技进步，拉近了不同国家与地区人民之间的距离。

但同时，能源开发利用所产生的环境、安全问题已成为人类面临的共同挑战。随着人口增长和经济发展，能源消耗水平大幅提升，全球生态环境面

---

[*] 在2017年英国能源投资峰会上的主旨演讲。2017年1月26日，伦敦。

第六章　生态环保　　387

临巨大压力,气候变化、能源安全等全球性挑战日益突出。对于全世界 70 多亿人民来说,地球是人类唯一赖以生存的家园。珍爱和呵护地球是我们的唯一选择。只有使能源更加绿色和低碳化,才能实现全球经济的可持续发展,建设一个清洁美丽的世界。正如习主席所说:"我们不能吃祖宗饭、断子孙路,用破坏性方式搞发展。绿水青山就是金山银山。我们应该遵循天人合一、道法自然的理念,寻求永续发展之路。"

令人欣慰的是,近年来绿色成为全球能源治理的主色调,推动清洁能源发展已成为能源合作的普遍共识。正是基于这种休戚与共、责任共担的精神,中英两国在参与和推进全球能源治理方面都做出了不懈努力。从 18 世纪工业革命到 20 世纪 50 年代率先建设运营民用核电站,英国一直是全球能源技术创新的领先者。近年来,英国加大对新能源、可再生能源领域投入,在应对气候变化问题上专门出台法律和政策文件,提出 2050 年碳排放量在 1990 年水平上减少 80% 的目标。2016 年英国煤炭发电量仅占总量的 9.2%,而风力发电量占比达 11.5%,风力发电量首次超过煤炭发电量。

同样,作为世界第一大能源生产国和消费国,中国在节能减排、可再生能源开发等方面也取得了有目共睹的成就。在创新、协调、绿色、开放、共享的新发展理念指导下,我们正加快构建清洁、高效、安全、可持续的现代能源体系,使能源消费逐步由粗放、低效走向节约、高效,推动能源结构持续优化,坚持走绿色、低碳发展道路。目前,中国已成为水电、风电、太阳能发电装机世界第一大国。2016 年中国能源消费总量约 43.6 亿吨标准煤,非化石能源消费比重达 13.3%,同比提高 1.3 个百分点。2016 年前三季度,单位 GDP 能耗同比下降 5.2%,绿色发展初见成效。

当然,随着中国城镇化、农业现代化的发展,节能减排任务还很艰巨,目前中国秋冬季的雾霾污染形势严峻就是一个例证。中国的目标是到 2020 年非化石能源占一次能源消费比重达 15%,天然气比重达 10% 以上,煤炭消费控制在 58% 以内,使清洁低碳能源成为能源供应增量的主体。我们争取到 2030 年碳排放提前达到峰值。中方积极参与《巴黎协定》谈判进程,不仅率先签署协定,还推动二十国集团首次发表《二十国集团协调人会议关于气候变化问题的主席声明》，就可再生能源等制订行动计划，为推动协定顺利生效提供强有力的支持。中国将继续采取行动应对气候变化，百分之百履行自己的义务。

女士们、先生们，

2016年，尽管英国公投"脱欧"、政府更迭给中英关系带来一些不确定性，但在双方共同努力下，两国关系实现平稳过渡并持续发展。两国领导人再次确认将继续打造中英面向21世纪全球全面战略伙伴关系。

能源合作是中英互利合作的重要组成部分。中英不仅就传统的石油、天然气等化石能源积极开展合作，还在清洁能源和可再生能源合作方面保持良好势头。例如，中国企业积极参与英国核电、海上风电、太阳能发电、生物质发电等新能源项目。中英企业在电动大巴、低排放出租车等新一代绿色交通工具方面的合作方兴未艾。

特别值得一提的是，2016年9月，中、英、法三方在伦敦正式签署欣克利角C核电项目一揽子投资协议，标志着中英核电实质性合作进入全新阶段。欣克利角项目不仅将给英国数百万家庭提供稳定电力供应和创造2万多个就业岗位，而且将有助于中英及有关各方在清洁能源领域深化合作，更好地应对气候变化挑战，为促进两国及全球可持续发展注入新动力。

女士们、先生们，

人类正处在大发展大变革大调整时期，也正处在一个挑战层出不穷、风险日益增多的时代。构建人类命运共同体这一美好目标，需要各国共同担当、同舟共济、携手努力。2017年是中英两国建立大使级外交关系45周年。中英关系面临新的发展机遇。能源应当成为双方合作的重点。我认为，两国应重点在以下领域加强合作。

第一，共同推进欣克利角旗舰项目顺利实施。欣克利角项目是互利多赢的项目。中国人常说："要把好事办好。"英语中有句俗语："结局好，一切都好。"中方衷心希望该项目能顺利实施，尽快投产发电，为保障英国能源安全做出贡献。中国发展核电30多年来，一直保持着良好的运行业绩和安全水准，在核电发展和监管方面的成就得到了国际机构的高度评价。我们也一直

第六章 生态环保

在通过国际合作发展核电事业。我们赞赏英国政府不久前正式启动中国核电技术"华龙一号"评审，期待相关技术早日落地。希望英方相关安全监管机制保持透明和开放，公平保障包括中资企业在内的外国投资者合法权益。

第二，共同开拓能源技术创新与合作空间。能源领域是最可能发生下一次科技革命和产业革命的领域之一。中国经济实现低碳转型需要大量新技术和资本，孕育着巨大商机。中国不仅在核电领域拥有完整的产业链及成熟的技术、装备和建设水平，而且在太阳能技术研发与使用方面也位居世界前列。英方在海上风电、潮汐发电、智慧能源、分布式能源、碳捕获与封存技术等方面处于全球领先水平。中英可积极开展能源领域技术创新的交流与合作，有效配置相关技术与资源要素，实现优势互补和互利共赢。

第三，共同开展"一带一路"能源合作。"一带一路"倡议是中国实行全方位对外开放的重大举措，致力于打造多主体、全方位、跨领域合作平台。"一带一路"共建国家多为发展中国家，能源设施、电力等领域需求缺口大，能源合作前景广阔。中英两国在能源设备、规划、工程施工和融资、专业服务等方面各有所长，可结合有关共建国家的现实需求与合作意向，探讨合作内容与形式，打造"能源丝绸之路"，使能源合作成果更好更多惠及双方及第三方市场。

第四，共同构建全球能源治理格局。二十国集团领导人杭州峰会在能源领域取得重要成果，突出能效和清洁能源对构建未来能源格局的重要意义，体现了二十国集团机制在全球能源治理中的独特作用。中英同为二十国集团领导人重要成员，可加强能源政策对话与协调，推动有关各方落实杭州峰会相关成果，不断加大能源投资，完善国际能源市场监测和应急机制，提高可持续能源安全，共同建设更有效、更包容的全球能源治理架构。

第五，共同推进气候变化国际合作。气候变化《巴黎协定》已于2016年11月正式生效，开启了全球合作应对气候变化挑战的崭新篇章，在全球气候治理史上具有里程碑意义，符合全球发展大方向，成果来之不易。中英在应对气候变化方面不仅有共同利益，而且有许多共识和相似立场，双方可发挥引领作用，共同推动协定落实，为全球碳减排事业做出新贡献。

女士们、先生们，

习主席说，"中国人历来主张'世界大同，天下一家'"，"只要我们牢固树立人类命运共同体意识，携手努力、共同担当，同舟共济、共渡难关，就一定能够让世界更美好、让人民更幸福"。

后天就是中国农历鸡年春节，鸡在中国文化中象征着勤劳、活力和吉祥。我对新的一年充满信心和期望。让我们共同努力，不断推进中英能源合作，为打造绿色、包容、可持续的人类命运共同体做出更大贡献！

谢谢！

Stronger China-UK Energy Cooperation Paves the Way for Building a Community of Shared Future[*]

Ladies and Gentlemen,

It is a real pleasure to join you for the UK Energy Investment Summit. This summit focuses on a highly pertinent issue because energy is closely linked to our daily life. It is an important subject that bears on the trend of global economy and the future of mankind.

Indeed, how do we judge the trend of the world economy and the future of global governance? To try to answer this question, let me quote President Xi Jinping.

In his keynote speech not long ago at the World Economic Forum in Davos, President Xi said:

We should not blame economic globalization for the world's problems.

Rather, we should keep to the goal of building a community of shared future for mankind.

We should adapt to and guide economic globalization. We need to relentlessly pursue innovation.

We need to build an open global economy to share opportunities through opening-up.

We should deliver the benefits of economic globalization to all countries and all nations.

From the perspective of building a community of shared future, let me share with you my thoughts on the issue of energy and my suggestions for China-UK energy

---

[*] Keynote Speech at the UK Energy Investment Summit 2017. London, 26 January 2017.

cooperation.

Talking about energy, the first thing we must admit is that energy makes it possible for building a community and a future where everyone has a stake. The history of human progress is, in a way, a history of discoveries of new forms of energy.

We have traveled a journey from the discovery of fire to the use of electricity, and from the excavation of fossil fuels to the rapid development of renewable energies. And every time, the discovery of a new source of energy and the replacement of the old always played a crucial role in human progress. The reasons are simple. Large scale exploitation and application of energy helps increase productivity in a dramatic way. This stimulates scientific and technological progress. This reduces the distance between countries and regions. And this drives economic globalization.

However, the development and use of energy also create environmental and security problems, which have posed challenges for us all. The growth of population and economy leads to immense increase of energy consumption. The global ecological and environmental system is now under huge pressure. Global challenges such as climate change and energy security are increasingly acute.

For all seven billion people on this planet, the earth is our only home. We have only one choice, and that is to cherish and care for our home. And there is only one way to do this, and that is to go green and go low-carbon. This is how we can grow the world economy in a sustainable way.

Just as President Xi said recently in Geneva,

"We must not exhaust all the resources passed on to us by previous generations and leave nothing to our children, or pursue development in a destructive way."

"Clear waters and green mountains are as good as mountains of gold and silver. We must maintain harmony between man and nature and pursue sustainable development."

In recent years, the idea of green development has prevailed in global energy governance. It is now an international consensus that energy cooperation should aim at the development of clean energy.

This is the spirit of sharing weal and woe and undertaking responsibility together. China and the UK, working in such a spirit, have respectively made unremitting efforts to advance the global energy governance.

The UK has been a world leader in energy related technology and innovation. It took the lead in the 18th century during the industrial revolution. It was among the first to build civil nuclear power plants in the mid-20th century.

In recent years, the UK has kept making progress in this field. Investment in new and renewable energy is increasing. Special laws are made and policies adopted to tackle climate change. The target is set for reducing emissions by at least 80% in 2050 from 1990 levels. And for the first time in 2016, wind energy provided 11.5% of the UK's total electricity output, overtaking coal generated power at only 9.2% of the total.

On the part of China, it is now the world's largest energy producer and consumer. In energy conservation, emission reduction and renewable energy development, the Chinese achievements over the years have been widely recognized.

We are committed to the new development concepts that focus on innovation, balanced growth, green economy, opening-up and inclusive development.

We are accelerating our efforts to build a modern energy system that is clean, efficient, secure and sustainable.

Our energy consumption structure has been constantly optimized. It is going through a gradual transition from the resource-intensive and low-efficiency model to one that is energy-saving and highly efficient.

In the future, China will remain committed to green and low-carbon development.

At present, China has greater installed capacity in hydropower, wind power and solar power than any other country in the world. Of the total energy consumption in 2016 (4.36 billion tons of standard coal), non-fossil fuel accounted for 13.3%, which was 1.3 percentage points higher than the previous year. In the first three quarters of last year, energy use per unit of GDP downed by 5.2% year on year. Such progress is largely attributed to green development.

Indeed, as urbanization and agricultural modernization remains an ongoing process in China, energy conservation and emission reduction becomes a daunting task. One example is the autumn and winter haze resulting from air pollution.

China is taking on this task. We will strive to make the growth in energy supply mainly green and low-carbon. To this end, we have set a number of targets to be met by 2020. These include:

- Increasing the share of non-fossil fuel in primary energy consumption to 15%.

- Increasing the proportion of natural gas to at least 10%.
- And keeping the percentage of coal consumption below 58%.
- This will enable us to reach the emissions peak before 2030.

On the world scene, China also played an active part in the negotiation of the Paris Agreement. China was among the first to ratify the agreement. China pushed the G20 to issue its first Presidency Statement on Climate Change. China also led the making of the G20 Voluntary Action Plan on Renewable Energy. The Presidency Statement and the Action Plan will help ensure the smooth and effective implementation of the Paris Agreement. China will continue to take steps to tackle climate change and fully honour its obligations.

Ladies and Gentlemen,

Last year's Brexit referendum and the UK's government reshuffle caused some uncertainties in China-UK relations. However, our two countries have since then worked together to steady our relationship in time of transition and to sustain its momentum of development. Leaders of both countries reaffirmed the shared commitment to China-UK global comprehensive strategic partnership for the 21st century.

Energy cooperation features prominently in the win-win cooperation between our two countries. China and the UK have had cooperation in the field of fossil fuels, such as oil and gas. Meanwhile, our cooperation on clean and renewable energy is showing a strong momentum. Chinese companies are actively involved in Britain's new energy projects, from nuclear power plants to offshore wind farms, from solar energy projects to biomass electricity generation. Their growing cooperation with the UK also includes next-generation green transport. The most familiar examples are the zero-emission electric bus and the ultra-low-emission London Black Cabs.

What is particularly worth mentioning is the package deal of the Hinckley Point C nuclear project. Its official signing by China, Britain and France last September was a milestone—a substantial step that China and the UK have taken in nuclear cooperation. This project will create more than 20,000 jobs and provide reliable energy supply to millions of British families. It will facilitate closer cooperation between China, Britain and other relevant countries on clean energy. It will help tackle climate change. It will drive the sustainable development in China, in the UK and beyond.

Ladies and Gentlemen,

We are now in an interesting time of profound transformation and massive changes. It is also a time of numerous challenges and increasing risks. Building a community of shared future for mankind is an exciting goal, and it requires all countries to undertake responsibilities and overcome difficulties together.

2017 marks the 45th anniversary of the Ambassadorial-level diplomatic ties between China and Britain.

There are certainly new opportunities for China-UK relations. Energy, among others, should be our focus for cooperation.

I think there are a number of specific areas where we can strengthen our energy cooperation.

First, we should work to ensure the smooth implementation of the Hinkley Point C nuclear project. This is a flagship win-win project. We Chinese like to say: "Good things deserve good results." British people say: "All is well that ends well." We sincerely hope that this project will proceed smoothly, start to generate electricity on an early date and contribute to the UK's energy security.

Over the past 30 years, China has kept a good operation and security record. Our achievements in nuclear power development and security supervision have been highly recognized by international institutions. And we have always cooperated closely with our international partners.

I appreciate the UK government's decision to start the generic design assessment of the Chinese nuclear reactor HPR1000, and we look forward to its early application in the UK.

We expect the British security assessment to be transparent and open, so that Chinese companies, like all foreign investors in the UK, will be treated equally and have their legitimate rights and interests protected.

Now let me talk about the second area of energy cooperation.

Of all the fields where the next scientific, technological and industrial revolution could take place, the energy sector has the greatest potential. Here, China and the UK are well placed to work with each other and explore energy-related technology and innovation.

China is in a transition toward low-carbon development. There is a huge demand for new technologies and investment, and hence great business opportunities.

China has a complete nuclear industrial chain, mature nuclear power technology, world-class equipment building and rich construction experience.

China is also a world leader in the field of solar power technology, both R&D and application.

The UK leads the world in offshore wind power, tidal power, smart energy, distributed generation, carbon capture and sequestration, etc.

China and the UK can draw on our respective strengths in technology and resources. We can engage each other in win-win cooperation.

The third area of China-UK energy cooperation is opened up by the Belt and Road Initiative.

The Belt and Road Initiative is a major effort of China to strive for all-round opening-up. It is a platform for all-dimensional, cross-field cooperation among multi-entities.

Most of the BRI partners are developing nations. The demand for energy facilities and electricity generation as well as the interest in cooperation with international partners are huge. And so are the prospects for cooperation.

China is good at energy equipment building, development planning and facility construction, while the UK has strengths in financing and special services. Based on such demands and interest, China and the UK can engage regional partners in discussions over the content and form of multi-party cooperation and build an Energy Silk Road. This will bring greater benefits to not only our two countries but also countries of the third market.

The fourth areas for China-UK energy cooperation is global governance regime.

Important outcomes on the issue of energy were reached at the G20 Hangzhou Summit. By highlighting the importance of efficient and clean energy in the future, the G20 demonstrated its unique role in global energy governance.

As members of the G20, China and the UK can work together on the following:

- Greater energy policy dialogue and coordination.
- Ensuring implementation of the G20 outcomes by all its members.
- Increased investment in the energy sector.
- Stronger monitoring system and an emergency response mechanism for the

international energy market.
- And improved energy security.

By working together, China and the UK can jointly contribute to a more efficient and inclusive global energy governance regime.

Last but not least, China and the UK can join hands to promote cooperation on climate change.

The Paris Agreement on Climate Change came into effect last November. It is a new chapter in the global response to climate change. It is a milestone in the history of climate governance. It is in line with the trend of global development. But it did not come easily and deserves to be cherished.

China and the UK have many common interests in tackling climate change. We have similar positions and share broad agreement on this issue. Both countries can play a leading role in the implementation of this agreement and contribute to the global cause of emission reduction.

Ladies and Gentlemen,

President Xi Jinping said this in his new year message:

"China believes that everyone belongs to one family in a united world."

He went on to say in his speech in Davos:

"As long as we keep to the goal of building a community of shared future for mankind and work hand in hand to fulfill our responsibilities and overcome difficulties, we will be able to create a better world and deliver better lives for our peoples."

In just two days, we will ring in the Chinese New Year of the Rooster. In Chinese culture, the rooster is a symbol of industry, vigor and good luck.

I am full of confidence and expectations for the Year of the Rooster. I believe by working together China and Britain will enable greater progress in energy cooperation.

By working together, our two countries will make even greater contribution to green, inclusive and sustainable development in building a community of shared future for mankind.

Thank you!

保护野生动物，共建美丽家园 *

尊敬的英国外交部政务次官埃尔伍德阁下，
尊敬的英国环境部政务次官科菲阁下，
尊敬的各位使节：

很高兴出席英国外交部和环境部联合举办的"打击野生动物非法贸易"早餐会。野生动物非法贸易是全球性挑战，各国亟须加强合作，共同应对。我期待听取各位同事的意见，也想谈谈自己的看法。

两千多年前，中国古代哲学家就提出人与自然和谐相处的思想，古代典籍《礼记·中庸》中载有"万物并育而不相害，道并行而不相悖"的理念。今天，我们同住一个地球村，野生动物是地球村不可或缺的成员。保护野生动物既是人类的共同责任，也是我们促进人类可持续发展事业的应有之义。

中国政府高度重视加强生态文明建设，从国家发展总体布局的战略高度重视保护环境，特别是野生动物保护事业。近年来，我们严厉打击野生动物及象牙等动物产品非法贸易，不断加强与国际社会合作，成效显著。概括而言，中方努力做到了三个"坚持不懈"。

一是坚持不懈完善法律体系。中国已制定以《中华人民共和国野生动物保护法》《中华人民共和国森林法》《中华人民共和国濒危野生动植物进出口管理条例》等为核心的野生动植物保护法律体系。2016年7月，中国修订了野生动物保护法，增加了禁止出售、收购、利用野生动物及其制品、禁止发

---

* 在"打击野生动物非法贸易"早餐会上的讲话。2017年5月2日，英国外交部。

布相关广告和提供交易场所的规定，建立了打击野生动植物走私和非法贸易联席会议制度，对违法行为加大惩处力度。该法案已于2017年1月1日开始实施，为进一步加强野生动物保护和打击非法贸易提供了强有力的法律保障。

二是坚持不懈开展执法行动。野生动物非法贸易案发数量在中国连续3年下降，其中象牙走私案下降80%以上。2016年12月，中国政府发布通知，决定于2017年底全面停止商业性加工销售象牙及其制品活动。截至2017年3月底，中国国家林业局已停业12个象牙定点加工企业和55个象牙定点销售场所。上述举措对保护非洲象有重要意义，有助于推动源头分布国、中转国和消费国共同有效打击违法活动。中国还通过公开销毁非法盗卖虎骨、犀牛角、藏羚羊皮毛制品等活动，加大宣传教育力度，展示打击野生动物走私犯罪活动的坚决态度。

三是坚持不懈推进国际合作。中国是《濒危野生动植物国际贸易公约》缔约国，认真履行该公约义务，举办了"非洲濒危物种履约管理培训班""亚洲履约执法和保护管理人员培训班"，协助成员国增强履约执法能力。中国支持联合国大会通过的"打击野生动物非法贸易"决议，积极参与联合国框架内国际合作。2011—2014年，中国组织开展3次跨国专项执法行动"眼镜蛇行动"，有效遏制了走私犯罪活动。

近年来，中英在打击野生动物非法贸易方面也开展了不少合作。中国积极参加英国发起的"打击野生动物非法贸易高级别会议"和"打击野生动植物非法贸易运输工作组"等行动。中方赞赏英国倡议召开的"打击野生动物非法贸易"高级别系列会议，支持伦敦、卡萨内和河内会议通过的宣言和行动计划，也愿建设性参与后续进程。

为进一步推动打击野生动物非法贸易的国际合作，我愿提三点建议。

第一，凝聚共识。我们应鼓励更多国家和机构参与打击野生动物非法贸易，构筑遍布全球的"朋友圈"，形成合作伙伴"关系网"，发挥集体智慧，丰富应对策略和行动计划。

第二，综合施策。我们应标本兼治，找准野生动物非法贸易成因、趋势和危害，对症下药。各方可在盗猎、走私出入境、国际转运、非法加工销售等环节联合行动，完善各自法律体系，加大执法力度，阻断非法贸易链。

第三，协调行动。高级别会议是国际社会打击野生动物非法贸易的重要措施之一，我们应使之与联合国、国际组织、地区机构、民间组织的行动保持协调，互相配合，形成合力，产生良好的综合效应，共同推进保护野生动物的伟大事业。

中国有句名言："坚持就是胜利。"中国愿与各国携手并肩，坚持不懈，共同为打击野生动物非法贸易，建设一个更加美丽、和谐的地球家园贡献力量！

谢谢！

Protect the Wildlife and Build a Beautiful Global Village*

Under Secretary Tobias Ellwood,

Under Secretary Thérèse Coffey,

Ambassadors and High Commissioners,

It is a real delight to join you at this Breakfast Meeting on Illegal Wildlife Trade co-hosted by the FCO and Defra.

The illegal wildlife trade is a global challenge. It therefore requires strong global collaboration and joint response. I appreciate the opportunity of this breakfast meeting to exchange views with you on this important issue.

Here I would like to share some of my thoughts.

In China, the idea that man and nature should coexist in harmony was first proposed by philosophers more than 2,000 years ago. The ancient Chinese classic, the *Book of Rites*, has these lines:

"All living creatures grow together without harming each other; all ways run parallel without interfering with one another."

Today, we live in a global village. The wildlife is certainly indispensable and man is obliged to protect them. That is the only way for us to achieve sustainable development for all of us.

The Chinese government places high priority on eco-environmental preservation. Environmental protection, especially wildlife preservation, is a key part in the Chinese

---

* Remarks at the Breakfast Meeting on Illegal Wildlife Trade. Foreign & Commonwealth Office, 2 May 2017.

overall national development strategy.

Over the years China has worked hard in cracking down on the illegal trade in wildlife and wildlife products including elephant tusks. In doing so, we have also constantly enhanced our cooperation with the world. The outcomes are remarkable.

There are three areas where China has made unremitting efforts.

Firstly, China has made unremitting efforts to improve relevant legislations.

China has made a set of laws in wildlife protection, which is underpinned by the Wildlife Protection Law, the Forest Law, the Regulations on the Import and Export of Endangered Species of Wild Fauna and Flora, etc.

In July 2016, amendments to the Wildlife Protection Law were introduced to provide for a number of prohibitions. These include:

- Prohibition on the sale, purchase and use of wildlife and related products.
- Prohibition on any wildlife related advertisement.
- And prohibition on providing trading venues for illegal wildlife products.

The amendments also provide for the establishment of a cross-department joint conference mechanism to tackle wildlife trafficking and illegal trade. This is aimed at strengthening the enforcement actions against violations of the law.

The amended Wildlife Protection Law came into force on the first day of this year. It is a powerful legal weapon for more effective protection of the wildlife and cracking down on illegal trade.

Secondly, China has made unremitting efforts to strengthen law enforcement.

For three years in a row, the number of illegal wildlife trade cases in China has continuously come down. Notably, the smuggling of elephant tusks has dropped by over 80%.

Last December, the Chinese government announced a total ban on the commercial processing and sales of ivory and ivory products in China. This ban will be phased in by the end of this year.

As of the end of March, the State Forestry Administration has ordered the closure of 12 ivory processing companies and 55 ivory shops.

These moves are highly significant for protecting African elephants. They will effectively promote the concerted efforts of elephant range states and transit and consumer states to combat the illegal activities.

Other concrete steps that China has taken include the destruction in public of tiger bone, rhino horn and Xizangan antelope hide involved in poaching and trafficking. These campaigns are both a means of public education and a demonstration of the Chinese firm stance against illegal wildlife trade.

Thirdly, China has made unremitting efforts to constantly strengthen international cooperation.

China has earnestly fulfilled its obligations as a signatory to The Convention on International Trade in Endangered Species (CITES).

One example is the training courses China has undertaken to run for member states from Africa and Asia in order to enhance their compliance and law enforcement capabilities.

China supported the UN General Assembly Resolution on "Tackling the Illicit Trafficking in Wildlife" and actively participated in international cooperation under the UN framework.

From 2011 to 2014, China conducted three cross-border operations against illegal wildlife trade known as "Mission Cobra". These operations have been effective in curbing wildlife trafficking.

Over the years, China and the UK have had much cooperation on tackling illegal trade in wildlife.

China took an active part in the High Level Event on Illicit Wildlife Trafficking and the United for Wildlife Transport Taskforce, both initiated by Britain.

China appreciates the British initiative in hosting the series of high level meetings on Illicit Wildlife Trafficking. We support the declarations and action plans adopted during the London, Kasane and Hanoi conferences. China is ready to take part constructively in the follow-up process.

To further advance international cooperation on combating illegal wildlife trade, I would like to make three suggestions.

First, build consensus.

We should encourage more countries and organizations to get involved and build a network of friends and partners. That will enable us to leverage our collective wisdom and enrich our toolbox so that our joint responses and action plans will be more effective.

Second, work for a comprehensive solution.

We must cure both the symptom and the root cause of this problem. This requires us to identify the specific causes, trends and damages of wildlife trafficking so as to prescribe remedies that will work.

We should take joint actions on the problem at different stages, from poaching, trafficking and transfer to illegal processing and sales. Such actions include improving our respective laws, enhancing enforcement and breaking the chain of illegal trade.

Third, coordinate actions.

The high-level conferences constitute one of the important means for the international community to prevail over illegal wildlife trade.

These conferences should be well coordinated with the actions of the UN and other international organizations, regional institutions and NGOs.

Effective coordination of efforts from all partners will strengthen our hands to make concerted progress in advancing the protection of wildlife.

As the Chinese saying goes, "Success belongs to the persevering."

China is ready to join hands with all other countries to make persevering efforts to tackle illegal wildlife trade.

China is ready to contribute our part to building a more beautiful and more harmonious global village.

Thank you!

深化中英气变合作，共建美好地球家园 *

尊敬的英国议会跨党派中国小组主席格雷厄姆先生，
尊敬的英国议会下院环境监察委员会主席邓恩先生，
尊敬的英国外交发展部COP26区域大使布里斯托爵士，
尊敬的各位议员，
女士们、先生们：

很高兴再次与英国议会跨党派中国小组各位议员座谈，我们今天座谈的主题是中英气候变化合作。2021年将是气候变化合作之年，中英将分别主办COP15和COP26，这既是中英两国的大事，也将对全球气变合作和环境治理产生重要影响。

当前，新冠疫情在全球蔓延，气候变化问题持续升温。我认为，人类社会正面临与气候变化紧密相关的五大挑战。

一是全球变暖挑战。目前全球平均温度已比工业化前高出1℃以上，全球海平面上升速度达到每年5毫米。未来，一些地区可能不再适宜居住。

二是生态环境挑战。人类工业化进程创造了前所未有的物质财富，也产生了严重的环境污染，生物多样性面临严峻挑战。

三是新冠疫情叠加挑战。疫情客观上削弱了各国对气候变化问题的关注度，COP15和COP26不得不推迟举行。

---

* 在英国议会跨党派中国小组气候变化问题在线座谈会上的主旨演讲。2020年10月13日，中国驻英国大使馆。

四是应对能力不平衡挑战。与发达国家相比，发展中国家受到气候变化冲击影响更大。国际社会消除南北发展不平衡、凝聚应对气候变化合力依然任重道远。

五是毁约退群挑战。个别国家悍然退出《巴黎协定》，这种单边霸凌行径使全球气变合作和治理遭受严重挫折。

不久前，习近平主席在出席联合国成立 75 周年高级别活动中宣布，中国将提高国家自主贡献力度，采取更加有力的政策和措施，二氧化碳排放力争于 2030 年前达到峰值，努力争取 2060 年前实现碳中和。这是中国基于国内可持续发展内在要求和构建人类命运共同体的责任担当，彰显了中国积极应对气候变化的坚定决心。国际社会对此予以高度评价。约翰逊首相称，习主席宣布的目标是一件了不起的事情，是向世界发出的强有力信号。中英是应对气候变化和环境治理的重要伙伴，双方合作大有可为。

一是共同做气变治理的领军者。中国积极落实应对气候变化国家战略，切实履行《巴黎协定》国际义务。2005—2019 年，中国单位 GDP 碳排放下降 48.1%，非化石能源占比达 15.3%，新能源汽车保有量占全球一半以上。英国确立了到 2050 年实现"净零排放"的目标。中英可以充分利用主办 COP15 和 COP26 两次会议之机，为全球气变治理发挥重要引领作用。习近平主席和约翰逊首相就两国加强 COP15 和 COP26 相互协调、相互支持达成重要共识。中国生态环境部部长黄润秋与夏尔马大臣，我本人与夏尔马大臣、布里斯托爵士等保持密切沟通，双方还在工作层建立了联合工作组。下一步，双方要加强沟通协调，调动政府、议会、商界、媒体、学界等各界人士的积极性，确保两次大会办得精彩，取得成功。

二是共同做绿色发展的推动者。疫情形势下，中国政府统筹推进疫情防控与经济社会发展，推广绿色生产和生活方式，加速完善气候投融资体系。英国在清洁能源、低碳技术等方面独具特色。中英应加强在新能源、低碳城市等领域合作，实现生态环境保护和经济高质量发展双赢。中国在核能等清洁能源领域技术成熟，运营管理经验丰富。欣克利角 C 核电站是中、英、法在清洁能源领域合作的重要旗舰项目，建成后可满足英国 7% 的电力需求，每年可以减排 900 万吨二氧化碳。双方应共同努力确保该项目顺利成功。我们还应鼓励两国产业界在可再生能源、绿色金融、绿色"一带一路"等领域加强合作，助力两国绿色复产，带动全球绿色复苏。

三是共同做绿色创新的开拓者。中英都在积极推动绿色科技、能源、金融创新发展。两国签署了《中英清洁能源合作伙伴关系实施工作计划2019—2020》，共同制定了《"一带一路"绿色投资原则》，绿色合作潜力巨大。吉利、比亚迪等中资企业积极投资英国，成为两国绿色交通合作的典范。

四是共同做多边主义的捍卫者。中英双方应坚定维护多边主义，按照共同但有区别的责任、公平原则和各自能力原则，尽最大努力落实国家自主贡献，共同推动《巴黎协定》全面、平衡、有效实施，帮助发展中国家提升应对气变能力，深化应对气变国际合作，完善气候治理体系，共同引领全球气变治理方向和进程。

女士们、先生们，

应对气候变化、保护生物多样性是中英合作的重要领域，也是中英两国作为具有全球影响的大国应肩负的使命。习近平主席在联合国生物多样性峰会上指出："我们要站在对人类文明负责的高度，尊重自然、顺应自然、保护自然，探索人与自然和谐共生之路，促进经济发展与生态保护协调统一，共建繁荣、清洁、美丽的世界。"英国议会在英国应对气候变化进程中发挥着重要作用。我衷心期望各位议员继续发挥积极作用，支持中英两国政府、两国企业开展绿色合作，为办好COP15和COP26献计献策，为构建人类命运共同体、共建美好地球家园贡献力量！

谢谢！

Make Our Planet a Better Home for All *

Chairman Graham,

Chairman Dunne,

Sir Laurie,

My Lords and MPs,

Ladies and Gentlemen,

It is a real delight to join you again at the APPCG webinar. Today we will focus on China-UK cooperation on climate change.

The year 2021 will be an important year for joint global response to climate change. China and the UK will host COP15 and COP26 respectively. These are not only important events in China-UK relations. They also bear great significance to global cooperation and governance on climate change and environmental protection.

Against the background of the raging COVID-19 pandemic, tackling climate change has become an increasingly urgent task. Mankind faces five major challenges of climate change.

The first challenge is global warming.

Global average temperature is now more than one degree Celsius above pre-industrial levels. The global sea level rise has averaged 5 millimeters per year in recent years. In the future, some places may no longer be suitable for people to live in.

The second challenge is deterioration of the eco-environment.

While creating unprecedented wealth, industrialization has caused serious pollution

---

* Keynote Speech at the APPCG Webinar on China-UK Cooperation on Tackling Climate Change. Chinese Embassy, 13 October 2020.

and posed severe challenges to biodiversity.

The third challenge is COVID-19.

This pandemic has drawn many countries' attention away from climate change. COP15 and COP26 have to be postponed.

The fourth challenge is the imbalance in response capacity.

Compared with developed countries, the impact of climate change on developing countries is more severe.

It remains a daunting task for the international community to redress the imbalance of development between the North and the South and to get everyone on board to tackle climate change.

The fifth challenge is the withdrawal from international treaties and organisations.

A certain country withdrew from the Paris Agreement. Such a unilateral and bullying move has led to severe setbacks in global cooperation and governance on climate change.

Last month, at a high-level UN meeting in commemoration of the 75th anniversary of the founding of the UN, President Xi Jinping announced that China will:

- scale up its nationally determined contributions,
- adopt even more forceful policies and measures,
- and strive to peak carbon dioxide emissions by 2030 and achieve carbon neutrality by 2060.

This is an attestation to the Chinese audacity to take up the responsibilities in line with the requirements of sustainable domestic development and the goal of building a community with a shared future for mankind. It is a display of the Chinese firm resolve to make an active response to climate change.

This announcement has been highly commended by the international community. In the words of Prime Minister Boris Johnson, this is "fantastic" and "a powerful signal to the world".

China and the UK are important partners in climate change response and environmental governance. There is enormous potential for closer cooperation between our two countries.

First, China and the UK can join hands and be the champions of global governance on climate change.

China has taken vigorous efforts to implement its National Climate Change Strategy and to fulfill its international obligations under the Paris Agreement.

- From 2005 to 2019, the Chinese carbon emissions per unit GDP dropped by 48.1%.
- The proportion of non-fossil fuel in total energy consumption increased to 15.3%.
- And China has more than half of the world's new energy vehicles.

The UK has set the target of net-zero emissions by 2050.

Hosting COP15 and COP26 respectively will enable China and the UK to play a leading role in promoting global governance on climate change.

President Xi Jinping and Prime Minister Boris Johnson have reached important political consensus on stepping up coordination and mutual support in hosting COP15 and COP26 respectively.

There have been close communications between Minister of Ecology and Environment of China Huang Runqiu and Secretary Alok Sharma.

I myself have stayed in touch with Secretary Sharma and Sir Laurie Bristow, the UK government's COP26 Regional Ambassador.

At the working level, a China-UK joint working group has been set up.

Going forward, our two sides should enhance communication and coordination, and fully engage the governments, legislatures, business community, media and academia, so as to make these two conferences successful.

Second, China and the UK can join hands and be the promoters of green development.

Against the ravaging epidemic, the Chinese government has taken a coordinated approach to economic and social development. We have lost no time in promoting green production and green way of life, and improving the system of climate finance and investment.

The UK has unique strength in clean energy and low-carbon technology.

It is important that China and the UK enhance cooperation in new energy and low-carbon cities. These will enable us to achieve win-win results in both ecological conservation and high-quality economic growth.

China has mature technology and rich experience in the operation and management of clean energy, such as nuclear energy. The Hinkley Point C nuclear power station is a flagship project of China-UK cooperation on clean energy. Upon completion, it will meet 7% of the UK's total demand for electricity and help reduce 9 million tons of CO_2 emissions every year. This project is completely in the common interests of both sides. We should work together to make it a success.

Our two countries should also encourage closer cooperation between our industries in renewable energy, green finance and green Belt and Road. This will help boost green recovery in both our two countries and the rest of the world.

Third, China and the UK can join hands and be the pioneers of green innovation.

Both China and the UK are pursuing innovative development in green technology, energy and financial services.

In clean energy, our two countries have signed the Clean Energy Partnership Work Plan for 2019—2020 to step up cooperation on the relevant technologies.

In green finance, China and the UK have signed up to the Green Investment Principles for the Belt and Road Development. There will be huge potential for cooperation in this aspect.

In green transport, Chinese companies Geely and BYD have actively invested in the UK, becoming shining examples of China-UK cooperation on green transport.

Fourth, China and the UK can join hands and be the defenders of multilateralism.

It is important that China and the UK stand up for multilateralism. Under the principles of common but differentiated responsibilities, equity and respective capabilities, China and the UK should make utmost efforts to:

- implement the nationally determined contributions,
- contribute to the comprehensive, balanced and effective implementation of the Paris Agreement,
- help developing countries scale up capacity building,
- deepen international cooperation,
- improve the governance system,
- and chart the course for global governance on climate change.

Ladies and Gentlemen,

Tackling climate change and protecting biodiversity are important areas of China-UK cooperation. They are also our mission as major global players.

As President Xi Jinping said at the UN high-level meeting,

"We need to take up our lofty responsibility for the entire human civilization, and we need to respect nature, follow its laws and protect it. We need to find a way for man and nature to live in harmony, balance and coordinate economic development and ecological protection, and work together to build a prosperous, clean and beautiful world."

The UK Parliament plays an important part in the UK's response to climate change. It is my sincere hope that you will continue playing a positive role and supporting green cooperation between our governments and businesses. I also look forward to your thoughts and ideas on hosting successful COP15 and COP26.

Let's work together to make greater contribution to building a community with a shared future for mankind and making our planet a better home for all!

Thank you!

应对气变挑战，促进能源转型 *

尊敬的穆尔主席，

尊敬的辛德勒总裁，

女士们、先生们：

很高兴出席此次国际能源信息论坛大会。在当前形势下，召开本届大会可谓恰逢其时。大会的主题是"能源大重启：新冠疫情、气候变化及后续"。围绕这一主题，我愿就全球气候变化与能源形势、中国引领全球气变治理和能源转型以及如何加强相关领域合作谈几点看法。

新冠疫情是百年来最严重的全球传染病大流行，给诸多行业带来巨大冲击。在疫情背景下，气候变化与能源转型发展面临什么样的形势？我认为，主要有三个动向。

一是气候变化与能源转型关系越来越密切。应对气候变化、推动能源转型发展，关乎人类赖以生存的地球家园，关乎人类的前途命运。极端天气频发、海平面上升、生态环境恶化、发展中国家应对能力不足、个别国家退出《巴黎协定》等气候变化挑战，都与能源行业息息相关。

二是疫情倒逼能源转型加快发展。疫情让世界经济和能源需求按下暂停键，促使各国深入思考能源转型方向和路径。加强全球抗疫合作、恢复经济社会秩序与活力是当务之急。实现疫后经济绿色复苏成为国际社会共识，未来能源行业结构将日趋多元化，能源转型发展将面临更大压力。

---

* 在国际能源信息论坛大会上的主旨演讲。2020 年 10 月 13 日，中国驻英国大使馆。

三是疫情启示我们要探索人与自然和谐共生之路。疫情告诉我们，人类不能再忽视大自然一次又一次的警告，不能只讲索取不讲投入，不能只讲发展不讲保护，不能只讲利用不讲修复。人与自然是命运共同体，人类要从保护自然中寻找发展机遇。只有顺应全球绿色低碳发展潮流，才能为能源行业重启注入动力。

在不久前举行的联合国成立75周年高级别活动上，习近平主席宣布，中国将提高国家自主贡献力度，采取更加有力的政策和措施，二氧化碳排放力争于2030年前达到峰值，努力争取2060年前实现碳中和。这是中国基于国内可持续发展内在要求和构建人类命运共同体的责任担当，是对自身气候环境政策做出的重大宣示，是向国际社会展示中国积极参与全球气变治理、引领全球绿色发展、推动全球能源转型的坚定决心。

第一，中国将继续为推进全球气变治理做出更大贡献。中国拥有14亿人口，是世界上最大的发展中国家，发展不平衡不充分问题仍很突出。但中国作为负责任大国，在应对气候变化上始终"言必信，行必果"。中国全面深入落实气候变化《巴黎协定》，在节能减排等领域成绩斐然。中国2018年单位GDP碳排放强度比2005年累计降低45.8%，相当于减少二氧化碳排放52.6亿吨。2019年中国单位GDP能耗较上年降低2.6%，较2012年累计降低25.6%。中国始终坚持多边主义，积极参与全球气变治理，实施"一带一路"应对气候变化南南合作计划，自2012年起每年气候南南合作资金支出达7200万美元；通过"一带一路"绿色发展国际联盟等平台，为应对气候变化国际合作汇聚更多力量。

第二，中国将继续为推动全球绿色发展做出更大贡献。中国积极倡导创新、协调、绿色、开放、共享的新发展理念，贯彻落实"绿水青山就是金山银山"重要理念，抓住新一轮科技革命和产业变革的历史性机遇，积极引领疫后世界经济"绿色复苏"。中国"十四五"规划将进一步指明绿色、循环、低碳经济的发展方向，中国统筹推进疫情防控与经济社会发展，探索以生态优先、绿色发展为导向的高质量发展之路，加速完善气候投融资体系，推广绿色生产方式和生活方式。在疫后经济恢复中，中国将培育壮大节能环保产业、清洁生产产业，促进产业和社会电气化、数字化与智能化，推动能源、交通、工业等多领域转型，继续引领全球经济走绿色和可持续发展之路。

第三，中国将继续为促进全球能源转型做出更大贡献。中国始终坚持提高能源供给质量和效率，加快能源技术创新，推进能源市场化改革。过去 10 年，中国是全球可再生能源领域的最大投资国。中国已建成全球最大清洁煤电体系，深水钻探、页岩气勘探开发等技术实现重大突破，核能、风能、太阳能等新能源应用蓬勃发展，"互联网+"智慧能源等一大批能源新模式加快培育。中国积极参与国际能源合作，持续深化能源领域对外开放，海外油气、核电合作不断拓展。中国正推动落实全球能源互联网，积极开展"一带一路"能源通道建设，参与全球能源技术合作，建立双边合作机制 58 项，参与多边合作机制 33 项，在全球能源转型发展与合作中发挥中国作用、贡献中国方案。

女士们、先生们，

人类社会发展史就是一部不断克服困难、战胜挑战的历史。展望未来，中国将继续应对气候变化，促进能源转型，这不仅将为全球可持续发展贡献力量，也将给包括英国在内的各国带来更多合作机遇。

一是共商全球气变和环境治理的机遇。2021 年是全球气变治理进程中的重要年份。不久前，习近平主席在联合国生物多样性峰会上发表讲话，指出在 2021 年于昆明举办的 COP15 大会上，中国将同各方共商全球生物多样性保护大计，共建万物和谐的美丽家园。2021 年英国将在格拉斯哥举办 COP26。各国能源界和产业界可以参与两个大会为契机，在清洁能源、绿色金融等领域加强交流对接，充分发挥互补优势，打造更多务实合作成果。

二是共享能源开放与合作的机遇。中国致力于建设开放型世界经济，正推动形成以国内大循环为主体、国内国际双循环相互促进的新发展格局，能源开放合作是其中的重要领域。中国仍是世界上最重要、最具活力的能源消费市场和进口市场，欢迎各国企业来华投资兴业。2020 年 11 月将举办第三届进口博览会，期待包括英国在内的各国能源企业踊跃参展。欣克利角 C 核电项目是中英合作的旗舰项目，建成后可满足英国 7% 的电力需求，每年可以减排900万吨二氧化碳。中英双方可以此为契机，不断深化民用核能等领域合作。

三是共促能源转型与创新的机遇。新一轮科技革命和产业革命方兴未艾，中国正积极推动绿色科技、能源、金融创新发展。中国以科技创新驱动能源事业高质量发展，以能源技术创新促进产业升级。智能电网、电动汽车、大规模储能、智慧用能等新技术新业态层出不穷，将给各国能源企业在华投资兴业带来广阔商机。

四是共建绿色"一带一路"的机遇。"一带一路"已成为规模最大的国际合作平台，绿色是"一带一路"建设的鲜明底色。中国和英国共同发布了《"一带一路"绿色投资原则》。能源企业可通过"一带一路"平台，在环保产业、节能减排、基础设施、绿色金融、金融科技等领域开拓双方、三方或多方合作的新模式，把能源转型发展更好地融入全球生态环境保护和可持续发展事业之中。

女士们、先生们，

西方有句谚语，"每朵乌云都镶着银边"。中国也有一句谚语，"风雨过后见彩虹"。当前人类正面对疫情蔓延的至暗时刻，但人类也展现出团结、勇气、决心、关爱的强大力量。中国愿与国际社会一道，坚定信心，共克时艰，共同应对气候变化挑战，共同促进能源转型发展，共同建设美好地球家园！

最后，预祝本届国际能源信息论坛大会圆满成功！

谢谢大家！

Address Climate Change and Promote Energy Transition[*]

Chairman Lara Sidawi Moore,

President Alex Schindelar,

Ladies and Gentlemen,

It is a real delight to join you at the Energy Intelligence Forum.

Themed on "The Big Energy Reset: COVID, Climate, Consequences," today's Forum could not be more timely. Let me take this opportunity to share with you my views on the theme of the forum. I will focus on three questions:

- How do we assess the current situation in energy and climate change?
- What will China do?
- How can we strengthen cooperation to address climate change and promote energy transition?

COVID-19 has been the most challenging pandemic in the past century. It has dealt a severe blow to many trades and industries. Against this backdrop, what is the situation like in climate change and energy transition? In my opinion, there are three major trends.

First, the connection between climate change and energy transition is increasingly close.

Addressing climate change and promoting energy transition matter a great deal to Planet Earth which mankind relies on for survival. In other words, how these issues are

---

[*] Keynote Speech at the Energy Intelligence Forum. Chinese Embassy, 13 October 2020.

addressed holds the key to the future of mankind.

Today, we are faced with many climate change challenges, from frequent extreme weather events to the rising sea level, from the deterioration of the eco-environment and the inadequate response from developing countries to the withdrawal of an individual country from the Paris Agreement. All these challenges can be traced back to the energy industry.

Second, COVID-19 is accelerating energy transition.

COVID-19 has pressed the "pause" button on world economy and energy demand, prompting countries of the world to reflect on the direction and routes of energy transition.

The most urgent task of the day is enhancing global cooperation on fighting COVID-19, restoring economic and social order and injecting fresh vitality. Pursuing green economic recovery has become the consensus of the international community in the post-pandemic world. The structure of the energy industry will become more diversified and this will put further pressure on energy companies to seek development through transition.

Third, COVID-19 highlights the need for harmonious coexistence of man and nature.

The pandemic sounded the alarm. Mankind must stop ignoring the repeated warnings from nature, stop taking without giving back, stop development at the expense of conservation, and stop utilization without rehabilitation.

Man and nature share a common future. We must explore opportunities for development in conservation. Only by following the trend of green and low-carbon development can we find the driving force to "restart" the energy industry.

Last month, at a high-level UN meeting in commemoration of the 75th anniversary of the founding of the UN, President Xi Jinping announced that China will:

- scale up its nationally determined contribution,
- adopt even more forceful policies and measures,
- and strive to peak carbon dioxide emissions before 2030 and achieve carbon neutrality before 2060.

This is an attestation of the Chinese audacity to take up the responsibilities in line with the requirements of sustainable domestic development and the goal of building a community with a shared future for mankind.

It is a major policy announcement on climate change.

It is also a display of the Chinese strong resolve to take an active part in global governance on climate change, to take the lead in global green development and to promote global energy transition.

First, China will make greater contribution to advancing global governance on climate change.

With a population of 1.4 billion, China is the world's largest developing country. It is faced with outstanding issues of imbalance and inadequacy in its development.

However, as a responsible global player, China always honors its promises on tackling climate change.

China has implemented the Paris Agreement and achieved remarkable outcomes in energy conservation and emissions reduction.

- From 2005 to 2018, China reduced carbon intensity by 45.8%, cutting CO_2 emissions by 5.26 billion tons.
- In 2019, the Chinese energy consumption per unit GDP was down by 2.6% from the level of the previous year and by 25.6% from the level of 2012.

Committed to multilateralism, China has been playing an active part in global governance on climate change.

- China has implemented South-South Cooperation Initiative on Climate Change under the framework of the Belt and Road. Starting from 2012, China spent 72 million US dollars on South-South cooperation on climate change every year.
- China has also worked on pooling international efforts for cooperation on climate change via platforms such as the BRI International Green Development Coalition.

Second, China will make greater contribution to promoting green development in the world.

China advocates a new development concept, namely innovative, coordinated, green, open and shared development. We are committed to the belief that "clear water and green mountains are mountains of gold and silver." We are seizing the historic opportunities of the new round of scientific and technological revolution and industrial transformation, and playing an active and leading role in the "green economic recovery" in the post-pandemic world.

The Chinese 14th Five-Year Plan will map out routes towards building a green, circular and low-carbon economy. This includes:

- A coordinated approach to epidemic response and economic and social development.
- A new path of high-quality development which gives priority to ecological conservation and is led by green technologies.
- An improved system of investment and financing for tackling climate change.
- And promotion of green production and green way of life.

In pursuing post-pandemic economic recovery, China will:

- foster and strengthen energy conservation, environmental protection and clean production industries,
- increase industrial and domestic use of electric, digital and smart technologies,
- promote transformation in multiple areas, such as energy and transportation,
- and continue to be a global leader in green and sustainable growth.

Third, China will make greater contribution to promoting global energy transition.

China has been committed to improving the quality and efficiency of energy supply, accelerating innovation in energy technology, and advancing market-based reform in the area of energy.

In the past decade, China has become the world's largest investor in renewable energy. We have:

- built the largest network of clean coal power generation,
- made important breakthroughs in deepwater drilling and shale gas exploration

and development,
- encouraged thriving application of new types of energy, including nuclear, wind and solar energy,
- and fostered "internet plus" and smart energy and other new business models in energy.

China has also taken an active part in international energy cooperation.

- China is opening its energy sector wider to the world and keeps expanding cooperation with other countries in oil, gas and nuclear energy.
- China is implementing the Global Energy Internet, taking an active part in the development of energy routes along the Belt and Road, and participating in global cooperation on energy technology.
- China has set up 58 bilateral mechanisms and taken part in 33 multilateral mechanisms for cooperation.

In a word, China has played its part and contributed its solution to global development and cooperation in energy transition.

Ladies and Gentlemen,

The history of mankind is a history of difficulties overcome and challenges tackled. Going forward, China will continue to address climate change and promote energy transition. This will not only contribute to sustainable growth in the world. It will also create more opportunities for cooperation with other countries, including the UK.

First, opportunities for global governance on climate change and environment.

The next year will be an important one for global governance on climate change.

In his speech at the UN Summit on Biodiversity last month, President Xi Jinping said that at COP15 to be held in Kunming next year, China and the other participating parties would discuss and draw up plans together for protecting global biodiversity, and turn Earth into a beautiful homeland for all creatures to live in harmony.

Next year the UK will host COP26 in Glasgow.

These two conferences will create opportunities for the energy and industrial communities of the world to enhance cooperation and foster greater synergy in areas such as clean energy and green finance. By matching their complementary strengths, the participating parties will be able to deliver concrete outcomes.

Second, opportunities of greater openness and cooperation in the energy sector.

China is committed to building an open world economy. Its current "dual circulation" model emphasizes domestic demand and encourages mutual complementarities between domestic and international demand. In this new development model, open cooperation in energy is an integral part.

China remains the world's most important and vigorous market for energy consumption and import. China will continue to open to investment from all over the world. In November, China will host the third International Import Expo, CIIE, where we hope to see energy businesses from all countries, including the UK.

The Hinkley Point C nuclear power station is a flagship project of China-UK cooperation. Upon completion, it will meet 7% of the UK's total demand for electricity and help reduce 9 million tons of CO_2 emission every year. It points to further opportunities for China and the UK to deepen cooperation in civil application of nuclear energy.

Third, opportunities in energy transition and innovation.

As the new round of scientific and technological revolution and industrial transformation unfolds, China is making vigorous efforts to promote innovation in green technology, energy and financial services.

Scientific innovation drives high-quality development of the energy industry, and new energy technologies will lead to the upgrading of the entire sector.

The development of new technologies and new business models in China, such as smart grid, electric vehicles, large-capacity power storage and smart energy, will create enormous opportunities for energy businesses from all countries.

Fourth, the opportunities of building a green Belt and Road.

Belt and Road Initiative, or BRI, has become the world's largest platform for international cooperation. Green is the salient background of the BRI development roadmap.

China and the UK have jointly issued the Green Investment Principles for the Belt and Road.

Via the BRI platform, energy companies could expand bi-party, tri-party and multi-party cooperation in the areas of environmental protection, energy conservation, emissions reduction, infrastructure development, green finance and FinTech.

Through such cooperation, energy transition will be better integrated into the global efforts of ecological conservation, environment protection and sustainable development.

Ladies and Gentlemen,

A Western saying goes, "Every cloud has a silver lining." A similar Chinese saying goes, "Rainbow appears after the storm."

In the "darkest hour" of the raging pandemic, mankind has displayed strength through solidarity, courage, determination and love.

China stands ready to work with the international community to shore up confidence and tide over the hard times. Together we can address climate change and advance energy transition to make our planet a better home for all.

In conclusion, I wish the Energy Intelligence Forum great success!

Thank you!

谱写生态文明新篇章，共建地球生命共同体 *

尊敬的英国议会跨党派国际环保小组主席加德纳，

尊敬的联合国《生物多样性公约》秘书处执行秘书穆雷玛，

尊敬的南非环境、森林及渔业部部长克里西，

尊敬的加蓬森林、海洋、环境和气候变化部部长怀特，

尊敬的英国外交发展国务大臣戈德史密斯，

尊敬的全球环境基金首席执行官罗德里格斯，

尊敬的各国议员，

女士们、先生们：

很高兴出席英国议会跨党派国际环保小组"保护自然：通向昆明之路"线上座谈会。2021年，中英两国将分别举办COP15和COP26。这既是中英两国的大事，也是全球环境治理的大事。因此，2021年可谓全球环境治理"大年"。

再过200天，COP15将在中国"春城"昆明召开。今天，我们在"云端"共聚一堂，为此次大会"预热"，具有重要意义。当前，新冠疫情仍在全球蔓延，给人类经济社会发展带来严重冲击。在此背景下，保护生物多样性更显突出、更加重要，主要体现在以下三方面。

一是保护生物多样性是人类社会当务之急。全球物种灭绝速度不断加

---

* 在英国议会跨党派国际环保小组"保护自然：通向昆明之路"线上座谈会上发表主旨演讲。2020年10月28日，中国驻英国大使馆。

快，生物多样性丧失和生态系统退化对人类生存和发展构成重大风险。

二是保护生物多样性是建设生态文明的内在要求。生态兴则文明兴。生物多样性是人与自然和谐共生的集中体现。加强保护生物多样性，有利于推动经济和生态协调发展，形成共建良好生态、共享美好生活的良性循环。

三是保护生物多样性要求践行多边主义。只有发扬多边主义精神，各尽所能，走合作共赢之路，才能加强生物多样性保护国际合作，促进可持续发展。

不久前，习近平主席在联合国生物多样性峰会上指出，"我们要站在对人类文明负责的高度，尊重自然、顺应自然、保护自然，探索人与自然和谐共生之路，促进经济发展与生态保护协调统一，共建繁荣、清洁、美丽的世界"。2021年COP15将以"生态文明：共建地球生命共同体"为主题，制定"2020年后全球生物多样性框架"，为扭转全球生物多样性丧失趋势迈出历史性一步，将在全球保护生物多样性进程中留下浓墨重彩的篇章。中国主办COP15充分体现了三个决心。

第一，推进生态文明建设的决心。中国积极做生态文明的倡导者和践行者，坚持绿水青山就是金山银山，坚持良好生态环境是最普惠的民生福祉，坚持共谋全球生态文明建设。中国将"生态文明"写入宪法，提出创新、协调、绿色、开放、共享的新发展理念，将生物多样性纳入经济社会发展和生态保护修复规划，努力建设人与自然和谐共生的现代化。这与《生物多样性公约》确定的保护生物多样性、持续利用其组成部分、公平合理分享由利用遗传资源而产生的惠益三大目标，以及人与自然和谐共生的2050年愿景高度契合。COP15是联合国首次以"生态文明"为主题召开的全球性会议，将发出共建地球生命共同体的强有力信号，进一步推动全球生态文明建设。

第二，保护生物多样性的决心。中国采取积极有力政策行动保护生物多样性，坚持山水林田湖草生命共同体，协同推进生物多样性治理。我们加快国家生物多样性保护立法步伐，划定生态保护红线，建立国家公园体系，实施生物多样性保护重大工程，提高社会参与和公众意识。过去10年，中国森林资源增长面积超过7000万公顷，居全球首位。中国长时间、大规模治理沙化、荒漠化，有效保护修复湿地，生物遗传资源收集保藏量位居世界前列。中国 90% 的陆地生态系统类型和 85% 的重点野生动物种群得到有效保护。COP15 将成为中国与各国分享生物多样性保护实践和经验的重要平台，进一步形成保护生物多样性的全球合力。

第三，参与和引领全球生物多样性治理的决心。中国是《生物多样性公约》的重要参与者和推动者，率先签署和批准该公约，严格履行该公约义务，积极促进与其他国际环境条约协同增效，已提前完成设立自然保护区等相关目标。中国与合作伙伴发起成立"一带一路"绿色发展国际联盟，积极加强生物多样性和生态系统保护。中国还在南南合作框架下积极帮助发展中国家提高环境管理能力。COP15 将制定"2020 年后全球生物多样性框架"，对未来十年乃至更长时间全球生物多样性治理做出规划。中国将在 COP15 大会上与各方共同努力，共同推进 2020 年后全球生物多样性治理进程。

女士们、先生们，

2021 年是全球生物多样性治理的关键节点，中英是全球环境治理的重要伙伴，在保护生物多样性和应对气候变化领域合作潜力巨大，应该相互支持、相互配合，共同确保 COP15 和 COP26 取得成功。

一是加强战略引领，全力做好 COP15 和 COP26 对接合作。习近平主席在联合国成立 75 周年高级别活动中宣布，中国将提高国家自主贡献力度，采取更加有力的政策和措施，二氧化碳排放力争于 2030 年前达到峰值，努力争取 2060 年前实现碳中和。习近平主席和约翰逊首相就两国加强 COP15 和 COP26 相互协调、相互支持达成重要共识。中国生态环境部部长黄润秋刚才在视频致辞中强调了中英加强两场大会合作的重要意义。下一步，我们将就两场大会加强政策和议题对接合作，包括积极推广"基于自然的解决方案"，将其作为应对气候变化和保护生物多样性的协同解决方案，促进两次大会相得益彰、协同增效。

二是深化绿色合作，引领全球可持续发展。中国制订并实施了《中国生物多样性保护战略与行动计划》（2011—2030 年），积极探索生物多样性保护与绿色发展，改善民生协同推进，倡导低碳、循环、可持续的生产生活方式。英国也发布了《未来25年环境保护计划》，倡导可持续发展，注重恢复陆地和海洋生物多样性。中英可加强对话交流，加强务实合作，挖掘绿色合作潜力，深化在应对气变、保护生物多样性、低碳经济、绿色金融、绿色科技、能源转型等领域的合作，在共建绿色"一带一路"方面加强三方合作，推动落实联合国2030年可持续发展目标，为全球可持续发展注入新动力。

三是坚持多边主义，凝聚全球生物多样性治理合力。中英应坚定维护多边主义，按照共同但有区别的责任原则，坚持公平公正惠益分享，照顾发展中国家资金、技术、能力建设方面关切，推动构建更加公平合理、各尽其责的多边环境治理体系。中方愿与包括英方在内的各方一道，遵循公开、透明、平衡、缔约方驱动等原则，推动COP15达成兼具雄心和务实平衡的"2020年后全球生物多样性框架"，为未来生物多样性保护绘制一幅宏伟且可实现的蓝图，为全球保护生物多样性开辟更广阔的前景。

女士们、先生们，

昆明是中国历史文化名城，四季如春，风景如画。习近平主席在联合国生物多样性峰会上发出邀请，欢迎大家2021年聚首美丽的春城昆明，共商全球生物多样性保护大计，共建万物和谐的美丽世界。作为COP15东道国和候任主席国，中方将全力做好COP15各项筹备工作，努力把COP15办成一届具有里程碑意义的全球环境治理盛会。我赞赏加德纳主席以及英国议会跨党派国际环保小组关心和支持中国举办COP15，也期望更多的英国议员以及支持环境事业的各国人士，共同为办好COP15和COP26两场大会、深化中英和全球环境治理合作建言献策。让我们携起手来，共同谱写生态文明新篇章，共同构建地球生命共同体！

谢谢！

Write a New Chapter of Ecological Conservation and Build a Shared Future for All Life on Earth *

Chairman Gardiner,

Secretary Elizabeth Maruma Mrema,

Minister Barbara Creecy,

Minister Lee White,

Lord Goldsmith,

Executive Secretary Carlos Manuel Roderiguez,

Parliamentarians from all countries,

Ladies and Gentlemen,

It is a real delight to join you at the "International Legislators' Summit—Protecting Nature: The Road to Kunming" hosted by the APPG on International Conservation.

In 2021, China and the UK will host COP15 and COP26 respectively. These are two big events not only for China and the UK but also for global governance on the environment. Therefore, 2021 can well be called "a big year" for global governance on the environment.

Exactly 200 days from now, COP15 will be held in Kunming, known in China as the "City of Eternal Spring." It is highly significant and meaningful that we gather online today to "warm up" for this conference.

---

* Keynote Speech at the "International Legislators' Summit—Protecting Nature: The Road to Kunming" Hosted by the APPG on International Conservation. Chinese Embassy, 28 October 2020.

As we speak, COVID-19 is still ravaging the world, dealing a severe blow to the economic growth and social progress of mankind. Against this backdrop, protecting biodiversity becomes an increasingly prominent and important task. This is reflected in the following three aspects.

First, protecting biodiversity is the top priority of mankind.

As mass extinction of wildlife accelerates, the loss of biodiversity and the degradation of the ecosystem are posing major risks to the survival and development of mankind.

Second, protecting biodiversity is the inherent requirement of ecological conservation.

A sound ecosystem is essential to the prosperity of civilization. Biodiversity reflects the harmonious coexistence of man and nature. Protecting biodiversity will help strike a balance between economic growth and ecological conservation. This will in turn form a virtuous cycle between conservation of nature and better life for man.

Third, protecting biodiversity requires countries of the world to uphold multilateralism.

Only in the spirit of multilateralism and only when every country does its best and works for mutual benefit can countries of the world enhance cooperation on biodiversity protection and promote sustainable development.

At the UN Summit on Biodiversity last month, President Xi Jinping said,

"We need to take up our lofty responsibility for the entire human civilization, and we need to respect Nature, follow its laws and protect it. We need to find a way for man and nature to live in harmony, balance and coordinate economic development and ecological protection, and work together to build a prosperous, clean and beautiful world."

At COP15, the parties will focus on the theme of "Ecological Civilization—Building a Shared Future for All Life on Earth" and strive to reach agreement on the Post-2020 Global Biodiversity Framework. This conference provides a platform for the parties to take a historic step towards reversing the loss of biodiversity and write a splendid chapter of joint global efforts to protect biodiversity.

By hosting COP15, China will display three determinations:

First, the determination to promote ecological conservation.

China has made vigorous efforts to advocate and practice the concept of ecological conservation. We believe that clear water and green mountains worth more than mountains of gold and silver, and a sound ecosystem is in the interests of everyone.

And we have championed international cooperation on ecological conservation in the world.

- China has written ecological conservation into its Constitution.
- It follows the concept of innovative, coordinated, green, open and shared development.
- It has made biodiversity protection part of its plans for economic and social development and ecological protection and rehabilitation.
- And it has worked vigorously to achieve modernization that ensures harmony between man and nature.

These efforts of China are in line with the three objectives of the Convention on Biological Diversity, namely:

- Conservation of biodiversity.
- Sustainable use of the components of biodiversity.
- And fair and equitable sharing of the benefits arising from the use of genetic resources.

They also match the vision for 2050, namely "Living in Harmony with Nature," which was outlined in the Strategic Plan for Biodiversity.

COP15 will be the first global conference of the United Nations that focuses on "ecological conservation". It will send a powerful message of building a shared future for all life on Earth and take global ecological conservation a step forward.

Second, the determination to protect biodiversity.

China has adopted vigorous and effective policies and measures in this aspect.

China is taking a holistic approach to conservation of mountains, rivers, forests, farmlands, lakes and grasslands and making coordinated efforts to advance biodiversity governance.

We have stepped up national legislation for preserving biodiversity, and we are drawing red lines for protecting the ecosystems. We have set up a national parks system, carried out major biodiversity conservation projects and increased public participation and awareness.

Over the past 10 years, China has increased forest coverage by more than 70 million hectares, which was more than anywhere else in the world.

We have also made long-term, large-scale efforts to combat sandification and desertification, and we have taken effective actions in wetland protection and restoration.

As a result of these efforts, China now has one of the world's largest banks of genetic resources reserve.

In China, 90% of terrestrial ecosystem types and 85% of key wild animal populations are under effective protection.

COP15 will serve as an important platform for China to share its practice and experience in biodiversity protection with the rest of the world and for the parties to pull together in biodiversity protection.

Third, the determination to take part and take the lead in global biodiversity governance.

China is an important contracting party to and defender of the Convention on Biological Diversity (CBD).

- It was one of the first to sign and ratify the CBD.
- It has fulfilled its obligations under the CBD and helped create synergy between the CBD and other international conventions on the environment.
- It has attained the goal of setting up nature reserves ahead of schedule.

Together with its partners, China has initiated the Belt and Road Initiative International Green Development Coalition to step up protection of biodiversity and the ecosystem.

Under the framework of South-South cooperation, China has also made vigorous efforts to help other developing countries build up their capacity in managing the environment.

At COP15, the Post-2020 Global Biodiversity Framework will be formulated, which will chart the course for global governance on biodiversity in the coming ten years and beyond.

China stands ready to work with all the parties at COP15 to promote the cause of post-2020 global governance on biodiversity.

Ladies and Gentlemen,

The year 2021 will be critical for global governance on biodiversity. China and the UK are important partners in global governance on environment. There is enormous potential for China and the UK to cooperate and take action on biodiversity protection and climate change. It is important that we support and coordinate with each other to make COP15 and COP26 great success.

First, China and the UK should follow the strategic guidance of our leaders and step up coordination and cooperation on hosting COP15 and COP26.

Last month, at a high-level UN meeting in commemoration of the 75th anniversary of the founding of the UN, President Xi Jinping announced that China will:

- Scale up its nationally determined contributions.
- Adopt even more forceful policies and measures.
- And strive to peak carbon dioxide emissions by 2030 and achieve carbon neutrality by 2060.

President Xi Jinping and Prime Minister Boris Johnson have reached important agreements on enhancing coordination and mutual support on COP15 and COP26.

In the video message just now, Chinese Minister of Ecology and Environment Huang Runqiu emphasized the importance of China-UK cooperation.

Going forward, China and the UK should step up coordination and cooperation with regard to the policies and agenda of the two conferences. We should promote Nature-Based Solutions and derive from them coordinated settlement for problems of climate change and biodiversity. And we should make the two conferences support each other and succeed together.

Second, China and the UK should deepen green cooperation and take the lead in global sustainable development.

China has issued and vigorously implemented its National Biodiversity Conservation Strategy and Action Plan (2011—2030). It has been exploring ways to coordinate biodiversity protection and green development with better life for the people. And it has been championing low-carbon, circular and sustainable way of life and production.

The UK has issued the 25-Year Environment Plan to advocate sustainable development and restore biodiversity on land and in the ocean.

China and the UK can enhance dialogue, exchanges and business cooperation. We can tap the potential for green cooperation in areas such as climate change, biodiversity protection, low-carbon economy, green finance, green technology and energy transition. We can also step up tri-party cooperation in building the green Belt and Road.

Together, we can advance the implementation of the UN 2030 Agenda for Sustainable Development and provide new impetus for global sustainable growth.

Third, China and the UK should uphold multilateralism and help build synergy among the parties for better governance on biodiversity.

Both China and the UK should uphold the principle of common but differentiated responsibilities, ensure fair and equitable sharing of benefits, and accommodate developing countries' concerns over funding, technology and capacity building. We need to build a fair and reasonable multilateral system of environmental governance where the parties shoulder their due responsibilities.

China stands ready to work with all the participating parties, including the UK, to conclude an ambitious and pragmatic Post-2020 Global Biodiversity Framework at COP15 through an open, transparent and parties-driven process. Together we can draw a blueprint that is both grand and feasible, and we can open up broader prospects for global biodiversity protection in the future.

Ladies and Gentlemen,

The city of Kunming is known for its long history, splendid culture, pleasant weather and beautiful landscape.

At the UN Summit on Biodiversity, President Xi Jinping said, "I want to welcome you to Kunming, the beautiful 'City of Eternal Spring,' next year, to discuss and draw up plans together for protecting global biodiversity and work in concert to build a beautiful world of harmony among all beings on the planet."

As the host and incoming president of COP15, China will exert every effort to get everything ready for the conference and make it a milestone in global governance on the environment.

I appreciate the enthusiasm and support of Chairman Gardiner and the APPG on International Conservation. I look forward to more ideas and suggestions from British parliamentarians and people of the world who support environmental actions on how to make COP15 and COP26 successful. I also want to listen to your thoughts on deepening China-UK cooperation on global governance on the environment.

Let's join hands to write a new chapter of ecological conservation and build a shared future for all life on Earth!

Thank you!

第七章 地方往来
PART VII Subnational Exchanges

国之交在于民相亲，民相亲在于心相通。中英关系的发展得益于良好的民意基础，受益于两国地方和民众的支持。使英 11 年，我见证了两国人民往来不断加强，地方合作不断深化。仅中国访英游客就从 2009 年的 19.2 万人次增至 2019 年的 101 万人次，增长 4 倍多。迄今，两国已缔结友城（省、郡、区）关系 67 对。中国在英国设有 3 个总领事馆（曼彻斯特、爱丁堡、贝尔法斯特），英国在华开设了 5 个总领事馆（香港、上海、广州、重庆、武汉）。2016 年，两国建立了地方领导人会议机制，进一步促进了双方地方交流与合作。每年都有数十个中国省市代表团赴英举办经贸、文化推介活动，英国也派代表团参加广交会、中国国际进口博览会、生态文明贵阳国际论坛、北京世界园艺博览会等活动。驻英国使馆践行外交为民的宗旨，积极为各省市开展对英交往与合作牵线搭桥。凡有省市推介活动，我都到场助阵。

本章从我近百篇关于中英地方往来的讲话中挑选了 16 篇，其中不少是推介中国中西部省市的，体现了向中西部倾斜，服务西部大开发战略。

The foundation of state-to-state relations lies in the friendship between the people, and the key to people-to-people friendship is mutual understanding. The development of China-UK relations benefits from the solid foundation of public opinion and the support from localities and the people of both countries. During my 11 years in the UK, I witnessed the continuous strengthening of people-to-people exchanges and deepening of subnational cooperation between the two countries. The number of Chinese tourists visiting the UK increased from 192,000 in 2009 to 1.01 million in 2019, more than fourfold. To date, the two countries have 67 pairs of sister cities (provinces, counties, districts). China has 3 consulates general in the UK (Manchester, Edinburgh, Belfast), and the UK has 5 consulates general in China (Hong Kong, Shanghai, Guangzhou, Chongqing, Wuhan). In 2016, the two countries established a mechanism of subnational leaders' meetings, further promoting subnational exchanges and cooperation. Every year, dozens of Chinese provincial and municipal delegations visit the UK to hold economic and cultural promotion activities, and the UK also sends delegations to participate in events such as the Canton Fair, China International Import Expo, Eco Forum Global Guiyang, and the Beijing International Horticultural Exhibition. The Chinese Embassy in the UK actively conducts diplomacy for the people, connecting Chinese provinces and cities with the UK for exchanges and cooperation. I attended all provincial and municipal promotion activities, providing support wherever needed.

This chapter includes 16 of my speeches on subnational exchanges, many of which focus on China's central and western provinces, tilting the scale in service of China's Western Development strategy.

"双龙共舞"与"双龙共赢"[*]

尊敬的罗－贝德勋爵，

尊敬的格拉摩根大学校长莫里斯勋爵，

尊敬的戴维斯主席，

尊敬的南威尔士大学校长莱顿女士，

各位企业家朋友，

女士们、先生们：

很高兴在大地回春、万物复苏的三月再次来到以田园风光著称的威尔士。英语谚语说："三月风、四月雨，带来五月的花。"我希望我此次访问威尔士也能带来一股"中国风"，并且使中国和威尔士的合作友谊之花芬芳盛开。

威尔士以龙为象征，中国更是龙的国度。说起中国的经济发展，有人形容是巨龙腾飞。的确，中国这个具有13亿人口的大国，30多年来创下了年均增长10%的"中国速度"；2010年超过日本成为世界第二大经济体。

中国经济发展有没有什么成功经验？我想，最关键是两条。一是政策上实行改革开放，解放了思想，解放了生产力，并从中国自己的国情出发，走适合自己发展的道路。二是人民辛勤劳动，奋发图强。2009年底，"中国工人"作为唯一群体入选美国《时代》周刊的年度人物。当时《时代》评价

---

[*] 在英国威尔士卡迪夫商业俱乐部午宴上的主旨演讲。2011年3月7日，卡迪夫希尔顿酒店。

说，中国经济带领世界走向经济复苏，这些功劳首先要归功于中国千千万万勤劳坚韧的普通工人。2010年，"中国工人"再次作为一个群体荣登美国知名财经杂志《财智》评选的2010年"全球最具影响力人物"排行榜，"中国工人"被该杂志评为世界经济中最强大的力量之一。

中国经济已经高速行进了30多年，是否会出现停顿呢？答案是否定的。中国正处于工业化、城镇化加速推进时期，现代化建设的进程不可逆转，而且中国人口多，市场广阔，回旋余地大，因此中国经济发展前景依然被看好。

就在这几天，中国全国人大正在审议决定未来五年发展的"十二五"规划，其核心是促进经济长期平稳较快发展和社会和谐稳定。我们将加快转变经济发展方式和调整经济结构，推动经济发展再上新台阶；我们将大力发展社会事业，保障和改善民生；我们将全面深化改革开放，不断加强政府自身改革建设。克服"成长中的烦恼"的最好方式，就是继续成长。

中国经济保持发展，给世界带来的是合作机遇。

第一，中国经济发展带动了世界经济增长。2009年金融危机时，中国经济对世界经济增长的贡献率达到了50%；2010年，各国不同程度地实现了经济复苏，中国对世界经济增长的贡献率仍然达到了20%。另有数据显示，中国经济每增长1个百分点，能拉动中等收入和低收入国家经济分别增长0.34和0.2个百分点。

第二，中国经济发展有利于国外企业扩大对华出口和投资。中国已经成为世界第二大进口国，2010年货物进口近1.4万亿美元，占世界贸易总量的10%。随着中国促进内需和扩大消费，中国有望成为世界最大的消费市场，进口必然还会增加。在过去十年里中国吸收了7000多亿美元的外资，各国企业在参与中国建设的同时，分享了中国市场成长的机会。今后，中国对外资的开放政策不会改变。当然，我们也不是来者不拒，我们将严格限制高污染、高能耗和资源型项目，鼓励外资投向符合发展潮流的高端制造业、高新技术产业、现代服务业、新能源和节能环保产业。

第三，中国经济发展带动了中国企业"走出去"，促进了所在国经济增长、就业和社会事业。2010年，中国对外直接投资接近600亿美元，在发展中国家中居第一位。2009年，中国企业的海外分支向所在国纳税总额达到109亿美元，雇用所在国员工43.8万人。中国企业在投资的同时也帮助所在国建设了大量基础设施，2000年以来中国企业在非洲建设了6万千米道路和7000万平方米房屋。《金融时报》的研究表明，过去两年，中国创纪录地向其他发展中国家至少发放了1100亿美元贷款，数额超过了世界银行。

总之，中国奉行互利共赢的开放战略，我们愿与各国共同发展，共享繁荣。

女士们、先生们，

经贸合作是中英关系的基础。近年来，中英经贸合作持续发展，不断深化。2010年，双边货物贸易额突破了500亿美元，两国领导人又确立了未来五年达到1000亿美元的目标。英国对华投资在欧盟内居于前列。中国银行保险、贸易运输、电信、传媒、旅游和汽车制造六大领域企业纷纷加大对英投资。以投资项目数量计，2010年中国升至英国的第六大外来投资国，中国在伦敦投资的企业数量已升居各国第二。今后，中英双方应充分实现优势互补，扩大企业强强联合，积极开展低碳、新能源、新材料、生物、信息技术等朝阳产业合作，努力寻找标志性大项目，促进两国中小企业技术、成本和效率的更好结合，并创造更加良好、便利的投资环境。

在中英合作良好的背景下，威尔士与中国开展合作的条件得天独厚。

第一，威尔士与中国交往较早，卡迪夫市在1983年3月即与厦门市结为友城，是中英两国间缔结的首对友城。近年来，威尔士又与重庆市交往密切，双方合作成果明显。

第二，威尔士具备欧洲一流的商业环境，既拥有许多先进、现代的科技成果，又具有优秀的研发人才和稳定的技术工人。

第三，威尔士是英国最安全、犯罪率最低的地区，是投资的理想之地。

第四，威尔士拥有自然美景，保持着原生态之美；威尔士又有"歌曲之乡"的美名，人文旅游资源丰富。

第五，威尔士的农产品具有美名，我来之前就听说这里的羊肉品质绝佳。

我衷心希望在座的各位企业家充分发挥优势，积极开拓中国市场，吸引中国投资，推动双方经贸等领域合作再上新台阶。

威尔士有句谚语，"辛勤播种，便会有加倍的收获"。我相信，只要我们珍视彼此的友谊，努力扩大交往与合作，我们就一定会有加倍的收获，中国和威尔士不仅能够"双龙共舞"，而且必将实现"双龙共赢"。

谢谢！

Two Dragons Will Not Only Dance Together but Prosper Together[*]

Lord Rowe-Beddoe,

Lord Morris,

Mr Gerald Davies,

Vice-Chancellor Julie Lydon,

Business leaders,

Ladies and Gentlemen,

It is a great pleasure for me to come back to Wales during March, a month of budding spring. As the saying goes, "March wind and April showers brings forth May flowers." I hope my visit will bring Wales a Chinese breeze that will bring forth the blossoming of China-Wales friendship and cooperation.

Just as here in Wales you have your red dragon, China is known as the country of the dragon. Our economic growth is sometimes described as the dragon roaring. Indeed, the last 3 decades have seen China roaring ahead with double digit growth. This resulted in China overtaking Japan as the world's second largest economy.

So, what has made the the Chinese success possible? There have been a number of contributing factors. First and foremost, our reform and opening-up have unleashed creative and productive forces that have steered the country onto a route of development which suits our national conditions, along with the hard work and ingenuity of the Chinese people. "The Chinese Worker" was named by *Time* magazine

---

[*] Keynote Speech at the Lunch Hosted by the Cardiff Business Club. Hilton Cardiff Hotel, 7 March 2011.

as "Person of the Year 2009", the only group of people to have shared the title. The magazine commented, "the tens of millions of workers ... are leading the world to economic recovery." The Chinese workers were also listed as one of the World's Most Influential Players in 2010 by the American *Smart Money* magazine, as they "make up one of the most potent forces in the world economy".

Some may be concerned that such fast rate of economic growth is unsustainable. However, their concern will be eased with a better understanding of the Chinese development. China is in the process of industrialisation and urbanisation. Its modernisation is irreversible. Given its large population and vast market, its economy promises huge potential and broad prospects for continued growth.

The Chinese National People's Congress is currently reviewing the 12th Five-Year Plan. This is the Chinese economic and social blueprint for the next 5 years. The plan will give priority to ensuring sustainable fast economic growth and social harmony. To this end, China will speed up the upgrading of its growth model and economic restructuring to raise the quality of development. China will also strengthen social programmes to improve people's living standards, expand reform and opening-up and improve governance. The best way to overcome "growing pains" is to keep growing.

The Chinese sustained economic growth will bring the world ever more opportunities for cooperation in a number of ways:

China serves as a driving force for global economic development. Its contribution to global growth was 50% in 2009 when the financial crisis was in full force. This figure was still as high as 20% when countries slowly emerged from the crisis in 2010. Statistics show that each percentage point of the Chinese growth drives growth in medium and low-income countries of 0.34 and 0.2 percentage points respectively.

The Chinese economic progress is an engine of growth for exports and investments by foreign businesses in China. With 1.4 trillion US dollars worth of goods imported in 2010, China is now the world's No. 2 importer. As China stimulates domestic demand and consumption, it is well on the way to becoming the largest consumer market in the world. China has attracted over 700 billion US dollars of foreign investment over the past decade. This has enabled foreign businesses to be very much part of the Chinese development and they have shared in the growing boom of the Chinese market. the Chinese opening-up policy will continue unchanged. However, the Chinese market is not free of competition. The fittest and the favourites are emerging industries such as high-end manufacturing, services, energy-efficient, environmental-friendly and high-tech sectors. Businesses which contribute to pollution and which are energy consuming will have no place.

The Chinese economic growth has invigorated Chinese businesses into "going-global." This has contributed to economic and social progress and job creation across the world. Last year, China invested almost 60 billion US dollars overseas, ranking first amongst developing countries. In 2009, overseas branches and subsidiaries of Chinese companies paid a total of 10.9 billion US dollars in local taxes and hired a local work force of 438 thousand people. Chinese businesses have also played an active part in the development of local infrastructure. Over the past decade, they have helped build 60 thousand kilometres of road and 70 million square metres of housing across Africa. Research by the *Financial Times* shows that in the past two years, China has given record loans of 110 billion US dollars to other developing countries, which is more than the World Bank.

In summary, China is following a win-win opening-up strategy and is committed to sharing development and prosperity with the rest of the world.

Ladies and Gentlemen,

Business cooperation is the bedrock of China-UK relations. We have seen ever deepening and expanding business cooperation between our two countries in recent years. Our trade in goods exceeded 50 billion US dollars last year, and an ambitious goal was set to double trade in the next 5 years. The UK is also one of the leading EU investor in China. Chinese businesses from banking, insurances, to telecommunications and the automobile companies have increased their presence in Britain. And this has resulted in China becoming the 6th largest investor in the UK in terms of number of projects and the No. 2 investor in London. China and the UK should draw upon their complementary strengths and encourage businesses to work together to explore cooperation in new industries such as low-carbon, bio-tech industries, new energy and material and information technology.

We need to identify flagship projects, foster synergy amongst SMEs between the advanced technologies and low cost, and ensure that we create a better investment climate for businesses of both countries. In the context of our booming China-UK cooperation, the cooperation between China and Wales enjoys a solid foundation. There is a long history of links between Wales and China, with Cardiff and Xiamen becoming the first British twinned cities in March 1983.

In recent years we have also witnessed close exchanges and productive cooperation between Wales and Chongqing. Wales is blessed with a first-class business climate in Europe, boasting scientific strength and a talent pool of R&D professionals and skilled workers. Wales has the lowest crime rate in the UK. It has stunning natural landscape and great cultural heritage. Not to mention its reputation of being the "Land of Song", and as I am sure we all know, the place to get delicious, mouth-watering lamb! I do hope all of you as business leaders play your role by exploring the Chinese market and attracting Chinese investment. We need your help to take our trade and investment cooperation to a new level.

A Welsh proverb tells us, "Scatter with one hand, gather with two." I am confident that as long as we deepen our friendship, work hard to strengthen our partnership, we will gather fruits of cooperation with two hands. And our two "dragons" will not only dance to the same tune but will prosper together.

Diolch yn fawr (Thank you)!

同舟共济，互利共赢 *

尊敬的保罗·卡拉汉主席，

女士们、先生们：

很高兴出席英格兰东北部经济论坛。这是我首次访问纽卡斯尔及英格兰东北部地区。

说起纽卡斯尔，对大多数中国人来说，早先想到的可能是足球，因为这里有英超老牌劲旅——纽卡斯尔联队。当然，英格兰东北部地区还有不少赫赫有名的球队，如桑德兰队和米德尔斯堡队，我知道在座的有不少是这三支球队的球迷。

除了足球，英格兰东北部地区无论是历史还是现在，都有很多值得骄傲的地方。这里曾经是英国著名的老工业基地，造船、采煤等重工业鼎盛一时。如今，这里聚集了英国一半的化工业，拥有英格兰最大的汽车制造商——尼桑公司，还有巴斯夫、亨斯迈等跨国巨头；这里正在涌现出一批充满活力的新兴产业，产业结构日益多元化；这里城市正在实现振兴，文化艺术和旅游更加繁荣。

来到英格兰东北部地区，我始终怀有一种特殊的感觉，觉得有许多共同语言。这可能是由于我本人出生于中国的东北地区，还在那里上学成长。更主要的是我发现中国东北三省和英格兰东北部地区情况非常相似，也是著名的老工业基地，而且近年来也在实行经济结构调整、资源枯竭城市转型和地

---

* 在英格兰东北部经济论坛上的主旨演讲。2012 年 3 月 1 日，纽卡斯尔市。

区发展振兴。

比如，大连已经从造船、机械制造、石化和炼油基地，发展为中国重要的 IT（信息技术）和软件中心，世界 500 强企业已有 89 家进驻大连。

阜新，这座昔日的"煤都"，已经从单纯依赖煤矿和电厂，发展到现在的依靠现代农业、煤化工和风电三大支柱产业，同时形成了液压装备、新型材料等六个产业集群，基本实现了城市经济的脱胎换骨。

两个东北地区情况很相似，那么中国和英国之间又怎样呢？答案是，既有相似，也有差异。中英目前面临着相同的世界经济不稳定环境，美国经济增长的前景和欧债危机的解决，这两个问题对中英来说都至关重要；中英也都在实行经济结构调整。但不同的是，中国作为一个发展中国家和新兴经济体，需要扩大国内消费，加快产业升级和加强科技创新；而英国作为一个发达国家，侧重点是重振制造业，发展创意产业和加大出口。

无论是中英经济发展的共同点还是不同点，实际上都为两国经贸合作提供了机遇。两国需要同舟共济，需要互利共赢。

令人高兴的是，中英经贸合作近年来取得快速发展。2011 年，两国货物贸易额达到创纪录的 587 亿美元，比 2010 年增长了 17%，其中英国对华出口增长了 28.8%。两国的共同目标是到 2015 年，双边贸易额达到 1000 亿美元。截至 2011 年底，中国在英国非金融类直接投资总额超过了 23 亿美元，仅 2011 年一年的新增投资就达到 11.3 亿美元，接近总量的 50%。可见，中国在英国投资步伐明显加快，双向投资格局正在形成。

英格兰东北部地区在中英经贸合作中发挥了重要作用。据统计，英格兰东北部地区对中国的出口从 2007 年的 1.9 亿英镑增加到 2011 年的近 4 亿英镑，整整翻了一番。中国目前已成为英格兰东北部地区十大出口市场之一。

当然，中国与英格兰东北部地区的经贸合作空间仍相当广阔，我们双方需要抓住机遇，挖掘潜力，提升层次，拓宽领域，推动合作多元化发展。为此，我认为双方要重点在以下几个方面采取行动。

第一，加大技术产品贸易。中国正在进行产业升级，需要大量进口高端设备和先进技术。英格兰东北部地区可发挥电动汽车、可再生能源、生物医药、纳米科技等产业优势，扩大对华高技术产品出口。

第二，开展联合研发合作。中国目前正加大科技创新，同时相对来说资金较为充裕，也愿与国外积极开展联合研发，共享合作成果。希望英格兰东北部的企业和大学利用自身研发优势，与中方共同设立研发中心或开展具体项目的研发合作。

第三，扩大双向投资。我们欢迎英格兰东北部地区的企业到中国投资现代服务业、绿色产业和高端制造业，并积极投资中国的西北部地区和东北老工业基地。同时，我们将继续鼓励中国企业到英格兰东北部地区投资兴业，当然，这需要你们向中国企业积极推荐合适项目，包括基础设施项目。

第四，促进中小企业合作。加强中小企业合作是中英两国经贸合作的一个重要方面。英格兰东北部地区不少中小企业技术独特，产品科技含量高，与中国企业和市场的互补性强。我们愿与英方共同为双方中小企业合作搭建平台，使双方经贸合作既有标志性大项目，又有"点点星光"。

第五，扩大人文领域交流。经贸合作的重要条件是双方人员之间的往来和交流。英格兰东北部地区可积极利用自身文化产业发达和大学质量一流的特色，积极开展与中方的教育和文化交流。同时，双方也应加强城市复兴和改造领域的相互学习和借鉴。

女士们、先生们，

昨天，我在前来英格兰东北部的路上，看到了英国最大的雕塑——"北方天使"。可能不同的人在不同的时候对它都会有不同的解读。看着天使张开的双臂，我在想，这或许预示着中国与英格兰东北地区的经贸合作即将展翅飞翔！

谢谢！

We Need a Win-Win Partnership*

Mr Paul Callaghan,

Ladies and Gentlemen,

It's a great delight to speak to the North East Economic Forum.

This is my first trip to Newcastle and the North East. But my knowledge of this city began much earlier. Like many Chinese, the first thing that comes to my mind about the city is Newcastle United of the Premier League.

Of course, there are other famous teams here in the North East, such as Sunderland and Middlesbrough. I'm sure in the audience there are many supporters and fans of these three teams.

In addition to football, the North East has won a global reputation in many other fields:

- Here is Britain's historic industrial heartland. Ship-building, coal mining and other heavy industries have thrived here for many centuries.
- Today, the North East makes up half of Britain's chemical industries. It's also a magnet for many multinationals to base operations here. These include BASF, Huntsman and the largest automaker in England, Nissan.
- This is a region where a wave of new industrialization is going full swing. New sectors are booming and are further diversifying the regional industrial structure.
- Equally encouraging is the renewal of cities and towns across the region. This

---

* Speech at the North East Economic Forum Annual Conference 2012. Newcastle, 1 March 2012.

has given rise to a dynamic arts and cultural scene and rising tourism.

For me, this visit to the North East is a special experience. I feel strong connections to this part of England. This may be because I am from the North East too!

I was born and educated in the Chinese Northeastern region. My home region shares a lot in common with the North East of England.

The Chinese Northeastern region is also going through economic restructuring. It is moving away from resource-intensive heavy industries. It is seeking sustainable growth and an economic future supported by new industries.

Dalian, where I went to university, offers a snapshot of what's going on in the Chinese North East.

This is a city known for shipbuilding, machinery, petrochemical and oil refining. But now, Dalian has established itself as the Chinese key IT and software centre. 89 of the global top 500 companies set up operations there.

The city of Fuxin is another example of how restructuring can utterly transform a regional economy.

Like Newcastle, Fuxin was the "coal capital" in China. The economic pillars were coalmines and power plants. But over the past decade, it has built up a more diverse economy. This has been driven by modern agriculture, the coal chemical industry and wind power. A range of new industries, including hydraulic equipment and new materials, are gaining strength.

These parallels between the Chinese Northeast and North East England are most striking. So what other comparisons can we draw about the economies of our two countries?

This is a much more complex question. I will give an answer in two parts.

First, China and Britain are major economies in a globalised world. As such both countries have to deal with the turmoil and risks in the world economy. This means we have to factor in America's weak economic outlook and the evolving debt crisis in Europe.

Clearly these factors means the stakes are high for both China and Britain.

Turning to the second part of the answer.

Both China and the UK are pushing through ambitious structural reforms. Yet at the same time, the nature and priorities of our approaches are different.

China is a developing country and emerging economy. We need to boost consumption. We have to move up the industry value chain. And we must build stronger technology innovation capacities.

Britain, by contrast, is a developed country. It is determined to revive its manufacturing strength. You are committed to developing creative industries. And overall you aim to increase exports to the rest of the world.

What deserves very close attention is what lies behind these differences:

- The reality is that our countries have needs and abilities that can be matched.
- There are real opportunities for China and Britain to build closer commercial ties.
- There is huge potential for mutual benefit.

The continuing financial crisis means we are in tough times.

In these conditions what we need is a win-win partnership. That is the way to emerge from the crisis stronger and more prosperous.

We are headed in the right direction with Sino-UK economic partnership.

Let me give you some of the indicators:

- In 2011, the two-way trade in goods reached a new high of 58.7 billion US dollars. That is up by 17% over the previous year.
- At the same time British exports to China grew by 28.8%.
- It is a shared objective of our two sides for bilateral trade to reach 100 billion US dollars by 2015.

Our business ties are developing outside of trade:

- By the end of last year, the Chinese direct investment in Britain had topped 2.3 billion US dollars.
- Almost half of this investment, 1.13 billion US dollars, was made in last year alone.
- The faster flow of Chinese capital means more balanced two-way investment is

emerging between our two countries.

The North East is clearly an important player in Britain's economic ties with China. Your exports to China are growing rapidly:

- Exports have more than doubled from 190 million pounds in 2007 to nearly 400 million pounds last year.
- China today is a top 10 export market of the North East.

Going forward, China and the North East have immense potential to strengthen our commercial ties.

What's pressing now is for both of us to seize opportunities. We must unleash our potential and lift our cooperation to a new level. And our cooperation must be extended to wider spheres.

For this to happen, I believe we need to take actions in the following five areas.

First, boost high-tech trade.

China has growing demand for advanced equipment and technologies to support our ongoing industrial upgrading.

The North East can leverage its competitive edge in electric cars, renewable energy, biomedicine and nanotechnology to increase exports to China.

Second, build a research and development partnership.

During the past 30 years of growth China has accrued high levels of capital. This has come from our manufacturing strengths producing the designs from other nations. Now China is determined to create its own designs. This means we are better positioned to develop a win-win partnership on research and development.

We would be happy to encourage joint R&D centres or research programs between companies and universities in the North East and Chinese partners.

Third, expand two-way investment.

We welcome companies in the North East to invest in China. There are opportunities in the advanced services sector, green industries, high-end manufacturing, and in our Northwestern and Northeastern regions.

At the same time, we will continue to encourage Chinese businesses to develop cooperation with the North East. This goal will be better served if more promising projects, including infrastructure projects, can be presented to Chinese investors.

Fourth, promote SME cooperation.

Research has shown the vital contribution of SME's to the growth of economies. This applies in both China and the UK. Stronger SME cooperation is a major component of our overall economic partnership. The SMEs in the North East can offer unique expertise and technologies to the Chinese partners and market.

China is committed to create platforms for our SMEs to harness the cooperation potential. We welcome and support projects of all sizes, not only the landmark projects, but also smaller ones.

Fifth, widen people-to-people exchanges.

Thriving business cooperation must be supported by closer people-to-people contacts.

With unique cultural industries and high-quality universities, the North East is well-positioned to build vigorous educational and cultural ties with China. Then there is urban renewal and regeneration. This is another area we can learn and benefit from each other's experience.

Ladies and Gentlemen,

On my arrival in the North East yesterday I was much impressed by Britain's largest sculpture, the Angel of the North.

The meaning of this sculpture could be understood in different ways.

The Angel of the North has spread its wings.

Surely this is a sign that the Chinese economic cooperation with the North East is now ready to take off.

Thank you!

天府之国，魅力无限 *

各位来宾，

女士们、先生们：

我谨代表中国驻英国大使馆对"2014伦敦成都周"的举办表示热烈祝贺。

成都位于中国西南地区，历史悠久，素有"天府之国"之美誉。自然环境与人文环境的长期协调发展，使成都成为一座既富有历史文化气息又充满生机活力的魅力之都。

魅力之一：成都有优美的自然景观，堪称"田园之城"。

成都拥有得天独厚的自然环境，孕育了丰富多彩的自然旅游资源。那里有许多国家级风景名胜区、自然保护区、森林公园和地质公园，一派田园风光，令人向往。

魅力之二：成都有丰厚的人文底蕴，堪称"文化之城"。

成都有两千多年的历史，是中国首批历史文化名城之一，也是中国国际非物质文化遗产节永久举办地。成都民风古朴，民俗遗存丰富，其精湛的传统工艺蜚声海外，银、漆、绣、竹、锦等工艺品堪称一绝，美食、茶艺、变脸、皮影艺术以及大熊猫成为这座城市永久的名片。

魅力之三：成都经济发展迅猛，堪称"财富之城"。

以成都为中心的中国西南市场备受国内外关注，目前已有超过半数的世界500强企业落户成都。2013年成都GDP总量已接近1万亿元，并首次举

---

* 在"2014伦敦成都周"开幕式上的致辞。2014年5月20日，伦敦肯辛顿宫花园。

办了《财富》全球论坛和世界华商大会等国际盛会。这说明成都已经登上世界舞台，正向国际化大都市的方向迈进。

近年来，成都与英国的交往日益密切。2010年，成都市与谢菲尔德市建立了友好城市关系。"2013欢乐春节"活动期间，成都艺术团在英国多地的巡演活动以及"成都伦敦文化艺术展"都给英国民众留下了深刻印象。2013年，成都实施了72小时过境免签政策，英航首开成都—伦敦航线，而且本月从每周3班增加至每周5班，这些举措为促进成都与英国的进一步交流打开了方便之门。尤其值得一提的是，2013年底，我有幸陪同卡梅伦首相访问了成都，此行不仅加强了英国与成都的联系与交流，而且使"成都火锅"扬名英伦，"首相套餐"备受追捧。

成都的魅力不胜枚举，"2014伦敦成都周"给英国民众提供了一个难得的体验机会。当然，我们更希望越来越多的英国民众亲身去成都感受这个城市的无限魅力。

最后，预祝"2014伦敦成都周"取得圆满成功！祝成都与英国在各领域的交流与合作不断取得丰硕成果！

谢谢！

Enchanting Land of Plenty*

Distinguished Guests,

Ladies and Gentlemen,

Greetings to you all on behalf of the Chinese Embassy in London!

I send my very warmest congratulations to the Chengdu 72 Hours Experience!

Chengdu, a city in southwestern China, is rich in history.

It has long had a reputation of being the "Land of Plenty". This is a city of harmony between nature and culture. It is a city of great attractions and can boast about a unique blend of traditions and dynamism.

The charm of Chengdu lies in its natural splendor.

The city has been richly endowed by nature. This means Chengdu offers a wealth of tourist destinations. These include national rated scenic areas, natural features, with many forest and geological parks. The splendor never fails to win over the hearts and minds of any visitor.

Chengdu also excels in its cultural riches.

With a history spanning over 2,000 years, Chengdu is among the Chinese earliest "famous historic and cultural cities". As a result Chengdu is the permanent seat of the "China International Festival of Intangible Cultural Heritage". Through this you will find that Chengdu is a city rich in traditions, cultural heritage and world-renowned handicrafts.

For example, Chengdu is famous for its silverware, lacquerware, embroidery,

---

* Speech at the Opening Reception of "Chengdu 72 Hours Experience 2014". Kensington Gardens, 20 May 2014.

bamboo and brocade crafts. In turn Chengdu offers its signature local cuisine, tea ceremonies, Sichuan opera, shadow puppet play and, last but not least, the giant pandas.

Alongside these cultural attractions Chengdu has evolved as a key business centre.

Chengdu is located right at the heart of the much desired market in the Chinese Southwest. It has attracted over half of the *Fortune* 500 companies. Business is prospering with its GDP in 2013 closing in on 1 trillion RMB. In turn, this success attracted major events. Examples are the first *Fortune* Global Forum and the World Chinese Entrepreneurs Convention. Chengdu has now won a place on the world stage and so is making steady progress towards becoming an international metropolis.

Recent years have seen Chengdu's engagements with the UK on the rise. Chengdu and Sheffield forged the bond of twin cities in 2010. During the Chinese New Year in 2013 an ensemble from Chengdu toured many cities in the UK. The Chengdu Art Exhibition also left a deep impression on people here in London.

Also in 2013, Chengdu implemented a 72-hour visa free transit policy. At the same time British Airways opened direct flights between Chengdu and London. This has just been upgraded from 3 flights a week to 5. These shared developments have enabled further engagements between Chengdu and the UK.

It is particularly worth mentioning that late last year, I had the honour of accompanying Prime Minister Cameron to visit Chengdu. The visit very much strengthened Britain's contacts and exchanges with Chengdu. But the visit was also a great boost for raising the fame of Chengdu "hotpot" in the UK.The Prime Minister's "hotpot" meal has since become a most sought-after set menu.

For myself, the charm of Chengdu can go on and on. But Chengdu 72 provides a valuable opportunity for British people to experience what the city offers. Of course, we look forward to more and more British people visiting Chengdu. That is the best way to learn about the many charms of Chengdu.

Finally, I wish Chengdu 72 a great success! May the exchanges and cooperation in many fields between Chengdu and the UK yield very fruitful outcomes.

Thank you!

不求大而全，但做小且精 *

尊敬的巴亚什议长，

尊敬的麦柯尔总督，

尊敬的戈斯特首席部长，

女士们、先生们：

很高兴在美丽的泽西岛和各位相聚。我谨代表我的夫人和同事，对各位的盛情款待和周到安排表示衷心感谢。

在泽西岛、根西岛、马恩岛三大英国皇家属地中，泽西岛是我访问的最后一站。虽然是最后一站，但也是最重要的一站。对于此行，我已期待许久。过去一天多，我领略了泽西美丽的海岛风光，感受了泽西人悠闲富足的生活。我与巴亚什议长、麦柯尔总督、戈斯特首席部长和泽西岛主要部门负责人的会谈会见，与企业家的座谈以及对本地学校和乳业公司的走访更是充满惊喜、富有成果，这些使我对此访的圆满成功充满信心。此次来泽西，我给自己确定了"三大任务"。

一是增进了解，深化友谊。在三个皇家属地中，泽西岛是对华交往最密切、与中国驻英国大使馆走动最频繁的，仅我本人就四次在使馆会见过泽西岛客人，其中三次是和戈斯特首席部长见面。两千多年前成书的中国古代经典《礼记》中说，"来而不往非礼也"。我们这次到泽西来，就是要回访老朋友，同时结识更多新朋友。我们希望通过此访，进一步增进对泽西岛的了

---

* 在英国泽西岛巴亚什议长欢迎晚宴上的讲话。2014 年 8 月 12 日，英国泽西岛议会大厦。

解，为双方日后更加广泛深入的交往夯实基础。

二是推动务实合作更上层楼。在双方共同努力下，中国与泽西岛务实合作进展顺利。中国银监会、证监会先后与泽西岛金融管理委员会签署了监管合作备忘录，中国国家税务总局还与泽西岛政府签署了税收情报交换协定。据我了解，泽西岛在中国企业界也已享有相当好的口碑，在伦敦上市的中国企业有1/3选择在此注册。下一步，双方应在现有基础上加强金融服务和乳业两大主要领域合作，这也是我此访的重点。戈斯特首席部长2014年访华时，提出在旅游业、电子商务、基础设施等领域加强合作的设想。这次随我来访的还有一些中国企业家，他们将以实际行动回应泽西岛方面与华合作的积极性。

三是开拓人文交流新领域。泽西岛地处英法之间，丰富的历史遗产和地缘优势滋养了独具特色的人文景观。我来此地虽然时间很短，但已领略了其中的精彩，也更加坚信，泽西岛在吸引中国游客特别是加强双方青年往来方面大有潜力可挖。

各位朋友，

中国有句俗话，"一方水土养一方人"，意思是一个地方的自然条件和物产对当地的人文风俗具有重要影响。泽西岛虽然面积不大，但地灵物美，本地孕育的泽西牛、泽西皇家土豆誉满全球，其共同特点是体形并不出众，但特色鲜明、品质优良。我曾收到你们从泽西岛邮寄来的皇家土豆，但尚未收到过泽西牛，可能是体积太大不易邮寄。我想，不求大而全，但做小且精，或许正是泽西成功的秘诀和中国与泽西交流与合作的发展方向。

最后，让我们共同举杯，

祝愿泽西岛和泽西人民繁荣安康，

祝中国与泽西岛互利合作不断发展，

祝在座的各位朋友万事如意！

谢谢！

Focus on Quality Instead of Size[*]

Deputy Bailiff William Bailhache,
Lieutenant Governor John McColl,
Chief Minister Ian Gorst,
Ladies and Gentlemen,

It is a real pleasure for me to visit the beautiful Jersey Island and join you in this magnificent building this evening. On behalf of my wife and my colleagues, I want to thank you for your very warm welcome and gracious hospitality.

Previously I have been to the Isle of Man and Guernsey Island. Jersey is the last stop of my visit to the three major Crown Dependencies. Last but not least, this is in fact a long-awaited trip for me.

In the past two days, I have much admired the natural beauty of Jersey. I also visited Hautlieu School and the Jersey Dairy Headquarters. This has given me a taste of the abundance in all aspects of life in Jersey from industry to leisure.

More importantly, I had productive talks with Deputy Bailiff Bailhache, Chief Minister Gorst, Lieutenant Governor McColl and other leading officials of Jersey. Overall this programme has been both substantial and stimulating, which gives me every confidence in the success of my visit.

I have come to Jersey with three goals.

First, increase mutual understanding and deepen friendship. Among all Crown Dependencies, Jersey has closest ties with China and most frequent contacts with the

---

[*] Speech at the Welcoming Dinner in Jersey Island. States Building, Jersey Island, 12 August 2014.

Chinese Embassy in London. During my time in London as Ambassador I have met Jersey guests four times in the Embassy. The leading guest on three of such occasions was Chief Minister Gorst.

The Chinese classic *Book of Rites* written more than two millennia ago says:

"It is impolite no to reciprocate."

So, here I am!

I am here to meet with people I can describe as good old friends.

But just as important, I want to make new friends here. I also hope this visit to Jersey will help build deeper understanding on both sides and lay a solid foundation for our broader exchanges in the future.

Second, heighten our practical cooperation.

With efforts from both sides, China-Jersey cooperation has made smooth progress. Both China Banking Regulatory Commission and China Securities Regulatory Commission have concluded MOUs with the Jersey Financial Services Commission regarding regulatory cooperation. The China State Taxation Administration has also signed agreement with Jersey Government on information sharing. As far as I know, Jersey Island is now well known to the Chinese business community. A telling example is one third of Chinese companies listed in London are registered here. But we can do much more.

Going forward, we should strengthen cooperation in the financial and dairy sectors. This is one of the priorities of my visit.

Moreover, when Chief Minister Gorst visited China earlier this year, he made proposals on boosting our cooperation in tourism, e-commerce and infrastructure. Echoing the immense enthusiasm, I have brought with me some Chinese entrepreneurs. They will work with their Jersey counterparts to translate the proposals into real actions.

My third goal is to expand people-to-people and cultural exchanges. Situated between France and England, Jersey is steeped in history. Though my stay is brief, I have been fascinated by the richness of your culture. I am convinced that Jersey has enormous potential to be tapped in attracting Chinese tourists and strengthening our youth exchanges.

Dear Friends,

As an old Chinese saying goes, "Man is a product of his environment." This applies not only to man, but virtually everything. Though small in area, Jersey has its own specialties unique to this island, specialties that you can certainly take pride in. The Jersey cow and Jersey Royal potatoes are highly prized throughout the world. One thing in common is, like the Jersey Island, they both have small size but high quality.

I once received potatoes you sent from Jersey, but never cows. Perhaps, after all a cow is too big to be sent by post. Anyhow I believe focus on quality instead of size is the knack of Jersey's success. It should also be the focus of China-Jersey exchanges and cooperation.

In conclusion, I wish to propose a toast:

To the prosperity of Jersey and the wellbeing of its people!

To the continuous progress of the mutually beneficial cooperation between China and Jersey!

And to the health of all friends present!

Cheers!

走在中英关系前列的江苏 *

尊敬的江苏省省长李学勇先生，
尊敬的英中贸协主席沙逊勋爵，
女士们、先生们：

很高兴出席"走进江苏"人文经贸交流活动开幕式。我谨代表中国驻英国大使馆表示热烈的祝贺！

江苏是历史悠久、人文荟萃的文化强省，也是中国率先发展的经济和科技强省。近年来，江苏与英国友好交往日益密切，各领域合作不断加强，双方关系"越走越近"，亮点不断，精彩纷呈。特别是在以下三个方面，江苏走在了中英关系的前列。

一是经贸关系走在前列。2013年，江苏与英国贸易额达93亿美元，在中英贸易中占比超过10%。英国企业纷纷到江苏投资兴业，总投资约占英国对华投资的20%。与此同时，江苏投资者也在大举进军英伦。

二是科技合作走在前列。在中英科技合作不断深化的大背景下，江苏与英国在国际技术转移交流、政府间项目合作、共建国际合作载体等方面开展了富有成效的合作。就在今天上午，在李学勇省长的见证下，中英双方刚刚签署了科技创新合作备忘录，创立了产业研发合作新机制。

三是人文交流走在前列。早在1992年，英国埃塞克斯郡就与江苏结好，

---

* 在"走进江苏"人文经贸交流活动开幕式上的致辞。2014年10月9日，威斯敏斯特中央大厅。

目前双方超过 100 所中小学建立了校际交流关系。江苏与英国的高校也建立了强强合作。伦敦与南京还先后举办了 2012 年奥运会和 2014 年青奥会。奥运拉近了两座城市之间的距离，也架起了两国人民之间的桥梁。

我高兴地看到，李学勇省长此次访英紧密围绕经贸、科技和人文这三大主题，此次访问必将进一步推动江苏与英国在经贸、科技和人文三大领域的交流与合作。在当前中英关系驶入全面发展的快车道，进入"共同增长、包容发展"新时期的背景下，此次访问和"走进江苏"人文经贸交流活动也将为中英关系全面深入发展增光添彩。

最后，我预祝"走进江苏"人文经贸交流活动取得圆满成功！

祝江苏与英国合作不断向更宽领域、更高水平迈进，不断取得新的更大成果！

谢谢！

Jiangsu, a Leader in China-UK Relations *

Governor Li Xueyong,

Lord Sasoon,

Ladies and Gentlemen,

It is a real pleasure for me to attend the opening ceremony of Jiangsu Comes to You 2014 and Yangzhou Day. On behalf of the Chinese Embassy in the UK I would like to extend warm congratulations.

Among all Chinese provinces, Jiangsu is known for its long history and rich culture. It also excels in economy and high technology. Recent years have seen closer exchanges and cooperation between Jiangsu and Britain in a wide range of areas. Relations between Jiangsu and Britain have created a catalogue of highlights. In particular, Jiangsu leads China-Britain relations in the following three areas.

First, business and trade. In 2013 trade between Jiangsu and Britain reached 9.3 billion US dollars, accounting for over 10% of total China-Britain trade. British businesses have shown a strong interest in investing in Jiangsu. As a result, 20% of total British investments in China found their home in Jiangsu. Likewise, Jiangsu's investments are also making headway in Britain.

Second, science and technology. As China-UK science and technology cooperation deepens, Jiangsu and Britain have carried out effective cooperation in international technology transfer, inter-governmental projects and building joint labs. This morning, Governor Li Xueyong has just witnessed the signing of the MOU on scientific

---

* Speech at the Opening Ceremony of "Jiangsu Comes to You". Central Hall Westminster, 9 October 2014.

innovation between Jiangsu and Britain. This set up a new mechanism for collaboration in industrial R&D.

Third, people-to-people and cultural exchanges. Back in 1992 Essex and Jiangsu became sister county and province. Now more than 100 middle and primary schools from both sides have established links. Collaboration between institutions of higher education of Jiangsu and Britain has enabled them to combine strengths. Moreover, London and Nanjing, provincial capital of Jiangsu respectively hosted 2012 Olympic Games and 2014 Youth Olympic Games. Olympics have brought the cities and their peoples closer.

I am glad to learn that trade, science, technology and culture are high on Governor Li's agenda during his visit. I am sure his visit will further promote exchanges and cooperation between Jiangsu and Britain in the three areas.

At present, China-UK relations are on a fast track. We are working together to build a partnership of common growth and inclusive development. Against this background, I have no doubt that Governor Li's visit and Jiangsu Comes to You 2014 will further boost the growth of overall China-UK relationship.

In conclusion, I wish Jiangsu Comes to You 2014 a great success.

I also hope cooperation between Jiangsu and Britain will be more productive and more fruitful!

Thank you!

拉起风箱，打出真铁 *

尊敬的王毅外长，

尊敬的英国女王代表奥鲍耶先生，

尊敬的北爱尔兰副首席部长麦金尼斯先生，

尊敬的北爱尔兰首席部长代表福斯特部长，

尊敬的王淑英总领事，

尊敬的各位市长、各位部长，

各位来宾，

各位侨胞，

女士们、先生们：

今天，我们在这里热烈庆祝中国驻贝尔法斯特总领馆的开馆。我愿感谢王毅外长远道而来，亲自为总领馆揭牌。我还愿感谢麦金尼斯副首席部长、福斯特部长和各位市长以及北爱尔兰（以下简称北爱）各界人士与我们共同见证这一具有历史意义的时刻。

中国驻贝尔法斯特总领馆的建立，不仅标志着中国驻英外交机构大家庭中增添新的一员，使中国驻英使团达到一个大使馆和三个总领馆，而且标志着中国与北爱的关系翻开新一页、进入新阶段，标志着中英两国的合作更加全方位、全地域。

---

* 在中国驻贝尔法斯特总领馆开馆仪式上的讲话。2015年6月8日，北爱尔兰贝尔法斯特希尔顿酒店。

北爱是中英合作的重要区域。近年来，北爱与中国各地在经贸、文化、教育、科技等领域的交流合作日益深化。中国在北爱开设总领馆，既满足双方扩大合作的实际需要，又表明中方对合作前景抱有高度期待，同时也反映出中方对北爱的和平与稳定抱有充足信心。

北爱也是中国在英华人华侨的重要居住地。侨胞们，你们在这里辛勤工作，努力奋斗；你们既深入融合当地社会，又努力弘扬中国文化；你们关心祖国发展，支持家乡建设。总领馆的建立，将为你们提供更加畅通的渠道、更加便捷的服务。希望你们一如既往地支持祖国的建设，一如既往地支持中国与北爱友好合作关系的发展，一如既往地为北爱的经济社会发展贡献力量。

我也愿借此机会感谢北爱政府和各界人士为中国驻贝尔法斯特总领馆的开馆所提供的多方帮助，希望你们继续关心总领馆，支持总领馆。

我相信，总领馆在王淑英总领事的率领下，将全力以赴，尽职尽责，为促进中国与北爱全方位交往，深化双方务实合作，做出积极贡献。

女士们、先生们，

北爱著名诗人谢默斯·希尼在他的诗篇《铁匠铺》中写道，"要打出真铁，就要拉起风箱"。今天，中国驻贝尔法斯特总领馆的设立，就是为中国与北爱之间交流合作架起了风箱。让我们一起拉起风箱，使双方交流之火越烧越旺，炼出互利共赢合作的"真铁"！

谢谢！

Work the Bellows to Beat out Real Iron[*]

Foreign Minister Wang Yi,
Lord Lieutenant of Belfast,
Deputy First Minister Martin McGuinness,
Minister Arlene Foster,
Consul-General Wang Shuying,
Lord Mayors,
Distinguished Guests,
Friends from the Chinese Community,
Ladies and Gentlemen,

Today, we are gathered here to mark the opening of the Chinese Consulate General in Belfast.

I want to thank Foreign Minister Wang Yi for coming all the way from China. We are honoured to have him to unveil the plaque of the Consulate General.

I also want to thank Deputy First Minister McGuinness, Minister Foster and Lord Mayors for joining us today.

In addition, I want to express my hearty appreciation to all the representatives of various sectors in Northern Ireland for joining us in witnessing this significant moment.

The opening of the Consulate General in Belfast marks the growth of the Chinese diplomatic community in the UK, with the Embassy being joined by three consulates general.

---

[*] Remarks at the Opening Ceremony of Chinese Consulate General in Belfast. Hilton Belfast, Northern Irland, 8 June 2015.

The opening of this new Consulate General also marks the beginning of a new era in the relationship between China and Northern Ireland. It heralds a time of all-dimensional China-UK cooperation that extends to every region in the UK.

Northern Ireland is an important region with whom China has enjoyed very good cooperation.

Recent years have seen growing and deepening exchanges and cooperation between China and Northern Ireland at local government level.

Such collaboration links the two sides in economy, trade, education, science and technology.

The opening of the Chinese Consulate General in Belfast will meet our mutual needs for expanding our links and partnerships. It is a clear sign of the Chinese high expectations of the growing cooperation with Northern Ireland. It is, at the same time, a demonstration of the Chinese confidence in peace and stability in Northern Ireland.

To the Chinese community living in Northern Ireland, I want to say this:

You have worked hard and your efforts are paying off.

You have integrated into the local community.

At the same time you have been sharing the best elements of the Chinese culture with the local people and contributing to the multicultural fabric of Northern Ireland.

And you also care about the development of China and have supported the construction of your hometowns.

The new consulate office will be your new "hot line" with people back home and your new source of consular services.

I hope the Chinese Consulate General in Belfast will inspire you to forge new and deeper connections between China and Northern Ireland:

Much can be gained when you continue to support the Chinese development.

Much can be achieved when you continue to support friendship and cooperation between China and Northern Ireland.

And much can be attained when you continue to contribute to the social and economic progress of Northern Ireland.

Turning now to the government of Northern Ireland and friends from all walks of life. I want to take this opportunity to express my warmest of thanks.

Thank you for a multitude of support you have rendered us in establishing the Chinese

Consulate General in Belfast.

And we will be deeply grateful for your continued care and support.

I have every confidence that this new consulate office, led by Consul General Wang Shuying, will do everything within its capability to live up to its duties.

I am sure we can all look forward to their excellent work in promoting all-round exchanges and beneficial cooperation between China and Northern Ireland.

Ladies and Gentlemen,

Seamus Heaney, a Nobel laureate and native of Northern Ireland, wrote in his poem *The Forge*:

"To beat real iron out, to work the bellows."

Today, we open the Chinese Consulate General in Belfast. We are setting up the bellows for China-Northern Ireland exchanges and cooperation. Let us work the bellows. Let us build up the fire and heat up our exchanges. Let us beat "real iron" out. That "real iron" is the win-win cooperation.

Thank you!

奏响互利共赢的交响曲 *

尊敬的中共中央政治局委员、中共北京市委书记郭金龙先生，
尊敬的伦敦市副市长罗杰·伊凡斯先生，
尊敬的西敏寺市市长克丽斯特贝尔·弗莱特女士，
各位来宾，
女士们、先生们：

欢迎大家在这凉爽宜人的伦敦仲夏之夜，与我们共同欣赏动听迷人的"北京之夜"音乐会。首先，我感谢远道而来的郭金龙书记，感谢他和北京市为我们带来这场音乐盛宴。

北京和伦敦都是世界级特大城市，有着许多不同。两者分处亚欧大陆的两端，一个代表着东方，一个代表着西方。作为各自国家的首都，北京和伦敦都是各自国家的象征。在中国，人们往往将英国和伦敦合在一起，称之为"英伦"。在英国等西方国家，提到中国，人们就会想到北京。

北京和伦敦又有着许多相同之处，两者都是历经千年的古老城市，今天又都已发展为现代化国际大都市，都是经济金融之都，都是文化艺术之都，都是精彩奥运之都。

北京和伦敦的交集丰富而多彩，北京和伦敦建立了友好城市关系；两市的贸易、投资和金融合作是中英经贸合作的典范；两地的博物馆先后成功在对方举办大型展览。在北京，英国奥运队闯入奥运四强；在伦敦，中国奥运

---

* 在"北京之夜"音乐会上的致辞。2015 年 6 月 21 日，伦敦北格林尼治体育馆。

梦之队雄踞奖牌榜第二。

如今，北京仍要续写奥运辉煌，正在积极申请 2022 年冬季奥运会主办权，音乐会前的图片展向大家展示了北京的实力、诚意和热情。

中国国家主席习近平将应女王陛下邀请于 2015 年 10 月对英国进行国事访问，中英政治往来与互信正在升至新水平，中英经贸合作正在迈上新台阶，中英人文交流正在进入新阶段。

在这样一个充满机遇的历史时刻，郭金龙书记率团访英，并且带来"北京之夜"音乐会，期待着与伦敦进一步增进了解，深化友谊，加强合作。我祝愿并相信，北京与伦敦将联手共同奏响更加精彩纷呈、互利共赢的合作交响曲。

最后，预祝大家度过一个愉快的夜晚！

谢谢！

A Spectacular Symphony of Win-Win Cooperation[*]

Secretary Guo Jinlong,

Deputy Mayor Roger Evans,

Lord Mayor of Westminster,

Distinguished Guests,

Ladies and Gentlemen,

Welcome to the "Night of Beijing" Concert.

It is a great pleasure to have you all with us on this beautiful midsummer night to enjoy delightful music.

My warmest of appreciation goes to Secretary Guo Jinlong. He has come to London all the way from China. I want to thank him and the City of Beijing for tonight's musical feast!

Beijing and London are both megacities.

As national capitals, Beijing and London are both world famous international cities.

But they differ in many ways:

- Beijing represents the East.
- London represents the West.
- They are on opposite ends of the Eurasian continent.

---

[*] Remarks at the "Night of Beijing" Concert. O2 Theatre, 21 June 2015.

Yet, Beijing and London have many things in common:

- Both have thousands of years of history.
- Both are modern leading global metropolis.
- Both are economic and financial centres.
- Both are cultural and art capitals.
- And both have hosted the Olympics.

Indeed, I can list many more things that have joined Beijing and London together.

Beijing and London are sister cities.

Their relations are an outstanding example of China-UK trade, investment and financial cooperation.

But it is not all about business—take culture and sport for example:

- Both cities have staged exceptional exhibitions in each other's museums.
- In Beijing back in 2008 Olympics, Team GB was one of the "fabulous four" of the medal count.
- In London three years ago, the Chinese Olympic Dream Team proudly ranked second.

Today, Beijing is determined to continue the Olympic glory, vigorously bidding for 2022 Winter Games. You may have seen and felt from the pre-concert exhibition Beijing's strength, sincerity and enthusiasm.

Ladies and Gentlemen,

- At the invitation of Her Majesty The Queen, the Chinese President Xi Jinping will pay a state visit to the UK in October.
- China-UK political exchanges and mutual trust is scaling new heights.
- China-UK trade and economic cooperation is making advances.
- And the China-UK people-to-people and cultural exchanges is entering a new phase.

This is indeed a historic time in the relations between our nations.

This is an age of immense opportunities.

At this opportune moment, we are delighted to welcome Secretary Guo Jinlong and his delegation to visit the UK.

We much appreciate the "Night of Beijing" Concert they have brought to us. They have come to further enhance understanding, deepen friendship and strengthen cooperation with London.

I wish, and I am confident, that when Beijing and London join hands, they will present an even more spectacular symphony of win-win cooperation.

In conclusion, I wish you all a most pleasant evening!

Thank you!

敢为人先，务实进取，再谱合作新篇章 *

尊敬的中共中央政治局委员、中共广东省委书记胡春华先生，
尊敬的英国国际贸易部国务大臣汉兹，
尊敬的英中贸协主席沙逊勋爵，
女士们、先生们：

正式演讲前，我谨对格兰菲尔公寓楼火灾事故中的遇难者表示哀悼，对遇难者亲属和伤者表示慰问，希望他们能够早日康复。

很高兴出席中国（广东）– 英国经贸合作交流会。首先，我谨代表中国驻英国大使馆，对中共中央政治局委员、中共广东省委书记胡春华率团访问英国表示热烈欢迎！

2017 年是中英建立大使级外交关系 45 周年。胡春华书记此访，对于促进两国地方合作、推进中英关系发展具有重要意义。

对于中国和广东省来说，2017 年也是具有历史意义的一年。25 年前，邓小平先生到深圳等南方城市视察，发表了著名的南方谈话，第一次提出"发展才是硬道理"，开启了中国改革开放的新篇章，也推动广东发展迈上了新台阶。

广东是中国开放最早、开放面最大、开放程度最深的"明星省份"。广东的"星光"主要闪耀在以下几个方面。

一是经济增长冠居全国。2016 年，广东的经济增长率高达 7.5%，GDP

---

* 在中国（广东）– 英国经贸合作交流会上的讲话。2017 年 6 月 14 日，伦敦万豪酒店。

总量达 1.2 万亿美元，已连续 28 年位居中国各省市之首。如果按经济体量排名，广东可以排到世界第 15 位，与西班牙差不多。

二是广东精神享誉全国。"敢为人先、务实进取"是广东精神的精髓。30 多年来，广东秉持"实践是检验真理的唯一标准"，坚定走在中国改革开放最前沿，成为中国改革开放的"排头兵"和"试验田"。可以说，广东精神代表了中国开拓进取的时代精神。

三是改革开放领先全国。过去 5 年，随着中国改革开放进入新的历史时期，广东积极推进供给侧结构性改革，实施创新驱动发展战略，吹响了新一轮改革开放的号角，开启了实现中华民族伟大复兴中国梦的新征程。

我高兴地看到，广东近年来在英国的知名度越来越高，许多广东的优秀企业在英国十分活跃，经营业务涉及通信、基础设施建设、房地产开发等广泛领域，其中包括华为、中兴、海能达等知名通信企业，还有生产新一代伦敦红色双层大巴的比亚迪公司，以及参与欣克利角 C 核电项目的中广核集团。粤英贸易占中英贸易的 20%，广东对英投资协议金额近 70 亿美元。广东与英国经贸合作已经成为中英地方合作的样板。

广东的成绩值得骄傲，值得庆贺。展望未来，我们对广东充满期待，对中英伙伴关系充满期待。为进一步深化中英和粤英合作，我有三点建议。

一是打造合作新亮点。英国创新研发能力全球领先，高端制造业发达，对中国投资持开放态度。广东正积极落实新发展理念，构建开放型经济新体制，拥有强大的创新、生产和制造能力。双方可以在基础设施、房地产开发、品牌创意、节能环保等领域打造更多合作新亮点。

二是发扬"敢为人先、务实进取"的精神。中英在过去 45 年中发扬"敢为人先"的精神，创造了多个互利合作"第一"。在当前国际格局深刻演变、世界经济复苏乏力、保护主义上升的形势下，双方更要发扬这种精神，不断探索合作新领域、新方式和新渠道，开创更多"第一"。

三是加强"一带一路"合作。英国作为"一带一路"重要共建国，金融服务、法律专业服务、项目运营、风险管控等领域经验丰富。近年来，广东企业积极赴"一带一路"共建国家投资合作，2016 年对共建国家和地区投资增长高达 65.3%。双方可以在中英"一带一路"合作框架下，携手挖掘新的合作潜力。

"明者因时而变，知者随事而制。"我希望并相信，只要中英双方本着求真务实的态度，发扬创新发展的精神，粤英合作就一定能结出更多成果，为中英关系增光添彩！

最后，祝胡春华书记访英圆满成功！

谢谢！

Adopt a Pioneering, Practical and Enterprising Spirit and Achieve New Success in China-UK Cooperation*

Secretary Hu Chunhua,

Minister Hans,

Lord Sassoon,

Ladies and Gentlemen,

Before I begin, let me first express my deep condolences on the tragic loss of lives in the Grenfell Tower fire and my sympathies go to the bereaved families and the injured. I hope they will recover from this horrific incident.

It is a great delight to join you for today's China (Guangdong)-UK Economic and Trade Cooperation Conference.

On behalf of the Chinese Embassy, I would like to begin by extending my warmest welcome to Secretary Hu Chunhua and his delegation.

For China and Britain, this year is a special year. It marks the 45th anniversary of the ambassadorial diplomatic relations between China and Britain. That's why Secretary Hu's visit to the UK is highly significant. This visit will give a strong push to both the regional cooperation and the overall bilateral ties between our two countries.

For China and for Guangdong Province, this year is also highly meaningful. 25 years ago, Mr Deng Xiaoping toured southern Chinese cities including Shenzhen in

---

* Remarks at the China (Guangdong)-UK Economic and Trade Cooperation Conference. London Marriott Hotel, 14 June 2017.

Guangdong Province. During the tour, he delivered the famous Southern Tour Speech and made, for the first time, the remark that "development is what really counts". His speech marked a new phase in the Chinese reform and opening-up. Guangdong has since entered a new stage of accelerated development.

Guangdong was the first province in China to open up for business. The width and depth of its opening-up are also unparalleled. It is no exaggeration if I call Guangdong "the Chinese opening-up superstar".

Now, let me show you some of the brightest "sparkles" of this superstar.

First, Guangdong has been a leader in economic development. In 2016, Guangdong's GDP grew by 7.5% and achieved a total of 1.2 trillion US dollars. Of all the Chinese provinces, Guangdong has ranked No.1 in GDP for 28 consecutive years. Globally, Guangdong is the 15th largest economy. That is about the size of Spain.

Second, I want to mention the "Guangdong spirit". This has won national acclaim in China. Guangdong province is known for its courage to break new ground, its down-to-earth approach to get things done and its enterprising spirit to reach for the best. And Guangdong has always followed the principle that "practice is the sole criterion of truth." These are the essence of the Guangdong spirit.

Over the past 30 years, Guangdong has been at the forefront of the Chinese reform and opening-up. The province has always been a bellwether or a test field for new policies. In a sense, the "Guangdong spirit" reflects the pioneering spirit of China over the past decades.

Third, Guangdong today continues to lead reform and opening-up in China. The past five years are widely regarded as the beginning of a period of economic transition in China. The key words for this transition are supply side reform and development driven by innovation. Guangdong has made unremitting efforts in actively advancing both the supply side reform and the innovation strategy. The province again sounded the clarion call for a new phase of reform and opening-up in China. It is at the forefront of the journey to realize the Chinese Dream of national rejuvenation.

In addition to the above "sparkles", I want to mention in particular that I am happy to see Guangdong building name recognition and increasing presence here in Britain. Many leading companies from Guangdong are doing very well in this country. Their businesses range from communication and infrastructure to real estate development.

To give you some examples, we have communication giants such as Huawei, ZTE and Hytera. We have BYD, the producer of the new generation London double-decker bus. And we have the CGN, a partner in the Hinkley Point C nuclear power project.

Trade and investments are also impressive. Guangdong's trade with Britain accounts for 20% of China-UK trade total. Guangdong's investment in Britain totalled 7 billion US dollars.

It is fair to say that the business cooperation between Guangdong and Britain is a model for the regional cooperation between our two countries. We have every reason to celebrate and be proud of Guangdong's achievements. This also gives us reason to expect more from Guangdong and from China-UK relations.

With regard to deepening China-UK and Guangdong-UK cooperation in the coming years, I have three suggestions.

First, we should continue to join hands and explore new areas of cooperation for new success.

The UK has world-class innovative and R&D capabilities. It boasts an advanced high-end manufacturing sector. And it always keeps an open mind to investment from China.

Guangdong is experimenting new development ideas and building an open economy. The province also has strong innovative, manufacturing and production capabilities.

If these strengths are matched well, there will be new cooperation opportunities and outcomes in infrastructure building, real estate development, branding and innovation, energy conservation and environmental protection.

Second, we should continue to uphold the "Guangdong spirit".

In the past 45 years, China and Britain have always dared to take the lead and have achieved many "firsts" in our mutually beneficial cooperation.

Today, profound changes are taking place in the international arena. The challenges of sluggish growth and rising protectionism remain daunting.

This calls on us to stick to the "Guangdong spirit", namely be pioneering, be practical and be enterprising.

We must keep exploring new areas, new means and new channels of cooperation.

This is how we can continue to set new records by achieving more "firsts".

Third, we should continue to enhance cooperation on the Belt and Road Initiative.

Britain is a key partner of the Belt and Road cooperation thanks to its unique strengths in financial services, legal services, project management and risks control.

Guangdong companies have been actively seeking investment and cooperation opportunities along the Belt and Road routes over the years. In 2016, investment by Guangdong in countries and regions along the Belt and Road routes grew by 65.3%.

There is huge potential for Guangdong and Britain to work more closely together under the framework of the Belt and Road.

Ladies and Gentlemen,

As a Chinese saying goes, "The wise man keeps abreast with the time and adapts to changes."

I hope and believe that, as long as we get down to business and continue to break new grounds, Guangdong-UK cooperation will deliver more fruits to China-UK relations.

In conclusion, I wish Secretary Hu Chunhua's visit to the UK a complete success.

Thank you!

促进东西方交流互鉴，推进中英战略伙伴关系 *

各位来宾，

女士们、先生们：

晚上好！

很高兴出席"感知中国——中国西部文化英国行"开幕式活动。我谨对出席今天活动的中英各界人士表示热烈的欢迎！

"感知中国"主题活动内涵丰富、形式多样，日益成为展示中华文化艺术魅力、推进中外文化交流的知名品牌。本次"感知中国"活动以中国西部文化为主题，将通过中国西部歌舞演出、图片展览、电影展映等系列活动，充分展示中国西部优美的自然风光、丰富的人文景观和深厚的历史文化。相信这些活动将有助于英国公众近距离感知中国、了解中国、领悟中国。

我曾经在中国西部省份甘肃工作，对中国西部的发展变化十分关注，也有深刻体会。近年来，中国西部地区充分发挥后发优势，主要发展指标增速明显高于全国平均水平。2013—2016 年，中国西部 GDP 年均增长 9.1%，高于全国平均增速约 2 个百分点；经济结构趋于优化，新能源汽车、电子信息、大数据等战略性新兴产业不断壮大。同时，中国西部也是文化大省集中的地区，地域与民族特色浓郁，历史文化资源非常丰富。近年来，中国西部文化产业快速发展，2016 年相关产业规模和收入增长均高于东部地区。经过不懈

---

* 在"感知中国——中国西部文化英国行"开幕式上的演讲。2017 年 7 月 20 日，伦敦美人鱼剧场。

努力，中国西部经济、社会、文化等多方面实现了跨越式发展，西部的面貌焕然一新。

中国地域辽阔，东西部差异很大。不少英国朋友去过中国东部发达省份，对东部了解较多。相比之下，对中国西部则了解较少。因此，此次活动登陆英伦，将遍访伦敦、爱丁堡、曼彻斯特，可谓恰逢其时，我认为有三重意义。

第一，感知中国西部文化，为中英关系增光添彩。2017年是中英建立大使级外交关系45周年。两国高层交往密切，经贸、金融、能源、人文等领域合作成果丰硕。近年来，中英成功互办"文化交流年"，共同纪念汤显祖和莎士比亚逝世400周年，围绕"青年与创新精神"开展系列人文活动，展现了双方人文交流的巨大潜力。中国西部民族文化多姿多彩，陕西秦始皇陵兵马俑、敦煌莫高窟、云南西双版纳等历史文化"经典品牌"驰名中外；对外文化交流方兴未艾，西部艺术节、博览会、电影节等不断提升西部的国际知名度。展望未来，中国西部完全可以成为中英人文交流合作的新亮点。通过感知中国西部文化，中英双方可以进一步挖掘在旅游、影视、新闻、出版、考古等领域的合作潜力，合作开发中国西部文化资源。

第二，感知中国西部文化，为"一带一路"民心相通增添助力。中国西部是古丝绸之路的诞生地和起点。约公元前140年的中国汉代，张骞率领一支和平使团，以现在中国的西安为起点出使西域，打通了东方通往西方的道路，开辟了丝绸之路。如今，在"一带一路"倡议指引下，中国西部积极推进丝路文化交流，与共建国家间开展了一系列丰富多彩的文化交流活动。2016年9月在甘肃敦煌举办的首届丝绸之路国际文化博览会上，各类独具民族文化特色的展品令众多国内外参观者驻足。前不久，在伦敦王储传统艺术学院举行的"敦煌佛教石窟"展览受到英国民众热烈欢迎。英国是"一带一路"建设的重要共建方，具有教育、语言、学术、媒体等诸多优势资源。通过感知中国西部文化，英国公众将更全面地了解中国的历史与文明，这将进一步促进中英两国民心相通，为中英"一带一路"合作筑牢民意基础。

第三，感知中国西部文化，为东西方文明交流互鉴拓宽内涵。中国西部文化是中华文明瑰宝的重要组成部分。历史上，东西方文明在中国西部交汇融合，竞相辉映。中英都是人文精英荟萃、文化积淀深厚的伟大国家，也是东西方文明的重要代表。纵观世界，文明没有高下、优劣之分，只有特色、地域之别，不同文明之间既要相互尊重、求同存异，也要相互借鉴、共同进步。通过感知中国西部文化，有助于中英两国加强交流合作，也有利于树立东西方文明相互尊重、交流互鉴的典范，为促进世界文明多样化和共同进步做出积极贡献。在此次活动期间，中国藏学专家代表团将与英方开展互动交流，这将进一步增进英国各界人士对中国西部特别是西藏自治区的了解。我们也希望更多英国朋友有机会到中国西部走一走，看一看，实地感受和深入体验中国的文化底蕴与时代脉搏。

女士们、先生们，

中国古人说，"夫物之不齐，物之情也"。西方人常说，"世界上没有两片完全相同的树叶"。文明因交流而多彩，文明因互鉴而丰富。前不久，习近平主席与梅首相在二十国集团领导人汉堡峰会期间举行会晤，两国领导人再次确认中英关系的大方向，提出要以中英高级别人文交流机制成立5周年为契机，密切两国民间交往和青年交流。我们愿与英国各界人士共同努力，不断深化交流与合作，增进相互了解与信任，共同促进东西方文明交流互鉴，共同推进中英关系不断结出丰硕成果。

最后，预祝本次"感知中国——中国西部文化英国行"活动取得圆满成功！

谢谢！

Mutual Learning between the East and the West Will Boost China-UK Strategic Partnership*

Distinguished Guests,

Ladies and Gentlemen,

Good Evening!

It is a real pleasure to join you for the opening ceremony of Experience China 2017 here in London. I would like to begin by extending my warm welcome to all my British and Chinese friends who are with us tonight.

Experience China is a cultural gala of a variety of artistic performances. It is widely recognized and highly reputed for exhibiting the Chinese arts and advancing cultural exchanges between China and other nations.

This year's event focuses on exploring the cultural heritage of west China in the forms of folk singing and dancing, photo exhibition, films and book show. The colorful composition of the event will bring the vast west of China to the door steps of Britain. It will allow the British audience to enjoy the natural beauty, historical sites and places of interest in west China and to learn and experience China from a close range.

Being no stranger to west China, I have worked in Gansu Province for a couple of years. Since then, I have always kept an eye on the development of the Chinese western region. I have to say I am more than amazed by the level of growth and scale of change

---

* Speech at the Opening Ceremony of Experience China—Cultural Exploration of West China. The Mermaid Theatre, London, 20 July 2017.

that have taken place over there all these years.

The western region has been a late-mover in terms of economic development compared with the more advanced east coast. In recent years, this has been turned into an advantage, enabling west China to achieve fast growth. Major development indicators of the western region have been higher than the national average.

From 2013 to 2016, the GDP of the western provinces and regions grew by 9.1% annually. That was close to two percentage points higher than the national average. The economic structure has been optimized. Strategic emerging industries, including new energy vehicles, IT and big data, are fast developing.

The western region of China is regarded as a fount of culture thanks to its unique and rich variety of ethnic cultural heritage. Recent years have witnessed fast development of cultural and creative industry in west China, overtaking that of the eastern region in 2016 in both output and revenue.

After years of efforts, the Chinese west has achieved leapfrog progress in economic, social and cultural development. It is now taking on a brand new look.

China is a vast country. There is a huge difference between the eastern and western parts of China. British friends who have been to the more advanced coastal regions in the east might not know a lot about the Chinese west. So I think Experience China 2017 could not have come to Britain at a better time. Its tour in Britain, including London, Edinburgh and Manchester, is significant in three aspects.

First, to experience the culture of west China is a part of the efforts to advance China-UK relations.

This year marks the 45th anniversary of the Ambassadorial diplomatic ties between China and Britain. Since the beginning of this year, our two countries have had close high-level exchanges and achieved fruitful outcomes in business, financial and energy cooperation and in culture and people-to-people exchange.

Over the years, China and Britain successfully held the "Year of Cultural Exchanges", jointly marked the 400th anniversary of the passing of Tang Xianzu and William Shakespeare, and co-hosted a number of cultural activities under the theme of "Spirit of Youth". These events have demonstrated the huge potential of cultural exchanges between our two countries.

West China is home to diverse ethnic cultures. There are world-renowned, classic cultural icons, such as the Terracotta army of Qin Dynasty, the Mogao Caves in Dunhuang and Xishuangbanna in Yunnan Province. There are booming cultural exchange events, including the Western China Art Festival, the Western China International Fair and Silk Road International Film Festival. These are helping to increase the global visibility of the Chinese western region.

There is every reason for the Chinese west to become a highlight of cultural and people-to-people exchange between China and the UK. We can work together in specific areas such as tourism, TV and films, press, publication, archaeology, etc. And in this process, we can explore and develop the rich cultural resources of west China.

Second, to experience the culture of west China helps form stronger people-to-people bond and enhance mutual understanding as we cooperate on the Belt and Road Initiative.

West China was the starting point of the ancient Silk Road. In the Chinese Han Dynasty in roughly 140 BC, Zhang Qian and his team of trail blazers set off from Xi'an on a peaceful mission. His journey to the west opened up trade routes later known as the Silk Road.

Today, the Chinese western region is actively engaged in a wide range of cultural exchanges and interactions under the Belt and Road Initiative. In September 2016, the first Silk Road International Cultural Expo was held in Dunhuang. It attracted visitors from China and abroad by showing the unique ethnic cultures of the Chinese west. Not long ago, an exhibition of artworks from Dunhuang's Buddhist cave temples took place here in London. The exhibition, housed in the Prince's School of Traditional Arts, opened a window on the sacred art of the Silk Road.

Britain is the Chinese key partner in building the Belt and Road. When it comes to culture, Britain has unmatched advantages and abundant resources. These include education, language, academic studies, media and others. Experience China 2017 could give the British public a new perspective on the Chinese culture and history. This will increase mutual understanding and cement the public support for China-UK cooperation on the Belt and Road.

Third, to experience the culture of west China contributes to the broad exchange and mutual learning between the Eastern and Western civilizations.

The cultural heritage of west China is an important part of the Chinese civilization.

Historically, west China is where the civilizations of the east and the west met.

China and Britain are both great nations of profound culture and history. We are important representatives of the eastern and western civilizations.

There is never a superior civilization. There is never a better civilization. There are only different civilizations with their respective and unique cultural and geographical features. And there have to be mutual respect, mutual learning and mutual accommodation between different civilizations. And this alone will enable common progress for all.

Experience China 2017 is such an event to enhance cultural exchanges and cooperation between China and Britain.

Our two countries are in a good position to set up an example of mutual respect and mutual learning between the East and the West. By working hand in hand, we are able to make the world a place of greater diversity, and we will be able to contribute to the common progress of all civilizations on our planet.

In the following days, a delegation of Tibetologists will visit Britain for academic exchanges and interactions. Such exchanges will increase understanding of the Chinese west, especially the Xizang Autonomous Region.

It is also my hope that more British friends will one day visit the Chinese west. It is absolutely rewarding to set foot on the land, to see with your own eyes, and to experience the Chinese culture steeped in history and traditions and shaped by the rapid changes of our times.

Ladies and Gentlemen,

We Chinese people often say:

"That things are born to be different is nature."

In the west, people often say:

"No two leaves are ever exactly alike."

Civilizations are richer and more colorful as a result of exchanges and mutual learning.

Less than two weeks ago, President Xi Jinping and Prime Minister Theresa May held a successful meeting at the G20 Hamburg Summit. The two leaders reaffirmed the shared commitment to building China-UK relations. They agreed to further strengthen non-governmental and youth exchanges based on the achievements over the past five years under the China-UK High-Level People-to-People Exchange Mechanism.

We look forward to working with British friends from all sectors for closer exchange and collaboration, and for deeper understanding and trust. I am confident that through our concerted efforts, we can advance the mutual learning between the Eastern and Western civilizations and China-UK relations will bear more fruits in our cooperation.

In conclusion, I wish Experience China 2017 in the UK a complete success!

Thank you!

深挖潜力，开拓中苏（格兰）合作美好未来 *

尊敬的苏格兰商会主席阿兰先生，
尊敬的苏格兰经济部长布朗先生，
尊敬的苏格兰商会国际事务大使瓦伦丁先生，
女士们、先生们：
很高兴出席苏格兰商会举行的晚宴。

出使英国七年半，我曾多次到访苏格兰，每次都有新发现、新感受，每次都留下难以忘怀的回忆。苏格兰自然风光秀丽多姿，人民热情好客，威士忌醇香馥郁。苏格兰与中国的交往合作更是持续强劲，我认为可以概括为"三多"。

一是互访多。苏格兰政府历任首席部长都访问过中国。现任首席部长斯特金女士于2015年访华，有力促进了双方务实合作。中国领导人也多次访问苏格兰，近两年有近20支中国部级以上代表团来访。双方还建立了西安与爱丁堡等5对友好省郡市关系，为中英地方交往合作树立了典范。2017年夏天，中共中央政治局委员、中共广东省委书记胡春华先生到访苏格兰，与各界人士广泛交流，访问取得圆满成功。

二是成果多。2016年中苏贸易额达36.8亿英镑，苏格兰对华出口比10年前翻了一番，50多家苏格兰企业在华设有机构，苏格兰国际发展局在华设立办事处。双方合作项目涵盖机电设备、建筑设计、可再生能源、造船、生

---

* 在苏格兰商会晚宴上的主旨演讲。2017年9月19日，英国格拉斯哥市。

命科学等。2017年4月，苏格兰商会首次访华并在烟台市设立了贸易代表处。目前，中国在苏投资遍地开花，涵盖能源、零售、汽车、创新等诸多领域。例如，由中资企业投资参股的苏格兰格兰杰莫斯炼油厂产品占苏成品油市场份额的80%，2016年11月中国携程旅行网出资14亿英镑收购总部设在爱丁堡的天巡网。就在上周，中国长江三峡集团公司和葡萄牙电力公司联合成功中标95万千瓦、位于苏格兰马里湾海域的海上风电项目，将中国工程技术应用优势与英国海上风能研发技术完美结合在一起，从而实现优势互补、互利共赢。

三是交流多。苏格兰是世界上孔子学院和孔子课堂覆盖率最高的地区之一，拥有5所孔子学院和44间孔子课堂，辐射300多所中小学，近3万名苏格兰中小学生正在学习中国语言和文化。就在几个小时前，我刚刚参加了苏格兰中小学孔子学院成立5周年的庆祝活动。苏格兰19所高校全部与中国高校建立了合作关系。中国有1万多名留学生在苏格兰学习，是苏格兰留学生数量最多的国家。双方影视文化界、博物馆和艺术团体交流频繁，合作有声有色。爱丁堡艺术节享誉全球，已成为苏格兰一张亮丽的文化名片，吸引越来越多的中国艺术家和文艺团体慕名而来。

女士们、先生们，

"浩渺行无极，扬帆但信风。"2017年是中英建立大使级外交关系45周年。在此背景下，中国与苏格兰合作蕴含新动力，面临新机遇，主要体现在以下三方面。

第一，中英伙伴关系为中苏（格兰）合作注入了新动力。2015年习近平主席对英国成功进行国事访问，两国建立面向21世纪全球全面战略伙伴关系。不久前，习主席与梅首相在二十国集团领导人汉堡峰会期间会晤，再次确认了中英关系的大方向。在中英伙伴关系引领下，两国在政治、经贸、金融和人文等领域结出越来越多成果。2016年中英双边贸易额达744亿美元，英国吸引中国直接投资180亿美元，高居欧洲之首。中英两国每年人员往来超过150万人次，"中国热"在英国持续升温，"英伦风"在中国拥有大量粉丝。

中英伙伴关系不仅为中苏（格兰）友好交往指明了方向，也为双方进一步深化合作提供了新动力。苏格兰政府连续多次发表对华合作"五年规划"，充分体现了苏方致力于深化对华合作的积极意愿。据我所知，2017年新版"五年规划"即将出台，我们对此十分期待。我相信双方将在地方政府、经贸、金融、科技创新、新能源、文化、教育、旅游、医疗等领域找到更多利益契合点、政策对接点与合作支撑点，更好地造福双方民众。

第二，"一带一路"倡议为中苏（格兰）合作搭建了新平台。中国国家主席习近平提出的"一带一路"倡议，是中国实行全方位对外开放的重大举措，也是共同推动地区及全球发展振兴的重要公共产品，有利于建设开放、包容、普惠、平衡、共赢的经济全球化，有助于构建人类命运共同体。2017年5月，中国成功主办"一带一路"国际合作高峰论坛。各国代表在会上共商合作大计，共谋发展良策，达成广泛共识，形成一份共5大类，76大项，270多项的成果清单，这标志着共建"一带一路"倡议已经进入从理念到行动、从规划到实施的新阶段。

英国是"一带一路"建设的重要共建方，两国"一带一路"合作在基础设施、金融、教育、法律等领域有许多互补优势。"一带一路"是开放包容的合作平台。我们欢迎苏格兰各界人士充分发挥自身优势，参与到"一带一路"建设中，携手做大共同利益"蛋糕"。众所周知，创新是引领发展的第一动力。中国正大力开展大众创业、万众创新，智能制造、互联网＋、数字经济、共享经济等创新浪潮方兴未艾。苏格兰是创新产业的"高地"，提出了"苏格兰能做到"创新行动计划。历史上，苏格兰人曾发明了蒸汽机、自行车、青霉素和电话。如今，苏格兰成为可再生能源、生命科学、信息网络、装备制造的国际创新中心。中苏双方可借助"一带一路"平台，加强创新发展战略对接，共同打造富有活力的经济增长模式。

第三，中国经济稳中向好为中苏（格兰）合作提供了新机遇。中国是世界第二大经济体，也是全球经济重要引擎，对全球经济增长贡献率连续多年超过30%。近年来，中国大力推进供给侧结构性改革、深入实施创新驱动发展战略，并已逐渐取得成效。2017年上半年，中国经济增长达6.9%，超出预期。中国货物贸易出口额和进口额分别同比增长 15% 和 25.7%，创 2011 年以来最高增速。在世界经济总体复苏依然乏力的形势下，中国在努力促进自身经济增长的同时，始终坚持建设开放型世界经济，促进贸易和投资自由化便利化，使之更好地惠及各国人民。中国已成为全球 120 多个国家和地区的最大贸易伙伴。预计未来 5 年，中国将进口 8 万亿美元的商品，吸收 6000 亿美元的外来投资，对外投资总额将达 7500 亿美元，出境旅游将达 7 亿人次。

这些无疑都会给中苏（格兰）扩大合作提供更多空间与机遇。一方面，中国企业走出国门、走进苏格兰的步伐更坚定、更有保障；另一方面，中方正在采取一系列举措降低企业制度性交易成本，改善外国企业在华营商环境。中国对外开放的大门不仅不会关上，而且会越开越大。当前，皇家苏格兰银行、标准人寿保险公司、GA 保险公司、苏格兰与纽卡斯尔酒业公司等一大批苏格兰企业在华开展合作业务，未来我们欢迎更多苏格兰企业在华投资兴业，欢迎更多像苏格兰威士忌这样有特色的商品进入中国市场。

女士们、先生们，

2015 年，苏格兰首席部长斯特金女士访华接受采访时，曾用四个"I"形容苏格兰经济，其中她把"投资"（investment）放在第一位。我刚才讲到，中国近年来在苏格兰投资步伐加快，并为苏格兰人民带来了实实在在的好处。但我也注意到，近来英国一些媒体频频出现所谓"中国投资威胁论"的论调，渲染中国投资威胁英国安全。对此，我想用三个"W"谈一谈我的看法。

第一是共赢（win-win）。中国有句古话："既以为人，己愈有；既以与人，己愈多。"互利共赢自古就是中国人的处世哲学，也是中国对外投资的出发点和最终目标。中国企业来英投资，寻求的是合作，是互利共赢。中国企业在获利的同时，也为英国创造了大量就业岗位，推动了英国绿色、低碳发展，促进了英国经济的繁荣与稳定。比如，中广核参与投资建设的欣克利角 C 核电项目预计将为英国创造 2.6 万个就业岗位，建成运营后每年相当于减排二氧化碳900万吨；比亚迪集团与英国亚历山大·丹尼斯公司在苏格兰福尔柯克共同生产的零排放电动公交车，已交付60余辆投入使用，整个项目预计可获6.6亿英镑收益。

第二是欢迎（welcome）。中国企业带着诚意和善意来到英国，它们也同样希望看到公平、友善、开放、欢迎的投资环境。中国企业在英投资主要集中在民用、民生领域，是公开透明的，它们给英国人民带来了实实在在的利益。一些人可能担忧所谓"国有"背景或安全隐患，但大多中国国企都是上市企业，经营标准与欧美跨国企业相仿，业绩公开透明，并且即便一些投资项目涉及通信、核电等重要基础设施领域，也严格遵守英国环保、卫生、安全等各项法律法规，积极履行企业社会责任，得到各界肯定。

第三是智慧（wisdom）。目前，英国正处于"脱欧"的历史进程中。我始终认为，在这一进程中，机遇与挑战并存，机遇大于挑战。如何抓住机遇、应对挑战、推进合作，考验的是中英双方的智慧。英国政府在公投"脱欧"后多次表示，将会继续坚持自由贸易，反对保护主义，致力于加强与欧盟之外伙伴的经贸关系，打造"全球化英国"。对于包括中方在内的投资者而言，目前最需要的是信心和确定性。这就需要英方运筹"大智慧"，信守对外开放承诺，而不是收紧外资审查政策，制造不必要的疑虑和不确定性。中国企业已经用实际行动为英国未来发展投下了信任票和支持票，希望英方也能以自己的实际行动为更多中国企业投资英国增强信心，使它们确信来英国投资是值得的，是正确的。

女士们、先生们，

苏格兰有句谚语，"如果想取得成果，必先付出努力"。中国人常说，"千里之行，始于足下"。我相信，在双方共同努力下，中苏贸易投资合作一定会迎来更加甜美和光明的未来。说到"甜"，中国大熊猫"甜甜"和"阳光"已经在爱丁堡动物园生活了近6年，"甜甜"在中文里就是"甜美"的意思，我衷心祝愿中苏经贸合作为中英关系贡献更多"甜美成果"！祝愿中国和苏格兰人民的日子越来越甜美！

最后，我提议，

为中苏（格兰）合作美好未来，
为在座朋友们的健康，
干杯！

Tap the Potential for a Brighter Future of China-Scotland Cooperation[*]

Mr Allan,

Secretary Brown,

Mr Valentine,

Ladies and Gentlemen,

It is a real delight to join you for today's SCC dinner.

In the past seven and half years since I arrived in Britain as Chinese Ambassador, I had visited Scotland numerous times. Every time I would discover something new. I would get to know Scotland a little better. And I would take home precious memories of the natural beauty, the warm-hearted people, and of course, the Scottish whisky, strong or mellow.

Most importantly, Scotland has always maintained strong and close cooperation and exchanges with China.

Let me summarize the ties between China and Scotland with the word "numerous", that is, numerous visits, numerous outcomes and numerous exchanges.

First, there are numerous official visits.

- All first ministers of successive Scottish governments have visited China. The latest was by Ms Nicolas Sturgeon in 2015. That visit gave a strong boost to the cooperation between China and Scotland.

---

[*] Speech at the Scottish Chamber of Commerce Dinner. Glasgow, Scotland, 19 September 2017.

- There have been many visits in the opposite direction, too. In the past two years, nearly twenty Chinese delegations at or above ministerial level visited Scotland.
- Five twin city relationships between Chinese and Scottish cities were established, including the one between Xi'an and Edinburgh. They are fine examples of regional exchanges and cooperation between China and Britain.
- In June, Member of the CPC Central Committee's Political Bureau and Party Secretary of Guangdong Province, Mr Hu Chunhua visited Scotland. He met widely with people from different sectors and his visit was a success.

Second, the business cooperation between China and Scotland has yielded numerous outcomes.

- Last year, China-Scotland trade totalled 3.68 billion pounds.
- In a matter of 10 years, Scotland's export to China has doubled.
- More than 50 Scottish companies have operations in China. Scottish Development International also has an office in China.
- Projects between Scotland and China cover a wide range of areas, from electro-mechanical equipment to building design, from renewable energy to ship building and life science.
- In April this year, during its first ever visit to China, the Scottish Chambers of Commerce established its office of trade representative in Yantai. I congratulate you!
- On the part of China, many Chinese investments have found their way into a wide range of sectors in Scotland, including energy, retail, automobile, innovation, etc.
- The refinery joint venture at Grangemouth, which accounts for 80% of Scotland's oil product market, is a good example.
- The 1.4 billion pounds acquisition of Skyscanner based in Edinburgh by the Chinese Ctrip last November is another example.
- Last week, China Three Gorges Group (CTG) and Portugese energy group EDP were awarded a 950 mega-watt offshore wind project in Scotland's Moray Firth. That means the Chinese engineering technology application will join hands with British offshore wind R&D capability. This will be a perfect match. It will bring

out the strengths of both sides and deliver a win-win outcome.

And the list can go on and on.

Third, there are numerous cultural and people-to-people exchanges.

- Scotland has the world's highest coverage of Confucius Institutes and Confucius Classrooms. The 5 Confucius Institutes and 44 Confucius Classrooms in Scotland cover more than 300 elementary and middle schools. Nearly 30,000 students are studying Chinese language and culture. Just a few hours ago, I attended the celebration to mark the fifth anniversary of the Confucius Institute for Scotland's Schools.
- All 19 Scottish universities have cooperative partners in China. More than 10,000 Chinese students are studying in Scotland, making up the biggest foreign student group in Scotland.
- Exchanges and cooperation between China and Scotland have been particularly vibrant and effective in film-making, TV industry, museums and performing art.
- The world-renowned Edinburgh International Festival is Scotland's best-known cultural brand. It is attracting more and more Chinese artists and art troupes.

Ladies and Gentlemen,

There is an ancient Chinese poem which goes:

"Boundless is the ocean where we sail with favourable winds."

As we work to advance the cooperation between China and Scotland, we have three favourable winds in our sail.

First of all, it is the wind of the partnership. In 2015 President Xi Jinping made a successful state visit to the UK, which heralded our global comprehensive strategic partnership for the 21st century.

This year marks the 45th anniversary of China-UK ambassadorial diplomatic relations. China-UK relations are creating a new momentum for China-Scotland cooperation.

During the G20 Summit in Hamburg not long ago, President Xi and Prime Minister May reaffirmed the shared commitment in their bilateral meetings. Now the partnership is delivering more and more fruits in our political, business, financial and culture cooperation.

- Last year, China-UK trade totalled 74.4 billion US dollars.
- The UK so far has attracted 18 billion US dollars of Chinese investment, far more than any of the other European country.
- Every year, more than 1.5 million visits are made between our two countries.
- Enthusiasm for learning Chinese language and culture is rising in Britain while British culture, including films and TV dramas, also has millions of fans in China.

The China-UK partnership not only points the way forward for China-Scotland friendship. It also provides a new driving force for our cooperation.

The Scottish government had issued five-year plans on cooperation with China. This had been a very positive gesture to show your commitment to deeper cooperation with China. I heard that a new five-year plan will be rolled out this year. We very much look forward to that.

I believe that China and Scotland can find more new areas where our interests converge, where our respective policies align with each other and where we can engage in cooperation. This could range from local government collaboration to business and financial ties, from scientific and technological innovation to new energy, and from culture and education to tourism and health care. Our joint endeavors in all these areas will deliver benefits to the people of both China and Scotland, and contribute to China-UK relations.

Second, the favourable winds also come from the Belt and Road Initiative. This Initiative can give China-Scotland cooperation a new platform.

Chinese President Xi Jinping proposed this Initiative in 2013. This is a major initiative through which China could achieve overall opening-up. This is also an important Initiative to boost regional and global development. It helps make the economic globalization process more open, inclusive, balanced and win-win. It helps build a community of shared future for all mankind.

Back in May, China hosted the Belt and Road Forum for International Cooperation.

The Forum was a great success. Representatives from countries around the world gathered to map out plans for cooperation and development in the future. A broad consensus was reached. The list of deliverables has five categories, 76 agreements and 270 specific outcomes. This was a landmark for the Belt and Road Initiative. This Forum has ushered in a new phase as countries engaged in Belt and Road cooperation begin to turn ideas into reality and plans into actions.

China regards Britain as a key partner in the building of the Belt and Road. The Belt and Road is an inclusive cooperation platform that is open to all. Under the Belt and Road framework, China and Britain have much to offer each other in areas such as infrastructure, finance, education, law, etc.

Here in Scotland, everyone from every sector is welcome to bring in your strength, take part in the Belt and Road building and make a bigger pie of common interests.

In this day and age, innovation, as we all know, is key to boosting growth. China is currently working hard to encourage innovation and entrepreneurship nationwide. Smart manufacturing, internet+, digital economy, sharing economy and other innovative forms of business are growing fast in China.

In Scotland, there is no shortage of inventions in your proud history, such as the steam engine, bicycle, penicillin and telephone. Today, Scotland is still a leader in innovative industries. I am impressed by your plan called "Scotland Can Do". Here, you are an international innovation centre in renewable energy, life science, information network and equipment manufacturing.

The Belt and Road Initiative could provide a platform for China and Scotland to dovetail our strategies on innovative development and build a vibrant growth model.

Third, the Chinese steady economic growth is another wind blowing in favour of and bringing new opportunities for China-Scotland cooperation.

China is the world's second largest economy and an important engine of global growth. For years in a row, more than 30% of world growth comes from China.

In recent years, China is making great efforts to advance supply side reform and innovation-driven development. These reform endeavours are showing effect.

- In the first six months of this year, the Chinese economy grew at higher-than-expected 6.9%.

- The Chinese export and import of goods grew by 15% and 25.7% respectively, the highest since 2011.
- Against the background of sluggish world recovery, China has kept a relatively high and steady growth.
- At the same time, China stayed committed to an open world economy, trade liberalization and investment facilitation for the good of people around the world.
- China is now the largest trading partner of more than 120 countries and regions.
- In the coming 5 years, China is expected to import 8 trillion US dollars of goods, attract 600 billion US dollars of foreign investment, and make 750 billion US dollars of outbound investment. Chinese tourists are expected to make more than 700 million visits overseas.

The Chinese development in these aspects will undoubtedly unlock more potential and create more opportunities for broader China-Scotland cooperation.

On one hand, Chinese companies will be more confident and reassured in operating internationally, including setting up business here in Scotland.

On the other hand, China has adopted a series of measures to facilitate inward bound foreign businesses. These include, among others, lowering the institutional cost and optimizing market environment.

I would like to stress that China will not close its door to foreign businesses. The Chinese market will be even more open to the world.

Now, the Royal Bank of Scotland, Standard Life, General Accident, Scottish & Newcastle and a number of other Scottish companies have set up businesses in China. China welcomes Scottish businesses. The more the better. And Chinese consumers welcome Scottish specialties like the Scottish whisky.

Ladies and Gentlemen,

When First Minister Sturgeon visited China in 2015, she used four "Is" to describe Scotland's economy, and she put investment in the first place.

As I mentioned just now, the past years have seen the Chinese investment in Scotland growing fast and bringing tangible benefits to the people of Scotland.

However, some British media have been claiming recently that Chinese investment poses threat to Britain's national security.

I would like to respond with three "Ws".

The first "W" is win-win.

As an old Chinese saying goes, "The more you do for others, the more you will gain. The more you share with others, the more you will have." For the Chinese people, win-win has long been a philosophy of life. Today, this same philosophy is guiding Chinese businesses in making overseas investment.

Chinese companies are coming to the UK for opportunities of investment so that they could engage in cooperation for mutual benefit. While making profits, they help create jobs, advance green and low-carbon development, and promote economic prosperity and stability locally.

Let me take the Hinkley Point C nuclear project for example. This project is partly funded by the Chinese CGN. It is expected to create 26,000 jobs. Upon completion, it will help reduce nine million tons of carbon dioxide on average every year.

Another example is the zero emission electric bus co-produced by the Chinese BYD and the UK's Alexander Dennis. More than 60 such buses are running on the road right now. This project is expected to create 660 million pounds of profit.

My second "W" is welcome.

Chinese companies have come to Britain in good faith and with sincerity. Naturally, they are hoping to find an open, friendly, fair and welcoming environment.

Chinese investment in the UK mainly focuses on civilian and livelihood related areas. They are open and transparent. And they are creating tangible benefits for the British people.

Some people point at the state-owned background of the Chinese companies operating internationally and claim that there might be potential security risks.

But the fact is that many state-owned enterprises in China are listed companies. Their operation is similar to that of European or American multinationals. Their business performances are completely open and transparent.

When making investment in the telecommunication, nuclear and other key infrastructure projects here, they strictly follow British laws on environment, health and security. They also make sure their corporate responsibilities are fulfilled. And their efforts are recognized.

My third "W" is wisdom.

The UK is in the process of Brexit negotiations, which means both challenges and opportunities. But it has been my consistent belief that there will be far more opportunities than challenges. The point here is how to seize the opportunities, address the challenges and advance cooperation. This is a test of the wisdom of our two countries.

The British government reiterates that it will stay committed to free trade, stand against protectionism, enhance business ties with partners outside the EU and build a truly "global Britain".

For international investors, including the Chinese investors, what they need most is confidence and what they want most is certainty. To reassure potential investors, the British need to "think big", namely, honouring the commitment to being open instead of tightening foreign investment reviews and creating unnecessary misgivings and uncertainties.

When Chinese businesses are putting their money here in this country, they are casting their vote of confidence for Britain's future. They hope Britain will take more actions to give them the confidence they need to stay here, to convince them that their decision to invest in the UK is a right one.

Ladies and Gentlemen,

I quite like this Scottish proverb:

"He that would eat the kernel must crack the nut."

It echoes with the Chinese saying:

"He that would travel a thousand miles must make the first step."

I believe that if we get down to business and take solid steps, China-Scotland business cooperation will enjoy a more promising and sweet future.

Talking about "sweet", I cannot help thinking about Tiantian and Yangguang, the two famous guests from China who have been living in the Edinburgh Zoo for the past six years. Interestingly, Tiantian in the Chinese language means sweetie.

So, with the cuddly, sweet pandas in mind, I sincere hope that China-Scotland business cooperation will bear more "sweet fruits" for China-UK relations and the people of China and Scotland will enjoy a happy and "sweet" life.

Now I would like to propose a toast,

To the future of China-Scotland cooperation,
And to the health of everyone present here tonight,
Cheers!

抓住"宝贵机遇",推进贵州对英合作 *

尊敬的贵州省省长谌贻琴女士,
尊敬的英中贸易协会主席沙逊勋爵,
尊敬的英国中部引擎联盟主席庄贝恩爵士,
各位来宾,
女士们、先生们、朋友们:
大家上午好!

很高兴出席"贵州全球推介活动——走进英国"活动,这是中国外交部和中国驻英国大使馆第一次与国内省市在海外联合举办的全球推介活动。我谨代表中国驻英国大使馆,对远道而来的谌贻琴省长一行及各界英国嘉宾表示热烈的欢迎!

2018年是中国改革开放40周年,在伦敦举办贵州省全球推介活动,既展示了贵州发展成果,拓展贵州对外合作,又展现了中国改革开放成就,可谓恰逢其时。

"贵州"顾名思义,意为"宝贵的地方"。把汉字"贵"拆开,可以解读为"中国的一个宝贝"。回顾历史,两千多年前,穿越云贵高原的"南方丝绸之路""茶马古道",将产自中国的丝绸、茶叶源源不断地运往南亚大陆,成为当时中国同世界互联互通的重要通道。

---

* 在"贵州全球推介活动——走进英国"活动上的讲话。2018年4月25日,伦敦地标酒店。

今天的贵州依然是中国的"一方宝地"。近年来，贵州依托"一带一路"连接线的区位优势，成为中国新一轮改革开放的排头兵，走出了一条民族团结、生态优先、创新发展的新路。我认为，贵州之"贵"，集中体现在以下四个方面。

第一，贵州是改革开放的缩影。推动区域协调发展，是中国深化改革、扩大开放的重要目标之一。随着中国全方位对外开放和"一带一路"建设向纵深发展，贵州独特优势和发展潜能不断释放。近年来，贵州综合实力显著提升，经济增速连续5年位居中国第二，2017年居全国第一，GDP增速达10.2%。

第二，贵州是精准扶贫的典范。作为中国脱贫攻坚战的主战场，贵州实施"大扶贫战略行动"，创新精准扶贫机制和举措，脱贫成效位居中国各省前列。2012—2017年，贵州贫困人口减少近800万，相当于整个大伦敦地区的人口。

第三，贵州是民族团结的样板。贵州是多民族聚居省份，有18个世居民族，少数民族占全省人口的36%，民族自治地方占全省面积的55%。贵州各民族团结协作、和谐共处、融合发展，形成了"各美其美，美美与共"的良好发展格局。

第四，贵州是创新发展的先锋。贵州坚持创新驱动发展，推进大数据、山地旅游等新兴产业发展，打造了"三大试验区"，即国家大数据综合试验区、国家生态文明试验区和内陆开放型经济试验区，聚集了强大的发展潜能。

近年来，贵州同英国的交流与合作势头喜人，这块"风水宝地"日益成为中英关系的"点金石"。双方企业和研究机构在大数据、新能源、创新科技、旅游等广泛领域开展合作，取得丰硕成果。贵州的大数据产业、山地自然风光、茅台酒、绣娘、生态文明论坛以及位于平塘的世界最大天文射电望远镜，被越来越多的英国民众知晓和关注。我非常高兴于2017年9月在中国驻英国大使馆举行"编织梦想——中国手工艺文化时装秀"活动，向英国各界人士介绍贵州少数民族文化的独特魅力和风采。

展望未来，我对贵州取得更大发展充满信心，对贵州在中英关系中发挥更加"宝贵"的作用充满期待。为进一步推动贵州与英国的合作，我有三点建议。

一是把握中英关系的"宝贵机遇"，加强发展战略对接。当前，中英两国地方合作面临重大机遇。中共十九大报告提出，加大西部开放力度，推进西部大开发形成新格局。英方正在推进英格兰"中部引擎"和"北部经济中心"等区域振兴计划，为打造"全球化英国"提供助力。双方可加强发展战略和政策对接，为双方各领域务实合作注入新动力。

二是挖掘双方优势互补的"宝贵潜力"，打造务实合作增长点。英国在科技创新、金融、新能源、旅游等领域具有较强实力和独特优势。贵州正加速实施大数据、大生态、大旅游等发展战略，积极推进"三个试验区"建设。双方可在大数据、金融、科技创新、绿色经济、旅游等重点领域加强合作，实现优势互补和共同发展。

三是利用贵州对外开放的"宝贵平台"，深化"一带一路"合作。英国在金融、法律、咨询、管理等领域经验丰富，是"一带一路"建设的天然合作伙伴。贵州是中国西部地区数据、交通和物流枢纽，正加紧打造服务"一带一路"共建国家的数据"聚、通、用"基地。双方可在"一带一路"合作框架下，利用"数博会""贵洽会"、生态文明贵阳国际论坛等平台，推动"一带一路"合作不断取得新成果。

不久前，习近平主席在博鳌亚洲论坛年会上发表主旨演讲，宣布了一系列扩大开放新举措，描绘了中国改革开放新前景，再次传递出中国同世界合作共赢的明确信息。

女士们、先生们，

"一滴水可以反映出太阳的光辉，一个地方可以体现一个国家的风貌。"贵州就是这样一个致力开放合作、闪耀璀璨光芒的宝地，就是不断发展进步的新时代中国的缩影。我衷心希望，越来越多的英国朋友关注贵州、走进贵州、热爱贵州，通过贵州更全面、更深入地了解新时代的中国。我也希望并相信，贵州一定会为中英互利合作增光添彩，为两国人民世代友好添砖加瓦!

最后,我预祝"贵州全球推介活动——走进英国"活动圆满成功!祝谌贻琴省长访英满载而归!

谢谢大家!

Seize the "Precious Opportunity" and Advance Guizhou-UK Cooperation[*]

Governor Shen Yiqin,

Lord Sassoon,

Sir John,

Distinguished Guests,

Ladies and Gentlemen,

Dear Friends,

Good morning!

It is a real delight to join you in welcoming the "Guizhou Going Global" event to the UK.

This is the first ever overseas promotion jointly hosted by the Chinese Foreign Ministry, the Chinese Embassy and a provincial government from China.

On behalf of the Chinese Embassy in the UK, I would like to begin by extending my warmest welcome to Governor Shen Yiqin and her delegation for coming all the way from China, as well as the distinguished guests representing various sectors in Britain.

I think the timing of this event is excellent.

- This year marks the 40th anniversary of the Chinese reform and opening-up policy.
- This is a good time to showcase Guizhou's achievements and expand its overseas cooperation.

---

[*] Speech at the Event of "Guizhou Going Global—the United Kingdom." The Landmark London, 25 April 2018.

- This is also a good opportunity to tell the success story of the Chinese reform and opening-up.

Guizhou in the Chinese language means "precious province". The character "Gui" is composed of elements that are interpreted as "a treasure of China". Guizhou has certainly lived up to its name.

Two thousand years ago, the "Southern Silk Road" and the "Ancient Tea-Horse Trail" on the Yunnan-Guizhou Plateau were important routes connecting China with the rest of the world. Via these routes, Chinese silk and tea found their way into South Asian subcontinent.

Today, this "precious province" is leveraging its strategic location on the Belt and Road routes.

- It has become a pioneer in the Chinese new round of reform and opening-up.
- It is where different ethnic groups live in harmony.
- It gives priority to the preservation of the eco-system.
- And its development is driven by innovation.

Let me give you four reasons why Guizhou is "precious".

First, Guizhou is an epitome of the Chinese reform and opening-up.

An important goal of deeper reform and further opening-up in China is promoting coordinated development between different regions. Guizhou's achievements testify to the attainment of this goal.

As China opens up on all fronts and deepens the Belt and Road development, Guizhou is showing unique strengths and huge potential. In recent years, Guizhou has significantly improved its comprehensive strengths. It had been one of the top two fastest growing provinces in China for five years in a row. And in 2017 it led the country in GDP growth rate with an increase of 10.2%.

Second, Guizhou is a model for targeted poverty alleviation.

Guizhou is the main battlefield in the Chinese fight against poverty. To win this battle, Guizhou has launched a massive strategic plan to reduce poverty. This includes new mechanisms and measures to achieve targeted poverty alleviation.

The result is encouraging. Guizhou has become one of the most successful provinces in poverty reduction. From 2012 to 2017, nearly eight million people, about the size of Greater London's population, have been lifted out of poverty.

Third, Guizhou is an exemplar of ethnic unity.

This province is home to 18 ethnic groups who have lived here for generations. Ethnic minorities account for 36% of the total population. And 55% of the localities enjoy ethnic autonomy.

The various ethnic groups in Guizhou respect the traditions of each other while maintaining their own. They live in harmony and work together for integrated development.

Fourth, Guizhou is a pioneer of innovation-driven development.

To promote innovation-driven development, Guizhou has focused on emerging industries such as big data and mountain tourism. It has gathered enormous potential for future development by setting up pilot zones for big data, ecological preservation and inland open economy.

In recent years, there has been a sound momentum in the exchanges and cooperation between Guizhou and the UK. This "precious province" is making greater contribution to China-UK relations.

Companies and research institutions from Guizhou and the UK have engaged in extensive cooperation and harvested fruitful results in areas ranging from big data and innovation technology to new energy and tourism.

Many "brand names" of Guizhou are gaining increasing recognition and interest here in the UK. These include nature tourism, Maotai the famous liquor and traditional crafts by seamstresses. These also include the Guizhou Eco Forum Global, big data industry and the world's largest radio telescope.

I am happy to have contributed personally to the exchanges between Guizhou and the UK by introducing Guizhou's charming ethnic culture to Britain at the "Weaving a Dream" Fashion Show I hosted at the Chinese Embassy last September.

Looking forward, I am full of confidence and expectations for Guizhou to make even greater achievements and play a more "precious" role in China-UK relations.

Here I would like to share with you three suggestions on advancing the cooperation between Guizhou and the UK.

First, the two sides should seize the "precious opportunity" arising from their matching development strategies.

Right now, China and the UK face huge opportunities for cooperation at the subnational level.

The 19th National Congress of the Communist Party of China decided to further open up the western region in order to map a new layout for the Chinese great western development.

The UK government is implementing regional development strategies, such as the "Midlands Engine for Growth" and the "Northern Powerhouse", while at the same time building a "global Britain".

There is an obvious match between these development strategies and policies which, if well leveraged, could create new impetus for cooperation across the board.

Second, the two sides should tap the "precious potential" of their comparative strengths to foster growth points in their cooperation.

The UK has unique strengths in scientific and technological innovation, financial services, new energy and tourism.

Guizhou is accelerating the implementation of strategic plans on big data, ecological preservation and tourism while actively building the three pilot zones.

The two sides could tap the great potential of their comparative strengths to achieve common development in all these areas.

Third, the two sides should make full use of the "precious opening-up platform" of Guizhou to deepen cooperation on the Belt and Road Initiative.

The UK, with its rich experience in financial and legal services, consultancy and management, is a natural partner of China for Belt and Road development.

Guizhou is a hub of data, transportation and logistics in the western part of China. It is building a centre of data collection, analysis and utilization that will serve BRI partners.

The two sides can engage in cooperation on the Belt and Road Initiative through such platforms as the Big Data Expo, the Eco Forum Global and the Cross-Border Investment and Trade Fair of the Guizhou Inland Opening-up Pilot Economic Zone. This could lead to great outcomes in Belt and Road cooperation.

Earlier this month, President Xi gave a keynote speech to the Annual Conference

2018 of the Boao Forum for Asia. He announced new measures to further open up the Chinese market and outlined the prospects of renewed reform and opening-up in China. This is a clear-cut affirmation of the Chinese continued commitment to win-win cooperation with the world.

Ladies and Gentlemen,

Just as the sunshine is reflected in a drop of water, a country can be epitomized by the work of a province.

Guizhou is such a province. It is committed to opening-up and cooperation. It is a fine example of China that is making constant progress in the new era.

I sincerely hope that more and more British friends will take an interest in Guizhou, and better still, visit Guizhou to see the place with your own eyes. You will fall in love with this "precious province". And you are sure to gain a more comprehensive and deeper understanding of China in the new era.

I also hope and believe that Guizhou will contribute its part to China-UK cooperation and to the ever-lasting friendship between the people of our two countries.

In conclusion, I wish the "Guizhou Going Global" event great success, and I wish Governor Shen a fruitful visit in the UK!

Thank you!

打造改革开放新高地，助力中英关系新发展 *

女士们、先生们、朋友们：

大家上午好！

很高兴出席海南自贸区伦敦综合推介会。

海南简称"琼"，意为美玉。海南省风景如画、气候宜人，堪称中国南部边陲的一块美玉。2018年是中国改革开放40周年，也是海南建省办经济特区30周年。经过30年砥砺奋进，海南省已发展成为中国最大的经济特区，也是唯一省级经济特区，海南这块美玉正在焕发夺目的光彩。

尤其令人振奋的是，2018年4月，习近平主席宣布在海南建设自由贸易试验区，探索建设中国特色自由贸易港，这对于海南省乃至中国未来发展都具有重大而深远的战略意义。

第一，彰显了中国对外开放新担当。中国正积极打造更高层次的开放型经济，推动构建更全面、更深入、更多元的对外开放新格局。习近平主席在博鳌亚洲论坛年会上向全世界宣示了中国进一步扩大开放的重大举措，此后第三天即宣布了海南建设自贸区和自贸港的重要决定。这是中国落实扩大对外开放承诺的有力举措，体现了中国支持自由贸易、推进经济全球化的坚定决心，展现了重诺笃行的大国担当。

第二，探索全面深化改革新经验。海南因改革开放而生，也因改革开放而兴。敢闯敢试、敢为人先、埋头苦干的精神已经深深融入海南人民的血

---

* 在海南自贸区伦敦综合推介会上的主旨演讲。2018年7月13日，伦敦地标酒店。

液。海南自贸区和自贸港的建设，将为海南加快经济转型升级、推进体制机制改革提供新机遇。海南也将继续发挥改革开放试验田的先行先试作用，为中国继续大力深化改革、推动经济高质量发展提供可复制、可推广的经验。

第三，助力海南开放发展新飞跃。改革开放和建省设特区以来，海南已成功打造了国际旅游岛、热带农业基地和医疗旅游先行区等响亮品牌，一年一度的博鳌亚洲论坛更是海南享誉世界的亮丽名片。三十而立，蓄势待发。海南建设自贸区和自贸港，是时代赋予海南改革开放的新使命，将为海南开放发展及参与"一带一路"建设注入新的强大动力，为建设更美好的新海南提供强大支撑。

女士们、先生们，

英国和海南虽然远隔重洋，但都拥有同样的胜景。英国人说自己是"陆地尽头"，海南人称自己是"天涯海角"。这说明，中英两国人民都有海纳百川的广阔胸襟、放眼四海的广博胸怀和勇立潮头的拼搏精神。英国素以贸易立国，正在实施"全球化英国"战略，积极拓展对外贸易投资合作。海南作为中国最开放、最具活力的地区之一，正致力于打造全面深化改革开放的新标杆。海南自由贸易试验区和自由贸易港建设，将为中英合作带来新机遇。为推动海南与英国合作迈上新台阶，我有三点建议。

一是以海南自贸区和自贸港建设为引擎，推进务实合作。海南自贸区和自贸港是中国进一步扩大开放的先行者，实行高水平贸易和投资便利化政策，开放层次更高、营商环境更优、辐射作用更强。英国一向敢为人先，善抓机遇。欢迎英国工商界抢占先机，积极参与海南自贸区和自贸港建设，到海南投资兴业，到海南分享机遇。

二是以海南发展三大主导产业为核心，打造合作亮点。海南自贸区将立足实际，以旅游业、现代服务业、高新技术产业为重点，加快培育生物科技、医疗健康、海洋经济、空间科技等新兴产业，着力发展创新型经济。英国在上述领域具有较强实力和独特优势，双方应进一步对接发展战略，优先推进相关领域合作。昨天，海南三亚至伦敦直飞航线正式开通，这将为海南与英国交流与合作提供更多便利。

三是以"一带一路"为平台，挖掘合作潜力。海南是建设 21 世纪海上丝绸之路的重要节点，与共建国家在农业、旅游、环境保护、蓝色经济等领域合作潜力巨大。英国在金融、法律、咨询和管理等领域经验丰富。双方可积极探讨合作项目，为中英"一带一路"合作添砖加瓦。

海南有一首动听的民歌《请到天涯海角来》，歌曲讲述了海南的美好时节。我希望并相信，随着海南自贸区和自贸港建设不断取得新进展，海南将不仅为中国改革开放打造新高地，也将进一步拉近两个"天涯海角"的距离，为深化中英务实合作贡献力量，为推进中英关系增光添彩！

最后，我预祝海南自贸区伦敦综合推介会圆满成功！

谢谢大家！

A New High Ground of Reform and Opening-up, a New Contribution to China-UK Relations*

Ladies and Gentlemen,

Dear Friends,

Good morning!

It is a real delight to join you at the 2018 Hainan Free Trade Zone (London) Promotion.

Hainan is known as "Qiong" for short, meaning "beautiful jade". With its picturesque scenery and warm climate, this southern frontier province definitely lives up to its reputation.

This year marks the 40th anniversary of the Chinese reform and opening-up policy. It is also the 30th anniversary of the establishment of Hainan province and special economic zone, the largest and only provincial level SEZ in China. The past thirty years of strenuous efforts have given this beautiful jade a dazzling shine.

What is more significant and exciting is that President Xi Jinping announced in April that Hainan was to establish a pilot free trade zone and explore the building of a free trade port. This will have a strategic and far-reaching impact on the future development of Hainan province and even the whole of China.

First of all, this is a demonstration of the Chinese renewed courage to open up wider

---

* Keynote Speech at the 2018 Hainan Free Trade Zone (London) Promotion. The Landmark London, 13 July 2018.

to the world.

China is building an upgraded version of an open economy. That means we are working on a more comprehensive, substantial and diverse structure of opening-up.

This decision to build a pilot free trade zone and a free trade port in Hainan came only three days after President Xi Jinping announced in Boao that China would take important measures to open up further to the world.

- Therefore, it became a major step of China to live up to the promise of further opening-up.
- It demonstrates the Chinese firm resolve to uphold free trade and promote economic globalization.
- It also shows that China, as a big country, means what we say. We honour our commitment with concrete actions.

Second, this is a new experiment with deeper reform on all fronts.

Hainan was born of reform and has prospered with opening-up. The audacious, enterprising and down-to-earth spirit runs in the blood of the people of Hainan.

The building of a pilot free trade zone and free trade port will create new opportunities for Hainan to upgrade its economy and to reform its institutional structure. Hainan will continue to serve as a "testing ground" for reform and opening-up. This is aimed at exploring effective approaches to deeper reform and higher-quality growth. These approaches can then be introduced to the rest of the country.

Third, this is a fresh impetus for the opening-up and development of Hainan.

Since becoming a province and a special economic zone, Hainan has made its name in a number of areas.

- It is an international tourist resort.
- It is a tropical agricultural base.
- It is a medical tourism pilot zone.
- In particular, the annual conference of the Boao Forum for Asia has helped spread Hainan's name all over the world.

Confucius said, "At 30, one has established himself." Now the 30-year-old Hainan province is ready to take up its new mission of reform and opening-up in the new era.

- Building a pilot free trade zone and a free trade port will inject fresh and strong impetus to the opening-up and development of Hainan.
- This will strengthen Hainan's position in the Belt and Road development.
- This will also become a strong pillar for building a more beautiful Hainan.

Ladies and Gentlemen,

Britain and Hainan are separated by vast oceans. But the similarity between their popular scenic spots make the two mirror images of each other. Here, the British people call theirs "Land's End". In Hainan, people call theirs "End of Sky and Ocean".

Both "Ends" have breathtaking views. Both peoples have inclusive mind, broad vision and pioneering spirit.

The UK has built the nation on trade. It is working to fulfill the vision of a "global Britain" by expanding foreign trade and investment.

Hainan is one of the most open and dynamic regions in China. By building the pilot free trade zone and free trade port, Hainan is committed to setting a new benchmark for all-round and deepening reform and opening-up in China. This will create new opportunities for cooperation between Hainan and the UK.

So, what should we do to take Hainan-UK cooperation to a new level? Here are my three thoughts.

First, the building of the pilot free trade zone and free trade port in Hainan could be the new engine to drive business cooperation.

This is a pilot project to experiment with further opening-up of the Chinese market.

- There will be policies to enhance trade and investment facilitation.
- As a result, Hainan will open up to the world at a higher level.
- It will be more business-friendly.
- Its experience will have a stronger and more extensive influence throughout the country.

British people are known for daring to be a pioneer and having keen eyes for opportunities. I therefore encourage the British businesses to play a leading and active part in building the pilot free trade zone and free trade port in Hainan. I hope you will take your business to Hainan and seize your share of the opportunities.

Second, the three pillars for Hainan's development should be the focus for cooperation.

In building the pilot free trade zone, Hainan will concentrate on its natural endowment, give priority to tourism, modern services and high-tech industries, and build an innovative economy. To be more specific, emerging sectors such as bio-technology, health and medical care, ocean economy and space technology will be the focus of accelerated efforts.

The UK has considerable strengths and a unique competitive edge in all these sectors. The two sides should strive to match their development strategies and identify the priorities for advancing their cooperation.

Yesterday, direct flight between Sanya of Hainan Province and London was launched. I am sure this will facilitate closer exchanges and cooperation between Hainan and the UK.

Third, the Belt and Road Initiative offers a platform to tap the potential for cooperation.

Hainan is an important hub on the 21st Century Maritime Silk Road. There is a huge potential for cooperation between Hainan and the BRI partners. The areas for such cooperation include agriculture, tourism, environmental protection and "blue economy".

The UK, with rich expertise in financial service, legal affairs, consultancy and management, could provide the services needed in specific projects. This will in turn contribute to the overall cooperation between China and the UK on the Belt and Road Initiative.

Ladies and Gentlemen,

A pop song from the early 1980s described the beauty of Hainan. The title of this song is *Welcome to the End of Sky and Ocean*.

With this song in mind, I hope and believe that Hainan's free trade zone and free trade port will make this province a new high ground for the Chinese reform and opening-up.

This will shorten the distance between "Land's End" and "End of Sky and Ocean".

This will strengthen the business cooperation between China and the UK.

This will be a great contribution to China-UK relations!

In conclusion, I wish the 2018 Hainan Free Trade Zone (London) Promotion great success!

Thank you!

推动新时代中英地方合作迈上新台阶 *

金秋十月，丹桂飘香。我谨代表中国驻英国大使馆，向第四届中英地方领导人会议在"北方明珠"大连召开表示热烈祝贺！

中英地方领导人会议机制自 2016 年建立以来有效运转，成果丰硕，为促进两国地方交流合作、推动中英关系发展发挥了重要作用。当今世界正处于百年未有之大变局，全球力量格局深刻调整，国际经济贸易形势复杂多变，逆全球化、单边主义、保护主义日益抬头，英国"脱欧"不确定性增大。这些因素给中英地方合作带来不少挑战。

同时，我们更要看到，中英地方合作面临诸多难得机遇。中英双方正在更大范围、更高水平、更深层次推动互利合作。随着中国特色社会主义进入新时代，中国对外开放的步伐不断加快，对外开放的大门越开越大。在"脱欧"背景下，英国致力于打造"全球化英国"，加快构建全球贸易关系新网络。英国视自己为"一带一路"天然合作伙伴，中英"一带一路"合作方兴未艾。这些机遇必将助力两国地方合作开辟新空间，注入新动力，迈上新台阶。

我衷心希望，中英两国地方领导人抓住机遇，化解挑战，以更广阔的全球视野、更积极的主动作为、更强烈的责任担当，共同打造中英地方合作"四大新亮点"。

一是以地方领导人会议为支撑点，用好中英战略对接新机遇。当前，中

---

* 致第四届中英地方领导人会议的贺词。2018 年 10 月 17 日，辽宁省大连市。

国积极实施区域协调发展战略，英国提出"英格兰北方经济中心""英格兰中部引擎"等规划。双方可通过中英地方领导人会议和地方经贸联委会等机制，深入了解彼此发展战略，加强政策对接，为双方企业合作提供更优质的环境和更便利的条件。

二是以互补优势为着眼点，拓展中英务实合作新渠道。英国是世界高科技、高附加值产业的重要研发中心，中国则拥有强大制造能力和巨大市场。双方可强强联合，进一步推进在能源、金融、创新、汽车制造、基础设施建设等领域合作，挖掘人工智能、绿色经济、共享经济等新产业、新业态合作潜力，积极探索开展第三方合作。

三是以特色项目为着力点，开创中英互利共赢新局面。每年数十个中国省市代表团赴英举办经贸推介活动，广交会、生态文明贵阳国际论坛等也为双方合作搭建了有效平台。2018年英方将派高级别代表团参加首届中国国际进口博览会、北京世界园艺博览会等活动。双方应充分用好各自优势，打造具有地方特色的旗舰项目，推动《中英科技创新合作战略》在地方层面落地，促成更多高质量、高水平的合作项目。

四是以人文交流为立足点，积蓄中英友好交流新能量。地方是中英人文交流的生力军，也是两国合作成果惠及民众的最前沿。今后，双方应进一步深化创意产业、文化遗产保护、旅游和艺术节庆等合作，促进地方文化、旅游、教育交流机制化、常态化，为两国民众带来更多实实在在的福祉。

中英关系发展得益于两国地方和民众的支持，未来更要依靠地方、扎根地方、造福地方。中国驻英国大使馆愿继续发挥桥梁和纽带作用，不断为中英地方合作提供有力支持和全方位服务。我们将与大家携手努力，共同推动新时代中英地方合作不断迈上新台阶！

最后，预祝第四届中英地方领导人会议圆满成功！

Take China-UK Subnational Cooperation to a New Level [*]

On behalf of the Chinese Embassy in the UK, I would like to extend warm congratulations on the Fourth China-UK Regional Leaders' Summit convened auspiciously in the golden month of October. Let me welcome all of you to Dalian, the "pearl of Northern China".

Since the first gathering in 2016, China-UK regional leaders' meetings has grown into an effective platform and produced fruitful results. It has played an important role in advancing exchanges and cooperation between local authorities as well as bilateral relations between China and the UK.

Today, the world is experiencing profound changes unseen in a century: Deep adjustment in the international landscape, complex and volatile economic and trade situation, surging anti-globalisation, unilateralism and protectionism, and rising uncertainties in Brexit. But we must not let these severe challenges take our attention away from the opportunities for China-UK subnational cooperation.

China-UK relations have been shifted to a higher gear, promising wider, higher and deeper cooperation that benefits both sides. As socialism with Chinese characteristics enters a new era, China has accelerated and expanded its opening-up. As Britain leaves the EU, it aims to build a "global Britain" and seeks to accelerate the building of a new global network of trade relations. On the Belt and Road Initiative, the UK sees itself as a "natural partner" of China, and China-UK cooperation on the BRI is thriving. All

---

[*] Message of Congratulations to the Fourth China-UK Regional Leaders' Summit. Dalian, Liaoning Province, 17 October 2018.

these are opportunities that will open up new prospects and give new impetus to local government cooperation between our two countries and take it to a new level.

I sincerely hope that local government leaders of our two countries will seize the opportunities and deal with the challenges. I hope, with a global perspective, with more proactive actions and with a greater sense of responsibility, you will advance China-UK subnational cooperation in the following four aspects.

First, maximise the Regional Leaders' Summit to dovetail the development strategies of our two countries and create new opportunities of growth.

China is seeking to balance domestic development between different regions. For the same purpose, the UK has proposed plans such as the "Northern Powerhouse" and the "Midlands Engine for Growth". This Summit, together with China-UK Joint Economic and Trade Commission, provides an excellent platform for the two sides to deepen understanding of each other's development strategies and dovetail relevant plans so as to create a better environment for business cooperation.

Second, tap the comparative strengths of China and the UK to explore new avenues of business cooperation.

The UK is an important R&D centre of high-tech and high value-added industries. China has strong manufacturing capability and a huge market. The two sides could dovetail these strengths in order to advance cooperation on energy, finance, innovation, automobile manufacturing and infrastructure development. You could tap the potential of cooperation in new industries and new business models such as artificial intelligence, green economy and sharing economy. You could also explore cooperation with a third party.

Third, initiate flagship projects to open up a new prospect of win-win cooperation.

There are already many effective channels of cooperation between our two sides, including the China Import and Export Fair and the Eco Forum Global Guiyang. In addition, Chinese provincial- or municipal-level delegations conduct dozens of trade promotion visits to the UK every year. And this year, high-level British delegations will participate in the Beijing International Horticultural Exposition and the first-ever China International Import Expo. Local authorities should pool your strengths to build some high-quality, high-level flagship projects with local features. This could be done through implementing the China-UK Joint Strategy for Science, Technology and

Innovation Cooperation at the subnational level, and local government leaders have a pivotal role to play.

Fourth, let cultural and people-to-people exchanges give new impetus to China-UK friendship.

Cultural and people-to-people exchanges are most active at the subnational level and they deliver outcomes directly to the people. Going forward, local governments of both countries should deepen cooperation on creative industry, tourism, art festivals and protection of cultural heritages, and enhance institutional and regular cultural, tourism and education exchanges between the regions of our two countries.

The development of China-UK relations needs the support of the local governments and people of our two countries. It will continue to rely on subnational level cooperation and deliver benefits to local communities.

The Chinese Embassy in the UK stands ready to serve as a bridge for such cooperation. We will continue to provide strong support and all-round services, and join hands with all of you to take China-UK subnational cooperation of the new era to a new level!

In conclusion, I wish the fourth China-UK Regional Leaders' Summit a great success!

创新引领未来，合作共谱华章 *

尊敬的湖南省省长许达哲先生，
尊敬的英国国际贸易部国务大臣费尔黑德女男爵，
尊敬的英中贸易协会主席沙逊勋爵，
尊敬的四十八家集团俱乐部主席佩里先生，
女士们、先生们：
大家上午好！

很高兴出席"湖南－英国未来创新峰会"。我谨代表中国驻英国大使馆，对远道而来的许达哲省长一行表示热烈欢迎！

创新是一个民族进步的灵魂，也是推动国与国关系发展的动力。本次会议以"创新"为主题，可谓恰逢其时。刚刚结束的中国两会，通过了新一年《政府工作报告》，明确了2019年工作基本思路和主要任务，其中创新就是重点之一。中国将深入实施创新驱动发展战略，大力优化创新生态，提升创新能力和效率，把大众创业、万众创新进一步引向深入。

2019年是中英建立代办级外交关系65周年。65年来，开拓创新、敢为人先始终是中英关系的一大特点。"湖南－英国未来创新峰会"会聚两国各界精英，让大家共享机遇、共商合作、共话未来，是对65周年最有意义的庆祝。

女士们、先生们、朋友们，

湖南省和英国的面积及人口相当，都素以勇于探索、敢于创新而闻名，

---

* 在"湖南－英国未来创新峰会"上的讲话。2019年3月28日，伦敦朗廷酒店。

双方创新合作潜力巨大。

第一，湖南和英国都是孕育先驱精神的摇篮。湖南人杰地灵、英雄辈出，不仅素有"湖广熟，天下足"的美誉，也久负"惟楚有材，于斯为盛"的盛名。湖南是新中国缔造者毛泽东主席的家乡，中国近代"开眼看世界"第一人魏源、近代化建设开拓者曾国藩都出自湖南。"杂交水稻之父"袁隆平也是从湖南走向全国，走向世界。许达哲省长曾在航天领域工作多年，获得过中国国家科技进步特等奖，曾当选国际宇航科学院院士，他本人就是这种先驱精神的杰出代表。

英国是工业革命的发源地，具有深厚的科技传统和独特的创新文化，培育了瓦特、牛顿、焦耳、达尔文、亚当·斯密、罗素等一大批享誉全球的科学家和思想家，在世界上产生了广泛而深刻的影响。

第二，湖南和英国都是践行创新精神的典范。近年来，湖南大力发展创新产业，诞生了运算速度最快的天河巨型计算机、速度最快的列车牵引电传动系统、最长的臂架混凝土泵车、起重能力最强的履带起重机、最大功率的六轴电力机车等多项"世界第一"的创新性高技术产品。

英国政府高度重视科学和创新，将其置于长期经济发展规划的核心。据统计，英国大学和研究机构的产出在发达国家中首屈一指。在世界知识产权组织发布的2018年全球创新指数排行榜上，英国稳居全球第三。2018年11月在上海举办的首届中国国际进口博览会上，以"非凡创新在英国"为主题的英国国家馆，再次向世界展示了英国的创新实力。

第三，湖南和英国都是富有合作精神的伙伴。湖南与英国在经贸、科技等领域已经开展了广泛而深入的合作。2018年湘英进出口贸易总额达6.8亿美元。截至2018年底，湖南实际使用英国外资达2.2亿美元，对英合同投资总额达1.3亿美元。

我高兴地看到，中车株洲电力机车研究所在英国设立了半导体研发中心和电气传动技术研究中心，湘潭电机股份有限公司与英国加勒德哈森伙伴有限公司合作研制2兆瓦以上低风速直驱式风力发电机组。越来越多的湖南企业积极寻求与英国加强科技创新合作。

女士们、先生们、朋友们，

展望未来，我们对中英和湘英在创新领域的合作充满期待，也充满信心。为进一步深化双方合作，我有三点建议。

一是纲举目张，加强战略对接。2017年底，中英共同发布了《中英科技创新合作战略》，为两国深化创新合作规划了蓝图。双方可进一步以《中英科技创新合作战略》为指引，加强中国创新驱动发展战略与英国促进增长的科学与创新战略、产业发展战略等对接，做好中英创新合作的顶层设计。同时利用好中英科技创新合作联委会、中英研究和创新伙伴基金、年度旗舰挑战计划、中英创意产业园等创新合作平台，让战略规划真正落地生根。

二是守正创新，深化产业合作。英国正大力实施产业发展战略，积极推进人工智能、健康和老龄化、绿色增长、文化创意等领域的创新发展与国际合作。湖南有很好的产业基础，产业门类齐全，产值过千亿元的产业多达11个，不仅工程机械、轨道交通等传统优势产业稳步推进，文化创意、电子信息、电子商务、服务外包等新兴产业发展迅猛。双方可结合各自发展需求和产业优势，明确优先合作领域和重点项目，在绿色制造、环境保护、医疗信息化服务、高端装备制造、高等教育资源合作等领域探讨加强合作。

三是深耕人脉，依托地方合作。中英创新合作的根基在地方、在人民。2018年10月，湖南省与林肯郡签署了友好省市协议。双方可更多地分享城市发展经验，探讨城市升级改造合作，推动可持续城镇化合作，建设绿色、智慧、包容性未来城市。湖南还可与英国其他地方加强沟通与合作，促进互联互通与联动发展。

女士们、先生们、朋友们，

中国北宋湖南籍著名思想家周敦颐曾说，"天下，势而已矣。势，轻重也。极重不可反"。创新才能发展，合作才能共赢，这就是当今世界不可逆转的大趋势。我坚信，只要中英双方开拓创新、锐意进取、深耕合作，就一定能为两国人民带来更多实实在在的利益，就一定能开创中英关系更加美好的未来！

最后，祝"湖南－英国未来创新峰会"取得圆满成功！

谢谢！

Cooperation on Innovation Leads to a Bright Future*

Governor Xu,

Baroness Fairhead,

Lord Sassoon,

Chairman Perry,

Ladies and Gentlemen,

Good morning!

It is a real delight to join you at the Hunan-UK Future Innovation Summit. On behalf of the Chinese Embassy in the UK, let me begin by extending a warm welcome to Governor Xu and his delegation!

Innovation is the soul of a nation's progress. It is the force behind the growth of state-to-state relations. It is timely that today's Summit focuses on innovation.

At the just concluded sessions of the National People's Congress of China and the National Committee of the Chinese People's Political Consultative Conference, the Report on the Work of the Government 2019 was adopted. In the basic plans and main tasks outlined in the Report, innovation is one of the priorities.

This means China will pursue innovation-driven development.

- By fostering an environment that is innovation-friendly.
- By improving our capacity and efficiency at innovation.
- And by encouraging private sector startups and innovation.

---

* Speech at the Hunan-UK Future Innovation Summit. The Langham, London, 28 March 2019.

This year marks the 65th anniversary of the establishment of China-UK diplomatic relationship at the level of chargé d'affaires. The most prominent characteristic of China-UK relations over the past 65 years has been our innovative and pioneering spirit.

What better way to celebrate this anniversary than with a Summit that focuses on future innovation—a Summit that brings together the best minds of all areas from both our two countries to explore the opportunities for future cooperation.

Ladies and Gentlemen,

Dear Friends,

Hunan Province and the UK are similar in size and population. Like the British, the people of Hunan are known for their pioneering and innovative spirit. There is great potential for the two sides to engage in cooperation on innovation.

First, both Hunan and the UK are cradles of great people with a pioneering spirit.

Hunan has been a land of abundance and the birthplace of great people. As the Chinese sayings go,

- When the provinces of Hunan and Hubei have a bumper harvest, there would be enough food for the whole country.
- And There is no other place which boasts so many talented people like the State of Chu—an ancient name for Hunan.

Hunan is the birthplace of:

- Mao Zedong, the founding father of the People's Republic of China.
- Wei Yuan, the first Chinese in modern times who "opened his eyes to see the world".
- And Zeng Guofan, the pioneer of the Chinese modern society.

Hunan is also the place where Yuan Longping, the "father of hybrid rice", conducted most of his research work.

Governor Xu himself is an outstanding representative of such a pioneering spirit.

- He has worked in the field of aerospace for many years.

- He won the special prize of the National Science and Technology Progress Award.
- And he has been an Academician of the International Academy of Astronautics.

The UK, as the cradle of the Industrial Revolution, has a profound tradition of science and technology and a unique culture of innovation. It is the birthplace of numerous world-famous scientists and great thinkers, such as James Watt, Isaac Newton, James Joule, Charles Darwin, Adam Smith and Bertrand Russell. These pioneers have had extensive and profound influence on the world.

Second, both Hunan and the UK have taken the lead in innovation.

In recent years, Hunan has taken great efforts to encourage innovation in industrial development. It is the birthplace of many high-tech, innovative products that count as the "world's No.1." These include:

- Tianhe-1, the world's fastest supercomputer,
- the world's fastest electric train traction system,
- the world's longest concrete pump,
- the world's strongest crawler crane,
- and the world's most powerful six-axle electric locomotive.

The British government attaches great importance to science and innovation, and puts them at the core of its planning for long-term economic growth.

- According to statistics, Britain has taken the lead among developed countries in the number of research results by universities and institutions.
- It ranks the third in the Global Innovation Index 2018 Report released by the World Intellectual Property Organisation.
- And its strength in innovation was further displayed to the world at the British Pavilion, which themed on "Innovation is GREAT", at the first China International Import Expo held in Shanghai last November.

Third, both Hunan and the UK are good partners for cooperation.

The two sides have engaged in extensive and in-depth cooperation in such areas as economy, trade, science and technology. In 2018, trade between Hunan and the UK reached 680 million US dollars. By the end of 2018, Hunan was home to 220 million US dollars paid-in investment and 130 million US dollars contract investment from the UK.

I am pleased to see that a growing number of companies from Hunan are exploring opportunities to carry out more cooperation with the UK on science, technology and innovation.

- CRRC Zhuzhou Institute has established R&D centres for semiconductor and electric drive technology in the UK.
- Xiangtan Electric Manufacturing Corporation is working with Garrad Hassan and Partners Ltd. on the development of above-2 Mega-Watt Direct Drive Turbines for Low-speed Wind.

Ladies and Gentlemen,

Dear Friends,

Looking forward, I am full of expectations for China-UK and Hunan-UK cooperation on innovation. May I share with you three suggestions for further cooperation.

First, make overall planning and match development strategies.

At the end of 2017, China and the UK signed the Joint Strategy for Science, Technology and Innovation Cooperation. This serves as a blueprint for our two countries to deepen cooperation on innovation.

With the guidance of this blueprint, our two countries can tap into the synergy between our national development strategies, such as the Chinese innovation-driven development strategy and the UK's Industrial Strategy and its innovation and research strategy for growth. This will enable us to enhance top-level design for our cooperation on innovation.

At the same time, we can fully leverage our existing bilateral platforms and resources to implement our strategic plans. These platforms and resources include:

- the Joint Commission on Cooperation in Science, Technology and Innovation,

- the Research and Innovation Partnership Fund,
- the Flagship Challenge Programme,
- and the Innovation Industrial Park.

Second, explore new ways and deepen industrial cooperation.

To achieve the goals of its industrial development strategy, the UK is promoting innovation and international cooperation in areas such as artificial intelligence, health care, elderly care, green growth and cultural and creative industries.

Hunan has a sound industrial basis and complete industrial categories, eleven of which are valued at 100 billion RMB yuan. Traditional industries such as engineering machinery and rail transport are making steady progress. At the same time, emerging industries such as cultural and creative industries, telecommunications, e-commerce and service outsourcing are also growing rapidly.

Hunan and the UK can work together to identify priority areas and key projects for cooperation according to each side's development need and industrial advantages. Possible areas for further cooperation include green manufacturing, environmental protection, medical information services, high-end equipment manufacturing and higher education.

Third, enhance people-to-people exchanges and subnational cooperation.

The fundamental driving force for China-UK cooperation on innovation is in our provinces and among our people.

Last October, Hunan Province and Lincolnshire established sister relationship. This creates opportunities for the two sides to share experience and explore cooperation on urban development, upgrading, regeneration and sustainable urbanization with a view to building green, smart and inclusive cities for the future.

I encourage Hunan to enhance communication and cooperation with other regions in the UK as well to enhance connectivity and inter-connected development.

Ladies and Gentlemen,

Dear Friends,

Zhou Dunyi, a Chinese philosopher who lived in Hunan a thousand years ago, said that knowing the trend of the times leads to success. In today's world, innovation is the way to development, and cooperation can lead to win-win results. This is the irreversible trend.

I am confident that as long as China and the UK continue to forge ahead and work together on innovation, we can deliver more tangible benefits to our people, and embrace a brighter future for China-UK relations!

In conclusion, I would like to wish the Hunan-UK Future Innovation Summit a great success!

Thank you!

永立改革开放时代潮头，推进中英全面战略伙伴关系 *

尊敬的深圳市委书记王伟中先生，

尊敬的英国国际贸易部投资事务国务大臣史徒华先生，

尊敬的英中贸易协会主席沙逊勋爵，

各位来宾，

女士们、先生们：

大家下午好！

很高兴出席"深圳－伦敦经贸交流会"。我谨代表中国驻英国大使馆，对远道而来的王伟中书记和深圳市代表团表示热烈欢迎！

2018年是中国改革开放40周年。在这样一个年份举办"深圳－伦敦经贸交流会"，可谓恰逢其时。40年前，深圳只是一个"靠近香港的边陲小镇"。40年后的今天，深圳成功跻身中国一线"明星"城市，书写了具有传奇色彩的"深圳故事"。

第一，它是中国发展的"缩影"。深圳用不到40年的时间，从一个小渔村变成一座国际大都市；GDP从1979年的1.97亿元跃升至2017年的2.24万亿元，增长了1万多倍，年均增速达23%。《经济学人》杂志称，"全世界的经济特区超过4000个，头号成功典范莫过于'深圳奇迹'"。深圳诠释了中国从"站起来"到"富起来"的历史性飞跃，有力地证明了中国特色社会主义道路是一条正确之路、成功之路。

---

* 在"深圳－伦敦经贸交流会"上的讲话。2018年6月11日，希尔顿伦敦帕丁顿酒店。

第二，它是改革开放的"旗帜"。40年来，深圳始终站立在中国改革开放的潮头，以"实干兴邦"的精神，以"敢为天下先"的魄力，在市场化经济体制改革中创造了1000多项"全国第一"。近年来，深圳更以供给侧结构性改革为主线，以完善产权制度和要素市场化配置为重点，引领了新一轮改革开放的潮流。改革开放既是深圳实现跨越式发展的"秘诀"，也是推动新时代中国高质量发展的动力。

第三，它是开拓创新的"乐土"。深圳被誉为"创新之都"，创新已经深深融入深圳的发展基因。2017年，深圳研发投入占GDP比重超过4%，接近全球最高水平；PCT（专利合作条约）国际专利2.04万件，连续14年居中国城市第一；2017年高新技术产业增加值占GDP比重达32.8%，全球城市竞争力排名第六。未来，深圳将以创新引领超大型城市可持续发展为主题，建设国家可持续发展议程创新示范区。可以说，深圳成功之路就是开拓创新之路，也预示着中国从"富起来"走上"强起来"的康庄大道。

近年来，随着中英关系加速发展，两国地方交流合作不断深化。深圳与伦敦金融城、苏格兰地区以及英属维尔京群岛先后建立了友城关系。华为、比亚迪、招商银行等深圳企业在英国发展业绩卓越。展望未来，深圳同英国在科技创新、金融服务、创意产业、智能制造等领域合作潜力巨大，前景广阔。

深圳不仅是中国的，也是世界的。我相信，深圳不仅将继续担当中国改革开放的"排头兵"，也将成为中英互利合作的"引领者"，不断为中英关系添砖加瓦、增光添彩！

最后，预祝本次"深圳—伦敦经贸合作交流会"圆满成功！

谢谢大家！

Stay at the Forefront of Reform and Opening-up, and Contribute to China-UK Strategic Partnership*

Secretary Wang Weizhong,

Minister Graham Stuart,

Lord Sassoon,

Distinguished guests,

Ladies and Gentlemen,

Good afternoon!

I am happy to join you at the China (Shenzhen)-UK (London) Economic and Trade Cooperation Conference.

On behalf of the Chinese Embassy, I would like to extend our warm welcome to Secretary Wang Weizhong and his delegation.

This year is the 40th anniversary of reform and opening-up in China. It is a perfect year to hold this conference in London.

Forty years ago, Shenzhen was a small border town near Hong Kong. Forty years on, Shenzhen is a star of the Chinese first tier cities. This is the legendary "Shenzhen story".

Shenzhen is first of all a microcosm of the Chinese rapid development.

- Its metamorphosis from a tiny fishing village to an international metropolis took

---

* Remarks at the China(Shenzhen)-UK(London) Economic and Trade Cooperation Conference. Hilton London Paddington, 11 June 2018.

only four decades.
- Its GDP has grown by over ten thousand folds, from 197 million yuan in 1979 to 2.24 trillion yuan in 2017.
- It has sustained an average annual growth rate of 23%.

The Economist marveled at the "Miracle of Shenzhen", calling it the biggest success story of more than 4,000 SEZs. Indeed, Shenzhen is the best example of the Chinese historic leap from "getting on its feet" to "becoming prosperous". It is the best illustration that socialism with Chinese characteristics is the right path to success.

Second, Shenzhen is the standard bearer of reform and opening-up. For 40 years, Shenzhen has been at the forefront of reform and opening-up in China. With its down-to-earth and pioneering spirit, Shenzhen has created over one thousand "national firsts" in the Chinese market-oriented economic reform.

In recent years, Shenzhen is leading a new round of reform and opening-up. This centres on supply side restructuring and emphasises better property rights system and market-based allocation of factors of production.

Reform and opening-up has been the "secret" to Shenzhen's leapfrogging development. Reform and opening-up will continue to be the driving force behind the Chinese high quality growth in the new era.

Third, Shenzhen is a promised land for innovation. Shenzhen is known as the Chinese capital of innovation. The city has innovation in its genes.

Here are some highlights of 2017:

- Shenzhen invested more than 4% of its GDP in research and development, which was one of the highest in the world.
- Shenzhen filed over 20,000 international patent applications under PCT, leading all Chinese cities for the 14th consecutive year.
- Shenzhen was the 6th most competitive city in the world, with added-value of hi-tech industries accounting for 32.8% of GDP.

Going forward, Shenzhen will make innovation the focus of sustainable megacity development, and around this theme, build a national innovation demonstration zone on the sustainable development agenda.

Innovation has been Shenzhen's road to success. Innovation will also be a broad thoroughfare leading China from being prosperous to becoming stronger.

As China-UK relations accelerate, exchanges and cooperation between the two countries at the subnational level continue to deepen.

Shenzhen has forged close ties with the City of London, Scotland and the British Virgin Islands. Companies from Shenzhen, such as Huawei, BYD and China Merchants Bank, are achieving great success here in the UK.

Looking ahead, we see huge potential and broad prospects for the cooperation between Shenzhen and the UK in scientific and high-tech innovation, financial services, creative industry and AI manufacturing.

Shenzhen is not only a Chinese city. It also belongs to the world.

I am confident that Shenzhen will continue to be at the forefront of the Chinese reform and opening-up. It will also play a leading role in the mutually beneficial cooperation between our two countries, and continue to contribute its part to China-UK relations.

In conclusion, I wish China (Shenzhen)-UK (London) Economic and Trade Cooperation Conference great success!

Thank you!

高举开放旗帜，携手开创未来[*]

尊敬的大曼彻斯特地区女王代表史密斯爵士，

尊敬的曼彻斯特市长希钦女士，

女士们、先生们、朋友们：

大家晚上好！

我曾多次到访曼彻斯特，每次都有新的体会。曼城是世界上第一座工业化城市。两百多年前，正是在这里诞生了世界上最早的棉纺织大工业，拉开了工业革命的大幕。可以说，世界工业革命源于英国，英国工业革命源于曼彻斯特。曼彻斯特引领的这次"革命"深刻地改变了英国和世界。

40年前，中国也发起了一场革命。40年前的今天，也就是1978年12月18日，中共十一届三中全会隆重召开，开启了中国改革开放的伟大征程。正如习近平主席所说，"改革开放这场中国的第二次革命，不仅深刻改变了中国，也深刻影响了世界"！

40年前，中国GDP总量仅为1750亿美元，居世界第十。今天，中国GDP总量已超过12万亿美元，按不变价计算增长33.5倍，跃居世界第二。40年来，中国进出口总额增长780多倍，已成为世界最大贸易国、第一大出口国和第二大进口国，连续多年对世界经济增长贡献率超过30%，成为全球经济复苏的稳定器和动力源。40年来，中国实现7.4亿人脱贫，占全球减贫人口总数70%以上。

---

[*] 在曼彻斯特工商界晚宴上的主旨演讲。2018年12月18日，曼彻斯特阿尔伯特广场。

中国的"第二次革命"为什么能取得如此巨大成功？我认为主要有三个原因。

第一，始终以与时俱进的精神探索发展道路。改革开放没有先例可循。40年来，从农村到城市、从试点到推广、从经济体制改革到全面深化改革，中国立足国情实际和发展需要，坚持以人民为中心的工作导向，以增强人民群众幸福感、安全感和获得感为出发点和归宿点，逐步探索出一条中国特色社会主义道路。这条道路不仅从根本上改变了中国的面貌，也拓宽了发展中国家走向现代化的途径，为解决人类面临的挑战贡献了中国智慧和中国方案。

第二，始终以开放包容的姿态融入世界。开放带来进步，封闭必然落后。40年来，中国始终敞开胸襟、拥抱世界，坚持到全球化的汪洋大海中学会游泳，从"引进来"到"走出去"，从加入世贸组织到共建"一带一路"，实现了从封闭半封闭到全方位开放的伟大转折。40年来，中国对外直接投资实现从无到有，今天成为世界第二大对外投资国，海外企业资产总额超过5万亿美元，遍布全球190个国家和地区；2017年，中国实际利用外资1300多亿美元，是40年前的60多倍，成为全球第二大外资流入国。习近平主席提出构建人类命运共同体的伟大设想，展现了中国与世界各国共享发展机遇的大国担当和天下情怀。

第三，始终以互利共赢的理念推进合作。互利共赢不仅是中华传统文化的精神内核，也是推进改革开放的重大战略。中国强调，实现自身发展，绝不能以损害别国利益为代价，各国只有同舟共济，实现联动增长，才能确保合作的可持续性。2018年是习近平主席提出"一带一路"倡议5周年。"一带一路"倡议秉持共商共建共享原则，已成为世界各国互利共赢的最大合作平台。5年来，中国与"一带一路"共建国家货物贸易累计超过5万亿美元。中国对共建国家投资超过860亿美元，创造24万多个工作岗位，给当地缴纳税款几十亿美元。2019年，中国还将举办第二届"一带一路"国际合作高峰论坛，我们热烈欢迎曼彻斯特的各界朋友积极参与。

女士们、先生们，

曼城在对华合作中历来敢为人先。120年前，来自曼城的英国人立德乐第一个驾驶轮船通过三峡抵达重庆，开启了英国与中国西南地区的经贸往来。1986年，曼彻斯特率先与中国武汉结成友好城市，为两国城市交流树立了典范。进入21世纪，曼联和曼城两个足球俱乐部在引进中国足球运动员方面也走在英超俱乐部前列。

2015年，习近平主席成功访问曼城后，中国与曼城的务实合作开启了新篇章。2018年9月，伯纳姆市长率企业代表团赴天津出席夏季达沃斯论坛并访问了北京、深圳等地。截至2018年11月，中国对大曼城地区累计投资总额达25亿英镑，仅北京建工英国公司就签约了4个大型合作项目。中国多家房地产企业积极参与了北部城市房地产和基础设施建设。比亚迪公司与数个北方城市签署了电动大巴供应合作协议，帮助这些城市升级公交系统。

当前，中英两国都处于关键发展阶段。中国将进一步深化改革、扩大开放，英国也正打造"全球化英国"，拓展与世界各国的经贸关系。中国同英国特别是英格兰北部地区深化合作可谓恰逢其时、前景广阔。为进一步推进双方合作，我谨提出"三个一"的建议。

一是加强"一个对接"，即"一带一路"倡议与"英格兰北方经济中心"战略的对接。英国是最早响应"一带一路"合作倡议的西方大国，是"一带一路"合作的"天然伙伴"。大曼城地区正以"北部经济中心"战略为引擎，整合英格兰北部各市、镇、郡优势，加强地区互联互通，促进地区联动发展。中英两国政府可进一步加强发展战略和产业政策对接，为两国企业合作创造良好条件，释放更多合作潜能。

二是用好"一个机制"，即中英地方领导人会议机制。该机制自2016年建立以来有效运转、成果丰硕，为促进两国地方合作、推进中英关系发挥了重要作用，包括曼城在内的多个城市积极参与。前不久，第四次中英地方领导人会议在中国大连市举办，会议倡导双方以更广阔的全球视野、更积极的主动作为、更强烈的责任担当推动互利合作。12月初，中英地方经贸合作交流会暨中英企业家委员会会议在深圳成功举行，双方探讨了"北部经济中心"与中方深化合作等议题。大曼城地区10个市镇中已有6个与中国城市结好。希望双方在中英地方领导人会议机制框架下，不断深化合作，推动大曼城与中国互利合作关系不断提质升级。

三是打造"一个地区中心"，即将曼彻斯特打造为英格兰北部对华合作的地区示范中心。大曼城地区是英国伦敦以外最大的金融、工业和专业服务中心，也是英国最具投资吸引力的地区之一，吸引了1600多家外国公司前来投资兴业，汇聚了众多世界级商业、科研机构，在先进制造业、汽车和航空、高科技、化工、设计和创意、能源、教育等领域有很强的实力。中国在资本、市场转化能力、高铁技术、装备制造、新能源等方面有较强优势。曼城的朋友告诉我，中国已取代法国成为大曼城地区第三大外资来源国。我希望，曼城地区抓住机遇，充分发挥自身优势，积极拓展对华合作，带动英格兰中部、北部对华合作再上新台阶。

女士们、先生们，

当今世界正处于百年未有之大变局。世界经济贸易形势复杂多变，逆全球化思潮暗流涌动，单边主义、保护主义日益抬头。中英两国作为经济全球化的维护者、贸易自由化的践行者、多边贸易体系的拥护者，更应高举多边主义和开放经济旗帜，共同推动经济全球化朝着更加开放、包容、普惠、平衡、共赢的方向发展。中英地方合作是两国务实合作的生力军，也是两国合作成果惠及民众的最前沿。我希望，曼彻斯特工商界朋友们抓住机遇，用好机遇，不断拓宽合作领域，不断丰富合作内涵，与中方一道，共同推动中国与曼城地区合作再上新台阶！

谢谢大家！

Hold High the Banner of Openness and Create a Brighter Future[*]

Lord Lieutenant,

Lord Mayor,

Ladies and Gentlemen,

Friends,

Good evening!

I have visited Manchester many times, yet every visit gives me new thoughts.

Manchester is the first industrialised city in the world. More than 200 years ago, it was in Manchester that the cotton industry was born. This was the prelude to the Industrial Revolution. It is fair to say that the world's industrial revolution was born in the UK, while the UK's industrial revolution was born in Manchester. This revolution led by Manchester brought profound changes to the UK and the whole world.

40 years ago, another "revolution" took place in China. It was reform and opening-up. As President Xi Jinping said, it is "the Chinese second revolution" that "has not only profoundly changed China but also great influenced the whole world".

December 18th, 1978. That was the day the "second revolution" began. Exactly 40 years ago, the third Plenary Session of the 11th Central Committee of the Communist Party of China made the decision to start the great journey of the Chinese reform and opening-up.

Forty years ago, the Chinese GDP was only 175 billion US dollars, ranking the tenth

---

[*] Keynote Speech at the Dinner of the Business Community in Manchester. Albert Square, Manchester, 18 December 2018.

in the world. Today, this figure has topped 12 trillion US dollars, increasing by 33.5 times in real terms and making China the second largest economy in the world.

40 years on, the Chinese trade volume has increased by more than 780 times. It is now the world's largest trading nation with largest export and second largest import. It is a stabiliser and powerhouse for world economic recovery, contributing more than 30% of world economic growth for many years in a row.

40 years on, China has lifted 740 million people out of poverty and contributed to more than 70% of the world's total poverty reduction.

Why has the Chinese "second revolution" achieved such enormous success? I think there are three reasons.

First, China has followed the trend of the times as it explores its development path.

In reform and opening-up, China has no textbook to follow. From rural to urban reforms, from pilot projects to wider application, and from economic restructuring to deeper reforms across the board, the only benchmarks for China are its national conditions and development needs. The centre of all work is the people. The intention and goal of reform and opening-up are always to ensure that the people live happier, safer and have a stronger sense of achievements.

Gradually, we have found a path of socialism with Chinese characteristics. This path has led China to a profound transformation. It is an effective way to development and modernisation. And it represents the Chinese wisdom and solution in addressing the problems of human society.

The second reason for the Chinese success is that China has been open and inclusive in seeking greater integration with the world.

Openness brings progress and isolation results in backwardness. In the past 40 years, China has embraced the world with open arms and set sail in the vast ocean of globalisation. From embracing foreign businesses at home to exploring access to the world market, from becoming a WTO member to proposing the Belt and Road Initiative, China has turned from a closed and semi-closed country to one that opens up on all fronts.

In 2017, paid-in foreign investment in China topped 130 billion US dollars, increasing by more than 60 times compared with 40 years ago. China has become the world's second largest destination for foreign investment.

China has also grown to become the world's second largest source of foreign investment. Starting from scratch, Chinese businesses have found their way into 190 countries and regions around the world and now possess a total overseas asset of more than 5 trillion US dollars.

As China grows, President Xi Jinping proposed to build a community with a shared future for mankind. This idea embodies the Chinese resolve to shoulder its responsibilities as a big country and share its development opportunities with the world.

The third reason for the Chinese success is that China has pursued win-win cooperation with other countries.

The win-win spirit is at the core of the Chinese culture. Pursuing win-win cooperation is a major strategy for advancing reform and opening-up.

China always believes that no country should seek development at the expense of others. Globalisation means that countries of the world are all in the same boat and should row together. Inter-connected development is the only way to sustainable cooperation.

This year marks the fifth anniversary of the Belt and Road Initiative. Since it was proposed by President Xi Jinping, the BRI has followed the principles of extensive consultation, joint contribution and shared benefits.

- It is now the largest platform for win-win cooperation between all countries in the world.
- In the past five years, trade in goods between China and BRI partner countries has exceeded 5 trillion US dollars.
- China has invested more than 86 billion US dollars in these countries.
- These investments have created more than 240,000 jobs and contributed billions of dollars in tax revenue to the local community.

Next year, China will host the second Belt and Road Forum for International Cooperation. It will be open to friends from all walks of life in Manchester. We hope to see you at the Forum.

Ladies and Gentlemen,

Manchester has been a pioneer in China-UK cooperation.

- 120 years ago, Archibald John Little, a merchant from Manchester, was the first man to steer a steam boat to Chongqing through the Three Gorges. This trip opened the trade and economic links between the UK and the southwestern region of China.
- In 1986, with the establishment of ties with Wuhan, Manchester became the first British city to have a sister city in China and a trail blazer in the exchanges between Chinese and British cities.
- In the 21st century, Manchester United and Manchester City are among the first Premier League clubs to recruit players from China.
- Then came 2015 when President Xi Jinping visited Manchester. A new chapter started in cooperation between China and Manchester.
- In September, Mayor Burnham led a business delegation to the Annual Meeting of the New Champions 2018, or Summer Davos Forum, in Tianjin. The trip also took him to Beijing and Shenzhen.
- By November 2018, Chinese investment in Greater Manchester had reached 2.5 billion pounds. Beijing Construction Engineering Group International (The UK) alone has signed agreements on four massive projects in Manchester.
- Chinese real estate companies have taken an active part in the real estate market and infrastructure building in Britain's northern cities.
- The Chinese automaker BYD has signed agreements with several northern cities to supply electric buses. This will help upgrade the public transportation in these cities.

China and the UK are both at a critical stage of development. China will deepen reform and open up its market wider to the world. The UK is building a "global Britain" to expand trade and economic ties with other countries in the world. There is a broad prospect for deeper cooperation between China and the UK, including northern England.

I would like to use three "Ss" to share with you my suggestions on building closer partnership.

The first S is "Synergy". There is a strong synergy between Belt and Road Initiative and the Northern Powerhouse strategy.

The UK was the first major Western country to take part in BRI cooperation. It is a "natural partner" of China in advancing the BRI. One of the major goals of the BRI is to enhance connectivity and promote coordinated development of different regions. This is exactly what Greater Manchester is aiming to achieve, namely, leveraging the comparative strengths of different cities, counties and towns of northern England under the guidance of the Northern Powerhouse strategy.

The governments of our two countries should look for such synergy between our development strategies and industrial policies to create conditions and opportunities for business cooperation.

The second S is "Summit". This refers to the China-UK Regional Leaders' Summit.

Since launched in 2016, this mechanism has made good progress and delivered fruitful results. With the active participation of cities from both countries, including Manchester, this mechanism has played an important role in enhancing regional cooperation and advancing the overall bilateral relations between our two countries.

The fourth Summit was held in the Chinese city of Dalian not long ago. It calls on both sides to engage in mutually-beneficial cooperation with a global vision, greater initiative and a stronger sense of responsibility.

I also wish to mention another mechanism, the China-UK forum on regional trade and economic cooperation and the meeting of the Chinese-British Entrepreneur Committee. It was held in Shenzhen at the beginning of this month. One of the agenda items of this meeting was how to deepen cooperation between the "Northern Powerhouse" region and China.

Of the ten boroughs of Greater Manchester, six have established sister relations with Chinese cities. I hope that, building on the existing ties, the two sides could continue to leverage the China-UK Regional Leaders' Summit, in order to lift our mutually-beneficial cooperation onto a new level.

The third S is "Subnational Centre". We should build Manchester into a subnational centre for cooperation between northern England and China.

Greater Manchester is Britain's second largest financial, industrial and professional services centre after London. As one of the most attractive destinations for investment, Greater Manchester is home to more than 1,600 foreign businesses and a number of world-class commercial and research institutions. It has great strength in advanced manufacturing, automobile and aviation, high technology, chemical engineering, design and creative industry, energy and education.

China has a competitive edge in capital, commercialisation capability, high-speed rail technology, equipment manufacturing and new energy. My friends here in Manchester told me that China has already overtaken France to be the third largest source of foreign investment in Greater Manchester.

I hope that Manchester will seize the opportunities and leverage its comparative advantages to expand cooperation with China. I am sure this will boost the cooperation between central and northern England and China.

Ladies and Gentlemen,

The world is undergoing profound changes unseen in a century:

- The economic and trade situation is complicated and volatile.
- Anti-globalisation sentiments are growing.
- Unilateralism and protectionism are surging.

Both China and the UK support economic globalisation, believe in trade liberalisation and uphold the multilateral trade regime. It is important that we hold high the banner of multilateralism and open economy. It is also important that we work to ensure economic globalisation becomes more open, inclusive and balanced.

Subnational cooperation is a crucial part of the overall cooperation between our two countries. The people of China and Britain stand to gain directly from subnational partnership.

I hope that the business community in Manchester will seize the opportunities and make the best of these opportunities to expand and enrich the cooperation between China and Manchester.

I also hope and believe, by working together, we will achieve new success in China-Manchester cooperation!

Thank you!